The Disadvantaged Child

The Disadvantaged Child

Selected Papers of

Martin Deutsch and Associates

BASIC BOOKS, INC., PUBLISHERS

NEW YORK / LONDON

Fourth Printing
© 1967 by Martin Deutsch
Library of Congress Catalog Card Number: 67–28504
Manufactured in the United States of America

THE AUTHORS

MARTIN DEUTSCH, Ph.D. Professor of Early Childhood Education and the Director of the Institute for Developmental Studies at New York University.

RICHARD D. BLOOM, Ph.D. Research Scientist, Institute for Developmental Studies, 1962–1963.

BERT R. BROWN, Ph.D. Assistant Professor, School of Industrial and Labor Relations, Cornell University, Ithaca, New York. Research Scientist, Institute for Developmental Studies, 1961–1967.

CYNTHIA P. DEUTSCH, Ph.D. Senior Research Scientist, Institute for Developmental Studies. Research Professor in Education, School of Education, New York University.

LEO S. GOLDSTEIN, Ph.D. Senior Research Scientist, Institute for Developmental Studies. Research Professor in Education, School of Education, New York University.

VERA P. JOHN, Ph.D. Associate Professor, Department of Educational Psychology, Ferkauf Graduate School of Humanities and Social Science, Yeshiva University, New York. Consultant, Institute for Development Studies.

PHYLLIS A. KATZ, Ph.D. Associate Professor, Psychology Department,

New York University, University Heights. Senior Research Associate and Consultant, Institute for Developmental Studies.

ALMA LEVINSON, Ph.D. NIMH Fellow, Post-doctoral Clinic, New York University. Field Selection Officer, Peace Corps. Senior Research Associate, Institute for Developmental Studies, 1962–1964.

ESTELLE CHERRY PEISACH, Ph.D. Research Scientist, Institute for Developmental Studies.

MARTIN WHITEMAN, Ph.D. Professor of Clinical Psychology, School of Social Work, Columbia University, New York. Consultant, Institute for Developmental Studies. Assistant Director, Institute for Developmental Studies, 1961–1963.

Preface

The material in this book has been selected to exemplify a particular approach to the problems of the so-called disadvantaged child and the social environment from which he comes. That approach may be characterized as a search for the mediating variables: those which influence or determine the relationship between the background factors on the one hand and the psychological factors on the other. That is, while it may be found reliably that children from disadvantageous environments have poorer school performance records than those from facilitative environments, not too much is yet known about how the environmental influences operate to depress school performance. Similarly, there is little understanding about what environmental characteristics influence what aspects of academic performance. It is, in all probability, safe to say, nevertheless, that there are particular environmental factors which exercise a negative influence both on certain skills which themselves underlie school performance and on such measures as intelligence tests.

Findings from research oriented to this approach are relevant for a theoretical understanding of environment-behavior relationships. They are also closely bound up with practical problems of formulating intervention programs which aim to overcome negative environmental effects on cognitive skills and school performance.

By emphasizing the variables which relate the child's background to his performance, we do not mean to ignore the school's role in the relatively poorer performance of disadvantaged children as compared with their middle-class peers. However, the original problem of failure cannot be placed on the schools; rather it stems from the massive inequality that characterizes all aspects of our society, and the fact that remedial efforts are so often tokens for the social superego, and represent no real attempt to reverse the deficit that so many children build up simultaneously with their educational experience. The school cannot be expected to cure all our social ills, and to assign to it all the responsibility for the children's failure is to place an unreasonable burden on one institution.

However, as is brought out in many studies, disadvantaged children fall progressively farther behind their middle-class counterparts as they spend more years in school. This phenomenon is referred to in this book as the "cumulative deficit." The orientation the school uses is obviously not successful with these children—and there is some evidence that it is not successful in terms of the realization of individual potential for the middle-class child either. In other words, the total assortment of material in this book indicates that the school is not reaching and educating a large proportion of the children. Certainly the burden of the cumulative deficit can be laid on the school. As disadvantaged children go through school and tend to lose a sense of confidence and competence, the failure cycle becomes progressively reinforced and their threshold for alienation becomes progressively reduced as compared with their middle-class counterparts. The school has not taken even the first step on the path to making these children feel worthwhile, competent, coping organisms. Many claim that the machine dehumanizes, but as one walks through the corridors of educational power, one develops a charity for the machine because at least it individualizes stimuli and contains within its mechanism a potential for consistency. The fact is that children who have the capability for learning simply are not learning in school.

One of the underlying problems, discussed in several of the chapters, is what is referred to as the "discontinuity" between the lower-class home and the middle-class-oriented school. The so-called "hidden curriculum" of the middle-class home is really continuous with—or identical to—the school curriculum; so in a sense the middle-class child has been exposed to at least some of the elements of school since infancy. The typical education dictum of "starting with the child where he is" often means starting with a child who already has many of the school-related skills. This preparation is not true for the child from the disadvantaged background, for whom school represents a discontinuous environment from the one he is used to. The responsibility for devising methods of teaching children from discontinuous environments rests solely on the school. If the children are not learning in school—as has been made abundantly clear in many studies—then the fault lies with the curriculum, organization, and methods of the school, not with the children or their parents. Perhaps part of the new approach might involve enlisting parent participation—and undoubtedly in any successful program the parents and others in the community must be meaningfully involved—but the major emphasis must be on finding appropriate ways of educating children. This task is a large one, and it cannot be accomplished in the context of constant crisis which has so far characterized the initiation of innovation. We work in a context of urgency. Simply to see it as crisis can lead to insufficient planning, discouragement, and insufficient evaluation of innovations and plans.

Included in the chapters which follow are both theoretical statements and specific research data addressed to the problems posed. About half the papers have not been generally available for distribution before. Almost all the original data included have been available only in bulky formal research reports or have not been previously presented.

The purpose of the book is to give a picture of a general orientation to the complex relationships among environment, society, school, and individual psychological development by putting together research and the theoretical material on which it was based. As indicated earlier, the approach emphasizes a search for the specificities of these relationships. Included are research reports which attempt to break down global environmental variables into those which relate most to school performance and formal intelligence measures. Also included are reports of research which attempted to define elements which underlie the school performance measures, or simpler elements which underlie complex tasks such as reading. In the latter categories are included papers on both language and perceptual variables. There is also some discussion of data on the influence of classroom organization on school performance.

While the emphasis in most of the material is on early childhood, the assumption should not be made therefore that the author believes that intervention at later points in life is a waste of resources and should not be attempted. The book simply reflects the recent work of the author and his associates, and that work has been oriented in the main to early childhood. Of course, as several of the papers indicate, that period of life does seem to hold great promise for success in intervention.

For ease of organization, the papers included have been divided roughly into three content areas, though overlap among the areas is substantial. To avoid unnecessary duplication, where the same data are used in different papers oriented to different elements, they have been included in only one chapter, and later chapters simply make reference to the relevant tables and pages.

It gives me great pleasure to acknowledge the contributions of colleagues and assistants to the work and thinking reported here. Some of the contributions are apparent in the authorship listings of some of the papers. But in a large research group such as that at the Institute for Developmental Studies many people contribute effort and ideas to every project. It is impossible to recognize each contribution, but it is, I hope, possible to convey appreciation to all who have participated in and contributed to the work of the past years.

For work on this book specifically, I should like to acknowledge with great appreciation the contributions of Mr. Jack Victor and Miss Carol Stanwood. The existence of this material within one set of covers is largely due to their perseverance and attention to important detail. I should also like to thank my wife, Dr. Cynthia Deutsch, for her help in the selection and organization of the papers included.

MARTIN DEUTSCH

New York
September 1967

Contents

PART I: The Social Environment for Learning

1 / *Social Intervention and the Malleability of the Child*
MARTIN DEUTSCH   3

2 / *Some Psychosocial Aspects of Learning in the Disadvantaged*
MARTIN DEUTSCH   31

3 / *The Disadvantaged Child and the Learning Process*
MARTIN DEUTSCH   39

4 / *Facilitating Development in the Preschool Child: Social and
Psychological Perspectives*   MARTIN DEUTSCH   59

5 / *Nursery Education: The Influence of Social Programming on
Early Development*   MARTIN DEUTSCH   77

6 / *Minority Groups and Class Status as Related to Social and
Personality Factors in Scholastic Achievement*
MARTIN DEUTSCH   89

7 / *Early Social Environment and School Adaptation*
MARTIN DEUTSCH   133

PART II: Cognitive and Language Factors in the Education of the Disadvantaged Child

8 / *Learning in the Disadvantaged*   CYNTHIA P. DEUTSCH   147

9 / *The Social Context of Language Acquisition*
VERA P. JOHN and LEO S. GOLDSTEIN   163

10 / *Communication of Information in the Elementary School Classroom*   MARTIN DEUTSCH, ALMA LEVINSON, BERT R. BROWN, and ESTELLE CHERRY PEISACH   177

11 / *The Relationship of Auditory and Visual Functioning to Reading Achievement in Disadvantaged Children*   PHYLLIS A. KATZ and MARTIN DEUTSCH   233

12 / *Auditory Discrimination and Learning: Social Factors*   CYNTHIA P. DEUTSCH   259

PART III: Aspects of Race and Social Class in the Education and Integration of the Disadvantaged Child

13 / *Dimensions of the School's Role in the Problems of Integration*   MARTIN DEUTSCH   281

14 / *Social Influences in Negro-White Intelligence Differences*   MARTIN DEUTSCH and BERT R. BROWN   295

15 / *Race and Social Class as Separate Factors Related to Social Environment*   RICHARD D. BLOOM, MARTIN WHITEMAN, and MARTIN DEUTSCH   309

16 / *Some Effects of Social Class and Race on Children's Language and Intellectual Abilities*   MARTIN WHITEMAN, BERT R. BROWN, and MARTIN DEUTSCH   319

17 / *Social Disadvantage as Related to Intellective and Language Development*   MARTIN WHITEMAN and MARTIN DEUTSCH   337

18 / *The Role of Social Class in Language Development and Cognition*   MARTIN DEUTSCH   357

19 / *The Principal Issue*   MARTIN DEUTSCH   371

Conclusion

20 / *Brief Reflections on the Theory of Early Childhood Enrichment Programs*   CYNTHIA P. DEUTSCH and MARTIN DEUTSCH   379

Acknowledgments   389

Index   391

PART I

The Social Environment
for Learning

1 /

Social Intervention and the Malleability of the Child

MARTIN DEUTSCH

There exists today a tendency toward what might be called an over-simplified parsimony in ascribing causal and singular responsibility for social failure to any one of a number of social institutions that happens to be under examination at the moment. For example, if the family is identified as disorganized, this is mechanically related to delinquency, or drug addiction, or alcoholism, or school failure, or what-have-you. If a history of job discrimination is identified for any group, the elimination of this form of discrimination is seen as the only necessary channel to total economic equality. If the urban slum child is found to come to school unprepared for the first-grade curriculum, preschool education is seen as the primary, and sometimes only, avenue for creating equality of opportunity in education. Examples of this kind of concrete thought can be extended throughout the fields of education, mental health, and the human sciences.

The point is that to justify social action in a particular area, the problem to which the action is directed is too frequently seen as having specific causal antecedents, and the action then becomes a method for the all-out eradication of the problem. A more realistic and modest approach is often not feasible, as our social ethic states that all efforts must be all-out wars against the newly discovered social atrocities. In the heat of our national psychology of social action, the interrelationship and interpenetration of multiple causes and effects become relegated to the promised panaceas that represent justifications for social effort and expenditure. When any set of actions fails to achieve the distant objective of near-total problem amelioration, the effort is likely to be considered insufficiently powerful, or the problem to which the effort was addressed loses its social saliency and is withdrawn to the stable in favor of some other hobby horse.

Today there is a tendency for innovations to be identified as pan-aceas in the market places of their birth, even prior to their initial implementation. No wonder that, when these innovations do not fulfill all initial expectations, they are dropped, when they might have evolved into effective strategies if they had been adequately assessed on a realistic scale which permitted feedback for selective strengthen-ing or modification. The history of the Higher Horizons program would be one of many examples of this process. A similar situation could conceivably obtain in Project Headstart. If the children enrolled in Headstart do not show first-grade achievement patterns similar to middle-class children, it is possible that the whole effort will be aban-doned or that preschool education will be seen as valueless. Similarly, if the new mental health centers do not have a substantial effect in ameliorating alcoholism, it is possible that these centers may be down-graded or that alcoholism will be considered too resistant to any men-tal health approach.

The statement of these problems is meant to serve notice that, even though the remainder of this paper discusses ways and principles of ameliorating a social problem, what follows is not to be considered the reflection of a unitary view, nor the prescription for a panacea.

For the purpose of this discussion, we shall be looking at a social institution, education; a number of strategies for utilizing this institu-tion; and a possibly mythical assumption that the royal road to equal-ity is only through the straight and narrow halls of learning. This may be partially true, but without considerable architectural re-engineer-ing of those hallways, the capability of education for becoming the major agent of social intervention is somewhat limited. However, edu-cation may become an increasingly significant component as it changes itself in order to accommodate to social pressures, for ex-ample, the civil rights movement.

Even if some innovation in education did prove to be a panacea, there would be a considerable time lag between the inception and development of the program and the appreciation of its universal sig-nificance, since its effects would not be fully observable on sufficient populations until a rather long period of time had elapsed.

As a society, we have arrived at a largely political decision, based on certain objective social conditions, to massively intervene in the development of the child. This decision applies not only to the recent surge of federal support for programs directed primarily to the poor; it represents as well a much older commitment to a public school system and other state-supported agencies, be it in the day care field, well-baby clinics, mental health centers, or the like.

The historical emphasis has been on reinforcing and supplementing the experiences in the home and giving the child the tools for adequate socialization for industry, the army, family life, and for functional participation in society. Now the emphasis has shifted from normative socialization to preventive, remedial, and facilitating functions, with the explicit assumption that our social system mutilates some, limits many, and for even more offers minimal possibility for full individual development and social participation. As a social system we seem to be more successful in limiting, restricting, narrowing, and controlling than in stimulating the growth of intellectual initiative, expanding horizons, or in encouraging a challenge of the status quo. The strength that exists in new intervention programs is in the assumption by society of responsibility for an environment within which individual development can be fostered.

Many of our urban centers are in the midst of much social reorganization and population transition, with all the concomitant conflict, pressure, frustrations, and hope. A metamorphosis is taking place in the demographic distribution of our big cities, both in terms of racial integration and occupational mobility. Further, the simultaneous and related technological upheaval creates a shifting of the job opportunity structure. Many semiskilled and skilled occupational categories are stagnant or disappearing, and the demand for unskilled labor is decreasing rapidly. On the other hand, there is an increasing demand in some new and highly skilled job categories. The child who is clearly alienated from school, who subsequently fails in reading or other academic subjects or becomes a dropout, is less likely to develop the skills appropriate for a highly technical and shifting job market.

Solutions to the problems of children, particularly of minority-group children, involve the creation of social forms that can assist the youngster to achieve self-respect, identity, motivation to achieve, and intellectual purposes consistent with the changing necessities of our social system. In many respects, the awareness of the retarding effects of social deprivation associated with ethnic-group and social-class membership offers an opportunity to develop procedures for *all* children who function below their intellectual capability. Much in middle-class affluent America tends to destroy individual identity and tends to alienate young people from any purpose outside the self. Many of these children, subject to contradictory and at the same time confluent social stresses, never become sufficiently motivated for intellectual achievement. At times, in middle-class children, the need for status replaces the need for individual accomplishment, thereby fostering an apathy toward substantive intellectual achievement similar to that found in children who have been subject to understimulation and discrimination.

The school can become a socially "therapeutic" instrument through its primary educational function by consciously developing broad-scale curriculum formats that will operate in such a way as to establish and reestablish cultural and educational, and school and community, continuities. This is true for the behavioral as well as the learning areas.

PRESCHOOL ENRICHMENT PROGRAMMING

For cogent theoretical and empirical, as well as practical, reasons, emphasis has been placed on the transitional years from the preschool period to and through the elementary school years. This is the span when the child is first independently subject to the influence and the requirements of the broader culture, and also when he is still highly malleable.

Programs for the preschool years have become variegated and confusing. As Alice, in reply to the Caterpillar's question, "Who are *You?*", said, "I hardly know, Sir, just at present—at least I know who I *was* when I got up this morning, but I think I must have been changed several times since then."

It is not that compensatory or enrichment programs have fallen down a rabbit hole, but that their rapid proliferation and modification have made it very difficult to define, describe, and evaluate their results in a systematic manner. While there has been overall before-and-after evaluation of children in most programs, there has been a general absence of evaluation of the relationship between specific aspects of enrichment programs and specific change. What is needed is systematic evaluation of what facets of program processes have what effects at what interacting periods in the life of the child and of the program.

As programs change and develop into more-or-less permanent

form, they require a guidance and feedback mechanism which evolves from an analysis of data on specific changes in and surrounding the learning situation. Therefore, a descriptive analysis of the learning process involved in the program, examining the roles of teachers and parents, as well as children, should be undertaken.

During these transitional years, two primary environments are present for the child: that of the home and that of the school. The child is engaged in some measure of interaction with both these environments, and since he is being influenced by this interaction, the environment is always in some measure intervening in his development.

Though we talk and think about intervention as a consciously evolved, highly focused, organized, and directed process, it is necessary to recognize that a child is always actively involved with the environment, and the absence of formulated stimuli can be as influential in the patterning of psychological and intellectual development as the existence of organized programs. Further, it is possible, either at home or in a nursery school setting, to have different degrees of organization: from chaos to disorganization to overstructure; or, under some conditions, to have too much stimulation, or inappropriate stimulation, over too short a period of time or at the wrong stage of development. The search for structured interventions which will be effective in enhancing the child's development involves the determination of the possible timing, degree, and types of stimulation required.

There are various assumptions about enrichment or compensatory education programs that require considerable empirical examination.

A cornerstone assumption that has provided much impetus to preschool programs is that earlier intervention is always superior to later intervention. This assumption, given sufficient time, can be empirically tested. My tendency would be to think that this position is, in general, justifiable, but it is also dependent on the sophistication of the intervention program and the powerfulness of the stimulation in terms of the sensory or cognitive receptivity of the child at that stage of development. An unfortunate corollary of the "earlier the better" assumption results in the unjustifiable position that after the seventh or eighth years of life it is not worthwhile to try to do anything. This, in turn, creates a counter-reaction to the effect that early enriched and variegated experiences are not sufficiently influential to justify intensive efforts. There is some evidence that early social and cognitive training can be effective, but there is no evidence that any program instituted early will necessarily be effective or that programs of similar magnitude initiated later cannot be effective. There is at present insufficient evidence to make a firm commitment to any one strategy at any particular age level.

All this could be ascertained by empirical studies, given both sufficient time and an adequate methodology. It may very well be that for later intervention different strategies will have to be developed, and that more training and more differentiation of techniques might be necessary. This in turn means that it will probably cost society more to intervene later, but it does not necessarily follow that children cannot be reached at later stages of development. This is an important distinction to draw because current early enrichment programs, even if they were generally adopted, could not yet reach all children in early childhood. If early childhood is thought to be the only effective period for intervention, then all the children who passed that period without a special program would have to be considered unreachable. Here the self-fulfilling prophecy could well operate, and pessimistic expectations about performance could give rise to low achievement.

Another prevalent assumption that needs examination is one that was previously touched on: namely, that *any* intervention program is better than none. Aside from the fact that this assumption gives rise to the creation of many types of programs without regard for their careful and specific evaluation, it is open to serious question on other grounds. It is possible that negative attitudes toward formal problem-solving and learning can be fostered in children by inept programming or by untrained or poorly trained people with ambivalence toward their roles and insufficient understanding of the attentional, orientation, and general learning processes and reward schedules of children in an adult-child learning situation. A good case can be made for saying that any program which gets the child into a classroom and handling and becoming familiar with school-related materials will have a positive effect on his general attitudes and his comfort in the school situation. But this argument too often is used as a rationale for providing a third of a loaf when a rich society has already stolen five loaves from the heritage of many minority-group children, and the return of at least one whole one is necessary to obtain any meaningful enhancement of performance.

Another myth or assumption requiring testing and careful examination is that, for a limited period of time, if a rich, structured program is begun for children when they are three or four years of age, it will ignite growth potential which had until then been dormant in the child. This approach starts with a powerful environmental intervention and then invokes a species of vitalism in which the environment no longer has primary saliency. Such a position is tenable if experience does not have a continuing role in cognitive development from the most concrete differentiations to the most symbolic processes. A distillation of this theoretical point of view would be that a deprived early environment simply prevents the normal cognitive-development process from beginning and that a powerful stimulus will kick it off, and that the process will create its own momentum independent of continued expanded environmental stimulation. The few studies of the long-term effects of early enrichment do not bear out this position, but admittedly they offer still insufficient evidence to discount it.

Another approach requiring more investigation seems to suggest that where there has been limitation of environmental encounters the child should be exposed to as much compensatory stimulation as possible. The assumption is that there is a limited period of time for the acceleration of cognitive development because of the presumed hypothetical period during which the child is said to be optimally receptive. Since the publication of Bloom's book *Stability and Change in Human Characteristics*,[3] especially, there has been much discussion of the necessity for establishing opportunities for the child to have differentiated environmental encounters during the crucial stage. This argument relates to that discussed earlier under the "earlier the stimulation, the better the result" rubric. Although the argument includes a critical-time concept, in essence it is a "the more the better" approach. It states that abundant stimulation even for a limited period of time—i.e., before the end of the critical period, which is roughly analogous to Piaget's preoperational stage—is necessary if the ceiling of accomplishment is to be elevated. A possible alternative concept is that it may very well be that initiation of special intervention before a certain period of time has elapsed is crucial for the enhancement of intellective functions, but that the overall quantity at that time is not so critical as long as there is continuity of enrichment after the period has passed.

It seems to me that the current state of information would indicate the advisability of an orientation that calls for enriched opportunities for environmental encounters as early as possible in the life of the child, and their maintenance at least through the formative years. It is not being suggested that either the failure or absence of early interventions should deny or relegate to unimportance the possible effect of later exposure. However, it might be that wholly different strategies and techniques would be indicated at later stages of development and socialization, i.e., that greater emphasis on achievement orientation, and general motivational and interpersonal factors, may have greater saliency in the preadolescent and adolescent years. In other words, the older child may still be malleable, but may require a very different kind of intervention strategy in order to promote differential growth. The fact that Bloom's analysis of normative studies shows that 80 per cent of intellectual development is completed by age eight does not mean that this percentage would not be changed by appropriate stimulation after age eight. The whole point is that we really know very little about what Hunt calls the "match" between individual development and external stimulation at various stages of growth.[5]

The popular mythology sees intervention, enrichment, compensatory programs, or what-have-you, as more-or-less homogeneous totalities. There is little understanding that we are at a relatively early period in the systematic collation of information which will allow for the construction of increasingly scientific programs to stimulate the intellectual growth of children, be they socially deprived, low achievers, or high achievers who are still not reaching individual potential. Jensen,[6] for instance, suggests that on the average there are another 20 IQ points that could be developed with proper stimulation. This is independent of the new possibilities for electromechanical or chemical stimulation of intelligent behavior, as described in the Rand report.[4]

The whole concept of the possibility of training to ameliorate deficits which underlie cognitive and learning abilities is based on these assumptions: that the environment plays a crucial role in development; that it is through the child's experience that much development is stimulated; and that appropriate stimulation is essential for development of the functions mentioned. The concept of compensatory education in these terms includes the provision of particular experiences in order to enhance the child's development in deficit areas. It is easy to assume that the kinds of experiences which should be provided are those the child has lacked; it is this assumption which lies behind taking children on trips to the zoo, the museums, and the like, and expecting that some development will take place in response to the trips. The assumption, however, is not a valid one. Programs which simply provide the overall experiences which a child has missed at an earlier age may well be ineffective. The experience which must be provided is that which will stimulate the growth of the desired skill at the child's current level of development, age, socialization, etc. Experiences missed cannot be retrieved. What probably can be retrieved, however, is the development that would have been stimulated by the missed experiences had they been present. But that development at a later time must be stimulated by experiences consistent with the later, rather than the earlier, time.

Children with deficits in learning and cognitive skills should be approached with methods to learn the skills other than the methods that would have been used at an earlier time had they not been disadvantaged in either their home or school environments. The task of a compensatory or an enrichment program, as I see it, is to diagnose the deficits and attempt to determine the kinds of procedures that will ameliorate them. Part of both the diagnosis and the determination might involve an evaluation of what is missing from the child's background, followed by a study of how the missing parts might have contributed to his more advanced development. But there is no logic to an assumption that (even if it were possible) a simple putting in *now* of what was missing *then* will have a beneficial effect on the current deficit areas. This is not to say that some of the experiences missed should not be provided—i.e., why *not* take children to the zoo? But that experience should now be structured differently for the child: in terms of his current developmental level.

Following from this discussion, it becomes apparent that, in some way, the child's developmental level must be ascertained. Then cognitive deficits which may be present can be analyzed, and followed by the devising of compensatory educational procedures.

This raises a great many questions, which are at the core of understanding the interaction of social conditions with development, as well as at the basis of the building of viable compensatory programs.

First of all, on what level does one seek deficits? If only the most complex areas, such as reading, are analyzed, then the factors which may contribute to deficits might be missed. On the other hand, if only the smallest definable components, such as visual perception of the diagonal, are measured, then a great deal of time might be spent in seeking procedures to train a skill that may not be too important to overall functioning and that, perhaps, would develop as a by-product of some other training procedure anyway. Here is one situation in which the middle ground truly seems the best answer—at least initially, until it can be tested. The middle ground between perception of the diagonal and reading might be visual discrimination. A compensatory approach, therefore, might be to devise procedures for training in visual discrimination, for example, and then later to note the speed of acquisition of reading skills.

The deficit-evaluation approach can also be applied to analysis of what elements are lacking in a particular disadvantaged background. As indicated above, such an evaluation does not mean that what should then be supplied to the child are the missing elements in the form in which they are missing. What it does mean is that if one could identify the absent stimuli, one might be helped to identify the particular functions which were not stimulated and so understand better the source of the deficits in cognitive and learning skills. Then educative procedures consistent with the child's developmental level could be devised.

NEXT STEPS, OR "SECOND GENERATION" PROGRAMMING

From observations and from preliminary data, I have the definite impression that current intervention programs are at best only partially successful, in terms of the achievement dimension. On the socialization dimension they may be doing a somewhat better job, though evaluation techniques and criteria are even more difficult in this area. Analysis of the nature and patterning of results obtained, however, yields a picture not only of the actual growth achieved by the children but also of the areas which should receive increased emphasis in program planning. With these data, what we are now ready for is a kind of "second generation" program: one which will attempt to retain the most useful elements of the past special curricula and to start identifying and delineating those experiences that have the greatest saliency at specified stages for the acceleration of cognitive growth.

One necessary prerequisite to the strengthening of programs so that a child has an opportunity to get a fair chance would be the development of five- and ten-year program concepts for the longitudinal study of the continuous flow and interaction of the experimental situation with normative growth expectancies in varying social contexts. A summer program such as Headstart may be useful, but by itself it is a minimal effort, when seen in the total context of a child's

opportunities to overcome socially imposed limitations on his achievement. In addition, if children are simply to be put into "special"
classes, with some increased funding and extra materials, there is no
reason why this in itself should have more than minimal—possibly
only temporary—effect.

I should like at this point to refer to some of the data from our
current enrichment program at the Institute for Developmental
Studies and then go on to examine the areas missing and propose program orientations to deal with these areas. Some of the data will be
independently reported in greater detail.

Children who have had a year of reasonably structured preschool
experience show significant increases in scores on the Binet and on the
Peabody Picture Vocabulary Test (PPVT), a test of receptive language performance. These changes are significant at the .001 level. A
control sample, not initially different on either measure and coming
from the same population, also shows significant increment, but at the
.05 level. Parenthetically, the control-group increase could be explained on the basis of test effects, or simply may reflect a combination
of the effects of the screening process and a one-month non-structured
summer nursery program for the control group. The data were obtained on groups selected at age four and first tested at that time, and
retested approximately one year later. At the initial testing there was
no difference between the groups.

Another control group was selected from five-year-old children
entering school at kindergarten, and coming from socioeconomic circumstances similar to those from which the first control and experimental groups came. At pretesting, these five-year-old children were
lower—though not significantly lower—than the experimental and
first control groups at the time of pretesting. That is, the mean IQs of
the five-year-olds were lower than similar scores for the four-year-olds
in the initial experimental and control groups. When the first posttest
data for the initial groups (data obtained when the children in these
samples were five years old) are compared with the pretest data of
the new five-year-old control sample, the latter group is found to be
significantly lower. This five-year-old group had no nursery school experience—and no testing at age four. It is also the group that for one
reason or another did not respond to the offer of a preschool program.
The general background characteristics of those children are, as
stated, similar to the other samples, but we are in the process of making a special analysis to determine if they differ on a cluster of special

"Deprivation Index" items. (This Deprivation Index will be discussed below.)

Data are now available on a third group: children who began school at the first-grade level, and had neither kindergarten nor nursery experience. Their pretest scores were significantly lower than those obtained by the original experimental and control groups (at age four), and their scores tended to conform with those typically found for children coming from depressed social environments. The mean Binet IQ for this six-year-old control group was 85.5, whereas the mean IQs of the other two groups were 98.9 and 99. This is another instance of a fairly consistent finding: that children tested two years prior to the first grade, who come from so-called socially disadvantaged conditions, test significantly higher than do children from the same background at the time of first-grade entrance. It may be that, in the data reported, we are dealing with selected samples, but indices such as percentage of broken homes, percentage of welfare cases, and the like, do not reflect differences between the groups, and *do* reflect frequencies typically found in this population.

The alternative explanation is that something occurs in an environment that limits the opportunities for the child to build mediational systems to interpret and relate a variety of experiences, and that the complexity of the environmental encounters increases disproportionately to the coping capabilities of the child restricted in the range of stimuli available to him. Also indicated is that the process associated with the deficit which seems to accumulate between the kindergarten or first-grade years and the fifth grade (see Part III, this volume) is already started by the time the child enters school. It would be reasonable to expect that the school system and the educational process could arrest or reverse the accumulating deficit. However, the school's failure to accomplish this is seen in the increased deficit at the end of the elementary years. (For a discussion of this, see Chapter 6, below.)

Another evaluation study used the Illinois Test of Psycholinguistic Abilities (ITPA) and the Wepman Auditory Discrimination Test. Data indicated that, at the first grade, the original preschool experimental enrichment group scored significantly higher than the matched control on both measures. Analysis of patterning yielded interesting results for both tests.

On the Wepman, the same phenomenon is noted on a variety of samples, in addition to the experimental and control groups in our preschool program. The Wepman presents a series of forty pairs of words, thirty of which differ from each other in one phoneme. This phoneme is placed at the beginning, the middle, or the end of each word, and the words are matched with respect to number of phonemes in each. The subject is asked to tell, for each pair, whether the same word has been repeated twice, or whether two different words were said. In our experience, the test cannot be used with preschool disadvantaged children, because they do not have the concept "same and different," but it is quite applicable to the same children at the end of kindergarten or the beginning of first grade. When test results were analyzed in terms of *position* of the different phoneme, what was found was more errors on final phonemes than on initial phonemes for both the experimental and the control groups. For both groups combined, the initial-versus-final phoneme comparison yielded significance at the .001 level of confidence. The groups are differentiated from each other in performance on the Wepman at the .05 level, but when this difference is further analyzed by phoneme position, it is found that group differences on initial phonemes are not significant, while for the final phoneme comparisons, the significance is at the .01 level.

Implications here are for the use of language and particularly the inflection of the language, and, perhaps most important, for attentional focusing. That is, it might simply be that, for the children who score poorly on the final phonemes, there is an attentional deficiency, and they are not really listening by the end of the word. Further, inflection in English is carried at the end of the word. Missing the final phoneme means missing the tense or number of the word. A consistent finding on verbal tests administered to similar samples is that these children are deficient in grammar and syntax. The degree to which these findings may be related is currently being investigated.

It is interesting to speculate that part of the cumulative deficit may be attributed to the child's "tuning out" before the final phoneme. If so, it may well be that attentional training and orientation might be of greater importance than is currently reflected in enrichment programs.

To return to the ITPA results: In addition to evaluating the overall differences between the experimental and control groups (tested, it will be remembered, at the time both entered first grade), potential differences in patterning of scores were evaluated. The ITPA has nine different subtests, measuring different aspects of language function according to Osgood's theory. Inspection of the patterning of the two groups revealed no difference between them: the subtest patterns of the groups were nearly identical. However, there was practically no overlap between them on level of score for each subtest. While not all the subtest differences were statistically significant, there was only one instance of an overlap in score between the experimental and the control group means. Since the ITPA is still an experimental test, there is as yet not sufficient data on subtest patterning among a variety of groups, so it is not possible to say whether the patterning observed for these lower-class disadvantaged children is typical for that age group. Whether or not it is typical, however, it remains highly interesting—if for the moment inexplicable—that the experimental group was superior to the controls on almost all of the subtests, even though the patterning was almost identical.

The tests reported so far have been mainly verbal or language-related. One other measure consistently used since the initial four-year-old testing is the Columbia Mental Maturity Scale (CMMS), which is a non-verbal conceptual task. Some rather different results were found on this test. The experimental group did not improve from the pretest to the posttest, but the control group in the same period showed a significant decrement in score. This finding could be important, as more abstract conceptual skills play an interestingly significant role in problem solving as children get older. The lack of such skills may make a significant contribution to the overall cumulative deficit. There is some evidence from a normative study, referred to as the "Verbal Survey" (and to be discussed again below), that it is with conceptual tasks that disadvantaged children and poor performers, regardless of social class, have consistent difficulty.

This finding is further supported by some initial studies in conservation of quantity. Experimental enrichment and control groups were tested on this function in kindergarten. The enrichment group was found to be superior to the controls, but both groups were below the level reported for middle-class children of the same age.

Mention has been made several times of the attempt to delineate the dimensions on which families of the same socioeconomic status (SES) can be differentiated. This attempt follows from the understanding that social-class designations are shorthand categorizations for a particular level of education and income, and that, while it is tempting to regard them so, the members of any given social class do not constitute a homogeneous group. Our effort to define the parameters of heterogeneity has taken the form of constructing what we call a "Deprivation Index." This Index is a collection of items from a questionnaire which was administered to a parent—usually the mother—of each of the children in the samples of a large-scale cross-sectional study, the Verbal Survey. The samples for this study were selected from populations of middle-class and lower-class, Negro and white, first- and fifth-grade children. The questionnaire included a number of items relating to aspects of family life, parents' aspirations for children, and the like. From these items, six were extracted to form the Deprivation Index. Then this Index was used to determine the feasibility of classifying the within-class groups into subgroups on the basis of such family-activity items, and then to investigate the potential relationship between deprivation categories and children's test performance on a variety of verbal, perceptual, and reading measures.

Results indicate that the Deprivation Index does indeed divide families into apparently meaningful categories, and that these categories cut across social-class lines. The Index tends to act as a factor independent of SES and race in contributing to variation in children's test performance. This suggests that groupings of specific environmental factors (e.g., family trips, parental motivation for child's schooling, and the like) can be associated with particular levels of performance on the measures used. A high index of deprivation (i.e., more deprivation as defined by the items on the Index) is associated with poorer test performance, regardless of the social-class level of the child's family. Decrements in test performance associated with lower-caste or lower-class status tend to be mitigated if associated with specific positive environmental factors, as reflected in a low Deprivation Index score. The major exception to this statement is the particular relationship found between fifth-grade Negro children and poor vocabulary score.

Further development and refinement of the Deprivation Index is expected to yield a scale which will meaningfully describe at least some of the environmental parameters relevant to children's school and test performance.

Another set of data to which the Deprivation Index has contributed has to do with a concept that has been mentioned several times before in this paper: the concept of cumulative deficit. This refers to the finding, in our studies and in those reported by others, that disadvantaged children tend to lose ground as they get older. That is, in the absence of special compensatory programs (and perhaps also with them—the data are not complete as yet) children from disadvantaged circumstances tend to test progressively lower, year by year, on IQ and other tests, and their relative school performance tends to decline. Some data relating to this phenomenon were reported above, in the discussion of the results of the special enrichment program. Data from the Verbal Survey cross-sectional study are also relevant. While the Verbal Survey study was not longitudinal, and therefore the differential age data cannot be so interpreted, nevertheless both first- and fifth-grade children were used, and each age group was divided into four major cells: middle-class white, middle-class Negro, lower-class white, and lower-class Negro. The findings do show lower scores for the fifth-grade children. The most notable interaction is that between age and race: whereas for the first grade, six of forty-two verbal measures correlated with race alone, nineteen with SES alone, and two with both; for the fifth grade, again six of forty-three verbal measures correlated with race alone, but there were only ten which correlated only with SES, and twelve which correlated with both. The conclusion stated about those data was:

> Essentially, it would appear that when one adds four years of a school experience to a poor environment, plus minority group status, what emerged are children who are apparently less capable of handling standard intellectual and linguistic tasks. One also might postulate that when the Negro child broadens his environmental contacts by going to school (and to and from school), he is made more aware of his inferior caste status, and this has the same depressing effect on his performance that his inferior class status had all along. (Chapter 18, below.)

The findings on the Deprivation Index also indicate the operation of a cumulative deficit: test decrements were more pronounced among the older children. When the Deprivation Index is included, along with SES and race, as background factors to be related to test performance, as indicated above, it tends to act independently. Further, test performance was not disproportionately decreased in children coming from backgrounds which included the most negative factors in all three areas. That is, while the lowest scores were found for children who came from lower-class Negro, high-deprivation homes, the effect was additive rather than multiplicative. Combined with the cumulative-deficit finding, these data would seem to indicate that more decrement results from deprivational factors accumulating over time than from more deprivational factors being added at a given time. These findings, if further confirmed and replicated, would strongly argue for the potentially greater efficacy of early childhood compensatory programs, as compared with those which might be introduced at a later time.

There were some differences in the relationship of various test scores with the background factors, with the verbal measures suffering more from deprivational factors than did the non-verbal. Further, the verbal measures were more negatively affected by some disadvantaging characteristics than others. The most striking of these differential findings is that fifth-grade Negro children showed the greatest deficit in vocabulary score. This fact points to the importance of further evaluation of the environment of the Negro child with respect to factors which promote or retard linguistic development. Such information should make it more possible to devise increasingly appropriate curricula.*

These are the specifics of the cumulative-deficit phenomenon. For a more general interpretation, I should like to refer to an earlier statement of mine:

> A tremendous reservoir of human potential is lost when dominant culture is not reflected in the motivational energies, fantasies, and aspiration symbols of minority groups—symbols that are required as foundation for successful climbing of the educational and economic ladders. It is possible that it is not just symbols which are missing here, but rather that, for people living so much on the margin of the dominant culture, and experiencing so many immediate and overwhelming problems of existence, identification with a set of majority culture symbols is not personally relevant, and becomes cumulatively less relevant with the increasing impact of social alienation and individual hopelessness. (Chapter 6, below.)

FUTURE PERSPECTIVES

After having had opportunities to profit from this wide spectrum of investigations, we are better able to devise an intervention strategy that is somewhat more sophisticated than has been possible in the past. First, three progressive goals of intervention can be defined, though all overlap and each goal is subsumed in the next.

The *first* intervention goal is to prevent or arrest the cumulative

* See Part III, especially Chapters 14–18, for more detailed findings of the Verbal Survey and the Deprivation Index.

deficit, so that disadvantaged children will not continue to lose ground. The *second* goal would be to achieve a distribution of performance among disadvantaged children similar to the national norms, which would involve the formulation of programs to reverse the effects of deprivation. The *third* goal has relevance for all children: it is to facilitate the maximum growth and utilization of intellectual potential. This goal involves devising environments, strategies, and techniques to make it possible for more children to "learn to learn" and to be more self-initiating and self-propelled in the learning process.

It seems to me that sufficient evidence now exists to state that certain kinds of programmatic orientations are more likely than other types to carry a certain measurable impact for a still-to-be-defined period of time, and for a specific population that can be identified. From our experimental enrichment program, for example, there is some initial evidence, yet to be fully analyzed and reported, that among children who show the most gain from their early enriched experiences (usually both enriched preschool and kindergarten years) are those with a tested low normal or somewhat below normal IQ and a highly deprived background. On the other hand, children who enter the experimental classes in the first grade,* and who come from somewhat less deprived circumstances, though from similar SES categories, and who have had traditional kindergarten or nursery experience, or both, frequently have higher tested IQs at first-grade entrance than do many of their previously enriched peers.

These findings may contribute to answering the question as to which children are likely to show the greatest gains from a particular intervention situation. In other words, one might speculate that there is a relationship between level of deprivation and amount of gain from exposure to so-called enriching experiences, such that a child from the most deprived background, and with an IQ in the lower part of the normal range, profits the most from the cognitive stimulation. This relationship may be the key to success of operations aimed at achieving the first objective: retarding or arresting the accumulating deficit.

A program to achieve this, referred to as a "first-goal" program, on the preschool or kindergarten level corresponds in a broad perspec-

---

* These children who enter at first grade are "fillers" for the overall program: children added to bring the number in the first-grade class up to that required by the Board of Education. These additions are made necessary because of attrition of the sample over the previous two-year period.

tive to the stimulation and the cognitive orientation found in most middle-class families and in some families from the lower class that would tend to rate low on indices of deprivation. (This is not to say that the special programs should or could be built on a simple transfer of the covert and overt curriculum of the middle-class home. Just as the techniques must relate to the child's current level of development, so must they be continuous with his own background of experience.)

This first phase would involve exposure to an environment demanding development and stimulating it along certain parameters. This environment would include sensorimotor stimulation, opportunities for making perceptual discriminations, interacting with a verbally adequate adult, receiving some individual attention, linking words and objects and meaningfully relating them in stories or to varying experiential contexts, being assisted in experiencing positive self-identifications, being encouraged toward task perseverance, and being helped to receive both tangible and verbal rewards for relatively competent performance. Such an environment includes stimulation which would be demanding of responses consistent with achieved developmental capabilities, and which would have sufficient and continual feedback from adults.

While it is not appropriate to go into a detailed curriculum statement, the foregoing represents the essential elements which underlie basic curriculum development in order to achieve the first goal.

Headstart-type programs represent quasi-first-goal programs to the extent to which they offer environments and curricula which stimulate development by including some of the essential aspects discussed above. Under these conditions they will probably be successful in obtaining significant results for the high-deprivation, low-achieving children. For the less deprived, higher-achieving children, I would hypothesize that the enrichment environment and the learning opportunities it offers will not be sufficient to substantially influence their long-term performance.

From the data previously reported, it can be expected that exposure to a full-program experience in the nursery and kindergarten years, aimed toward the first goal, will significantly elevate children's performance at the first-grade level, though the performance will probably not overlap substantially with middle-class distributions. Therefore, I have referred to the goal of this strategy as being the arresting of the accumulating-deficit process. Whether or not a permanent change is produced cannot be determined from the initial data or experiences now available: we do not know if significant change will be maintained through the primary grades, and it would be socially irresponsible to communicate the impression that early gains can be extrapolated to performance later in the school years.

It is quite possible that initial changes will be seriously attenuated when these children leave the consciously enriched situation for the routine curriculum. It may very well be that, to maintain the initial changes, continuity of exposure to the environmental ingredients previously referred to is necessary, at least through the preoperational stage described by Piaget.

It is probable that, when children complete even a current "idealized" program, they are not having linked onto their basic experiences the linguistic and coping skills necessary for handling symbolic and abstract material. It might even be that our failure to establish real program continuity through the preschool and elementary years may result in the children's not having an opportunity to utilize a crucial stage for the development of higher-order conceptualizing capabilities. It is essential that we explore the possibility that we are currently giving children sufficient stimulation and coping opportunities to establish a higher level of functioning, but that, by not maintaining an environment that demands development, we later vitiate our own earlier efforts, even though the children's overall performance level improves. The question of continuity is not the only relevant issue here. For example, simple training in labeling or in gross visual and auditory discriminations may improve vocabulary or perceptual discrimination and give a feeling to both the teacher and the child of adequate performance which may not in fact generalize to the higher-order functions increasingly required for adequate achievement. In other words, the question raised here is whether our current programs are sufficient to achieve the goals previously defined and always explicitly associated with program rationales.

To accumulate any definitive data on these points it will be necessary to continue evaluating the effects of special programs for a period of years. There is no reason to suppose, *ipso facto,* that all effects will be immediately visible, nor that immediate gains will be maintained. It is highly likely that certain functions need a long time to mature once they are stimulated, while other functions develop at a fairly rapid rate. It is also likely that some curricula will stimulate development in areas which seem far removed from the content. Further, it is eminently plausible to assume that stimulation of a basic function at a time later than that at which it would ordinarily develop might not automatically yield the consequent development of the more specific skills which it underlies. Many similar questions can be formulated, all pointing to the necessity of an evaluation over time in order to ascertain the effects of an intervention program.

With all this, it also should be recognized that, if the child fails either to maintain progress or to have made progress, what may be reflected are not the child's potentialities but the failure to articulate adequately the various necessary encounters suggested in the brief curriculum description. Currently, I know of no program, including ours at the Institute for Developmental Studies, that sufficiently delineates the desired curriculum and carries it out with maximum fidelity, though we are now in the process of detailing a curriculum that hopefully will be inclusive of first-type programs.

It should be emphasized that the general orientation included in these first-goal programs can be developed by many institutions with somewhat differing orientations, making possible a great deal of heterogeneity in specific curriculum formats. Nevertheless, I would speculate that certain requirements must be met in order to achieve stable developmental changes for the bulk of the deprived population, changes of a magnitude sufficient to allow maximum growth potential. An example of one major requirement, I would think, would be to insure that the child knows from his experiences that he can both comprehend and use a language system which makes it possible to probe the world of knowledge with mediational, symbolic, and abstract concepts. He should be able to put this language system to use in the daily interaction with curriculum and reading materials, as well as with the adults in the total school environment, and eventually in the interaction with the larger environment.

It should be possible now to begin the systematic development of the next stage of the evolution of curriculum strategies—what was previously termed the "second generation" curriculum. I will call these programs "second-goal" programs, and their objective is to insure the maintenance of gains achieved in the first-type programs, and to achieve the second and prepare for the third goals previously defined. In essence a more potent curriculum is called for, and one which includes more clearly defined components, particularly in the language area.

The second goal, as previously defined, is the achievement in disadvantaged children of mean achievement scores that substantially overlap with middle-class performance. Following from the concepts discussed, together with those previously suggested by my colleagues and myself, and by other investigators, it appears that the next step would be to evolve a curriculum which would emphasize the development in the child of a linguistic-conceptual schema, including a developing vocabulary which would contribute to an increasingly elaborated syntax.

Several elements of such a second-goal curriculum emphasis can be defined:

1. The first element would be to help the child to link past experiences and future anticipations and fantasies through overt verbalization and its internalization in the form of verbal mediation. Only through the attainment of a temporal concept can the past experience and learning be wheeled into the present and applied in the future.

2. The second element involves creating an environment in which the verbal matrix would be reflected in a person orientation instead of the closed-end status orientation that, according to Bernstein,[1,2] Hess and Shipman,[7] and other investigators, is typical of many lower-class homes (though it might also be said that the same conditions may hold in middle-class families, especially those characterized by a high degree of authoritarianism). Enrichment programs which apply the concepts coming from this orientation would encourage a child to seek reasons and ask questions, to choose alternatives, and would help him to develop a cognitive style that permits probing into experiences and thereby to attain informational feedback and reinforcement.

This cognitive style, including the concomitant attitude of curiosity, certainly can develop in a successful program at the first stage, and we have observational and anecdotal evidence of it. The question is whether or not the earlier programs made it possible for the child to initiate his own explorations and inquiries into the structure of his environment and to classify the new knowledge and information being assimilated. A child may acquire both a lot of information and certain skills, and his performance may correspondingly improve, yet, if the assimilation is passive, if it is not interiorized and self-motivating, he may be unable to build a reasonably connected system for interrelating his experiences and knowledge. As previously mentioned, there is some initial evidence in support of this point: many of our enrichment children show vastly increased vocabularies and funds of knowledge and much-improved orientation to the environment, but do not have a correspondingly improved syntax or verbal mediational capability. It may be that the optimal period for achieving the capability for conceptual classifying phases out in the middle or late stage of the preoperational period. If so, we need a much more rapid acceleration in the development of curriculum experiences and in the evolution of systematic procedures to be incorporated into enrichment programs.

3. In essence, the third element for emphasis in a second-goal curriculum follows from the first two, and is directed toward an area that often is a great barrier to the overcoming of learning deficits. That is the decoding of society's formal instructional code. In order to be able to make spontaneous classifications of perceptions and all environmental encounters, the child must be able to interiorize information and experiences. Such internalization is necessary if the child is to profit substantially and permanently from an enrichment situation. As previously mentioned, an elaborative cognitive style is probably required for this goal, and the child needs training in abstracting relevant and necessary features from trips, stories, and other learning experiences, if he is to succeed.

The way stories are used in the curriculum can be illustrative of these points. Stories can be used in different ways at different times. Initially in an enrichment program they can be used to familiarize children with long speech sequences and with particular content and vocabulary, or simply to teach them to focus on and attend to someone reading to them. To read a story to a passively attending group of children and to ask them a few random questions about it may have great initial value for increasing vocabulary and information; but such a procedure has deficiencies when used later on. The procedure does not have built into it a linguistically operative system for the child to conceptualize the story, and consequently he is not being effectively prepared to succeed with the formal curriculum. For example, a story has context as well as content, syntax as well as vocabulary, feeling tone as well as information, certain cause-and-effect relationships, and logical intervening sequences, as well as a beginning and an end. The child, through the proper programming of questions, can have his attention called to all these features.

The most effective use of story materials also includes their invasion and modification by the child. This process has at least three definable components:

a. Saliency. The story is new or old for the class or for the child, and is either similar to or different from stories heard before, either in school or at home. The story has both an objective context and an associational, subjective context. It expresses affect and relationships that may or may not have been previously explicated in the classroom. Nevertheless the child should be able, and should be assisted, to identify salient features on all of these dimensions, and to connect them with his developing cognitive network. When this is done consistently, the network should become expanded and deepened in a way that would make it continually more receptive to the coordinated incorporation of new material.

b. Condensation. By condensation I mean the ability to organize and compress the essence of an experience or story by telescoping the relevant and eliminating the irrelevant details. This process involves a high order of verbal mediation. Again, questions could be programmed to help the child develop the kind of cognitive parsimony necessary for adequate condensation.

c. Extrication. This component is to some extent contingent on the other two, and is really what is measured by most verbally oriented achievement tests. Extrication involves seeing logical and complex interrelationships in "shorthand," and selecting the cogent features to be adapted to particular play or other learning situation. Here we have particularity, the active transposition of symbols, and the ability to utilize the essential condensed ingredients in the framework of their experiential saliency. In essence, this may be an operational definition of what in other contexts is called "learning to learn."

This exposition of the use of stories is equally applicable to other curriculum experiences, such as trips, science demonstrations, and the like.

The foregoing discussion is not meant to imply that the other ingredients of first-goal enrichment programs, as delineated on pages 20–22, are not incorporated in the succeeding levels. Actually, the contrary is true. But, as previously mentioned, the reinforcement a child receives from successful coping on the earlier levels may no longer occur if he does not have the verbal training and skills to make abstractions and generalizations from his concrete experiences. For example, a necessary component of the earlier enrichment stages is helping the child to identify similarities and differences in stimuli presented to the different sensory modalities. The repetition of such experience in itself serves to enhance only the child's discrimination capabilities. However, if the experience is to make it possible for the child to handle new and increasingly complex stimuli, it is necessary that abstract verbal symbols be attached. By such a process the growth of verbal mediational processes should be stimulated, and thereby a particular experience can contribute to cognitive growth in more than one area.

To repeat: The emphasis for the second-type curriculum has been placed on abstract verbal processes because they relate centrally to problem solving and to the acquisition of new knowledge and skills. In other words, as previously indicated, simply increasing the quantity of vocabulary and factual knowledge is important but is not in itself a sufficient achievement. If this increase is what an intervention program accomplishes, it may well yield initially significant gains that are not maintained later on, when the learning process involves a greater degree of autonomy and when successful solution of problems presented calls for the relating and applying of prior learning through the utilization of complex language functions.

Specification of techniques to accomplish what was identified as the third goal of intervention programs will have to wait until there is some experience with the second-goal curriculum. However, it can be predicted that the third-goal programs will be both more general—to stimulate overall learning-to-learn and attentional functions—and will more specifically relate to the development of particular skills. The linguistic component will probably become increasingly important. It may be necessary for this component to be introduced at a reasonably early stage, though not necessarily during the first year of an enrichment experience. Also, in order to arrest the cumulative-deficit process and to go beyond that by actually reversing deprivation effects and carrying performance levels up to national-norm expectations, more potent interventions along the lines discussed will be necessary. These interventions will probably involve an accelerated curriculum which reaches the child during a maximally receptive or optimal period. In addition, there might be exposure to a continuous, systematically evolving enriched environment for a full five years, with at least two of these years being pre-first grade.

In making these predictions about some necessary attributes of effective programs, I have indicated a long-term time trajectory, both for program development and for the period of special intervention expected for each child. If we are to assume a responsibility for using the most powerful tools that will be evolving, then we must assume responsibility for their adequate adaptation and for permitting sufficient continuity—measured in years—for a child to interact meaningfully with the experiences available in the new intervention environment. In this context, it might be appropriate to note that NASA's program was not established on a short-term basis, nor was it expected to achieve its final goals in its early life or to be satisfied with its initial goals or results.

The overwhelming evidence from the last few decades is that the child is basically malleable. This is truer for some functions than for others, and for some stages or periods than for others. It may not be true for mastering certain skills if specified or critical periods have elapsed—but for this last there is less empirical evidence and, therefore, the statement is less definitive. Hunt [5] indicates that the extent to which modification of function is possible is dependent on the correspondence, or "match," between individual developmental stages and external stimulation. The extent of malleability, then, is related to the appropriateness and power of the entire social intervention process.

Actually, what all this involves is stimulating what is really the prime national resource: the intellectual capabilities of the entire population. Attempts to accomplish this by underfunded and instant programs that do not fundamentally change the curriculum and the character of the schools will simply be ineffective placebos.

It will be expensive and will require a maximum effort and much real social modification to make education an effective instrumentality for overcoming the social and psychological consequences of poverty and discrimination. Maybe we have started along this road in the new education, mental health, and antipoverty legislation. But in the early childhood area alone it will eventually cost enormously more than what is now being allocated in order to do the necessary research, application, retraining, and social reorganization to achieve permanent results.

REFERENCES

1. Bernstein, B. Linguistic codes, hesitation phenomena and intelligence. *Lang. & Speech,* 1962, **5** (1), 31–46.
2. Bernstein, B. Social class, linguistic codes, and grammatical elements. *Lang. & Speech,* 1962, **5** (4), 221–240.
3. Bloom, B. *Stability and change in human characteristics.* New York: Wiley, 1964.

4. Gordon, T. J., & Helmer, O. *Report on a long range forecasting study.* New York: Rand Corp., Sept., 1964.

5. Hunt, J. McV. The psychological basis for using pre-school enrichment as an antidote for cultural deprivation. Merrill-Palmer Quart., 1964, *10*, 3, 209–243.

6. Jensen, A. R. Preschool development of children's educational potential. A paper prepared for *Time-Life Books, Early Learning Program* (restricted distribution), 1965.

7. Shipman, Virginia C., & Hess, R. D. Children's conceptual styles as a function of social status and maternal conceptual styles. Prepared for Amer. Psychol. Ass. Symposium on "The Effect of Maternal Behavior on Cognitive Development and Impulsivity," Chicago, Sept., 1965.

2 /

Some Psychosocial Aspects of Learning in the Disadvantaged

MARTIN DEUTSCH

It has long been known that some general relationship exists between the conditions of social, cultural, and economic deprivation and cognitive deficit. The environment having the highest rate of disease, crime, and social disorganization also has the highest rate of school retardation. Deficiencies in linguistic skills and reading are particularly striking. School dropout and failure, apart from what they represent in lost potential to the individual and his community, mean that, as adults, those who have failed or dropped out will be confined to the least skilled and least desirable jobs and will have almost no opportunity for upward social mobility.

A large body of empirical literature supports the assumption that certain environmental conditions may retard psychological processes, including intellectual development. This conclusion is borne out in research on both animals and human beings.[8],[9] One of the most comprehensive reviews of the effects of environmental impoverishment on intellectual development, by Clarke and Clarke,[7] presents data collected on adolescents and young adults who have experienced severe deprivation as a result of cruelty, neglect, or parental separation. Bruner[5] writes that "exposure to normally enriched environments makes the development of (cognitive) strategies possible by providing intervening opportunities for trial and error . . . that there is impairment under a deprived regimen seems . . . to be fairly evident." Although he does not refer specifically to the environment of the lower-class child, Bruner's remarks seem especially relevant here. The obvious implication is that disadvantaged children, who have a meager environmental basis for developing cognitive skills, are often unprepared to cope with the formal intellectual and learning demands of school.

FACILITATING GROWTH

Nevertheless, a fostering environment for such children can facilitate intellectual development. Bruner,[6] for example, suggests that certain environmental conditions increase the likelihood of learning cognitive strategies. And Clarke and Clarke[7] report striking increases in IQ in a deprived group during a six-year program aimed at reversing deprivation effects. That improved environmental conditions may have a positive impact on the intellectual development of children is also supported by the studies of the Iowa group.[10,11,12] Informal observation shows that, even in the most economically depressed areas, where school retardation rates are highest, some children manifest considerable school success and academic proficiency. If we assume a causal relationship between environmental conditions and cognitive development, then variation in such development could partially reflect variations within the environment. We can assume that no so-called underprivileged area is homogeneous: There are, indeed, considerable variations in the home environments of children from such areas—variations ranging from large fatherless families supported by public assistance to small intact families with inadequate but regular income.

Moreover, learning contexts are as heterogeneous as environmental backgrounds. Although the two contexts are not actually disparate, early socialization, mediated through home and neighborhood environments and mass media, requires responses different from those necessary for school learning and subject mastery. The formal learning processes carry well-defined criteria of failure and success not mediated through such behavioral indices as group leadership influence, and the like, whereas the informal learning environment has no explicitly stated criteria or marking systems. In the latter, success may be more highly related to leadership, and failure to rejection or subordination by the group.

PSYCHOLOGICAL CONTEXTS

Even as his learning context changes when the child enters school, so does his psychological context for achievement. At this point the amount of continuity between the home environment and that of school can strongly influence the child's responses to the learning and achievement context of school. The discontinuity between the lower-class child's background and the school impairs his sucessful responses in the new situation.

The middle-class child is more likely to have been continuously prodded intellectually by his parents and rewarded for correct answers, whereas, in the main, the lower-class child's parents have seldom subjected him to the pressure of a formal adult-child learning situation. The middle-class child is likely to have experienced, in the behavior of adults in his environment, the essential ingredients implicit in the role of teacher. For the lower-class child, relating to the teacher and school officials requires a new kind of behavior, for which he has not necessarily been prepared.

School curricula and learning techniques usually imply an assumption that the child has had prior experience in the complex learning area, where there are logical assumptions as to appropriate behavior and where success is rewarded and failure is disapproved. The teacher, trained in our not-so-modern teacher-education institutions, assumes—probably consciously as well as unconsciously—that the school child is a quasi-passive recipient of knowledge, and that he clearly understands the teacher's educative and remedial functions. In this regard, the teacher is as likely to be as confused about the child's expectations as the child is confused about the school's expectations.

Lacking sufficient sociological sophistication, school authorities understandably tend to expect from children a level of comprehension and motivation that can be built only through positive experiences in the learning situation. Children who are used to a great deal of motor activity, and who have certain environmentally determined deficiencies in learning to learn, often respond with an inappropriate academic orientation. Teachers meet this situation in several ways, most of which cause serious problems for the socially marginal child. Some teachers establish low expectations, anticipate failure, and, true to the Mertonian self-fulfilling prophecy, find an increasing rate of failure.

Another reaction seems to be, "They can't learn; they don't care; their parents are not concerned." This projective device serves to relieve the professional of responsibility, since it does contain a grain of truth: Often older siblings and neighbors of the lower-class child have experienced so much failure and so much class and cultural arrogance as to generate a great apathy out of which none of them expects positive consequences from the school experience. This very apathy is sometimes reflected in the attitudes of the educational apparatus toward the lower-class community.

Still other teachers say, "It is all the environment impoverishment, economic insecurity, segregation, second-class citizenship, historical chains. Of course, none of these is the child's fault, but neither is it the school's fault." This approach has greater validity, invoking as it does social circumstances obviously crucial to the developing organism. Yet such a view often leads to negation not only of the essential responsibility of the school but also of the actual and potential strengths of the children. Most important, it induces an elaborate rationale for the further alienation of teachers from their primary function, teaching. The essential element, which is both professionally and psychologically threatening, is simply that, for the child inadequately equipped to handle what the school has to offer, it is up to the school to develop compensatory strategies through a program of stimulation appropriate to his capabilities. Essentially, the disadvantaged child is still further disadvantaged when the school, as the primary socializing and teaching agent, refuses to accept its own failure whenever any such child fails. For the school to assume its full responsibility requires constant self-criticism and self-evaluation; these have not been characteristic of educational systems, despite noteworthy exceptions.

To put it more bluntly, when teacher-training institutions and educational systems foster an atmosphere of critical evaluation of their procedures and establish high criteria for professional training and development, teachers will maintain a psychological connection with their children that today is often severed, especially when the teacher, with neither a theoretical nor a working model, must bridge social-class discontinuities. Were more of today's children succeeding in learning to read at grade level, we would be forced to reconstruct our theory considerably. They are not, and the total atmosphere in the majority of our urban schools having large groups of disadvantaged youngsters becomes less and less conducive not merely to the learning process but also to the positive child-teacher relationship that establishes motivation and gives rise to high standards of achievement.

REFLECTIONS OF FAILURE

Responsibility for this unfavorable learning situation is not the school's alone. It lies in a combination of social circumstances, historical apathy, economic exploitation, and a society that does not put its money where its explicit values are. Even so, the school most directly reflects society's failure: It is the one institution that has the opportunity directly to affect the situation.

In this total atmosphere, what are some of the additional handicaps that the disadvantaged child brings into school? If we expect the school to organize so as to meet the child on his own developmental level, then we must know a good deal about the specific intellectual sequelae likely to be associated more with economic impoverishment than with affluence. Further, we need simple and adequate ways of measuring the actual development of each child's abilities, because they are the foundation for the skills the school is to teach him. Such specific information will enable the teacher to teach him more adequately and to present him with the most appropriate stimuli. Moreover, the child's probable success will increase when the material presented is truly consistent with his developmental level, since engendering a sense of competence, in White's terms,[13] can sustain motivation, thereby facilitating learning.

The self-image is vital to learning. School experiences can either reinforce invidious self-concepts acquired from the environment, or help to develop—or even induce—a negative self-concept. Conversely, they can effect positive self-feelings by providing for concrete achievements and opportunities to function with competence, although initially these experiences must be in the most limited and restricted areas. The evidence leads us to the inescapable conclusion that, by the time they enter school, many disadvantaged children have developed negative self-images, which the school does little to mitigate.

Another significant element, usually ignored, probably helps shape the perception of himself that the child develops in school, namely, the use of time. Generally, time is inefficiently used, there is minimal individualized attention, and the child often spends much time in unproductive rote activities, while the teacher focuses her attention on remedial subgroups or the omnipresent paper work. Given the high pupil-teacher ratio, the critical need is for autoinstructional devices or preprogrammed curriculum elements to which the child can turn. This is part of a situation where responsibility cannot be placed on the teacher, and the frequent use of this downtrodden professional as a scapegoat reflects chiefly only her position as the psychologically operative instrument in the education of the child.

In a sense, after passing through the whole of society's educational echelons, the buck stops with her (but not in her pocket). Nevertheless, this understanding does not improve the situation. Too often, the child is seriously understimulated, even with the best of teachers, and there is little overall curriculum planning for the needs of disadvantaged children. Most important, society has furnished neither funds nor the educational leadership and training necessary for the new supplementary technologies that would enormously increase the effective use of time. These would, in turn, help the child develop a sense of purpose and belonging in the school context.

DECREASING ALIENATION

Autoinstructional and programmed devices and methods might also give the child a sense of greater mastery over the unfamiliar school environment: They could reduce his passivity by giving him greater control over the timing of stimuli, thus minimizing cultural differences in time orientation. Further, in the self-corrective feedback of programmed materials, the teacher's role of giving reward and disapproval would be shared; for a child unaccustomed to these as means of motivation for intellectual performance, it might help decrease his alienation from the school. If these hypotheses are valid, then the new educational techniques could socially facilitate the learning process.

The extent of the disadvantaged child's alienation as a crucial factor in handicapping his school performance and achievement has been emphasized. Much of this is structural, and much of the psychosocial problem lies in the interaction between the child and the school. However, cognitive variables which have been socially influenced or determined also contribute to the whole process of increasing the mutual alienation of the school and the child. Among these, one of the major difficulties is the often nonfunctional language system he brings to school.

LANGUAGE AND LEARNING

I would like to point out here that social-class determination of linguistic styles and habits is an effective deterrent to communication and understanding between child and teacher. To illustrate, the child is unaccustomed to both attending to, and being the object of, what are for him long, orderly, focused verbal sequences. Yet this is the primary method of scholastic teaching and discipline. Further, because the disadvantaged child is less familiar with the syntactical regularities and normative frequencies of the language, he has difficulty in ordering sequences and in both deriving meaning from, and putting meaning into, context. This is all the more disadvantageous for the lower-class child because he has a short attention span for the verbal material to which he is exposed in school. Consequently, he is likely to miss a great deal, even when he is trying to listen. For such a child it is extremely important to feel some mastery in handling at least receptive language. This is made more difficult by what Bernstein, the English sociologist,[1,2,3,4] has described as the different dialects spoken by lower- and middle-class people.

This discussion keeps returning to the need for helping the educator to develop a comprehensive consciousness of the psychological as well as the learning difficulties of the disadvantaged child; the real potential for change; the specifics involved in training children, for example, to ask questions, or to become aware of syntactical regularities, or to use autoinstructional materials; and the imperative need to maintain as high as possible the level of stimulation and relevancy in the classroom. Here the research and insights of the behavioral sciences should be able to contribute significantly, provided the educational albatross takes a few "risks" to accommodate social change.

REFERENCES

1. Bernstein, B. Language and social class. *Brit. J. Sociol.*, 1960, 11, 271–276.
2. Bernstein, B. Social structure, language and learning. *Educ. Res.*, 1961, 3 (3), 163–176.

3. Bernstein, B. Linguistic codes, hesitation phenomena and intelligence. *Lang. & Speech*, 1962, **5** (1), 31–46.
4. Bernstein, B. Social class, linguistic codes and grammatical elements. *Lang. & Speech*, 1962, **5** (4), 221–240.
5. Bruner, J. S. *The process of education.* Cambridge: Harvard Univer. Press, 1960.
6. Bruner, J. S. The course of cognitive growth. *Amer. Psychol.*, 1965, **19**, 1–15.
7. Clarke, A. D. B., & Clarke, A. M. Recovery from the effects of deprivation. *Acta Psychol.*, 1959, **16**, 137–144.
8. Hebb, D. O. *The organization of behavior.* New York: Wiley, 1949.
9. Hunt, J. McV. *Intelligence and experience.* New York: Ronald, 1961.
10. Skeels, H. M., Updegraff, Ruth, Wellman, Beth L., & Williams, A. M. A study of environmental stimulation: An orphanage preschool project. *Univer. Iowa Stud. Child Welf.*, 1938, **15**, No. 4.
11. Skodak, Marie, & Skeels, H. M. A final follow-up study of one hundred adopted children. *J. genet. Psychol.*, 1949, **75**, 85–125.
12. Wellman, Beth L. Iowa studies on the effects of schooling. *Yearb. nat. Soc. Stud. Educ.*, 1940, **39**, 377–399.
13. White, R. W. Motivation reconsidered: The concept of competence. *Psychol. Rev.*, 1959, **66**, 297–333.

3 /

The Disadvantaged Child and the Learning Process

MARTIN DEUTSCH

This paper will discuss the interaction of social and developmental factors and their impact on the intellectual growth and school performance of the child. It will make particular reference to the large number of urban children who come from marginal social circumstances. While much of the discussion will be speculative, where appropriate it will draw on data from the field, and will suggest particular relationships and avenues for future investigation or demonstration.

Among children who come from lower-class socially impoverished circumstances, there is a high proportion of school failure, school dropouts, reading and learning disabilities, as well as life-adjustment problems. This means not only that these children grow up poorly equipped academically, but also that the effectiveness of the school as a major institution for socialization is diminished. The effect of this process is underlined by the fact that this same segment of the population contributes disproportionately to the delinquency and other social-deviancy statistics.

The thesis here is that the lower-class child enters the school situation so poorly prepared to produce what the school demands that initial failures are almost inevitable and that the school experience becomes negatively rather than positively reinforced. Thus the child's experience in school does nothing to counteract the invidious influences to which he is exposed in his slum, and sometimes segregated, neighborhood.

We know that children from underprivileged environments tend to come to school with a qualitatively different preparation for the demands of both the learning process and the behavioral requirements of the classroom. There are various differences in the kinds of socializing experiences these children have had, as contrasted with the middle-class child. The culture of their environment is a different one from the culture that has molded the school and its educational techniques and theory.

We know that it is difficult for all peoples to span cultural discontinuities, and yet we make little if any effort to prepare administrative personnel or teachers and guidance staff to assist the child in this transition from one cultural context to another. This transition must have serious psychological consequences for the child, and probably plays a major role in influencing his later perceptions of other social institutions as he is introduced to them.

It must be pointed out that the relationship between social background and school performance is not a simple one. Rather, evidence which is accumulating points more and more to the influence of background variables on the patterns of perceptual, language, and cognitive development of the child and the subsequent diffusion of the effects of such patterns into all areas of the child's academic and psychological performance. To understand these effects requires delineating the underlying skills in which these children are not sufficiently proficient. A related problem is that of defining what aspects of the background are most influential in producing what kinds of deficits in skills.

ENVIRONMENTAL FACTORS

Let us begin with the most macroscopic background factors. While it is likely that slum life might have delimited areas that allow for positive growth and that the middle-class community has attributes which might retard healthy development, generally the combination of circumstances in middle-class life is considerably more likely to furnish opportunities for normal growth of the child. At the same time, slum conditions are more likely to have deleterious effects on physical and mental development. This is not to say that middle-class life furnishes a really adequate milieu for the maximum development of individual potential: it does not. The fact that we often speak as though it does is a function of viewing the middle-class environment in comparison to the slum. Middle-class people who work and teach across social-class lines often are unable to be aware of the negative aspects of the middle-class background because of its apparent superiority over the less advantageous background provided by lower-class life. We really have no external criterion for evaluating the characteristics of a milieu in terms of how well it is designed to foster development; as a result, we might actually be measuring one area of social failure with the yardstick of social catastrophe.

It is true that many leading personalities in twentieth-century American life have come from the slums; this is a fact often pointed out by nativistic pragmatists in an effort to prove that if the individual "has it in him" he can overcome—and even be challenged by—his humble surroundings. This argument, though fundamentally fallacious, might have had more to recommend it in the past. At the turn of the century we were a massively vertical mobile society—that is, with the exception of certain large minority groups such as the Negroes, the Indians, and the Mexican-Americans who were rarely allowed on the social elevator. In the mid-twentieth century, it is now increasingly possible for all groups to get on, but social and economic conditions have changed, and the same elevator more frequently moves in two directions or stands still altogether. When it does move, it goes more slowly, and, most discouragingly, it also provides an observation window on what, at least superficially, appears to be a most affluent society. Television, movies, and other media continually expose the individual from the slum to the explicit assumption that the products of a consumer society are available to all—or, rather, as he sees it, to all but him. In effect, this means that the child from the disadvantaged environment is an outsider and an observer—through his own eyes and those of his parents or neighbors—of the mainstream of American life. At the same time, when the child enters school he is exposing himself directly to the values and anticipations of a participant in that mainstream—his teacher. It is not sufficiently recognized that there is quite a gap between the training of a teacher and the needs, limitations, and unique strengths of the child from a marginal situation. This gap is, of course, maximized when the child belongs to a minority group that until quite recently was not only excluded from the mainstream, but was not even allowed to bathe in the tributaries.

What are some of the special characteristics of these children, and why do they apparently need exceptional social and educational planning? So often, administrators and teachers say, they are children who are "curious," "cute," "affectionate," "warm," and independently dependent in the kindergarten and the first grade, but who so often become "alienated," "withdrawn," "angry," "passive," "apathetic," or just "trouble-makers" by the fifth and sixth grades. In our research at the Institute for Developmental Studies, it is in the first grade that we usually see the smallest differences between socioeconomic or racial groups in intellectual, language, and some conceptual measures, and in the later grades that we find the greatest differences in favor of the more socially privileged groups. From both teachers' observations and the findings of this increasing gap, it appears that there is a failure on some level of society and, more specifically, the educational system. Was the school scientifically prepared to receive these children in the first place? And, in addition, were the children perhaps introduced to the individual demands of the larger culture at too late an age—that is, in first grade?

Before discussing these psychological products of social deprivation, it is appropriate to look more closely at the special circumstances of Negro slum residents. In the core city of most of our large metropolitan areas, 40 to 70 per cent of the elementary school population is likely to be Negro. In my observations, through workshops in many of these cities, I have often been surprised to find how little real comprehension of the particular problems of these youngsters exists as part of the consciousness of the Negro or white middle-class teachers. While in middle-class schools there is great sensitivity to emotional climates and pressures and tensions that might be operating on the child in either the home or the school, in lower-class schools the problems of social adaptation are so massive that sensitivity tends to become blunted.

In the lower-class Negro group there still exist the sequelae of the conditions of slavery. Although a hundred years have passed, this is a short time in the life of a people. And the extension of tendrils of the effects of slavery into modern life has been effectively discouraged only in the last few decades, when there have been some real attempts to integrate the Negro fully into American life. It is often difficult for teachers and the personnel of other community agencies to understand the Negro lower-class child—particularly the child who has come, or whose parents have come, from the rural South. There is a whole set of implicit and explicit value systems which determine our educational philosophies, and the institutional expectation is that all children participate in these systems. Yet for these expectations to be met, the child must experience some continuity of sociocultural participation in and sharing of these value systems before he comes to school. This is often just not the case for the child who comes from an encapsulated community, particularly when the walls have been built by the dominant social and cultural forces that have also determined the value systems relating to learning.

A recent article in *Fortune* magazine asked why the Negro failed to take full advantage of opportunities open to him in American life. At least part of the answer is that the Negro has not been fully integrated into American life, and that even knowledge about particular occupations and their requirements is not available outside the cultural mainstream. Implications of this for the aspirations and motivations of children will be discussed later.

Another source of misunderstanding on the part of school and social agency people is the difficulty of putting in historical perspective the causal conditions responsible for the high percentage of broken homes in the Negro community. Implications of these conditions for the child's emotional stability are very frequently recognized, but the effects on the child's motivation, self-concept, and achievement orientation are not often understood.

The Negro family was first broken deliberately by the slave traders and the plantation owners for their own purposes. As was pointed out earlier, the hundred years since slavery is not a very long time for a total social metamorphosis even under fostering conditions—and during that period the Negro community has been for the most part economically marginal and isolated from the contacts which would have accelerated change. The thirteen depressions and recessions we have had since Emancipation have been devastating to this community. These marginal economic and encapsulated social circumstances have been particularly harsh on the Negro male. The chronic instability has greatly influenced the Negro man's concept of himself and his general motivation to succeed in competitive areas of society where the rewards are greatest. All these circumstances have contributed to the instability of the Negro family, and particularly to the fact that it is most often broken by the absence of the father. As a result, the lower-class Negro child entering school often has had no experience with a "successful" male model or thereby with the corresponding psychological framework in which effort can result in at least the possibility of achievement. Yet the value system of the school and of the learning process is predicated on the assumption that effort will result in achievement.

To a large extent, much of this is true not only for the Negro child but for all children who come from impoverished and marginal social and economic conditions. These living conditions are characterized by great overcrowding in substandard housing, often lacking adequate sanitary and other facilities. While we do not know the actual importance, for example, of moments of privacy, we do know that the opportunity frequently does not exist. In addition, there are likely to be large numbers of siblings and half-siblings, again with there being little opportunity for individuation. At the same time, the child tends to be restricted to his immediate environment, with conducted explorations of the "outside" world being infrequent and sometimes nonexistent. In the slums, and to an unfortunately large extent in many other areas of our largest cities, there is little opportunity to observe natural beauty, clean landscapes, or other pleasant and aesthetically pleasing surroundings.

In the child's home, there is a scarcity of objects of all types, but especially of books, toys, puzzles, pencils, and scribbling paper. It is not that the mere presence of such materials would necessarily result in their productive use, but it would increase the child's familiarity with the tools that will confront him in school. Actually, for the most effective utilization of these tools, guidance and explanations are necessary from the earliest time of exposure. Such guidance requires not only the presence of aware and educated adults, but also time—a rare commodity in these marginal circumstances. Though many parents will share in the larger value system of having high aspirations for their children, they are unaware of the operational steps required for the preparation of the child to use optimally the learning opportunities in the school. Individual potential is one of the most unmarketable properties if the child acquires no means for its development, or if no means exist for measuring it objectively. It is here that we must understand the consequences of all these aspects of the slum matrix for the psychological and cognitive development of the child.

PSYCHOLOGICAL FACTORS

A child from any circumstance who has been deprived of a substantial portion of the variety of stimuli which he is maturationally capable of responding to is likely to be deficient in the equipment required for learning.

Support for this is found in Hunt,[2] who, in discussing Piaget's developmental theories, points out (pp. 258–259) that, according to Piaget,

> . . . the rate of development is in substantial part, but certainly not wholly, a function of environmental circumstances. Change in circumstances is required to force the accommodative modifications of schemata that constitute development. Thus, the greater the variety of situations to which the child must accommodate his behavioral structures, the more differentiated and mobile they become. Thus, the more new things a child has seen and the more he has heard, the more things he is interested in seeing and hearing. Moreover, the more variation in reality with which he has coped, the greater is his capacity for coping.

This emphasis on the importance of variety in the environment implies the detrimental effects of lack of variety. This in turn leads to a concept of "stimulus deprivation." But it is important that it be correctly understood. By this is not necessarily meant any restriction of the quantity of stimulation, but, rather, a restriction to a segment of the spectrum of stimulation potentially available. In addition to the restriction in variety, from what is known of the slum environment it might be postulated that the segments made available to these children tend to have poorer and less systematic ordering of stimulation sequences, and would thereby be less useful to the growth and activation of cognitive potential.

This deprivation has effects on both the formal and the contentual aspects of cognition. By "formal" is meant the operations—the behavior—by which stimuli are perceived and responded to. By "contentual" is meant the actual content of the child's knowledge and comprehension. "Formal equipment" would include perceptual discrimination skills, the ability to sustain attention, and the ability to use adults as sources of information and for satisfying curiosity. Also included would be the establishment of expectations of reward from accumulation of knowledge, from task completion, and from adult reinforcement, and the ability to delay gratification. Examples of "contentual equipment" would be the language-symbolic system, environmental information, general and environmental orientation, and concepts of comparability and relativity appropriate to the child's age level. The growth of a differentiated attitudinal set toward learning is probably a resultant of the interaction between formal and contentual levels.

Hypothesizing that stimulus deprivation will result in deficiencies in either of these equipments, let us examine the particular stimuli which are available and those which are absent from the environment of the child who comes from the conditions discussed above. This reasoning suggests also certain hypotheses regarding the role of environment in the evolving of the formal and contentual systems.

As was pointed out in the previous section, the disadvantaged environment as well as certain aspects of the middle-class circumstance offers the child, over all, a restricted range of experience. While one does see great individual variability in these children, social conditions reduce the range of this variation; with less variety in input, it would be reasonable to assume a concomitant restriction in the variety of output. This is an important respect in which social poverty may have a leveling effect on the achievement of individual skills and abilities. Concomitantly, in the current problem of extensive underachievement in suburban lower-middle-class areas, the overroutinization of activity with the consequent reduction in variety may well be the major factor.

In individual terms, a child is probably farther away from his maturational ceiling as a result of this experiential poverty. This might well be a crucial factor in the poorer performance of the lower socioeconomic children on standardized tests of intelligence. On such tests, the child is compared with others of his own age. But if his point of development in relation to the maturational ceiling for his age group is influenced by his experience, then the child with restricted experience may actually be developed to a proportionately lower level of his own actual ceiling. If a certain quantum of fostering experience is necessary to activate the achievement of particular maturational levels, then perhaps the child who is deficient in this experience will take longer to achieve these levels, even though his potential may be the same as the more advantaged child. It might be that in order to achieve a realistic appraisal of the ability levels of children, an "experience" age rather than the chronological age should be used to arrive at norms.

This suggests a limitation on the frequent studies comparing Negro and white children. Even when it is possible to control for the formal attributes of social-class membership, the uniqueness of the Negro child's experience would make comparability impossible when limited to these class factors. Perhaps too, if such an interaction exists between experiential and biological determinants of development, it would account for the failure of the culture-free tests, as they too are standardized on an age basis without allowing for the experimental interaction (as distinguished from specific experimental *influence*).

Let us now consider some of the specifics in the child's environment, and their effects on the development of the formal, contentual, and attitudinal systems.

Visually, the urban slum and its overcrowded apartments offer the child a minimal range of stimuli. There are usually few if any pictures on the wall, and the objects in the household, be they toys, furniture, or utensils, tend to be sparse, repetitious, and lacking in form and color variations. The sparsity of objects and lack of diversity of home artifacts which are available and meaningful to the child, in addition to the unavailability of individualized training, gives the child few opportunities to manipulate and organize the visual properties of his environment and thus perceptually to organize and discriminate the nuances of that environment. These would include figure-ground relationships and the spatial organization of the visual field. The sparsity of manipulable objects probably also hampers the development of these functions in the tactile area. For example, while these children have broomsticks and usually a ball, possibly a doll or a discarded kitchen pot to play with, they do not have the different shapes and colors and sizes to manipulate which the middle-class child has in the form of blocks which are bought just for him, or even in the variety of sizes and shapes of cooking utensils which might be available to him as playthings.

It is true, as has been pointed out frequently, that the pioneer child did not have many playthings either. But he had a more active responsibility toward the environment and a great variety of growing plants and other natural resources, as well as a stable family that assumed a primary role for the education and training of the child. In addition, the intellectually normal or superior frontier child could and usually did grow up to be a farmer. Today's child will grow up into a world of automation requiring highly differentiated skills if he and society are to use his intellect.

The effect of sparsity of manipulable objects on visual perception is, of course, quite speculative, as few data now exist. However, it is an important area, as among skills necessary for reading are form discrimination and visual spatial organization. Children from depressed areas, because of inadequate training and stimulation, may not have developed the requisite skills by the time they enter first grade, and the assumption that they do possess these skills may thus add to the frustration these children experience on entering school.

The lower-class home is not a verbally oriented environment. The implications of this for language development will be considered below in the discussion of the contentual systems. Here let us consider its implication for the development of auditory discrimination skills. While the environment is a noisy one, the noise is not, for the most part, meaningful in relation to the child, and for him most of it is background. In the crowded apartments, with all the daily living stresses, there is a minimum of non-instructional conversation directed toward the child. In actuality, the situation is ideal for the child to learn inattention. Furthermore, he does not get practice in auditory discrimination or feedback from adults correcting his enunciation, pronunciation, and grammar. In studies at the Institute for Developmental Studies we have found significant differences in auditory discrimination between lower-class and middle-class children in the first grade. These differences seem to diminish markedly as the children get older, though the effects of their early existence on other functioning remain to be investigated. Here again we are dealing with a skill very important to reading. Our data indicate too that poor readers within social-class groups have significantly more difficulty in auditory discrimination than do good readers. Further, this difference between good and poor readers is greater for the lower-class group.

If the child learns to be inattentive in the preschool environment, as has been postulated, this further diminishes incoming stimulation. Further, if this trained inattention comes about as a result of his being insufficiently called upon to respond to particular stimuli, then his general level of responsiveness will also be diminished. The nature of the total environment and the child-adult interaction is such that reinforcement is too infrequent, and, as a result, the quantity of response is diminished. The implications of this for the structured learning situation in the school are quite obvious.

Related to attentivity is memory. Here also we would postulate the dependence of the child, particularly in the preschool period, on interaction with the parent. It is adults who link the past and the present by calling to mind prior shared experiences. The combination of the constriction in the use of language and in shared activity results, for the lower-class child, in much less stimulation of the early memory function. Although I know of no data supporting this thesis, from my observations it would seem that there is a tendency for these children to be proportionately more present-oriented and less aware of past-present sequences than the middle-class child. This is consistent with anthropological research and thinking. While this could be a function of the poorer time orientation of these children or of their difficulty in verbal expression, both of which will be discussed below, it could also relate to a greater difficulty in seeing themselves in the past or in a different context. Another area which points up the home-school discontinuity is that of time. Anthropologists have pointed out that, from culture to culture, time concepts differ and that time as life's governor is a relatively modern phenomenon and one which finds most of its slaves in the lower-middle, middle-middle, and upper-middle classes. It might not even be an important factor in learning, but it is an essential feature in the measurement of children's performance by testing and in the adjustment of children to the organizational demands of the school. The middle-class teacher organizes the day by allowing a certain amount of time for each activity. Psychologists have long noticed that American Indian children, mountain children, and children from other non-industrial groups have great difficulty organizing their response tempo to meet time limitations. In the Orientation Scale developed at the Institute, we have found that lower-class children in the first grade had significantly greater difficulty than did middle-class children in handling items related to time judgments.

Another area in which the lower-class child lacks preschool orientation is the well-inculcated expectation of reward for performance, especially for successful task completion. The lack of such expectation, of course, reduces motivation for beginning a task and, therefore, also makes less likely the self-reinforcement of activity through the gaining of feelings of competence. In these impoverished, broken homes there is very little of the type of interaction seen so commonly in middle-class homes, in which the parent sets a task for the child, observes its performance, and in some way rewards its completion. Neither, for most tasks, is there the disapproval which the middle-class child incurs when he does not perform properly or when he leaves something unfinished. Again, much of the organization of the classroom is based on the assumption that children anticipate rewards for performance and that they will respond in these terms to tasks which are set for them. This is not to imply that the young lower-class child is not given assignments in his home, nor that he is never given approval or punishment. Rather, the assignments tend to be motoric in character, have a short time span, and are more likely to relate to very concrete objects or services for people. The tasks given to preschool children of the middle class are more likely to involve language and conceptual processes, and are thereby more attuned to the later school setting.

Related to the whole issue of the adult-child dynamic in establishing a basis for the later learning process is the ability of the child to use the adult as a source for information, correction, and the reality testing involved in problem solving and the absorption of new knowledge. When free adult time is greatly limited, homes vastly overcrowded, economic stress chronic, and the general educational level very low—and, in addition, when adults in our media culture are aware of the inadequacy of their education—questions from children are not encouraged, as the adults might be embarrassed by their own limitations and are in any case too preoccupied with the business of just living and surviving. In the child's formulation of concepts of the world, the ability to formulate questions is an essential step in data gathering. If questions are not encouraged or if they are not responded to, this is a function which does not mature.

At the Institute, in our observations of children at the kindergarten level and in our discussions with parents, we find that many lower-class children have difficulty here. It follows that this problem, if it is not compensated for by special school efforts, becomes more serious later in the learning process, as more complex subject matter is introduced. It is here that questioning is not only desirable but essential, for if the child is not prepared to demand clarification he again falls farther behind, the process of alienation from school is facilitated, and his inattentiveness becomes further reinforced since he just does not understand what is being presented.

It is generally agreed that the language-symbolic process plays an important role at all levels of learning. It is included here under the "contentual" rubric because language development evolves through the correct labeling of the environment, and through the use of appropriate words for the relating and combining and recombining of the concrete and abstract components in describing, interpreting, and communicating perceptions, experiences, and ideational matter. One can postulate on considerable evidence that language is one of the areas which are most sensitive to the impact of the multiplicity of problems associated with the stimulus deprivation found in the marginal circumstances of lower-class life. There are various dimensions of language, and for each of these it is possible to evaluate the influence of the verbal environment of the home and its immediate neighborhood.

In order for a child to handle multiple attributes of words and to associate words with their proper referents, a great deal of exposure to language is presupposed. Such exposure involves training, experimenting with identifying objects and having corrective feedback, listening to a variety of verbal material, and just observing adult language usage. Exposure of children to this type of experience is one of the great strengths of the middle-class home, and concomitantly represents a weakness in the lower-class home. In a middle-class home, also, the availability of a great range of objects to be labeled and verbally related to each other strengthens the overall language fluency of the child and gives him a basis for both understanding the teacher and for being able to communicate with her on various levels. An implicit hypothesis in a recent Institute survey of verbal skills is that verbal fluency is strongly related to reading skills and to other highly organized integrative and conceptual verbal activity.

The acquisition of language facility and fluency and experience with the multiple attributes of words is particularly important in view of the estimate that only 60 to 80 per cent of any sustained communication is usually heard. Knowledge of context and of the syntactical regularities of a language makes correct completion and comprehension of the speech sequence possible. This completion occurs as a result of the correct anticipation of the sequence of language and thought. The child who has not achieved these anticipatory language skills is greatly handicapped in school. Thus, for the child who already is deficient in auditory discrimination and in ability to sustain attention, it becomes increasingly important that he have the very skills he lacks most.

The problem in developing preventive and early remedial programs for these children is in determining the emphasis on the various areas that need remediation. For example, would it be more effective to place the greatest emphasis on the training of auditory discrimination, or on attentional mechanisms or on anticipatory receptive language functions in order to achieve the primary goal of enabling the child to understand his teacher? In programming special remedial procedures, we do not know how much variation we will find from child to child. We also do not know if social-class experiences create a sufficiently homogeneous pattern of deficit so that the fact of any intervention and systematic training may be more important than its sequences. If all this is so, the intervention would probably be most valid in the language area, because the large group of lower-class children with the kinds of deficits mentioned are probably maturationally ready for more complex language functioning than they have achieved. Language knowledge, once acquired, can be self-reinforcing in just communicating with peers or talking to oneself.

In observations of lower-class homes, it appears that speech sequences seem to be temporally very limited and poorly structured syntactically. It is thus not surprising to find that a major focus of deficit in the children's language development is syntactical organization and subject continuity. In preliminary analysis of expressive and receptive language data on samples of middle- and lower-class children at the first- and fifth-grade levels, there are indications that the lower-class child has more expressive language ability than is generally recognized or than emerges in the classroom. The main differences between the social classes seem to lie in the level of syntactical organization. If, as is indicated in this research, with proper stimulation a surprisingly high level of expressive language functioning is available to the same children who show syntactical deficits, then we might conclude that the language variables we are dealing with here are by-products of social experience rather than indices of basic ability or intellectual level. This again suggests another possibly vital area to be included in an enrichment or a remedial program: training in the use of word sequences to relate and unify cognitions.

Also on the basis of preliminary analysis of data, it appears that retarded readers have the most difficulty with the organization of expressive language.

Differences between middle- and lower-class language usage have been defined by Bernstein.[1] He reports that the middle class tends to use a more formal language, oriented to relating concepts, while the lower class uses a more informal language, whose referents are more likely to be concrete tasks or objects. This difference might explain why we have found that the middle-class fifth-grade child has an advantage over the lower-class fifth-grader in tasks where precise and somewhat abstract language is required for solution. Further, Bernstein's reasoning would again emphasize the communication gap which exists between the middle-class teacher and the lower-class child.

Though it might belong more in the formal than in the contentual area, one can postulate that the absence of well-structured routine and activity in the home is reflected in the difficulty that the lower-class child has in structuring language. The implication of this for curriculum in the kindergarten and nursery school would be that these children should be offered a great deal of verbalized routine and regulation so that expectation can be built up in the child and then met.

According to Piaget's theories, later problem solving and logical abilities are built on the earlier and orderly progression through a series of developmental stages involving the active interaction between the child and his environment. This is considered a maturational process, though highly related to experience and practice. Language development does not occupy a superordinate position. However, Whorf, Vygotsky, and some contemporary theorists have made language the essential ingredient in concept formation, problem solving, and in the relating to an interpretation of the environment. Current data at the Institute tend to indicate that class differences in perceptual abilities and in general environmental orientation decrease with chronological age, whereas language differences tend to increase. These might tentatively be interpreted to mean that perceptual development occurs first and that language growth and its importance in problem solving comes later. If later data and further analysis support this interpretation, then the implication would be that the lower-class child comes to school with major deficits in the perceptual rather than the language area. Perhaps the poverty of his experience has slowed his rate of maturation. Then by requiring, without the antecedent verbal preparation, a relatively high level of language skill, the school may contribute to an increase in the child's deficit in this area, relative to middle-class children. Meanwhile, his increased experience and normal maturational processes stimulate perceptual development, and that deficit is overcome. But the child is left with a language handicap. The remedy for such a situation would be emphasis on perceptual training for these children in the early school, or, better, preschool, years, combined with a more gradual introduction of language training and requirements.

This theory and interpretation are somewhat, but by no means wholly, in conflict with the previous discussion of language. In an area where there is as yet much uncertainty, it is important to consider as many alternatives as possible, in order not to restrict experimentation.

In any event, whether or not we consider language skills as primary mediators in concept formation and problem solving, the lower-class child seems to be at a disadvantage at the point of entry into the formal learning process.

The other contentual factors that so often result in a poorly prepared child being brought to the school situation are closely interrelated with language. Briefly, they revolve around the child's understanding and knowledge of the physical, geographic, and geometric characteristics of the world around him, as well as information about his self-identity and some of the more macroscopic items of general information. It could be reasonably expected, for example, that a kindergarten or first-grade child who is not mentally defective would know both his first and last names, his address or the city he lives in, would have a rudimentary concept of number relationships, and would know something about the differences between near and far, high and low, and similar relational concepts. Much of what happens in school is predicated on the prior availabilty of this basic information. We know that educational procedures frequently proceed without establishing the actual existence of such a baseline. Again, in the lower-class child it cannot be taken for granted that the home experience has supplied this information or that it has tested the child for this knowledge. In facilitating the learning process in these children, the school must expect frequently to do a portion of the job traditionally assigned to the home and curriculum must be reorganized to provide for establishing a good base. This type of basic information is essential so that the child can relate the input of new information to some stable core.

From all of the foregoing, it is obvious that the lower-class child, when he enters school, has as many problems in understanding what it is all about and why he is there as school personnel have in relating traditional curriculum and learning procedures to this child. Some reorientation is really necessary, as discussion of these problems almost always focuses on the problems the school has, rather than on the enormous confusion, hesitations, and frustrations the child experiences and does not have the language to articulate when he meets an essentially rigid set of academic expectations. Again, from all the foregoing, the child, from the time he enters school and is exposed to assumptions about him derived from experience with the middle-class child, has few success experiences and much failure and generalized frustration, and thus begins the alienating process in the direction of the apathetic and disgruntled fifth-grader described earlier.

The frustration inherent in not understanding, not succeeding, and not being stimulated in the school—although being regulated by it—creates a basis for the further development of negative self-images and low evaluations of individual competencies. This would be especially true for the Negro child who, as we know from doll play and other studies, starts reflecting the social bias in his own self-image at very early ages. No matter how the parents might aspire to a higher achievement level for their child, their lack of knowledge as to the operational implementation, combined with the child's early failure experiences in school, can so effectively attenuate confidence in his ability ever to handle competently challenge in the academic area, that the child loses all motivation.

It is important to state that not all the negative factors and deficits discussed here are present in every or even in any one child. Rather, there is a patterning of socially determined school-achievement-related disabilities which tends initially to set artificially low ceilings for these children: initially artificial, because as age increases it becomes more and more difficult for these children to develop compensatory mechanisms, to respond to special programs, or to make the psychological readjustments required to overcome the cumulative effects of their early deficits.

It is also important to state that there are strengths and positive features associated with lower-class life. Unfortunately, they generally tend not to be, at least immediately, congruent with the demands of the school. For example, lack of close supervision or protection fosters the growth of independence in lower-class children. However, this independence—and probably confidence—in regard to the handling of younger siblings, the crossing of streets, self-care, and creating of their own amusements, does not necessarily meaningfully transfer to the unfamiliar world of books, language, and abstract thought.

SCHOOL CONDITIONS

Educational factors have of course been interlaced throughout this discussion, but there are some special features that need separate delineation.

The lower-class child probably enters school with a nebulous and essentially neutral attitude. His home rarely, if ever, negatively predisposes him toward the school situation, though it might not offer positive motivation and correct interpretation of the school experience. It is in the school situation that the highly charged negative attitudes toward learning evolve, and the responsibility for such large groups of normal children showing great scholastic retardation, the high dropout rate, and to some extent the delinquency problem, must rest with the failure of the school to promote the proper acculturation of these children. Though some of the responsibility may be shared by the larger society, the school, as the institution of that society, offers the only mechanism by which the job can be done.

It is unfair to imply that the school has all the appropriate methods at its disposal and has somehow chosen not to apply them. On the contrary, what is called for is flexible experimentation in the development of new methods, the clear delineation of the problem, and the training and retraining of administrative and teaching personnel in the educational philosophy and the learning procedures that this problem requires.

In addition, the school should assume responsibility for a systematic plan for the education of the child in the areas that have been delineated here by the time the child reaches kindergarten or first grade. This does not mean that the school will abrogate the family's role with regard to the child, but rather that the school will insure both the intellectual and the attitudinal receptivity of each child to its requirements. Part of a hypothesis now being tested in a new pre-school program is based on the assumption that early intervention by well-structured programs will significantly reduce the attenuating influence of the socially marginal environment.

What might be necessary to establish the required base to assure the eventual full participation of these children in the opportunity structure offered by the educational system is an ungraded sequence from age three or four through eight, with a low teacher-pupil ratio. Perhaps, also, the school system should make full use of anthropologists, sociologists, and social psychologists for description and interpretation of the cultural discontinuities which face the individual child when he enters school. In addition, the previously discussed patterning of deficits and strengths should be evaluated for each child and placed in a format which the teacher can use as a guide. In the early years this would enable diagnostic reviews of the intellectual functioning of each child, so that learning procedures, to whatever extent possible, could be appropriate to a particular child's needs. New evaluation techniques must be developed for this purpose, as the standardized procedures generally cannot produce accurate evaluation of the functioning level or achievement potential of these children.

Possibly most important would be the greater utilization by educators in both curriculum development and teacher training of the new and enormous knowledge, techniques, and researches in the social and behavioral sciences. Similarly, social and behavioral scientists have in the school a wonderful laboratory to study the interpenetration and interaction of fundamental social, cognitive, psychological, and developmental processes. Close and continuing collaboration, thus, should be mutually productive and satisfying, and is strongly indicated.

REFERENCES

1. Bernstein, B. Language and social class. *Brit. J. Psychol.*, 1960, 11, 271–276.
2. Hunt, J. McV. *Intelligence and experience*. New York: Ronald, 1961.

4 /

Facilitating Development in the Preschool Child: Social and Psychological Perspectives

MARTIN DEUTSCH

Massive evidence makes it clear that a child's social experience is a very influential factor in his development; yet it is also obvious that the relationship between experience and development is an extremely complex one. A basic assumption of the approach to be presented in this paper is that there is a continual and influential interpenetration of environmental experience and psychological development along a broad front, and that therefore simple cause-effect models can be accurate on only the grossest level.

In a sense, our current social dilemma has the usual contradictions that every period feels are unique to its particular time. Historically, the present era may or may not have more contradictions than other periods. But the rapid development of automated, highly skilled, labor-reducing techniques does have revolutionary consequences for man's relationship to the social order, to work and leisure, and to intellectual activity. Further, the level of our technology, particularly in the field of communication, creates conditions in which these new techniques are rapidly disseminated. Thus, the time within which institutional and structural adjustments can take place is greatly reduced. This necessitates the deliberate and planned manipulation of social conditions in order to avoid, or at least attenuate, the sometimes invidious consequences of rapid change.

In a society of abundance there is an amazingly large segment of our population living in a subsociety of social, economic, and educational impoverishment. The estimates range from 20 to 40 per cent of our population, depending on criteria.[4] The problems associated with marginal employment and crowded, dehumanizing living conditions are, of course, characteristic of the lives of most of the peoples of the world. But here in this country we have the facilities, the productive capacity, and at least some of the knowledge required consciously to reorient social development. A necessary focus for such orientation should be the child, so that he can develop the requisite basic skills for the new technology and changing social institutions.

A thesis presented in this paper is that the behavioral scientist and the educator can facilitate the evolution of the educational institution so that it will be capable of preparing all children for optimal social participation, as the racial, social-class, and sex gatekeepers become inoperative. The contemporary problems of education are to some extent a reflection of current technological, racial, and urban conflicts inherent in accelerated social change. At the same time, the human sciences (though beset by similar problems) could become major instrumentalities for the resolution of social conflict, since they are among the few systems oriented toward change. For example, the intervention concepts in social psychology and psychiatry are relatively quite new. These disciplines can thus be seen as possible agents for the construction of blueprints to harmonize human needs with cultural transformations.

In general, the human sciences are moving from social and individual diagnosis to remedial therapies. Those sciences are now, in some of the more advanced thinking, concerned with primary prevention, ranging from mental illness and juvenile delinquency to disabilities in learning and socialization. To speculate on a possible avenue of future development, it might be that from this stage an orientation will develop toward assisting the individual to potentiate his intrinsic capacities for productive living and full individual realization.

This is by no means meant to minimize the importance of activities in other disciplines; rather, it is an attempt to specify the potential role and contribution of the human sciences. It must also be remarked that the knowledge available in the combined human sciences is still quite limited, and that too frequently formulas have been presented which are insufficiently related to scientific knowledge.

While to a major degree the behavioral sciences and education have run parallel courses, they have insufficiently interacted with and enriched each other. What better place is there to investigate meaningfully the development of learning processes—or of attitudes or of mental health—than in longitudinal studies in the context of the school, from the nursery school through college? It is always surprising to us how many educators are not aware of the exciting investigations of socialization, learning, and cognitive processes in the field of child development. On the other hand, too many social scientists look upon education and work in the educational field as "applied," "atheoretical," and somehow unrelated to the growth of a child into an adult. Just as medicine is the application of physiology, biochemistry, and similar sciences to human problems, so too could education be the application of the human sciences. As medicine discovers principles and laws that are continually being circulated back to its basic sciences, so could education not only evaluate and validate the principles which it derives from the human sciences, but also could lead toward the genesis of methods of influencing and accelerating individual growth.

In order to achieve such integration, a crucial historical difference between education and psychiatry, sociology, and psychology must be recognized. While the latter have the impetus coming from both their newness and their response to challenge, education has the disadvantage of a long and encumbering history. In a sense, the institution of education—the school—*is* the status quo. Often it must operate through politically oriented bureaucracies that continually inhibit its potential for change and for developing strategies to meet social crises such as those inherent in the new urban America. These bureaucracies are often so large that introduction of meaningful change, even when agreed on by the higher echelons, is limited by the clogging of communication channels with paper, red tape, and assorted other artifacts, and by the constraints under which the average classroom teacher operates.

Somehow, this great gap in the educational hierarchy, separating the educator and his concept from the classroom teacher with her idea, creates a discontinuity that results in much wasted energy and distortion of effort. A clear educational philosophy can come best from educators who are free enough from bureaucracy to communicate with the classroom teacher as a full professional, and to attenuate the burden of the past while setting up new relationships with the human sciences. Inherent in this approach is the necessity for effective cooperation between educators and behavioral scientists, so as to incorporate the growing knowledge of the sociopsychological development of the child into educational procedures in the interests of facilitating realization of his greatest intellectual and social potential.

The children most in need of help are from the economically and socially marginal and quasi-marginal segments of the community. These groups are the ones most caught in the technological and social changes; in many of our metropolitan areas they are becoming the majority of the center city population. It is in these groups that we find the highest proportion of unemployment, welfare support, and broken families. And it is in their children that we see the highest proportion of learning disabilities and school dropouts. While in the past it was possible to absorb most of such youth in unskilled, low-paying jobs, now the current adult generation is increasingly being replaced in such jobs by machines. With the number of unskilled and semiskilled jobs decreasing, in order to find any place in the job market youth must now learn more complex functions, for which a successful educational experience is a prerequisite. This is a central problem for the total community, and a challenge for education. How it is met has wide ramifications for other underdeveloped areas outside our large cities and national boundaries.

There are various avenues of approach to the problem of both preventing learning disabilities and facilitating intellectual growth.

In recent years, there have been major curriculum renovations, enrichment programs, new systems for teaching mathematics and the sciences, programmed courses and teaching machines, as well as a multiplicity of new methods for teaching reading. However, in the disadvantaged, underdeveloped areas of our communities, where there is the large proportion of underachievers, these new methods are probably least applicable, being most often based on an assumption that the child has reached a particular level in skills which underlie them. As will be pointed out later, for the disadvantaged child this is an unwarranted assumption. For the most part, it is a correct assumption for the middle-class child; but here there are other problems. Too often, new methods are seen mainly as more effective techniques to help the child get into college and achieve occupation status goals, and the aim of education along with its innovations becomes narrowly pragmatic. This is not to say that new methods should not be devised and attempted, but, rather, that they might be seen neither as solutions to underachievement nor as substitutions for the development and encouragment of intrinsic motivation toward intellectual mastery and scholastic achievement.

An approach that combines the preventive with the facilitating— and which would establish a basis for the absorption of new methods —is that of planned intervention at the earlier periods of development of the various components of the intellectual spectrum. Evidence which is accumulating points more and more to the influence of background variables on the patterns of language and cognitive development of the child, and a subsequent diffusion of the effects of such patterns into all areas of the child's academic and psychological performance. Deprived backgrounds thus lead to the inadequacy of such patterns. What is proposed is that experiential inadequacies in the social background can be compensated for by a planned enrichment, channeled through improved schools.

Reference has been made to the constellation of factors in lower-class life which are associated with a limited range of experiential variability available to the child. Of course, there are probably differing clusters of economic, social, and family factors associated with greater or lesser retardation. But the fact remains that lower social-class status apparently predisposes to scholastic retardation, even though not all children are equally affected. Therefore, before discussing learning processes in the school it might be helpful to delineate some of the major features of urban slum life.

Geographically, there are crowded and dilapidated tenements quite at variance with the TV image of how people live. If the people are Negro, Puerto Rican, or Mexican-American, or poor mountain white, life is in a more-or-less segregated community. There are likely to be extremely crowded apartments, high rates of unemployment, chronic economic insecurity, a disproportionate number of broken families, and (particularly in the case of the Negro) continual exposure to denigration and social ostracism of varying degrees. The educational level of the adults tends to be quite limited. In the homes, there is likely to be a nearly complete absence of books, relatively few toys, and, in many instances, nothing except a few normal home objects which may be adapted as playthings. In addition—particularly but not exclusively where relatively new in-migrants are concerned— there is a great deal of horizontal mobility. The result is a pattern of life that exposes a child to a minimum of direct contacts with the central channels of our culture. The conditions of social inequality, the absence of an accessible opportunity structure, and the frequent nonavailability of successful adult male models create an atmosphere that is just not facilitating to individual development. Moreover, the everyday problems of living, particularly those of economic insecurity and a multiplicity of children, leave minimal time for the adults who may be present to assist the child in exploring the world, to reward him for successful completion of tasks, or to help him in the development of a differentiated self-concept. Even in homes which are not broken, the practical manifestations of economic marginality result in the father's sometimes holding two jobs and having little time for interaction with the child. We have found in various studies that children from these circumstances have relatively few shared or planned family activities, again resulting in a narrowing of experience.

The implications of these environmental conditions for the development of the child can be appreciated in terms of Hunt's discussion[5] of Piaget's developmental theories. (See preceding chapter, p. 45.) In essence, it is richness and variety of situations which a compensatory enrichment program must provide.

In the previous chapter, I said that emphasis on the importance of variety in the environment implies the detrimental effects of lack of variety. I then postulated that a child from any circumstances, who has been deprived of a substantial portion of the variety of stimuli to which he is maturationally capable of responding, is likely to be deficient in the equipment required for school learning. This does not necessarily imply restriction in the quantity of stimulation; rather, it refers to a restriction in variety—i.e., restriction to only a segment of the spectrum of stimulation potentially available. In addition to such restriction in variety, from the description of the slum environment, it might be postulated that the segments made available to children from that background tend to have poorer and less systematic ordering of stimulation sequences, thereby being less useful to the growth and activation of cognitive potential.

The most promising agency for providing environmental compensations is the school. It is through this institution, which reaches every child, that the requisite stimulation for facilitating learning, psychological maturation, and acculturation can be most efficiently organized and programmed. Yet it is now estimated that up to 60 per cent of lower-class children are retarded two years or more in reading by the time they leave the elementary school.

Before we place the entire responsibility on the school, however, an important fact must be noted. The overwhelming finding of studies on the relationship between social class and learning, school performance, and the like, is that children from backgrounds of social marginality enter the first grade already behind their middle-class counterparts in a number of skills highly related to scholastic achievement. They are simply less prepared to meet the demands of the school and the classroom situation. Conversely, though, the school has failed to prepare to meet their needs. The failure of the educational institution to overcome the children's environmentally determined handicaps too often results in early failure, increasing alienation, and an increasingly greater gap between the lower-class and middle-class youngsters as they progress through school. In other words, intellectual and achievement differences between lower-class and middle-class children are smallest at the first-grade level, and tend to increase through the elementary school years. It is here that the interaction between school and early environment, instead of having a facilitating influence, has a negative effect. While the school does not contribute to the initial problem (except through its effects on the previous generation), neither does it contribute to the overcoming of the initial handicaps.

It would seem quite reasonable, in the light of this discussion and its supporting evidence, to prepare the child better to meet the school's demands before he enters the first grade, and before there has been an accumulation of failure experiences and maladaptive behavior. It would also seem eminently reasonable that the school should accept this responsibility. At the same time, it does not seem reasonable that an institution which so far has generally failed to meet its responsibility to this group should simply be given a mandate, without the incorporation of new and appropriate knowledge and techniques. Here is where the knowledge from the behavioral sciences can be put to its most effective use.

For example, all peoples have difficulties in spanning cultural discontinuities, and the entrance of the child into school for the first time places him in an environment which, in many respects, is discontinuous with his home. This discontinuity is minimal for the middle-class child, who is likely to have had the importance of school imprinted in his consciousness from the earliest possible age. For him, therefore, the school is very central and is continuous with the totality of his life experiences. As a result there are few incongruities between his school experiences and any others he is likely to have had, and there are intrinsic motivating and molding properties in the school situation to which he has been highly sensitized. Further, there is more likely to be contiguity in the school-faculty orientation with his home-family orientation. Failure can be interpreted to him in appropriate and familiar terms, and methods of coping with it can be incorporated, increasing the motivation or offering the necessary rewards, goals, or punishments to effect the desired change in performance.

For the lower-class child there is not the same contiguity or continuity. He does not have the same coping mechanisms for internalizing success or psychologically surviving failure in the formal learning setting. If the lower-class child starts to fail, he does not have the same kinds of operationally significant and functionally relevant support from his family or community—or from the school. Further, because of the differences in preparation, he is more likely to experience failure.

In this context, let us consider White's concept of competence motivation as a primary drive. The middle-class child comes to school prepared, for the most part, to meet the demands made on him. The expectations of his teachers are that he will succeed. As he confronts material that is congruent with his underlying skills, he is able to succeed; and thus he achieves the feeling of efficacy which White[8] points out is so necessary to the "effectance motivation" which promotes continuing positive interaction with the environment. The lower-class child, on the other hand, experiences the middle-class-oriented school as discontinuous with his home environment, and, further, comes to it unprepared in the basic skills on which the curriculum is founded. The school becomes a place which makes puzzling demands, and where failure is frequent and feelings of competence are subsequently not generated. Motivation decreases, and the school loses its effectiveness.

It is in the transitional years from the preschool period through the elementary school years that the child is first subjected to the influence and the requirements of the broader culture. It is then that two environments are always present for him: the home environment and the school environment. But it is also in these transitional (and especially in the pretransitional) years that the young organism is most malleable. Thus, that is the point at which efforts might best be initiated to provide a third—an intervention—environment to aid in the reconciliation of the first two. Such reconciliation is required because, especially for the child from a disadvantaged background, there are wide discrepancies between the home and school milieus. In the intervention environment, preventive and remedial measures can be applied to eliminate or overcome the negative effects of the discontinuities.

The importance of early intervention is underlined in the summary by Fowler[3] of findings on cognitive learning in infancy and early childhood. He points out that seemingly minimal cognitive stimulation in the preschool years, when organized appropriately to the capabilities of the child, can be highly effective in accelerating the development of intellectual functions.

Critical and optimal time periods for many aspects of development and learning in both humans and animals have long been studied. These concepts are always related to stimulation or interaction between the organism and the environment, and thus represent an important additional dimension when we discuss influences on development and behavior. Apparently, it is not sufficient merely to provide particular stimulation for the growing individual; it must be supplied at a special time, or within particular time limits, if it is to have the most desired effect. Thus, a program intended to compensate for environmental deprivation would be most effective if supplied at a particular stage in the life of the child.

Scott's[7] summary of the relevant research information on critical stages in development indicates that the period of greatest plasticity is during the time of initial socialization. Since the bulk of the literature in this area is on animals, generalizations must be carefully confined. But seemingly, as one ascends the phylogenetic scale, there are greater ranges of time during which the organism has high levels of plasticity and receptivity. There is an insufficient body of data to hypothesize a most critical period for learning in the human child, and there are probably different critical or optimal periods for different functions. However, at about three or four years of age there is a period which would roughly coincide with the early part of what Piaget calls the "preoperational stage." It is then that the child is going through the later stages of early socialization; that he is required to focus his attention and monitor auditory and visual stimuli; and that he learn through language to handle simple symbolic representations. It is at this three- to four-year-old level that organized and systematic stimulation, through a structured and articulated learning program, might most successfully prepare the child for the more formal and demanding structure of the school. It is here, at this early age, that we can postulate that compensation for prior deprivation can most meaningfully be introduced. And, most important, there is considerably less that has to be compensated for at this age than exists when, as a far more complex and at least somewhat less plastic organism, the child gets to the first grade.

This position and its implications for specially organized early stimulation of the child find support in an article by Bruner[2] on cognitive consequences of sensory deprivation. He says: "Not only does early deprivation rob the organism of the opportunity of constructing models of the environment, it also prevents the development of efficient strategies for evaluating information—for digging out what leads to what and with what likelihood. Robbed of development in this sphere, it becomes the more difficult to utilize probable rather than certain cues, the former requiring a more efficient strategy than the latter" (pp. 202–203). Bruner goes on to a discussion of nonspecific transfer of training in which, I think, he provides the most incontrovertible foundation for a structured, systematic preschool enrichment and retraining program which would compensate, or attempt to compensate, for the deficiencies in the slum environment. His discussion is not of slums or compensation, but in his pointing up the importance of the "normally rich" environment, the serious cognitive consequences of the deprived environment are thrown into relief. Bruner says, ". . . nonspecific or generic transfer involves the learning of general rules and strategies for coping with highly common features of the environment" (p. 203). After pointing out that Piaget ". . . remarks upon the fact that cognitive growth consists of learning how to handle the great informational transformations like reversibility, class identity, and the like" and that Piaget speaks of these as "strategies for dealing with or, better, for creating usable information," Bruner proposes ". . . that exposure to normally rich environments makes the development of such strategies possible by providing intervening opportunity for strategic trial and error" (p. 203).

What Bruner talks about under "trial and error" requires a certain level of motivation and exploratory efforts. I have previously discussed the possible role of early failure experiences in influencing the motivational and goal orientations, and the self-expectancies, of the lower-class child. When the lower-class child gets into first grade, too frequently his cognitive, sensory, and language skills are insufficiently developed to cope with what for him are the complex and confusing stimuli offered by the school. It is the interaction of these motivational and maturational dynamics that makes it extremely important for society, through institutions such as the school, to offer the lower-class child an organized and reasonably orderly program of stimulation, at as early an age as possible, to compensate for possible cognitive deficit.

The focus has been on deficit because of the general hypothesis that the experiential deprivations associated with poverty are disintegrative and subtractive from normative growth expectancies. The extent of academic failure and reading retardation associated with lower-class status—and especially with minority-group membership within the lower class—makes it imperative that we study the operational relationship between social conditions and these deficits, and the subsequent failure of the school to reverse the tendency toward cumulative retardation in the primary grades.

Our work has been directed particularly toward delineating the effects of conditions of life on cognitive structures. For an understanding of these relationships and the scientific development of enrichment programs, we have emphasized the role of specific social attributes and experiences in the development of language and verbal behavior, of concept formation and organization, of visual and auditory discrimination, of general environmental orientation, and of self-concepts and motivation; and of all of this to school performance. It is the areas mentioned which apparently are essential to the acquisition of scholastic skills, and around which a basic curriculum for early childhood should be developed. Pragmatically, this must be a program which successfully teaches disadvantaged children.

Examination of the literature yields no explanation or justification for any child with an intact brain, and who is not severely disturbed, not to learn all the basic scholastic skills. The failure of such children to learn is the failure of the schools to develop curricula consistent with the environmental experiences of the children and their subsequent initial abilities and disabilities.

As has been emphasized previously in this paper, a compensatory program for children, starting at three or four years of age, might provide the maximum opportunity for prevention of future disabilities and for remediation of current skill deficiencies. In addition, such a program might serve to minimize the effect of the discontinuity between the home and school environments, thereby enhancing the child's functional adjustment to school requirements.

For an early enrichment program, one model available is that developed by Maria Montessori[6] in the slums of Italy. Though her theoretical system need not be critically evaluated here, there is much in her technology that could productively be re-examined and incorporated in compensatory programs. Basically, this includes the organization of perceptual stimuli in the classroom, so that singular properties become more observable, one at a time, without the distraction of competing, overly complex elements. For example, materials used to convey and illustrate the concept of size and size differential are all the same color and shape. This maximizes the attentional properties of size, and minimizes competing elements. Use of such materials should make it possible for size discriminations to be learned more easily. This method is, of course, carried over to many fields, and the availability of such stimuli under the Montessori system gives the child an opportunity to select materials consistent with his own developmental capabilities. This makes possible success experience, positive reinforcement, and subsequent enhancement of involvement and motivation. The attention to the minutiae of learning, and the systematic exposure to new learning elements based on prior experience, could allow for the development of individualized learning profiles. This would be particularly appropriate for a compensatory program, where there is a great deal of variation in individual needs.

There is, however, a major variable which is apparently inadequately handled by this method, and that is language.

Language can be thought of as a crucial ingredient in concept formation, problem solving, and in the relating to and interpretation of the environment. Current data available to the author and his co-workers tend to indicate that class differences in perceptual abilities and general environmental orientation decrease with chronological age, whereas language differences tend to increase.

In a social-class-related language analysis, Bernstein[1], an English sociologist, has pointed out that the lower class tends to use informal language and mainly to convey concrete needs and immediate consequences, while the middle-class usage tends to be more formal and to emphasize the relating of concepts.* This difference between these two milieus, then, might explain the finding in some of our recent research that the middle-class fifth-grade child has an advantage over the lower-class fifth-grader in tasks where precise and somewhat abstract language is required for solution. Further, Bernstein's reasoning would again emphasize the communication gap which can exist between the middle-class teacher and the lower-class child.

One can postulate that the absence of well-structured routine and activity in the home is reflected in the difficulty that the lower-class child has in structuring language. The implication of this for curriculum in the kindergarten and nursery school would be that these chil-

---

* Bernstein has since indicated that he was replacing the terms "public" and "formal" with the terms "elaborated" and "restricted." He feels that the latter offer better analytic distinctions and operate at a higher level of abstraction.

dren should be offered a great deal of verbalized routine and regulation, so that positive expectations can be built up in the child and then met. It can also be postulated that differences in verbal usage are directly attributable to the level of interaction of the child with the adult, and at this age, to a lesser extent, with peers.

In observations of lower-class homes, it appears that speech sequences seem to be very limited temporally and poorly structured syntactically. It is thus not surprising to find that a major focus of deficit in the children's language development is syntactical organization and subject continuity. But in analysis of expressive and receptive language data on samples of middle- and lower-class children at the first- and fifth-grade levels, there are indications that the lower-class child has more expressive language ability than is generally recognized or than emerges in the classroom. The main differences between the social classes seem to lie in the level of syntactical organization. If, as is indicated in this research, with proper stimulation a surprisingly high level of expressive language functioning is available to the same children who show syntactical deficits, then we might conclude that the language variables we are dealing with here are by-products of social experience rather than indices of basic ability or intellectual level. This again suggests a vital area to be included in any preschool enrichment program: training in the use of word sequences to relate and unify cognitions.

A language training program would require the creation of a rich, individualized language environment, where words are repeatedly placed in a meaningful context, and where the child is allowed multiple opportunities for expressive language demonstrations as well as for receiving language stimuli under optimal conditions and being encouraged to make appropriate responses. More specifically, stress could be placed on the following areas: orienting feedback, so that if the child says "give me the ——" or "where is ——," the teacher consciously instructs him in a complete sentence as to direction, location, placement, context, etc.; the systematic attempt to increase vocabulary; allowing the child to sort symbols, pictures, and artifacts with letters and words; verbal labeling practice; relating objects and experiences verbally, for example, constructing stories using specified objects and events; every child completing differently incomplete stories suggested by the teacher; reinforcing and encouraging the simultaneous articulation of motor behavior. Through the verbal area it is also possible to train memory, to some extent to train auditory discrimination, and to improve environmental orientation. However, it is not the purpose of this paper to go into a detailed description of potential enrichment procedures.

Working out compensatory programs is based on the assumption that retardation in achievement results from the interaction of inadequately prepared children with inadequate schools and insufficient curricula. This, in turn, is based on the contention that this large proportion of children is not failing because of inferior innate resources. Also implied is the assumption that one does not sit by and wait for children to "unfold," either on the intellectual or behavioral levels. Rather, it is asserted that growth requires guidance of stimulation, and that this is particularly valid with regard to the child who does not receive the functional prerequisites for school learning in the home. Hunt[5] points out that ". . . the counsel from experts on child-rearing during the third and much of the fourth decades of the twentieth century to let children be while they grow and to avoid excessive stimulation was highly unfortunate" (p. 362). This is particularly true with regard to lower-class children. We have found that, controlling for socioeconomic status, children with some preschool experience have significantly higher intelligence test scores at the fifth grade than do children with no preschool experience (see Chapter 14).

But it is not necessary to consider special education programs only on the preschool level, even though that is what has been emphasized here. Rather, to assure stability of progress, it would be desirable to continue special programs for several more years. The construction of a preschool program does not absolve a community or a school system from the responsibility to construct an effective strategy for teaching the marginal youngster from kindergarten on. In fact, if there *is* to be a reversal of some of the sequelae associated with poverty discussed in this paper, programs must have continuity, at least through the period of the establishment of the basic scholastic learning skills. This means that it is necessary for the community to support kindergartens with reasonable enrollments and adequate equipment, as well as specialized training of staff. As far as the primary grades are concerned, the continuation of special programming through establishment of basic skills would involve probably the time through the third-grade year. This level is used, because there is empirical reason to believe that levels of achievement for different social classes start their greatest divergence here. This is probably so because here the work begins to become less concrete and more abstract, more dependent on language symbolization, and, probably most important, more related to good reading skills. For these reasons, it would seem that the child from the preschool and enriched kindergarten classes might best remain in a special ungraded sequence through the third-grade level, a period in which he could be saturated with basic skill training, and not be allowed to move on until he has attained basic competence in the skills required by the higher grades. Such an ungraded school would also be of considerable interest theoretically, inasmuch as the child would be in its program through the preoperational stage delineated by Piaget. This should make it possible to devise a systematic curriculum that is consistent with the actual developmental levels of the child during the early childhood period.

Fowler[3] points out:

> Few systematic methods have been devised for educating young children, especially in complicated subject matter. We have in mind methods for simplifying and organizing the presentation of cognitive stimuli. Equally important, methods must be sufficiently flexible and play oriented to be adaptable to the primary learning levels and personality organization characteristic of the infant and young child.
>
> The advantages of utilizing the now relatively untapped "preschool" years for cognitive education are, of course, manifest. Most obvious is the availability of more years of childhood to absorb the increasingly complex technology of modern society, a technology already requiring many of the more productive years of development to acquire. A second is the less evident but more crucial possibility that conceptual learning sets, habit patterns, and interests areas, may well be more favorably established at early than at later stages of the developmental cycle (pp. 145–146).

There are those people who seem to fear the word "cognitive," sometimes correctly, because they are reacting to the overstringent mechanical models of the past. These models are not what is meant. The potentiation of human resources through the stimulation of cognitive growth could represent a primary therapeutic method for developing positive self-attitudes and a meaningful self-realization. For the lower-class child especially I would postulate that time is extremely valuable if the deficits are not to be cumulative and to permeate the entire functioning of the child.

The overgeneralized influence on some sections of early childhood education of the emphasis in the child-guidance movement upon protecting the child from stress, creating a supportive environment, and resolving emotional conflicts has done more to misdirect and retard the fields of child care, guidance, and development than any other single influence. The effect has especially operated to make these fields ineffective in responding to the problems of integrating and educating the non-white urban child. These orientations have conceived of the child as being always on the verge of some disease process, and have assigned to themselves the role of protecting the child in the same manner that a zookeeper arranges for the survival of his charges. Too frequently a philosophy of protectiveness that asks only about possible dangers has prevailed over any questions of potential stimulation of development. The attitude that perhaps helped to create this policy of protectionism can also be seen in the suburban "mom-ism" that so many sociologists and psychoanalysts have commented on. The child is a far healthier and stronger little organism, with more intrinsic motivation for variegated experience and learning, than the overprotectionists have traditionally given him credit for.

As Hunt[5] says: "The problem for the management of child development is to find out how to govern the encounters that children have with their environments to foster both an optimally rapid rate of intellectual development and a satisfying life" (pp. 362–363).

A curriculum as discussed here should serve both for the primary prevention of the social deviancies associated with deprivation and for the stimulation of healthy growth and utilization of individual resources. This orientation would represent one effective method of offering opportunities to all peoples to overcome and break the chains of social and historical limitations that have been externally imposed on them. This, of course, has immediate significance to the current critical questions in both race relations and education in America.

References

1. Bernstein, B. Language and social class. *Brit. J. Sociol.*, 1960, **11**, 271–276.
2. Bruner, J. S. The cognitive consequences of early sensory deprivation. In P. Solomon (Ed.), *Sensory deprivation.* Cambridge: Harvard Univer. Press, 1961. Pp. 195–207.
3. Fowler, W. Cognitive learning in infancy and early childhood. *Psychol. Bull.*, 1962, **59**, 116–152.
4. Harrington, M. *The other America.* New York: Macmillan, 1962.
5. Hunt, J. McV. *Intelligence and experience.* New York: Ronald, 1961.

6. Montessori, Maria. *Education for a new world.* Wheaton, Ill.: Theosophical Press, 1959.
7. Scott, J. P. Critical periods in behavioral development. *Science,* 1962, **138,** 949–955.
8. White, R. Motivation reconsidered: The concept of competence. *Psychol. Rev.,* 1959, **66,** 297–333.

5 /

Nursery Education: The Influence
of Social Programming on Early Development

MARTIN DEUTSCH

There is a convergence today of knowledge and of social problems which I believe will place increasing importance on early childhood and preschool education.

One converging current comes from social necessity, from the rapid urbanization of our cities and the patterns of substandard living conditions that exist for so many children in the cities. Another current derives from the present status of the psychological and behavioral sciences and the increasing implication, in the work being done especially in the developmental and social psychological areas, that early systematic intervention is the most effective means for alleviating or eliminating later social and learning disabilities.

Currently, 40 to 70 per cent of the total school population in our twenty largest cities consists of children from the most marginal economic and social circumstances. By the time these children reach junior high school, 60 per cent are retarded in reading by one to four years. We know that this academic retardation carries with it a much broader social retardation and that it represents a tremendous loss to America of very needed resources.

It is a simple fact that unskilled jobs are decreasing rapidly and that it will be increasingly necessary for people to enter the job market highly prepared to perform skilled tasks. This preparation is well-nigh impossible for people who were alienated from school at an early age. Thus current social necessities demand attention to the educational process, and especially to the participation in it of the children from the most deprived circumstances.

Let me say a few words about the kinds of backgrounds these

children come from. First, one must remember that the slums in our large cities are generally segregated institutions. This fact means that the mainstream of American life has been denied to these children. They have not had the opportunity to share its values, to internalize the motivational systems that may or may not make the child a successful student. The middle-class child has had school held up to him as a goal with an emblem and as a means, a vehicle, for his own advancement. Writing, books, and reading have played very important roles in his life from the time he could understand simple speech.

However, many of the children from lower socioeconomic circumstances come into the school situation and go through a kind of cultural trauma. They have entered a foreign land. There is a teacher speaking in continuous sentences for longer periods of time than they have been spoken to before, often in a different dialect, expecting and anticipating attention from the children, and assuming that they are functioning in terms of the same parameters as she.

These children have come from a different cultural context, and have had no real preparation to meet the demands of the school. It is not simply that the children lack skills—there is an incongruity between the skills that the children have and the kinds of skills that the school demands. And the school cannot appropriately use and functionally attach the skills of the children to itself.

It might be that some changes in curriculum would help in establishing a continuity between the child's previous experience and the demands of the school, but essentially it is the child who is going to have to make the major adjustment in order to handle the school materials. It is highly important that the child be able to handle these materials, not only because of the kinds of social problems mentioned above, but because emotional health is based on achieving the individual dignity associated with competence and success.

If a child begins early to experience largely failure in his contacts with the broader culture, his relationship to it and its various institutions cannot but deteriorate, and simultaneously his sense of self, his emotional growth and health will suffer. If school becomes more and more a place of failure and stimulates feelings of inadequacy, school will be more and more avoided—mentally if not physically—and will come to have little influence.

The sequence of events described and the individual and social problems to which they relate point up the importance of preparing the child for his first school experience. As was indicated earlier, the middle-class family seems to do this quite adequately for the middle-class child. But for the lower-class child, some social intervention is strongly indicated. This reasoning points squarely at preschool programming for these children.

The importance of preschool experience, however, does not derive solely from the fact that it is preschool—i.e., before school—but largely from what is known about the greater resiliency and accessibility of children of preschool age. While there are few specific studies of the effects of early training on later school performance, nearly all cited by Fowler[1] demonstrate substantial gains coming from early training. In a preliminary analysis of some of our own data at the Institute, we find higher group intelligence test scores among children who had preschool and kindergarten experience, as compared with those whose initial contact with school was in the first grade. (These data are on children from low socioeconomic status.) Data adduced by Scott[5] also point to early childhood as a time of maximum plasticity and accessibility to training and to learning.

Therefore, the preschool situation can serve as a real stimulant to development and learning, as well as a sociocultural bridge between the background of the slum child and the demands of the school. It is not implied that the attempt should be to regulate the cultural values of people who come from different social and cultural histories and circumstances, but that the children must be helped to understand the values that motivate the school philosophy and its demands for achievement and accomplishment.

The use of the preschool experience as both a bridge between the two cultures with which the child must deal and as a stimulant to his development dictates that its program be carefully planned to accomplish these goals. There must be a balance between the social and the cognitive, between the cultural and the emotional. I must say categorically at the outset that planning by educators does not mean regimenting the children. Such planning means organizing a program that will best accomplish the ends in view by supplying the most effective bridge and the most effective early stimulation.

What program content will be most effective can be determined in part by a careful examination of where the cultural discontinuities are most evident in first-grade performance, and of the kinds of experiences the middle-class child has which seem best to facilitate his early school learning and adjustment. Much of the kind of enrichment experience I will suggest for children from deprived circumstances is actually common procedure in the experience of middle-class children, and the core of it is daily procedure in the kinds of activity and of training that are put into situations where middle-class children are found. Certain improvements could be introduced into these middle-class situations but the focus here must be on the large body of children who come into our school situations fundamentally not properly prepared for the educational experience.

I would like to put several factors in the building up of a program into the context just discussed. These factors relate to the motivational, linguistic, memory, and general cognitive areas which seem most crucial in the planning of successful preschool programs.

First, we must recognize that the children from these deprived environments live under very crowded conditions and have few toys or even household objects to play with and to use, to develop the perceptual and spatial understanding taken for granted in school. These children will be coming to a school situation much richer in these objects than any environment they have experienced before, and cannot be expected to make use of them in the same way, or with the same minimal need for external direction that middle-class children will. For this reason, these disadvantaged children must be helped to play with and use these unfamiliar objects.

This difference brings us immediately to the problem of the teacher's expectation of children's performance. Usually, these expectations are built on the behavior of middle-class children, and the tendency is to look upon children from the lower socioeconomic groups as being quite slow; they just don't perform in the same way or with the same alacrity and understanding as the child from the more privileged background. Yet one must remember that these children have the same range of potential as any group of children who come from more favorable circumstances. The teacher's expectation that a child will fail or do well is communicated to the child in various ways, even if the teacher is unaware of it. Therefore, for any program for these children to be successful, teachers must be educated to be aware of the particular deficiencies most likely to be encountered in children from underprivileged backgrounds, and to adjust their expectations accordingly.

These children have somewhat different expectations of adult behavior than do middle-class children. Many more slum children come from broken homes, and have had family experiences qualitatively different from those of middle-class children. Frequently the parents, because of economic and social pressures and lack of education themselves, have not been able to reinforce the child in an appropriate way so he will develop a constructive relationship to his own intellectual and psychomotor behavior, where he will set goals, work toward them, and be disappointed when he fails to receive concrete rewards when he is successful. Native intellectual potential tends to be artificially reduced in the absence of feedback mechanisms.

When we consider what kinds of experiences and motivational systems can be introduced into a preschool experience, we can first specify a whole process of real feedback. We must insure that the teacher responds to the child, permits him to make demands on her, and indicates by her behavior that she is there not only to offer emotional warmth but also to answer questions and to provide a larger perspective and introduction to the world.

It is important to respond to each child individually, because, with these children, there tends to be a major deficiency in the whole area of self-identification. While I believe this to be largely class based, rather than racially based, most urban Negro children belong to the lower socioeconomic groups, so that often the problem of self-concept and self-awareness is complicated by the realities of social inferiority thrust on Negro children.

Discrimination plays a devastating role in the developing consciousness of the child, and if this role is to be minimized we need, on one level, extensive social engineering. On another level, we need direct work with the child in the school and preschool years which can be extremely effective in at least limiting the kinds of violence done to a child's self-concept by these invidious characteristics of the larger culture.

I would like to turn to the whole question of cognitive development—what the opportunities are for early cognitive development and its stimulation in a preschool program. I mentioned in the beginning that the behavioral sciences are coming increasingly to the realization that there are common opportunities for the early cognitive development of children if it is systematically programmed. The child must first develop the expectation that he can complete a task, and that he can explore the environment and ask questions. The program of cognitive stimulation must give opportunity for the child to express curiosity, to explore, and to learn that he can expect feedback and reward from adults.

I should like to quote a short section, from a major article in *Psy-*

chological Bulletin by Fowler[1], which indicates the importance and
the history of cognitive stimulation of young children. While he was
not dealing necessarily with children from lower socioeconomic circumstances, the conclusions remain pertinent for all children. The exciting aspect of this article and of others on the subject is the kind of
minimal intervention at these early ages that seems to result in maximum changes. Fowler says, near his conclusion,

> . . . Much if not most of the energy in child psychology and
> development in late years has been concentrated on the child's per-
> sonality, perceptual-motor, and socioemotional functioning and devel-
> opment. Originating primarily as a reaction to historically inadequate
> and stringent methods, fears have generalized to encompass early
> cognitive learning *per se* as intrinsically hazardous to development.
> As legitimate areas of study, the contributions of studies on per-
> ceptual-motor and socioemotional problems are obvious. But in the
> field of child guidance, interest in these areas has come to permeate
> and dominate work in child development almost to the exclusion of
> work on cognitive learning. In harking constantly to the dangers of
> premature cognitive training, the image of the "happy," socially ad-
> justed child has tended to expunge the image of the thoughtful and
> intellectually educated child. Inevitably, in this atmosphere, research
> (and education) in cognition has lagged badly, especially since the
> 1930's, not only for the early years of childhood but for all ages.
> Even prior to the more recent era, however, very little careful
> research was done on early cognitive learning. As historical evidence
> shows, most studies have comprised the work of those "beyond the
> pale" of formal psychology. Yet, taken collectively, the findings are
> so provocative as to make us entertain hopes that many, if not all,
> children can and indeed should be offered much more cognitive stimu-
> lation than they have been generally receiving.
> There is, however, a further problem, at once a derivative of and
> an important contributor to the failure to undertake work on cognitive
> learning. Few systematic methods have been devised for educating
> young children, especially in complicated subject matter. We have in
> mind methods for simplifying and organizing the presentation of
> cognitive stimuli. Equally important, methods must be sufficiently
> flexible and play oriented to be adaptable to the primary learning
> levels and personality organization characteristic of the infant and
> young child.

Among the kinds of organized stimulation necessary for the cognitive development which we would promote, one of the most important is language stimulation. (By organized stimulation, we mean a
systematic introduction of stimuli in a way that is congruent with

what is known about the maturational development of the child, and which will offer the child opportunity for the facilitation of what might be passively developed or hypo-developed cognitive operations.)

Language is probably the most important area for the later development of conceptual systems. If a child is to develop the capabilities for organizing and categorizing concepts, the availability of a wide range of appropriate vocabulary, of appropriate context relationships for words and the ability to see them within their various interrelationships, becomes essential. Sometimes the most productive training can be done in the third and fourth and fifth years of life in the language area.

Milner recently concluded a study[4] of children who were high in verbal ability and high in reading skill, and of children who were low in both areas. In the kind of observations that one would like to see made also in preschool settings, she points out, in regard to home differences, "There appears to be a radically different atmosphere around the mealtable from a child's point of view for the high scorers than for the low scorers." (This is also a social class difference.) She goes on to say:

> More frequently for the high scorers, mealtime at home, particularly the first meal in the day, serves as a focus for the total family interaction. Further, this interaction seems to be positive and permissive in emotional tone for these children, and has a high verbal content. That is, the child is talked to by adults with mature speech patterns and talks back to the adults. The opposite situation apparently exists for the low scorers. There were, in fact, indications in responses of some of their mothers that they actively discourage or prohibit the children's chatter and refuse to engage them in conversation during meals. This prohibition is based on a belief that talking during meals is a bad practice. One low scorer's mother's response to, "Did anyone talk to the child while she was eating a meal" was, "I do not allow her to talk while she is eating; it is a bad habit." To what extent the apparently more limited opportunities for low scorers to interact verbally with personally important adults has contributed to a low degree of verbal skill is unknown.

Other data on this point indicate that an element lacking in the environments of children from slum areas is the failure of adequate and continuous, sustained, connected, and relevant verbal communication. Somehow, in the verbal interaction matrix of the home, the child is not considered a participant; and in not being a participant, he does not give exercise to those incipient processes that must receive the nourishment of experience and active participation. Within the context of the school and the preschool situations this can be reversed; a child can become familiar with language, can increase tremendously his ability to identify and label different aspects of the environment, and can organize these aspects and catalogue them into certain conceptual categories.

Language training will take careful programming if it is to be done most effectively. We have found that children often have a much greater language capability and knowledge of language than is ever evident in a school situation with an adult present. Through experimental techniques we are able to record language of a child with no adult present, and we—and the child's teacher—are often amazed at the richness of the language that comes out. To stimulate this language so it will be available to the child in a school situation, in a situation where an adult is present, enrichment programming must be carefully planned.

Another area which should be mentioned is memory training, which is, after all, an adult-child kind of interaction. It is the ability of adults to refer the child to the past and to demonstrate or show him things in the past that have relevance in the present or the future. This interaction depends largely on language training, too. If the child has not had sufficient language, or if language is not a major element within the child-adult interaction, there will be a certain retardation in the development of memory systems. Here, too, specific and detailed programming by educators in the preschool context can play an important role.

Numerous techniques and methods can be and are being developed. However, if such methods are used, they must be used in terms of the basic principles of the individuation of the child. The child must have individual opportunities to relate to adults, and the stimuli presented to him must be consistent with his own development and history.

If the child is able to remember three or four elements from a problem established for him, and if he is rewarded for it, one does not next jump to a six-element problem or give him a one- or two-element problem. Not knowing where a child stands in relationship to a particular and delineated intellectual area can result in a great deal of frustration for the child. One must keep a very accurate accounting of the child's accomplishments and experiences.

The development of perceptual mechanisms is another area for preschool enrichment. Such development closely relates to the lack of environmental opportunities. The lack of artifacts in the environment and the absence or reduction of language training in the home can lead to a deficiency in development of auditory and visual modalities. Here, too, early auditory training, and particularly semantic discrimination training, using tape recorders and organized sound systems, should help to compensate the child for his deficiencies. The same is true for the visual area, but again, both types of training have to be closely meshed with the child's language ability. One must present only words and labels for objects already in the child's vocabulary. It is not possible to teach either visual or auditory discrimination in the absence of an external anchor in the child's language system; he must know the object or word that is being used for the visual or auditory training.

One other factor must be mentioned before concluding this discussion: Whatever the means of establishment of the nursery school situation, be it by a board of education, by a neighborhood house, or by any other kind of organizational system, it should be meaningfully related to the community it serves. We have found very often that parents of children from the low socioeconomic environments feel very self-conscious about their own lack of understanding and lack of knowledge and formal education, and sometimes look upon teachers as a competitive threat in their relationship with the child. One parent said recently, "My child comes home and I want to read to him, but the teacher reads so nicely it makes me look stupid."

There is a necessity to see if parallel programs in reading and in library work can relate the child's parents to the essentials of the school situation, which means that one has to understand the sociology of the family and the social sensitivities that have developed. Yet it is extremely important to give the parent some insight into what is expected in the school, and even more so to let the parent know it is important for the child's education for him to be a participant in the language interaction in the home and that he receive a certain degree of individuation, attention, and reinforcement. Recently reported research indicates that just the reading to a child by the parent for twenty minutes an evening when the child is two or three years old results in significant changes in the child's language abilities.[2]

There is a larger role in interpreting to the community the necessity of preschool experience, so that such education on a systematic basis becomes an indigenous part of the community structure, especially in our metropolitan areas. On this point, and particularly on the special responsibilities of preschool educators to recognize the potential of each child, some observations of Martin[3] are most pertinent. He said:

> . . . there is evidence from a variety of sources that there is in the making a cognitive theory of behavior and development. It would view the child not merely as a passive victim of either his environmental history or of his biological nature, but as one who strives to be the master of both his nature and his history. It will thus emphasize the unique characteristic which makes that mastery a possibility, namely, intelligence. It will be a science of man that includes man. To the development of such a science, research workers and field workers in child development should have a significant contribution to make. For they are, by training and commitment, both scientists and humanists. As such, they are in a most favorable position to humanize science and to bring an end to the mechanization of the human being. We face the question of whether man is to be the master or slave of his technology. The answer lies in the extent to which we can succeed in developing and utilizing our most important human resource, the ability to think. That we seem to be rediscovering in our research and theory the mind of the child provides hope that the answer will be in our favor.

Essentially, what is being said here is that the child, as a thinking organism and as a potential contributor to society, must be reached at as early an age as possible, particularly if he is marginal to our major cultural streams. He must be reached by educators with scientific knowledge, working in consort with behavioral scientists, and recognizing the underlying social necessities that make it imperative for America to solve the problems that will be associated with mass youth unemployment if children are not integrated into the school context. This integration must be accomplished during the children's first school experiences, and the attempt to do it must be made then, rather than at a later stage, where, unfortunately, it has so often proved a failure.

REFERENCES

1. Fowler, W. Cognitive learning in infancy and early childhood. *Psychol. Bull.*, 1962, 59, 116–152.
2. Irwin, O. Infant speech: Effect of systematic reading of stories. *J. Speech Hear. Res.*, 1960, 3, 187–190.
3. Martin, W. Rediscovering the mind of the child: a significant trend in research in child development. *Merrill-Palmer Quart.*, 1960, 6, 67–76.
4. Milner, Esther. A study of the relationship between reading readiness in grade I school children and patterns of parent-child interaction. *Child Develpm.*, 1951, 22, 95–112.
5. Scott, J. Critical periods in behavioral development. *Science,* 1962, 138, 949–955.

6 /

Minority Groups and Class Status as Related to Social and Personality Factors in Scholastic Achievement

The evolution of social problems into critical issues offers social and behavioral scientists a special opportunity to study sociopsychological processes. Frequently, it is through addressing a practical problem that the psychology of the individual can be related to the social environment, and thus the psychologist can study the basic questions in his field. It may be that in physics a concentration on theoretical problems of relativity and atomic structure is the shortest path to the development of atomic power; but, in the social sciences, it is the concrete presence of the problem which leads to an investigation, and theorizing about basic issues, and this, in turn, leads back to greater practical application. The very fact that social psychology deals with society, and the individual in it, dictates that its starting point be in the concrete problems and processes of society. Social necessities do provide impetus to social psychological inventions.

Various eras produce different necessities. Since the Supreme Court's desegregation decision in 1954, the necessity has been peaceful integration of schools and solution of problems arising when children of widely varying socioeconomic levels and prior educational backgrounds are for the first time put together in the same classroom. Although school segregation has been the law only in the South, for many years the semiencapsulated living conditions of Negroes and other minorities in the North created semisegregated school districts. From about 1950 on, the increased wartime and postwar birthrate was being felt in overcrowded classroom conditions, and the teacher shortage became more and more acute. At the same time there was a great in-migration of both Negroes and whites from rural areas in the South to large urban centers in both the North and the South. These factors, too, provided additional focus on the social situations and social climate of minority group children in our population, and, to a lesser extent, on all children from lower socioeconomic groups.

It is well established that the favorability or unfavorability of environmental factors influences the development process, even though this process is biologically the same for all children, regardless of racial or ethnic group. The experiences and subsequent self-concept and "world" concept of a child are determined by the conditions under which he lives and grows up. Dissimiliarities in the growth processes of children become maximized when their actual life conditions are dissimilar. As a result, attitudes and patterns of behavior and learning, though basically reflecting the larger culture, assume particular and often marked subgroup characteristics.

It is generally recognized that emotional and learning factors are closely related. The influence of environmental factors on the intensity of motivation and on the growing child's self-attitudes regarding his own capabilities is significant. Psychologists have long recognized the intimate relationship that exists among internalized attitudes, motivation, and the general efficiency of individual learning and functioning. In general, educational concepts and techniques have developed from experiences with majority group children, and have then been generalized, with sometimes only minor modifications, to all children. It is reasonable to suppose that attitudes toward and response to the school situation might also have distinctive characteristics related to environmental conditions and subgroup membership.

It has been the general purpose of the present study to investigate the existence of special problems in minority-group education, as well as to provide increased understanding into social and behavioral factors as they relate to perception of the self, frustration tolerance, group membership, and the rate of learning.

The present study was an extensive three-year research program conducted in a major northern city and centered in the schools and community of a large encapsulated all-Negro area. The area is characterized by severe social impoverishment and greater than usual stress in social and family life: social rejection, high rates of family breakdown, chronic economic anxiety, low aspiration level, and the absence of culturally approved symbols and individuals with whom to identify occur with monotonous regularity. The relative encapsulation of the community within a large urban area (a goodly proportion of the school children included in the study had never been more than twenty-five blocks in any direction from their homes) and the homogeneity of occurrence of the kinds of variables mentioned make this area a particularly good community for research for the behavioral scientist.

Since educational conditions represented one of the most pressing practical problems in this area (the children were found to be seriously behind the national norms for their grade levels, especially in reading), since school children constituted a readily available population, and since classroom factors and the learning process represent good dependent variables for the study of cultural impact, the area singled out for intensive study was the school situation. Also, this represented an excellent microcosm within which cultural and personality variables could be studied in the context of daily activities. Two sets of problems were of focal interest: (1) the interrelationships among the social environment, class, ethnic, and racial factors, and specific aspects of intra-group behavior and personality in a population of children; and (2) the implications of this for learning and for scholastic achievement in the school, the organization of the school to meet the needs of these children, and the attitudes and values of the teachers in working with and stimulating these children.

Thus, in the interests of the real challenge which it was felt would be presented to the social sciences by the coming desegregation of schools, the study reported here was oriented to the determination of the manner in which social stress affects motivation, personal aspiration, concepts of self, and learning, and how it differentiates the minority-group child from the majority-group child of similar background. The study of these rather practical matters, it was felt, should also provide data relating to the way in which social and cultural factors influence personality development, the role of the school in personality development, and the relationship of all these factors to individual motivation and learning.

PROCEDURES AND METHODS

The various phases of this study were organized around several problems which were approached as broadly as possible within the practical restrictions imposed by financial and staff limitations and by various other circumstances. Some of the more specific questions whose answers would offer evidence and understanding of the possible interrelationships among social, emotional, and learning conditions were conceived as follows:

How are variables of emotional, personality, social, and behavioral functioning related to each other and to scholastic position in the class? What is the difference in this patterning between minority-group children in a minority-group area and majority-group children in a majority-group area?

Is the rate of learning related to previous standing in the class? To the child's attitudes toward himself? To home and family relationships? To social, behavioral, and concentration factors in the classroom?

Is there a differential acquisition of the basic scholastic skills, and if so, is this differential related to special circumstances in the lives of minority-group children?

Is scholastic retardation and/or relative failure to accelerate in learning (not based on mental deficiency) related to specific social, emotional, and intellectual patterning, and are these general patterns related to problems of delinquency?

Do children in the minority-group area who have the opportunity to participate in a specially organized afterschool activity program differ in their behavior, self-attitudes, place in the social group, and in the general rate of scholastic change from those who do not?

What is the importance of the teacher's awareness of and sensitivity to the group processes in the class, to the learning process, and to the problems of the individual child? Will teachers' attitudes and behavior toward the class and themselves as teachers change as a consequence of their examination of their own socially influenced biases?

The overall plan of the project designed to deal with these questions involved studying intensively a 99 per cent Negro school in a Negro area and, somewhat less intensively (because of budgetary and staff restrictions), an almost all-white school in a white area. The white school served primarily as a control. The techniques used for the children measured academic performance, socioeconomic variables, personality and self-attitude factors, and classroom group variables such as sociometric choice and classroom activity and behavior. Teachers' behavior and attitudes were also evaluated, primarily by the use of process recorders in the classrooms. In addition, a special arrangement was made whereby the teachers of some of the participating classes received in-service credit for attending a seminar conducted by the author. These seminars were oriented toward discussion and self-evaluation of attitudes and behavior in the classroom. A special value of these seminars was the opportunity to correlate the teachers' discussions with the process records of actual behaviors in the classroom. In addition, since the experimental school was a participant in a program of planned afterschool activity, which 20 per cent of the children attended, it was possible to compare children who participated in this enrichment program with those who did not.

• *Population*

The study used two samples of elementary school children from fourth, fifth, and sixth grades.* Two whole classes at each grade level from each of two schools were used, making a total of twelve classes, and including approximately 400 children.† One school from which subjects were drawn was in a racially encapsulated area and over 99 per cent of its enrollment was Negro. This is the experimental school. The other, control school was in a white neighborhood of similar socioeconomic level, with a white enrollment of 94 per cent.

It was impossible to achieve complete socioeconomic comparability, but the children from the control school had living conditions very similar to the experimental school children. However, the white families had a slightly higher income level and greater job stability, rentals were in general slightly lower, and the landlords' upkeep of the houses was somewhat better. In addition, the number of relief cases was higher in the Negro group. Despite these differences the two groups can be considered basically comparable; there was considerable overlap over most of the continuum.

The experimental school was studied over a total time period of three years, although data from only the third year are reported here. (For the procedures constructed for this study, the first two years gave time for pilot study and refinement.) The control school data were collected during half of one school year, and for reasons of time are necessarily less complete, especially in qualitative data. Specific note will be made later on of what data were not obtained for the control school subjects.

---

* At the time of the study an automatic promotion policy was in effect, so the ages of the children at each grade level were homogeneous. Hence 90 per cent of the entire population was between 9 and 12 years of age.

† In the experimental school, an additional four classes served as controls for the teachers' seminar. The use of these controls will be explained more fully later.

• Procedures and Measurements

ACADEMIC ACHIEVEMENT

This was measured by means of the Stanford Achievement Test, which is so constructed as to yield grade-equivalent scores for reading and arithmetic separately, as well as to give a total grade equivalent for the whole test. In the experimental school, also, it was possible to administer the test twice: once at the beginning and once at the end of the school year. Hence for the experimental subjects there is a measure of progress (end-of-year total score)/(beginning-of-year total score) in addition to the three scores already mentioned. Further treatment of the scores derived from this test included an arithmetic/reading ratio, applied to both experimental and control subjects.

POPULARITY OF CHILD AMONG PEERS

This was measured by a sociometric index using three questions with three ranked choices for each.* The questions were: "I would most like to sit next to ——," "I would most like to play with ——," "I would most like to go to the movies with ——." This was scored in the usual way, and the children in each class were ranked on the basis of total weighted score.

SOCIOECONOMIC MEASURES

A short questionnaire was administered to each child individually, dealing with objective home and family factors. No attempt was made to inquire about family incomes because of the expected lack of validity of children's reports. However, it was possible to determine how many people in each home worked, and which families were on relief. Perhaps the most useful index derived from this questionnaire is the *crowding ratio,* defined as the number of people living in the home divided by the number of rooms in the apartment. Housing authorities generally consider that a ratio of over 1.0 represents crowded conditions, while a ratio of 1.5 or more indicates extremely crowded living conditions.

---

* This measure and all the others with the exception of the Stanford were given orally and individually to avoid contamination of results by reading problems.

INTACTNESS OF FAMILY

This was measured on a four-point scale, with 1 representing both parents in the home, 2 representing one parent in the home, 3 standing for the child living with relatives but with neither parent, and 4 indicating that the child lived with no relatives. For purposes of dichotomy, however, only the home in which the child lived with both true parents was classified as intact.

FAMILY FOCUS ON CHILD

This was evaluated through simple questions dealing with who made dinner for the child, the bedtime routine, whether he was taken places by his family, etc.

SENTENCE COMPLETION TEST

This was constructed to yield two kinds of data: attitudes toward self, and attitudes toward family. It included twenty-two sentences, selected from an original group of thirty-six. Twelve of the sentences relate to self-image, and seven to family atmosphere. Specific examples of these items may be found in the section discussing the results from this procedure. Each response was rated independently by three raters on a five-point scale where one represented the most positive, and five the most negative response. Thus two quantitative measures were derived from this procedure: the Negative Self-Image Score measures degree of self-acceptance, with a high score representing poor self-acceptance and a low one indicating positive self-acceptance. The second score obtained is the index of Negative Family Atmosphere, measuring the degree to which the child made negative statements about interpersonal relationships in the home and about the general family atmosphere. The higher the score here, the more negative is the family atmosphere. Another direct measure obtained from this test was an occupation-aspiration level.

FIGURE DRAWING

Each subject was requested to draw a human figure; these productions were rated by three judges along a four-point scale ranging from "relatively good personal adjustment" to "signs of serious personal maladjustment." The average of the ratings was used as the child's final score. Analysis of these scores, however, indicates that this measure is highly dubious; this will be discussed later.

DIGIT SPAN TEST

This test was used to determine the child's ability to retain and manipulate a number series. Similar tests have also been widely interpreted in previous studies as measure of attention span and, perhaps, level of anxiety. The test in the present study included both forward and backward repetition. Three scores were used: a *forward* score, a *backward* score, and a *total* score. Each represents the number of digits successfully reproduced.

TEACHER-ATTITUDE QUESTIONNAIRE

This was a questionnaire administered to the children to evaluate their attitudes toward the teacher.

BEHAVIORAL OBSERVATIONS IN CLASSROOM

Running process records were taken by research assistants in each of the classrooms in the experimental school, and to a lesser extent in the control school. This was done for about three hours a week in each class, with the times being randomly distributed so that the teachers could not anticipate the arrival of the observer. In addition, an activity measure was devised, and by using time samples, each pupil was rated several times during each observed class period on the quality of his activity and participation. The data derived here are largely qualitative.

TEACHERS' SEMINARS

These were conducted over a period of two years in the experimental school, and included altogether about twelve teachers. Process and content analyses were done for each seminar meeting. The discussions dealt with attitudes toward teaching; education; Negroes, and on being Negro (nine of the twelve teachers were Negro); on conflict in class and racial identification; and on methods of handling group disorganization in the classroom. The seminars were established in such a way that the researcher could assure the teachers that all communications were privileged, and it was clearly understood that the researcher had no formal connection with the educational bureaucracy. This was essential for rapport, as the teachers had considerable negative feeling toward school administration and Board of Education. Nevertheless, it took a few months to accomplish this confidence building, and for the group to become sufficiently cohesive for individual problems to be tackled. The only other person at the seminars was a research assistant (white, female) who took the process records. The opportunity afforded to compare the teachers' reports of their classes with the process records of the same classes was an unusual one and yielded a wealth of information.

In addition to the research function one of the prime purposes of these seminars for the teachers (they received in-service graduate credit for attendance at the seminars) was their learning of group-dynamics techniques and how to apply them to classroom problems in an effort to stabilize the atmosphere, and to help them gain a primary self-perception as motivated teachers.

ADDITIONAL PROCEDURES

The researcher met with a few small groups of children from the experimental classes for discussion and play. Some of these sessions were tape recorded, and on others there are process records.

In addition, following from emphasis on the relation between nutrition and general intellectual functioning,[3,5] some inquiry was made into the children's dietary habits.

RESULTS

As indicated in the procedure discussion both quantitative and qualitative results were obtained from the study. While of course the two types of data are interrelated, for purposes of clarity in report they should be separated, to be recombined in discussion at the conclusion.

Some of the observational categories aimed at quantifying specific variables, while others were directed toward collecting qualitative data about school and classroom atmosphere, community-school interaction, and teachers' social-class attitudes and their possible effects on the learning and behavior of the children. In addition, in a study of this complexity dealing with real social situations, there are many observations gathered on repeated occasions, often unanticipated, which are highly consistent and which enrich understanding of the educational process and its social basis. With this in view, some of the anecdotal material as well will be scattered through the following discussion.

The more specific quantitative results will be discussed first.

Table 6–1

MEDIAN STANFORD ACHIEVEMENT TEST SCORES FOR EXPERIMENTAL AND CONTROL
GROUPS, AND MEDIAN TEST RESULTS

Score	E Group	C Group	X^2 value	P
Reading	3.2	4.8	28.00	< .001
Arithmetic	3.6	4.5	25.47	< .001
Total	3.2	4.4	31.55	< .001

• School Achievement and Retardation

Analysis of achievement data indicates that the experimental group
was significantly retarded when compared with the control group, as
can be seen in Table 6–1.

However, the Stanford Achievement Test is based on national
norms: a pupil in the fourth grade should achieve a fourth-grade score
on the test. Therefore, it is possible to compare both the experimental
and control groups with the national norms and calculate retardation
on the basis of this external criterion. These findings, in terms of discrepancy of mean score from national average, are presented in Table
6–2.

Table 6–2

RETARDATION OF EXPERIMENTAL AND CONTROL GROUPS, GROUPED BY GRADE,
AS MEASURED BY THE STANFORD ACHIEVEMENT TEST

Grade	Experimental Group	Control Group
4	1 yr., 9 mos. (N:26)[a]	9 mos. (N:64)
5	2 yrs. (N:82)	9 mos. (N:69)
6	2 yrs., 1 mo. (N:62)	1 yr., 3 mos. (N:66)

[a] The N's will be somewhat variable throughout, because of the variability of the
children's absences on days when procedures were administered.

It is seen that both the groups are behind grade-level expectations, and are falling farther behind as they progress in school. These
findings are somewhat different from those of another study[6] which
showed that although Negro third-grade pupils do slightly poorer
than white pupils of that grade, the discrepancy increases as the children go farther in school, until white eighth-graders are seen perform-
ing at an 8.4-grade level on a reading test, while Negro pupils in the
same grade average at the sixth-grade level. In Table 6–2 there is a
more or less stable discrepancy between the two groups. However, the
differences between the two studies are probably explained by the
homogeneity of social class in the present study, and the inclusion of

white middle-class children in the other one referred to. In addition, the present study does not tap either the third- or the eighth-grade levels, the anchor points of the other study.

It was possible to administer the Stanford at both the beginning and the end of the school year in the experimental school. Unfortunately, the rate of absence was quite high at the end of the school year, so that only about two-thirds of the group was tested the second time. The teachers indicated that it was the children toward the bottom of the class in achievement who tended to absent themselves most frequently at this time. So it would appear that whatever bias exists in the retesting data would tend to maximize improvement. According to the standards of the Stanford, one would expect a nine- to twelve-month improvement during the school year. In contrast to this expectation, the range of change in the six experimental classes was from a loss of 0.22 months to a gain of 0.26 months, with the mean change being a gain of .077 months.

It is of particular significance that, with more schooling, there is proportionately decreased learning over time. For the moment, if we do not consider the absence of stimulation in the environment of these children, but rather look only at the school *Zeitgeist*, we find in the random time samples of classroom activity that 50 to 80 per cent of all classroom time in the experimental group is devoted to disciplining and various other essentially non-academic tasks.* This is not true of the control group, where similar activity occupied about 30 per cent of the class time, at a maximum. Thus, although the experimental and control groups have the same overall time exposure to school, when the cumulative time is considered, each year there is a greater discrepancy in academic time between the two groups.

Of interest also among achievement variables is the interrelationship for the individual child between reading and arithmetic scores. Since both arithmetic and reading levels are measured in terms of grade level achieved according to nationwide norms, the scores should parallel each other: fifth-grade pupils, for example, normally score at 5.0 on both arithmetic and reading. Therefore, the "average" ratio between the two would be 1.0, the ratio being defined as arithmetic achievement score divided by reading achievement score. This ratio,

* It may be noted that the 50 per cent ratio was generally maintained by the somewhat more authoritative, more directive, and usually more experienced teachers. The children, on the other hand, seemed to be continually asking for greater structure and more discipline, but would accept it only from the consistent teacher whom they knew could not be intimidated. On the teacher-attitude measure, in fact, the most frequent association was "She's real strict—she's good!"

which we called the "A/R ratio," was computed for each child, and when groups are compared, differences in the median ratios are seen. This median ratio was 1.12 for the experimental group (indicating a higher arithmetic score than reading achievement score) and .93 for the control group. The difference between these two values, computed by the median test, is significant at better than the .05 level of confidence. This finding reflects the fact that the experimental group children have an arithmetic average score on the Stanford which is higher than their reading average, while for the control group the opposite is true. Reading, though emphasized in school for both groups, may represent a motivation arising from specific value systems, while arithmetic involves a concrete grocery-store transaction common to all groups.

• *Self and Social Variables*

GENERAL FINDINGS

Having established these findings, concomitant similarities and differences between the experimental and control groups were investigated. The groups were compared on all the variables quantitatively assessed.* These results may be found in Table 6–3. In order to make these comparisons, the combined distribution of each variable was dichotomized as closely as possible to a 50–50 split. This method (which approximates the median test) allows comparison of both groups as to the percentage above and below the cutoff point on the combined distribution. Then the *chi-square* test with Yates' correction was used to determine significance. For clarity, the tables report these results in terms of the percentage of each group above the combined median, the value of which is given in the left column.

On four of the variables compared, the two groups were significantly different. Interestingly, however, the two groups were *not* different on the crowding ratio, which is a fairly sensitive socioeconomic indicator. While a majority of both groups comes from very overcrowded living conditions, the children in the experimental group have significantly more broken family backgrounds. The Index of Negative Family Atmosphere and the Index of Negative Self-Image also differentiate between the experimental and control groups. These

---

* The sociometric measure was omitted here, of course, since it is an intraclass measure and therefore has no significance for intergroup comparison. Also, the figure-drawing measure is excluded because of its apparent invalidity, to be discussed in greater detail later.

Table 6–3

COMPARISON OF EXPERIMENTAL AND CONTROL GROUPS ON SELF AND SOCIAL
VARIABLES

Variable	Experimental Group %		Control Group %
Crowding Ratio (more than 1.4 persons per room)	57		59
Broken Home	55	a	9
Digit Span Forward (score 6 or higher)	46		49
Digit Span Backward	39	a	53
Index of Negative Family Atmosphere (score 11 or higher)	49	a	37
Index of Negative Self-Image (score 27 or higher)	63	a	35

a Differences significant at .05 level or better

are scores derived independently from the Sentence Completion Test and reflect the subjects' responses to incomplete sentences dealing with self and family.* In terms, then, of family organization and intactness, the Negro children come from more unfavorable backgrounds, and, further, regard their home environment less favorably than do their white counterparts.

Although as was indicated earlier, and despite the overcrowding, the two groups are not fully comparable in socioeconomic class, the family background data are far more disparate than the class backgrounds and thus these findings cannot be explained on a class basis. This is similarly true for the Index of Negative Self-Image, where the discrepancy between experimental and control groups is even greater. Also, the negative self-image of the Negro children cannot be wholly attributed to their more deprived family backgrounds, as the percentages having a negative self-image exceeds both of the family background measures.

Repetition of digits is considered to measure span of attention. In this more school-related variable, repetition of digits forward shows no significant difference between the two groups, but where the child must recall a series of digits and repeat them in *reverse order* (a task often interpreted as more stressful and more difficult) the experimen-

* It should be noted, though, that the Family Atmosphere Index is consistent with the child's reported perceptions of his family, as gathered in the questionnaire dealing with the family's focus on the child.

tal pupils drop in their performance as compared with the controls. Thus, in a task which requires a measure more of concentration and persistence, the experimental group falls behind the control.

The quantitative digit-span results may reflect the observation data to be found in the process records and reaffirmed by the teachers: there is a general absence of persistence on the part of these children when they find a task to be difficult. Time after time, the experimental child would drop a problem posed by the teacher as soon as he met any difficulty in attempting to solve it. In later questioning, the child typically would respond "So what?" or "Who cares?" or "What does it matter?" In the control group, there was an obvious competitive spirit, with a verbalized anticipation of "reward" for a correct response. In general, this anticipation was only infrequently present in the experimental group, and was not consistently or meaningfully reinforced by the teachers. It may well be that the cultural deprivation (or, as might be more descriptive, the stimulus deprivation) of the home and its general instability does not, for the lower-class Negro child, create an expectation of future rewards for present activity.

This inconsistency between the lack of internalized reward anticipations on the part of the Negro child, and his teachers' expectations that he does have such anticipations, reflect the disharmony between the social environment of the home and the middle-class oriented demands of the school. This is reminiscent of Florence Kluckhohn's[4] description of Negro lower-class culture as being "present" and "past-present" in cognitive orientation.

Of the major socialization foci for the child, the most potent agents are the home and the family. Later on, the efficacy of the school and the larger environment increases. However, there is some evidence, in dropout statistics and the like, that the school never does achieve much of its potential socialization influence for the children included in the experimental group. This presumably indicates that a poor home experience predisposes the child to be *less*, rather than more, easily reached by the school as a socialization institution. The problem here is more than a simple disharmony between the implicit value system of the home and the explicit values of the school. Rather, there seems to be a complete absence of preparation for the school experience. It is not that the parents are "anti-school," but that the rewards of schooling are foreign to their experiences. This situation would imply that the school cannot presuppose that the child comes to it acculturated to its purposes.

For these reasons, the highly significant broken-home comparison between the experimental and control groups is of particular importance, and warrants full analysis, because it is reasonable to assume that a broken home is a poorer socializing agent than is an intact home.

When the experimental and control groups are combined and the children from broken homes are compared with those from intact homes, the broken-home group is found to be significantly inferior in scholastic performance.

Little emphasis can be placed on this finding in the current study, however, because of the exceedingly low N (15) in the control group broken-home category. Whether this is a stable and very significant finding or simply an artifact of the present sample cannot be determined by these data. What could be—and was—determined, however, by three series of median tests, was that the patterning of significant differences for broken- versus intact-home comparisons for the total group was identical with the patterning for comparison of the broken-home children in the experimental group with the intact-home subjects of the control group. (The reverse—control-broken vs. experimental-intact—yielded no significance for any comparison.) Apparently, then, the differences between the broken- and intact-home groups for the total population are actually contributed by the broken-home experimental group and the intact-home control group categories, and therefore the total group comparisons using this dichotomy have questionable validity.

When differences between the experimental and control groups within the broken-home category are tested, two of the three Stanford scores are significantly lower for the Negro group. (The arithmetic subtest average does not differentiate between the Negro and white children.) However, when differences between the Negro and white children in the intact-home category are assessed, there are also significant differences in achievement in favor of the control group. There results are presented in Table 6–4. (The intact-home category results are presented because the low control-group N in the broken-home category renders those results statistically less reliable. It should be noted, however, that the only differences in significant items between the broken-home and the intact-home comparisons were in the arithmetic subtest and Negative Family Atmosphere variables, both of which did not achieve significance in the broken-home group.)

From these results it is apparent that the broken-home factor is not the basic determinant of the experimental-control group differences.

Table 6–4

COMPARISON OF EXPERIMENTAL- AND CONTROL-GROUP CHILDREN FROM INTACT HOMES

Variable	Experimental Group %		Control Group %
Crowding Ratio (more than 1.3 persons per room)	45		52
Digit Span Forward (score 6 or more)	52		49
Digit Span Backward (score 4 or more)	41		53
Stanford Test Total (score 4.2 or higher)	28	a	57
Stanford Reading Subtest (score 4.7 or higher)	30	a	55
Stanford Arithmetic Subtest (score 4.4 or higher)	31	a	58
A/R Ratio (score 1.0 or higher)	67		49
Index of Negative Family Atmosphere (score 11 or higher)	57	a	37
Index of Negative Self-Image	67		43

a Differences significant at .05 level or better.

To investigate further the differential effect of broken and intact homes, the experimental group was divided on this basis and the differences assessed. These results are presented in Table 6–5.

Interestingly, intact homes are more crowded than broken ones, although the children from intact homes do better in scholastic achievement. This finding can be quite important, as it seems to indicate that crowding in the home is less likely to have a negative effect on scholastic achievement than is the fact of coming from a broken family background. This was further tested and confirmed by examination of differences between high and low achievers. Apparently, *who* lives in the home is more important than *how many*. As the broken home was presumed to be the poorer agent of socialization, it could be expected that in the intact home there would be relatively more stability and focusing on the child, and perhaps some awareness

Table 6–5

COMPARISON OF EXPERIMENTAL-GROUP CHILDREN FROM BROKEN AND INTACT HOMES

Variable	Broken Home %		Intact Home %
Crowding Ratio (more than 1.4 persons per room)	42	a	60
Digit Span Forward (score 6 or higher)	38		52
Digit Span Backward (score 4 or higher)	38		41
Stanford Test Total (score 2.8 or higher)	38	a	65
Stanford Reading Subtest (score 2.6 or higher)	40	a	61
Stanford Arithmetic Subtest (score 3.5 or higher)	41	a	64
A/R Ratio (score 1.1 or higher)	54		55
Index of Negative Family Atmosphere (score 12 or higher)	45		41
Index of Negative Self-Image (score 29 or higher)	53		40
Popularity in Class (top half of class)	58		45

a Difference significant at .05 level or better.

and concern for his school performance. Hence it is surprising that significant differences were not obtained on the indices of Negative Family Atmosphere or Negative Self-Image although in the latter case significance was approached. It might well be that these factors are most strongly influenced by the larger environment, or, again, that they are so massive in the Negro group that their influence exceeds the effect produced by home conditions. While the broken home is more likely to be receiving its income from public assistance, the intact home has very little additional economic security. Frequently both parents are working, and the father holds down two jobs. A more psychological reason for the absence of difference in perception of the home atmosphere might be that children from the intact homes have higher expectations of their parents which the parents can meet only inconsistently under the conditions of great stress in their lives, thereby increasing the frustration and dissatisfaction of their children.

Considering that those Negro children who come from broken

homes have a lower level of academic performance than those who come from intact families, but that there is no gross difference in degree of negative self-image between these two categories, it must be inferred that academic performance has little effect on self-image for these children, and that in fact the school experience exercises little influence on developing self-attitudes.

The general assumption can be made that, in order to feel comfortable in, and cope effectively with, both the subculture and the larger culture, it is necessary for the child to be developing an image of himself which allows him to establish some positive expectations as to his present abilities and potential future achievement. Thus, the concept of self of the minority group child must be one of the first factors studied in evaluating the effects of segregation, cultural separation, and inferior social status on his personality development and general socialization, including school performance.

In all comparisons made with the data reported here, the Negro children had significantly more negative self-images than did the white children. That this fact is not artifact caused simply by a lower achievement level (also a universal finding) is shown by the lack of difference in self-image when experimental and control intra-group comparisons are made, including comparisons between high and low achievers within the groups. Further, in the cluster analysis to be reported here, a negative self-image is seen to relate strongly to being Negro.

Some examples make this association even more revealing. In completion of the sentence "If someone makes fun of me ———," 47 per cent of all the white children respond with the suggestion of some kind of counter-action, while only 6 per cent of the Negro children respond in this way. In completion of the sentence "When I look in the mirror I ———," the most frequent answer in both groups (about 50 per cent in the white, 30 per cent in the Negro) is "I see myself." But 20 per cent of the Negro boys give such dysphoric responses as "I cry," "am sad," "look ugly," and the like, while such responses occur in only 9 per cent of the white boys.

From these examples it is also clear that a relatively high proportion of the white lower-class children in this sample have negative self-responses, but not nearly so many as in the Negro group. In general, the Negro group tends to be more passive, more fearful, and more dysphoric than the white. Although the Negro children do show less aggressive content in their responses, it is of great interest that, when asked to complete the sentence "If I could be an animal I would most like to be ——," 31 per cent identified with an aggressive animal as compared with only 16 per cent of the white children. Although, in general, boys of both groups are significantly more likely to identify with a highly aggressive animal (40 per cent) than are girls (12 per cent), more Negro girls give such responses than do white girls (21 per cent to 3 per cent). On the other extreme, 23 per cent of the white children, while only 9 per cent of the Negro, named animals which they associated with warm and positive contact.

It is highly unlikely that any one factor could account for the poor performance and deprived psychological state of the experimental group; it is more realistic to see the urban Negro child as subject to many influences which converge on him, all contributing to the effects noted. Among these influences certainly not the least is his sensing that the larger society views him as inferior and *expects* inferior performance from him, as evidenced by the general denial to him of realistic vertical mobility possibilities. Under these conditions, it is understandable that the Negro child—the experimental group in the present study—would tend strongly to question his own competencies, and in so questioning would be acting largely as others expect him to act, an example of what Merton has called the "self-fulfilling prophecy"—the very expectation itself is a cause of its fulfillment. The middle-class orientation of the school helps little in recognizing the realities of the problem, and contributes little toward the development of value systems and activities directed toward breaking this circular dynamic process. All in all, however, it is necessary not to lose sight of the fact that objective depriving circumstances such as a broken home and family instability contribute to the poorer performance and self-image noted, even though these factors may not be considered the primary ones.

Within a given class or racial group, with its various cultural components, there are usually differences in the socializing experiences of the two sexes. To some extent these experiences of course reflect the larger and more modal attitudes of the culture toward sex roles, but since the subgroup has its own history, semi-isolation, and social pressures, sex-role delineations often come into conflict, or are incongruent, with these role expectations of the larger culture. For example, the Negro man does not have the same opportunities as the white for status mobility, job security, or individual power expression in his work relationships. These limitations inherent in the class position of the Negro man influence the developing system of self-identification of the Negro boy, his motivation, and his ability to operate on a delayed reward system. Considering the high proportion of broken homes among the Negro group, and the fact that most of the homes are broken by virtue of the absence of the father, the Negro boy very often has no close male adult with whom to identify. Further, even in an intact family, the Negro boy does not generally have the opportunity to identify with a male figure who has had a history of reinforcement for accomplishment.

In contrast, the majority of Negro girls has an adult female with whom to identify, and the dominant role that female subserves is not too inconsistent with the role prescription of the larger culture, i.e., housewife and mother. Further, many higher-status positions frequently aspired to by lower-class women are open to Negro women as well as white: e.g., nurse and secretary.

For these reasons, sex differentials in the present data were carefully evaluated.

There is educational evidence that in the early school years, girls on the average do better than boys in certain school subjects, especially reading. However, in the current study, there are greater sex differences in the experimental group than in the control group, and these differences are found in many areas in addition to reading. The results of the sex comparisons within the experimental group are presented in Table 6–6.

Among the Negro pupils, the girls outperform boys in both reading and arithmetic, as well as on the Stanford test total score. Girls often demonstrate superior span of attention, less often report a negative family atmosphere, and are much more popular with their classmates. Of special interest is the fact that the A/R ratio indicates that the boys are more frequently superior in arithmetic, as compared to their reading average, than are the girls. In the control group, only one comparison is statistically significant (girls do better than boys in reading achievement), but the A/R ratio also shows a relatively large difference, even though it is not quite significant statistically at the level accepted for this analysis. Thus there seems to be some general sex difference operative in regard to reading achievement and in the relationship between arithmetic and reading scores. All the other sex differences found in the experimental group, however, are exclusive to that group, and on all of them it is the Negro boys who are found to be significantly poorer than the girls.

Table 6–6

COMPARISON OF BOYS AND GIRLS WITHIN THE EXPERIMENTAL GROUP

Variable	Boys %		Girls %
Crowding Ratio	56		54
(more than 1.4 persons per room)			
Digit Span Forward	33	a	55
(score 6 or higher)			
Digit Span Backward	33		43
(score 4 or higher)			
Stanford Test Total	32	a	62
(score 3.3 or higher)			
Stanford Reading Subtest	35	a	63
(score 3.2 or higher)			
Stanford Arithmetic Subtest	41	a	63
(score 3.8 or higher)			
A/R Ratio	68	a	43
(score 1.1 or higher)			
Index of Negative Family Atmosphere	58	a	42
(score 11 or higher)			
Index of Negative Self-Image	47	a	42
(score 29 or higher)			
Popularity in Class	36	a	58
(top half of class)			

a Difference significant at .05 level of confidence or better.

A rather interesting difference found between the experimental males and females is in the Digit Span Test, an attention-retention measure. Here the boys do significantly more poorly on the forward digits, but, although they also score lower on backward digits, this latter difference does not meet the significance criterion. This finding might indicate that, although both the boys and girls have difficulty with a harder and more stressful situation (digits backward was significant between the total experimental and control groups), the girls respond much better to a simpler test of attention. (Again, there was no significant difference on this comparison between the control-group boys and girls.) This difference is stressed here because of the importance of attention for any academic learning and therefore the potential contribution of lowered attentivity to the achievement differences found.

When the control- and experimental-group males are compared with each other, and when the females of the two groups are compared, the resulting patterns of significant differences are similar to those previously found in the other comparisons of the control and experimental groups. These differences are similar but minimized when the control-group boys are compared to the experimental-group girls, and they are maximized in the comparison between the control-group girls and the experimental-group boys. Thus the Negro males' performance contributes the most to the differences between the experimental and control groups. It is important, though, to remember that all four subgroups are behind the national norms in school achievement, with the white girls being the least behind.

In these sex comparisons, the sociometric analysis shows significance for the first time. A determinant of this is that, although boys list girls among their preferences, very few girls list boys. Questioning revealed that the girls do not list the boys because they "are bad," "play tricks on us," "make the teacher angry," and the like. Process data indicate that the girls, in general, are less mischievous, and it was usually the boys who would initiate a period of classroom disruption. In most classes there seemed to be a core of relatively well-behaved girls who were the teachers' favorites, and there was a tendency for these girls to be given high sociometric ratings. Also, behaviorally the female subgroups formed tighter and more permanent alliances than did the male. Again the process material suggests that this might be a defensive reaction against a core of the boys who were continually literally pushing, kicking, and playing tricks on the girls.

The finding of strong sex differences in the current report seems to indicate that, within the social processes and psychological reactions discussed earlier, there is a selective factor operative which determines that the Negro boy receives the brunt of the negative implications of his situation, while the Negro girl is possibly more removed from these effects.

The relative position of the Negro boy seen in these data necessitates an examination of the social and cultural context of his life. As was indicated previously, it seems likely that the social role expectations for the Negro girl are less in conflict with middle-class value systems, presenting her with choices which are both more realistic and more acceptable than those offered to the male. In the great majority of the broken homes it is the father who is absent, and consequently the only stable sex role is the female one. Even in intact homes, the Negro family tends to be matriarchal.[1]

Thus it is the Negro girl who is far more frequently provided with an identification model, while the boy is often left with no strong personal male figure with whom to identify. The impersonal ones, from

TV, movies, and other mass media, are nearly invariably white and middle class, with the exception of a few sports and entertainment figures. Interestingly, during Negro History Week, the process records showed a tremendous spurt of interest on the part of the Negro boys, including those who were real behavior problems, with a number of tussles over who would take the parts in skits of such figures as Carver, Turner, and Booker T. Washington. Also, the one male teacher in the experimental classes—a strong Negro man—had the most control over his class, and received considerable respect from the boys.

In addition to this special handicap of the Negro boy—i.e., lack of a strong male with whom to identify—there is the particularly dismal aspect of his future relative to competition for jobs. In our culture a man is expected to achieve, to provide, to compete, and this necessarily involves more contact with the larger society. Whatever handicaps the Negro boy starts with are likely to be increased by his contact with the majority group as a minority-group member, with consequent lower status. We really cannot calculate the full extent of the deleterious effects on personality development of the continual reaffirmation of inferior status, segregation and quasi-segregation, and discrimination. These realities are especially met with in the job area, where in our upward mobile society the Negro is most often forced to remain stationary. These effects are somewhat cushioned for the Negro girl by her more definitely defined and attainable roles within the family and by the lesser importance of occupational prestige in work outside the home. It also cannot be overlooked that the female role within the family is not only attainable for the Negro female, but also is a role prescribed and valued by the larger society; hence she is able to aspire to a socially valued goal.

The data on occupational aspirations are consistent with this formulation. Boys in both groups tend to aspire to very unlikely jobs— about a third want high-prestige professions such as medicine or engineering. In contrast, the most popular job among the girls is nursing, also high in prestige but more realistic.

When aspirations of the experimental and control group boys are compared, there are no significant differences between the two groups. These comparisons are presented in Table 6–7. Both white and Negro lower-class boys of this age equally tend to aspire in an unrealistic way to the high-prestige professions.

It is surprising that more of the Negro boys do not identify more strongly with, and aspire to, sports careers. Perhaps the successful

Negro sports figures are too remote to these isolated lower-class children. It would be most interesting to determine if such identifications are more frequent in a sample of middle-class Negro boys. (Of course, class differences would be informative on all levels of the study.)

Table 6-7

COMPARISON OF OCCUPATIONAL ASPIRATIONS OF EXPERIMENTAL- AND CONTROL-GROUP BOYS

Occupational Choice Category	Experimental Group %	Control Group %	Total Group %
High-prestige profession (doctor, lawyer, etc.)	26	38	34
Sports (baseball player, prize fighter, etc.)	13	16	15
Policeman or fireman	11	14	13
Skilled or semiskilled laborer	13	8	10
Pilot, air force	5	8	7
Army, navy, marines	11	4	7
Entertainment (movie star, actor, etc.)	8	1	4
Music or art (artist, trumpet player, etc.)	3	3	3
Markedly childish response (cowboy, Superman)	3	2	3
Other occupations (druggist, farmer, etc.)	2	3	3
Non-occupational response (a man, rich, etc.)	5	2	3

Chi-square $= 13.30$
$df = 10$
$P = >.20<.30$

When the occupational aspirations of the two groups of girls are compared, the differences are of such magnitude that the likelihood of their being due to chance fluctuations is less than one in a thousand. Table 6–8 shows these comparisons.

The great majority of the girls indicated much more realistic occupational aspirations. The most popular job in both groups is that of nurse. Among the white girls, housewife (or mother), teacher, and movie star are the next three most popular occupations, with 12 per cent or more giving each of these as her wished-for occupation. The pattern for Negro girls is markedly different, with white-collar jobs and teaching being the only two other occupations chosen by more than 12 per cent of the girls.

Table 6–8

COMPARISON OF OCCUPATIONAL ASPIRATIONS OF EXPERIMENTAL- AND CONTROL-
GROUP GIRLS

Occupational Choice Category	Experimental Group %	Control Group %	Total Group %
Nurse	35	25	30
White collar[a] (secretary, bookkeeper, etc.)	25	4	14
Teacher	13	13	13
Dancer	10	13	12
Housewife, mother[a]	3	16	10
Movie star, actress[a]	4	12	8
Other (hairdresser, fashion designer, etc.)	7	10	8
Musician, singer	1	4	3
Other self-display (model, ice skater, etc.)	0	4	2
Non-occupational response (myself, etc.)	3	1	2

Chi-square = 28.25
  df = 9
  P = <.001

[a] Individual categories significantly different at the .05 level or better.

The fact that the experimental group here chooses white-collar jobs apparently at the expense of both the glamorous (movie star) and mundane (housewife) categories probably reflects the different social conditions under which the two groups live. For Negro women, often consigned to domestic-type work, white-collar jobs enjoy considerably more prestige than among their white counterparts. Movie star, while an unrealistic aspiration for both groups, would be even farther afield for a Negro girl in view of the almost 100 per cent white ranks in that occupation nationally. As was noted earlier, in the Negro family the mother is likely to be the strongest figure, but she is also very likely to work outside the home. Hence, not only is this less a full-time occupation for the Negro girl (and therefore perhaps less likely to be picked as an occupational choice) but also it is one which will involve much more work, responsibility, and hardship for the Negro than for the white woman.

OBSERVATIONAL DATA

In this section will be reported data obtained from various methods and techniques not amenable to quantitative analysis, and information gathered more informally, bearing on these questions.

The major particular methods and techniques were:

1. Student observers came to the classrooms at random intervals and remained for periods of from forty-five to ninety minutes. Generally, the same observers returned to the same classrooms, and sat in a position to observe the class activity without themselves being too conspicuous. The teachers were told that the observers would be in the classroom from time to time, but were never informed as to the exact day or hour that they would appear. Generally, two observations were made each week in each classroom over a period of two years.

Observers were trained to take process records of the classroom activity. Sometimes these would focus on the teacher, and at other times on the children. Guidelines for the selection of various foci of observation were developed in weekly student (observer) seminars, and these shifted, partly as a consequence of the teachers' seminars and partly because of the accumulation of experience in classroom observations. For these reasons, quantification of the observations was not formally attempted, and many of the records consist of rich narrative reports of classroom activities and interactions. At a later stage in the program, several forms were developed to obtain salient behavior indices. These forms included for the most part two types of variables: motor activity and verbal teacher-related behavior. Classifications for the former range from "active-constructive" to "passive-destructive" with intermediate points also represented. For instance, one child rising from his seat, walking over, and striking another child is obviously showing "active-destructive" behavior. On the other hand, a child who, when asked to erase the blackboard, rises from his seat, performs the task, and returns to his seat without disruptive activity, is showing "passive-constructive" behavior. In other words, the words "active" and "passive" refer to more self-organized activity, as opposed to more other-organized activity, while "constructive" and "destructive" refer to the relationship of the behavior to the group purposes and context at the time. For the verbal behavior, categories included length of remarks, relevance to subject, continuity, and whether it involved initiative on the part of the pupil. While observations were made in the control classes as well, these could not be so extensive.

2. The other main pathway into the social and educational structure of the school was through a specially organized seminar led by the writer and composed of teachers whose classrooms were visited by the observers. The children in half these classes were subjects in the experimental group. The seminar was established with the explicit understanding that its proceedings were private, and that none of the information revealed would be transmitted to the then principal or other educational authorities. This arrangement required real understanding on the part of some of the authorities, inasmuch as the teachers received in-service credit for attendance at the seminar. About one-third of the participating teachers belonged to a special all-day school program in which children of working parents could participate in organized activity after regular school hours. An extremely competent student observer maintained a running narrative record of all teachers' seminars. The confidential nature of these sessions was later recognized as crucial to their success.

Unfortunately, it was not possible to arrange a similar teachers' seminar in the control school because of limitations of time and staff.

3. There were occasional meetings with small groups of children. These meetings ranged from after-school discussions about attitudes toward school and classes, to neighborhood and drugstore ice-cream-soda conversations, with a wider range of topics.

4. In addition to these methods, there were some rather randomly used techniques. These techniques included time samples used to determine teaching/play ratios in the classroom; teacher-attitude questionnaires administered to the children (a generally unsuccessful device, as the children tended to be much more positive than their other behavior would indicate); nutritional surveys consisting of repeated questioning of children as to what their last meal consisted of; and a series of repeated questions about a limited area of family experiences, such as, "Who gave you your supper last night?" "Who helps you with your homework?" "Does anyone kiss you good-night?" "What did you do last Sunday?" and the like.

The data and impressions gathered from these techniques and methods will be reported in a descriptive, largely anecdotal manner, within defined categories. The intention here is to convey an impression of the actual learning situation and of the quality of the children's experience in it. For this reason, information gathered from the four technique and method categories will be combined and related.

• *Classroom Observations*

Nine classes were visited consistently over a two-year period and five additional classes were observed on an intermittent basis. These five classes had teachers who were not participating in the teachers' seminar, but who had individually agreed to cooperate in the research and to have their classes observed. Our understanding of the nature of the actual process and activity in the classrooms comes from these observations and from statements, interviews, and written reports of the teachers in the seminar.

In conveying a feeling of the situation that existed, perhaps it is most appropriate to quote from a written statement by one of the teachers, a Negro woman who was one of the most experienced and effective in the school:

> At the present time I don't feel that we are giving the children what they need. Most of them are not being educated. About 95 per cent of them are working at least one year below their grade level. There are very few children who are working up to their capacity. In my fifth-year class of children of normal intelligence not one child achieved 5-10 in both mathematics and reading on the Stanford Achievement test. My class is the norm rather than the exception in this school. The children are clearly not learning what they should. What brings such a situation about? I don't feel that I have all of the answers. I shall merely state my opinion.
>
> Most of the teachers would, I think, agree with me that we spend about 75 per cent of our time disciplining the children and about 25 per cent of our time teaching. Even the time spent in teaching is only about 10 per cent effective because of having to stop several times during a lesson to speak to certain children. The attention span of most of the children is very short. They become bored easily. I feel that one of the reasons for this is that the curriculum is not of sufficient interest to the children. Units of study should be integrated with some aspects of the children's lives. Teachers should attempt to make the curriculum as vital as possible and involve the children emotionally in what they are studying.
>
> I feel that an important aspect of such a program would be the extension of the interests of the children. I have found that the real interests of the children are often so limited that they would have to be increased in order to provide a full program.
>
> One of the reasons that we have such a terrific discipline problem is that the children just don't care. School is just a place where they are sent. Even children who are eleven and twelve years old

have no ideas of their own as to what they want to get from school. The older children don't respect teachers or school property.

A number of points raised in the foregoing quotation continually emerge, both in the observational data and in reports by other teachers.

Although there is considerable inter-teacher variation in classroom atmosphere and in the amount of time devoted to actual subject teaching, our time samples indicated that as much as 80 per cent of the school day was channeled into disciplining, and, secondarily, into organizational details such as collecting milk money, cookie funds, special principal reports and the like. In the control school, this figure never rose above 50 per cent while even with the best teachers it never fell below 50 per cent in the experimental school.

The implications are extremely important and suggest that the lower-class Negro child receives one-half to one-third the exposure to learning that a child from the control environment receives. In addition, it is possible that the control children are likely to receive assistance at home, while it is very rare that a child in the experimental population receives any help with his homework. These discrepancies by themselves can account for a substantial portion of the differences in achievement between the experimental and control groups. Further, the more exposure to school-type learning problems which a child has, the more "test-wise" he is likely to become, responding better and with less anxiety to all types of tests, including those measuring IQ.

In addition, if these findings are consistent, and the school is really capturing the attention of these children for so limited a period of time, it is necessary to scrutinize this primary failure in the teaching function of the school. For it is this failure that transforms the role and self-concept of the teacher from that of an instructor to that of a monitor. It might very well be that the lack of permanence of the teaching staff in lower-class schools is traceable to a 25 per cent difference in how the teaching day is spent.

Within the general picture of classroom disorganization there are large differences between teachers, which suggests that emulation of the techniques used by the most successful could lead to more time spent in actual teaching. Excerpts from observational reports might best illustrate these inter-teacher differences.

First, here are some excerpts from observational records in Mrs. A's fifth-grade class. It should be pointed out that Mrs. A is an average to better-than-average teacher.

October 3—The class was noisy, and at least three large groups were doing their assigned tasks. One was working with A on arithmetic, another was copying a composition from the board, and the third was doing arithmetic examples. There were also about six or seven children walking from group to group, fighting, yelling, and in general, disrupting order . . .

November 5—Mrs. A was yelling at different children and the children were yelling at each other. Santiago was sawing wood at the back of the room, which did not add to the peace and quiet. Although Mrs. A yelled, I could not hear a word she said. The general volume of noise in the room was so great that you couldn't hear a person speaking if he were more than a foot away. Mrs. A said: "I can't force you to work, but don't think you can leave your seat and disrupt all of us," to Albert. He was crying. A took him in her arms and tried soothing him. He broke away, stamped his foot, and turned around. I couldn't make out what he was saying, but the tone of his voice, and both A's and Albert's actions revealed that he wanted to do something that she wouldn't permit. He ran out of the class and she ran after him and came back, with Albert trailing behind. Two minutes later, he ran out again but came back quickly. A looked at him and said nothing until he tried to lock Barbara out of the room.

December 3—For the first time, the class was relatively quiet. Mrs. A was having the children put their heads on the desk in a resting position. One boy raised his hand and called to A. She replied: "Don't Mrs. A me, I know whose head is down and whose isn't." She gave out the report cards. Most of the children did not even bother looking at theirs.

April 14—I came at a bad time again. The lunch money boxes had to be given out. As usual the boxes and envelopes and pieces of paper which go into them are in a very confused state. Today, the condition seems to be at its worst. And all the while that A is trying to straighten the situation out, the class is doing nothing.

A few additional quotes from records will illustrate how Mrs. A deals with the question of remedial work, and how she attempts to motivate the children.

November 5—Barbara and Yvonne were talking. A yelled at them. Barbara said she was helping Yvonne with her spelling. A misunderstood and ridiculed: "How can Yvonne help *you* with spelling?"

December 5—A said to a child that his work was wonderful. Another child said: "But Teacher, he copied it from the board." She replied:

"I know, but at least he was doing some work, which is more than most of you were doing."

April 2—Mrs. A was passing around pictures for the new unit. Edith stopped to read a caption and A yelled: "Don't hold us up by starting to read now."

These illustrations are of the modal class pattern. There are exceptions: for example, Miss B:

October 7—Miss B is able to integrate passing events with what the children are supposed to be learning. One of the children in the class was run over by a car. B asked why children weren't allowed to go to the hospital for a visit, and the children had a discussion of hospitals. They decided to buy flowers for the child and B asked how much money they could collect if 36 children gave 10 cents apiece. Then they discussed the kinds of flowers you could buy in a store.

February 23—B only has to tap her pencil on the desk when the class is noisy and the children quiet down.

February 26—B went around the classroom and looked over everyone's notebooks to make sure that the corrections on the spelling papers were made.

March 9—There are four reading groups, and B helps them one at a time. She compliments the children who read with good expression (Edward and Mareline) and tells those who are improving how pleased she is. The speed of reading in general is very slow. Most of the children stumble over two-syllable words and frequently have a hard time reading one-syllable words. B helps them to pronounce the words, but she usually gives the children time to sound them out.

That these different teacher approaches beget different reactions from the children can be seen in analysis of the children's behavior toward the teacher in each of the two classes. For instance, the observer in B's class noted that the children have internalized her expectations to the point of anticipating her disapproval by looking to see where she directs her attention, while no such instance was recorded in A's class. The "active-constructive" category on the activity record sheet is much more frequently and consistently marked in observations of B's class, while the highest frequency of defiance by a child is found in A's class. B's orientation might be described as definitive but supportive in making demands on the children. She shows a high degree of consistency, which makes it possible for the children to learn to anticipate consequences of their behavior. On the other hand, A undermines her own authority by making punitive and often impossible threats on which she has no intention of following through. B in her teaching continually brings in examples from the children's own experiences and develops figures with whom they can identify. A, on the other hand, sticks much more closely to the formal materials, and her expressed feelings are that the children just don't want to learn, and will not, no matter what she does. B, in her discussion of the situation, says that motivating these children is very difficult but that it is not an impossible task, and expresses the wish that she might have the same class for more than one year. It is not surprising, either, from the excerpted observational records, that A reports she is always "worn out" at the end of the day, while fatigue does not seem to be an important factor for B.

Given the undoubted sincerity and basic competence of both these teachers, and given the fact that they both are Negro women from approximately the same social milieu and that neither is psychologically disturbed, it would seem that the most salient difference between them which is reflected in their contrasting classroom methods is that, although both see and are concerned about the problem of educating these children, B sees means of solution which she can apply, while A does not. Both state that they feel the school and the whole educational apparatus offer little concrete help with these problems and do not constitute sources to which the individual teacher can turn for assistance.

While the achievement scores for A's and B's classes do not differ significantly, there is a slight difference in favor of B, and the question arises as to the possible differences which might accrue from cumulative experience over several years in a class like B's. Certainly the fact that these children can be motivated and disciplined in a class is of significance, and the practical principles by which this can be accomplished warrant further study.

Here another illustration of methods of disciplining and motivating can be drawn from the class of a young, athletic, male Negro teacher. As was indicated in the earlier discussion of sex differences, boys tended to contribute disproportionately to classroom chaos, but they could be adequately controlled by this autocratic but warm teacher who was the only male teacher in the school. It must be remembered that a good proportion of the boys do not have stable father figures in the home with whom to identify, and Mr. J undoubtedly supplied this for many; it might be that more male teachers are indicated for this reason. The children referred to him as "tough," said "he means business" and, in general, responded well to him and to the explicit limits he always set on their behavior and learning. He was continually establishing limited goals and offering rewards only when they had been attained. This man, Mr. J, was continually creative in his use of educational techniques, and, like Miss B, made great use of the children's own life experiences for teaching materials. For example, for an arithmetic lesson he used the children's own cost of living as a problem; he achieved thereby the almost unprecedented complete attention and involvement of the class.

It should be noted, though, that whenever a teacher—including Mr. J or Miss B—turned around or left the room, there was always a higher degree of disorganization and misbehavior than occurred in the control school under similar circumstances.

The majority of teachers found the experience of teaching in this kind of situation frustrating and unrewarding, and the rate of turnover in schools such as the one studied has been shown to be significantly higher than the average.[6]

• Teacher Orientation

It was through the combination of the teachers' seminar and the classroom observations that a fairly comprehensive picture was developed of the teacher's role and attitudes. The teachers were interested in communicating with each other and in working out solutions to the problems they recognized. However, they saw no ready path of communication, either with each other or with the educational hierarchy. The teachers universally felt that they were excluded from a curriculum-planning and school organization role, that they lacked the respect of those higher in authority, and that their problems as teachers were not objectively viewed or seriously considered. In general, they felt under-utilized because they saw no way to enrich the school curriculum through the consideration or introduction of their own ideas and experiences.

All the teachers participating in the seminar felt that to some extent they had been set adrift. They were particularly vehement in regard to curriculum advisers, district coordinators, and similar personnel, feeling that these people especially had no appreciation of the special problems existing in the education of the lower-class and, most specifically, Negro and Puerto Rican, child. Without exception, they charged that school authorities were always imposing an educational orientation which was exclusively developed for a middle-class population who have very different preparations for learning. The vehemence of their feelings on these matters occupied many hours of the teachers' seminar after the initial months of establishing basic rapport. The core of affect expressed cut across the continuum of good and poor teachers, although the better teachers were more likely to come up with some suggestion or innovation.

Some of these teachers described the seminar as a cathartic experience, and all felt some gratification in learning that the others were as totally frustrated. It is interesting here, and it was discussed many months later, that the teachers in their daily contact tended to restrict their communications with each other on these matters to expressions of annoyance. It was not until the end of the first year of the seminar, after the teachers had established confidence in each other and in the writer, that it was possible to bring in detailed observers' descriptions of their classes for interpretation and evaluation by the other seminar members.

As the seminar progressed, the teachers discussed the motivation and self-image of the children in their classes, and this led to an evaluation of the role of the teacher in the development of these attitudes. Thus, as the teachers felt free to complain and to criticize the educational hierarchy, they also felt free to criticize themselves and each other and were able to evaluate their own roles more objectively.

From studies conducted in Detroit and in Texas, Wattenberg *et al.*[7] conclude that "the social origin of teachers does influence considerably their attitudes toward their administrators, their colleagues, the parents, and children." This finding was certainly borne out in the analysis of the present data. The participating teachers were middle class and the majority were Negroes; the childen they taught were lower-class Negroes. For the most part, the teachers felt alien to the community within which they worked, and with one or two exceptions, they themselves lived in other neighborhoods. Yet the shared minority racial status created more identification and also more conflict for the Negro teachers than is usually the case for the white teacher in a lower-class white school. This conflict resulted in their emphasis of the minority group identification of the child by, for example, reminding him on museum trips that, since he was Negro, he must be especially well behaved: better behaved in his line than the white children in the next line. It is interesting to note that observers of such trips reported that, among these usually so undisciplined and so unruly children, there was then an unusual amount of discipline and control—more than that of the comparable mixed and white groups. In the seminar it was pointed out to the teachers that the children acted as if they were in a foreign country, and that normal childhood spontaneity was absent. Two of the teachers especially took the position that, even if this was harmful for the child, *they* would not feel comfortable with everybody observing them if the children acted any differently. The teachers were able to verbalize the dynamics of this: that their identification was middle class, and if these children in any way lost their "decorum," the lower-class label would be attached to the teacher too. Here it would be interesting to know if the racial factor was subordinated to the class factor, and what would be the attitude of the middle-class white teacher toward lower-class white children under similar circumstances. Throughout the seminars and the classroom observations there was constant and frank interplay of class and racial factors, and the conscious discussion of this interplay made a real contribution toward putting both factors into perspective for the teachers. Here again, a cultural anthropologist or social psychologist whose role was properly defined could play an important part in the educational functions of the school.

It was observed in the classroom process records that the teacher often directed derogatory remarks toward individual children. The most frequent such remark was to call a child "stupid," and as a result, the teacher and, through the teacher, the school played a role in reinforcing the negative self-image of the child, and contributed a negative reason for learning. From the fact that higher achievers did not have more positive self-attitudes, it was pointed out in the discussion of quantitative results that school achievement had little influence on self-attitudes. Perhaps such classroom reinforcement combined with negative motivation for learning is one explanation for this finding.

After discussion of these derogatory comments and the negative motivation sequence, future process records indicated that the majority of the teachers substantially decreased or eliminated such comments, and much seminar discussion was devoted to finding positive methods of approaching the children.

The conclusions to be drawn from the foregoing rather anecdotal discussion are that the teacher is an essential part of the learning process, and when she is made—or feels she has been made—a supernu-

merary in matters of policy and curriculum and in evaluation and discussion of teaching problems, she also loses her initiative and interest
in evaluating her own role. This occurrence must be true in any school
context, but is particularly valid when the actual frustrations are so
enormous, the problems so great, and the guidance so minimal as in
these special problem schools. Further, when a valid opportunity is
offered, and they feel sufficiently protected, teachers are anxious to
deal with these problems. They are much more comfortable when
they feel that the school recognizes the special educational problems
they confront. All of the participants emphasized the importance of
assigning to these schools experienced teachers and of making a special effort to eliminate the succession of substitutes to which many
classes are subjected. (One class in the experimental group had six
different teachers in one academic year.)

Another important composite observation is that the teachers,
with the social scientists, feel that the children's learning process can
be facilitated by the school's recognition of the deficiencies in the
backgrounds of these children and a constant and comprehensive
effort to compensate for them.

Perhaps if schools were to establish such seminars, using for lead-
ers behavioral scientists unconnected with the school system, it would
help teachers better to evaluate and understand their roles, and help
to orient educational materials in a more meaningful context for the
lower-class child. Further, the communication now felt by teachers to
be so lacking could be at least partially supplied, and eventually channels could be opened between such seminar groups and the administrative hierarchy of the school system. Such a program should substantially help in making "difficult" teaching situations "challenging,"
thereby reducing the turnover rate and giving both children and
teachers more consistency in their roles.

DISCUSSION

It can be assumed that the social context of a child's life is crucial to
his particular growth of consciousness and the unique role he perceives
himself playing in the world. In an affluent society whose goal is success and whose measurement is consumption, the lower-class child
starts the race to the goal with an assortment of disadvantages. Economic uncertainty, slum living, crowded homes, and small value given

to intellectual activity are not an adequate foundation for achievement. It is another problem that the struggle against poverty sometimes leads to deepened understanding and maturity: scores of unique individuals are only exceptions to the rule and do not alter the effects of these conditions in the aggregate. The majority of Negroes is found in the lower socioeconomic groups and consequently is subjected to the whole array of deleterious factors associated with such social status.

To avoid confounding social with racial status, a number of studies attempted to equate middle-class Negroes with similar white groups. It is doubtful if such an equation can be validly made. The results of the present study, and of other studies, delineate some of the negative psychological attributes associated with self-awareness of Negro status, or any racial status deviating from the valued white norm. But even if this could be controlled for, middle-class identification is more than simply socioeconomic position. The great majority of Negro middle-class members is at most one or two generations removed from lower-class status, and in order to achieve truly comparable populations for social psychological research, comparable class stability is essential.

In planning the present study, it had been considered also desirable to have a population of both Negro and white middle-class children, as it was felt that it would then be possible to measure more accurately some of the effects of being Negro in a white society. The criterion of class stability, though, makes it extremely difficult to find in a small area a sufficient Negro population.

As a result, in the present study, the Negro children are differentiated from the white majority by the cumulative effects of having inferior status as members of a racial minority, as well as social-class handicaps, while the white children in the study have only the class handicap. In the classroom process records there are frequent remarks by the teachers to the effect that if the Negro child is to achieve he must be twice as good and capable as his white counterpart. It was noticed on field trips that the Negro children were admonished continually to be on their best behavior so they would not bring disgrace (sic) on themselves or their race. This pressure and the anxiety it produced in the children became one of the basic discussions in the teachers' seminar. The groups of children with whom the writer met often insisted he must be Negro, and when this was explored they said that someone who was nice to them and did not criticize them must be

Negro. Their expectations, reinforced by the anxiety of their middle-class teachers, were that the larger white world would fundamentally be rejecting and critical. It must be remembered that this is a world with which they had practically no personal contact (with the exception of the principal and a few teachers). It is undoubtedly this experience of a segregated life with the consequent anxieties reinforced by the school that plays a vital role in the development of the negative self-image of these children.

It is for these reasons that a study such as the present one is a study of the effects of chronic social stress on personality development, motivation, and subsequent school achievement. This chronic stress is what is probably seen in the increasing divergence between the experimental-group boys and control-group girls over successive school years. In addition, in median tests of longitudinal achievement data between the high and low achievers in the experimental group, the low achievers showed no progress, and, in fact, had a slight decline (not statistically significant), while the high achievers showed a flattening in progress curves. Unfortunately, there are no comparable longitudinal data for the control group. The important fact here is that even the more advanced experimental children do not show significant progress; while the national norm expectation is one year's progress in one school year, it would be expected that the advanced children would even exceed this norm. Seemingly, the weight of the whole complex of negative factors which have been delineated here is depressing the scholastic functioning of these children, as well as distorting personality growth. While the data as collected here do not give specific causal information, the internal relationships in them make this a compelling conclusion.

In this flattening of progress there must be some nullifying of the expected effect of the school. Further, if there is some nullification of the school's academic influence, it is likely that its socializing effects are also partially vitiated. A partial parallel to this situation may be found in Gordon's study of canal-boat and gypsy children,[2] in which he discovered that the IQ's of these children declined as they got older. He related this result to the infrequent school attendance of the children, and to the fact that a poor environment is more stimulating for a younger than for an older child, inasmuch as there is proportionately less prior knowledge or experience. This may relate rather closely to the present data, as the canal-boat children attended approximately 5 per cent of the normal school time, the gypsy children approximately

35 per cent, while the process records in the present study indicate that a good percentage of time in the experimental school classes was given over to non-academic and often disorganized activity. It might be that for children from non-intellectually stimulating environments the school must offer proportionately more stimulation. This additional stimulation would be particularly necessary for children who came from a broken home or one in which parents work such long hours that little time is left at home. However, the poor cultural environment which increases the child's need for stimulation in school does little to prepare the child to accept his school experience. So the children who most need the socialization influence of the school may well be those who are the least amenable to it because of their previous narrow range of experience. It would seem, therefore, that it should properly become society's responsibility, through the school, to provide not only schooling but also the preparation for it.

Coming from an intact home is significantly correlated with achievement, and the achievement scores of the total experimental group were influenced by the large proportion of children from broken homes. Again, here it might be that the school should supply some of the support and stimulation that are absent in the broken home. In the classroom process records it was observed that some of the teachers would be quite critical of the children when they answered incorrectly. These criticisms might not only affect motivation negatively but might also reinforce the negative self-image of the child. It is interesting that one of the most frequently used negatively-toned words with which the children described themselves was "stupid."

Special training in group processes and on the effects of social deprivation might be helpful for teachers in these schools. These children require considerably more reinforcement than do others, possibly because absent, missing, and excessively burdened parents cannot supply it. One student observer put it aptly in describing the classroom as a continual competitive battle among the children to gain the teacher's attention. In a sense, the children are trying to gain the attention of a parental substitute and are extremely responsive to any encouragement or warmth (although the responsiveness rarely includes any prolonged periods of self-control or orderliness). Although approval was important to the children, the teachers agreed in the seminars that attention was more important even if it was a severe reprimand. It is probably this factor which in good measure leads to classroom chaos which is responsible for the limited percentage of time actually going into academic work. With middle-class children the problem is usually different, with parents tending to be overindulgent, families more intact, and subsequent decrease in the need for the attention of the teacher.

A cross-racial class factor, the crowding variable, is a major one in both populations, and because of this its effects could not adequately be measured in this study. It is possible, though, that it is playing a major role in depressing the levels of performance of the total populations, and would be worth further investigation. Some relationship was found between crowding and reading achievement in this study, as reported earlier, and there are also some qualitative data to support this finding.

An anecdotal corroboration of this relationship might be interesting. In one of the experimental classes there was a boy who after school habitually went into a large closet and closed the door. With the prevalence of psychoanalytic assumptions about such behavior, he was put on the "urgent" waiting list for an evaluation by the school psychologist without further ado—and without further investigation. The process recorder in the class meanwhile discovered that the boy left the light on in the closet—surely a modification of intra-uterine conditions. When asked why he went into the closet and what he did there, the boy replied, after urging and quite hesitantly, that it was the only place he knew of to be alone, and that he usually read while he was there. In the course of the study, it was found that this child came from a home which consisted of a three-room apartment shared by 14 people. The anomaly both here and in other cases is that this child, obviously bright, was functioning on a relatively low scholastic level, and was quite embarrassed at acknowledging the fact that he read. Under questioning, he explained that at home there were always some people sleeping, so he could never leave a light on and would be laughed at anyway if caught reading.

In the popular literature in post-Sputnik America there has been a torrential criticism of our school system and its apparent failure to fulfill its goals. Teachers, administrators, physical plant, and equipment have all been held responsible. In the experimental school dealt with here there were competence and sincerity in the vast majority of personnel, and the physical plant was adequate. But the orientation of our schools at present is almost entirely toward middle-class values and way of life, which sometimes have no concrete meaning for the lower-class child. In addition to the more general ones raised earlier,

the problem here appeared to be one of a standard curriculum, tai-
lored to our pervasive middle-class value system and to the overall
norms of child development. But norms, after all, are mathematical
averages, and it is crucial here to keep in mind that we are dealing
with children who come from among the poorest home environments;
who have the poorest nutritional status; who have the least parental
support and reward; and who are most subject to premature birth,
para-natal complications, and accidents, all of which may lead to a
higher proportion of central nervous system damage. It is unrealistic a
priori to expect such children to perform at the norm. In other words,
a proportion of the retardation here could be expected. Both the segregated nature of their lives and the encapsulation of the school in a
minority group living area are serious handicaps, as the broad experiences reflected in modern curricula are not shared by these children.

As has been shown, these children from lower-class and culturally
deprived environments are more limited in access to new knowledge
and in opportunities for new experience, and this is even more true in
a racially encapsulated community. The teachers in the seminar felt
that the curriculum was unrealistic in terms of the experiences of the
children in the school, and they had many concrete suggestions for
changes in teaching method and content. Unfortunately, the teachers
did not feel free to channel these suggestions and felt that the special
problems of their children were not understood by the educational
hierarchy. For example, an early grade primer presents country situations, and yet the vast majority of these children have never been to
the country. Similarly, the primers are not biracial, often have meaningless story content, and fail to present situations with which these
children can become involved or to picture children with whom they
can identify. These primers represent a further extension of the alienating experiences these children have in a segregated community, in
segregated schools, surrounded by the majority racial group. Instead
of making school a more meaningful experience for these children
who most need it, such instructional materials serve only to turn to
them another of society's unsmiling faces.

The principle drawn from the foregoing is that when the home is
a proportionately less effective socializing force, the school must become a proportionately more effective one; further, the deficiencies of
the home and immediate environment create deficiencies in the children's experiences which make it more difficult for them to deal with a
curriculum which presupposes a variety of experience which they can-

not enjoy. The question to be dealt with in this context is how the school can become a more potent socializing force for these children.

The data of the current study could offer some suggestions. For example, the inferior performance of the Negro boy relative to the Negro girl and the not infrequent absence of the father from the home lead to a consideration of the potentially beneficial role which male teachers could play. Similarly the instability of the broken home might be somewhat compensated by children having the same teacher over a longer period of time. A set of rewards might be worked out to channel the attention needs into the scholastic areas, and somehow intellectual activity and the child's confidence in himself could be consciously reinforced. Also, the apparent greater facility with numbers rather than words might be put to more extensive use in the teaching situation, and perhaps an expanded remedial reading program around story content which has intrinsic interest and familiarity for the children would be helpful in overcoming a basic deficiency. In addition, the child can be offered broadening experiences which must include integrated schooling and afterschool activities: he must no longer feel that visiting another neighborhood is tantamount to a trip to a foreign country.

However, if the schools are to compensate meaningfully for the impoverished intellectual background of these children, it is necessary to know scientifically the specific effects of their impoverished environment on their cognitive and language development. When the parameters of these deficits have been delineated, then it will become possible for the school to offer an effective enrichment program in the early years to stimulate the intellectual maturation of these children, so that the gap between their actual functioning and average grade expectations can be closed. This task is a major one for social scientists, and no effective enrichment can be possible until these more microscopic effects of environment have been understood and their implications systematically tested in the actual school situation. Also, if the school is to be the comprehensive socializing institution, the all-day school program should be expanded, as it is one of the most successful current attempts to increase the influence of the school and to develop constructive behavioral alternatives for the children.

This discussion has centered mainly on the role of the school in helping to compensate for the deficiencies of the home. The fact of these deficiencies, however, and their close relationship to overcrowded, encapsulated, and economically marginal living conditions cannot be ignored. Society must solve these social problems, but in the meantime there is an important role here for the social scientist and particularly the social psychologist and the cultural anthropologist, who could study extensively the dynamic relationships between environmental and social circumstances and personality and intellectual performance.

The lower-class child, and especially the lower-class minority group child, lives in a milieu which fosters self-doubt and social confusion, which in turn serves substantially to lower motivation and makes it difficult to structure experience into cognitively meaningful activity and aspirations. As Erich Fromm consistently points out, one of the social characteristics of modern man is his increasing alienation from both his work and his fellow man. The dynamics of this psychological process in a technological society might be best understood through the study of the progressive alienation of the Negro child in a white world.

REFERENCES

1. Frazier, E. F. *The Negro family in the United States.* Chicago: Univer. Chicago Press, 1939.
2. Gordon, H. *Mental and scholastic tests among retarded children.* Board of Educ. Pamphlet No. 44, London, 1923.
3. Klineberg, O. *Race differences.* New York: Harper, 1935.
4. Kluckhohn, Florence. Family diagnosis: Variations in the basic values of family systems. *Soc. Casewk.,* 1958.
5. Kugelmass, I. N., Poull, L. E. and Samuel, L. E. Nutritional improvement in child mentality. *New York State J. Med.,* 1944, **54,** 2604–2605.
6. Public Education Association. *The status of the public school education of Negro and Puerto Rican children in New York City.* New York: Public Education Association, 1955 (mimeo).
7. Wattenberg, W., *et. al.* Social origins of teachers and American educacation. In L. J. Stiles (Ed.), *The teacher's role in American society.* New York: Harper, 1957. Pp. 61–70.

7 /

Early Social Environment and School Adaptation

MARTIN DEUTSCH

This essay will make no attempt to incorporate the total complex of social institutions involved in school failure, for this can lead only to a loss of the direction necessary to the carving out of relevant and malleable chunks of the problem. For this reason, the focus will be largely on the school, an institution that in itself cannot initiate major social change, but one which can play a determining role in orienting its products. The school is, after all, the only social institution which has some contact with *all* children.

There is variation in the impact of this contact from group to group, fostered through (1) the child's preparation by his parents for entry into school, (2) the general meaning of the school to the economic substance of the community, and (3) the various expectations of the school and the appropriateness of its curriculum for the child. These differences in the interaction among the child, the school, and the community are determined, among other things, by social attitudes toward education, stability of community, the social class and ethnic membership of family, and the sex of child.

Generally speaking, the middle-class child is more likely to have the importance of school imprinted in his consciousness from the earliest possible age. This is not necessarily bad or good for the child or the school, but it is very different from the preparation of the lower social status child. I have never seen a school curriculum that is organized on the basis of the existence of these differences. Both sets of children are typically asked to climb the same mountain at the same rate, as if they had similar prior experience and training. The lower-class child, because of poorer preparation, is at a real disadvantage in this exercise, although it is the middle-class child who probably has more personal anxiety about the success of his climb. The middle-class child, however, has available to him other avenues for handling the school situation. There is more likely to be continuity from the school's orientation to his home-and-family orientation. Failure can be interpreted to him in appropriate and familiar terms, and methods of coping with it can be incorporated, increasing the motivation or offering the necessary rewards, incentives, or punishments to effect the desired changes in performance. For the middle-class child, the school is very central and is continuous with the totality of his life experiences. As a result, there are few incongruities between his school experiences and any others he is likely to have had, and there are intrinsic motivating and moulding properties in the school situation to which he has already been highly sensitized.

For the lower-class child, there is not the same continuity, and he does not have the same coping mechanisms for internalizing success or psychologically surviving failure in formal learning. If the lower-class child starts to fail, he does not have the same kinds of operationally significant and functionally relevant support from his family or community—or from the school—that his counterpart has. Further, because of the differences in preparation, he is more likely to experience failure. It may even be that both groups are equally motivated quantitatively; but failure or lack of recognition for the middle-class child may only serve to channel his energies more narrowly, whereas for the lower-class child it early becomes dysfunctional, converting the original motivation into a rejection of intellectual striving.

EFFECTS OF SCHOOL FAILURE ON THE CHILD

Failure in school for the middle-class child can be more personally disorganizing because the continuity of values from home to school insures that such a child will be considered a failure in both places. However, as was already pointed out, there are also more resources avaliable for helping the child to cope with the failure and to recover from it, and to mitigate its degree.

For the lower-class child, school failure may result in less personal upset or disturbance but may be more final, both in the recovery of adequate functioning in school and in occupational choices. Such failure may have the result of gradually but effectively alienating the child from the school and the structure of opportunities associated with it. In addition, though lower-class parents may or may not be opposed to the specific act involved in the child's leaving school prematurely, they may have made clear to the child their own negative affect in response to their personal experiences with social institutions. Particularly the minority-group lower-class parent is likely to explain, rationalize, and attribute job and economic frustration, both correctly and incorrectly, to impersonal societal institutions. He may thus identify, accurately and inaccurately, these same institutions with his child's troubles in school. This negative affect can rapidly, though perhaps inadvertently, be generalized to the whole school-learning process. This kind of constellation has particular significance where the school system operates as a bureaucratic mechanism, isolated from the community and unable to counteract the consequences of inadequate preparation for functioning in the school factory. So the school, at the time the child decides to leave it, has little influence with either the child or the parent, and even if it did, it is frequently just not programmed for interpreting its own processes to children or adults from outside the middle class.

ALIENATION OR INCREASING RAPPORT

Thus, if the school is to influence the continued attendance of children, the influence must begin and the channels for its transmission must be opened well before failure and dropout problems arise.* This brings us to the first contact of the child and his parents with the school. The process of alienation or, on the other hand, of increasing rapport, begins here. It is at this level that certain crucial questions must be asked: First, is the child intellectually and psychologically ready for the school experience, for the specific curriculum, and for the demands of comprehension, communication, motor control, and timing made by the school? The reference here is not to specific "readiness"

---

* Of course, not all dropouts are school failures (and there might even be instances when high-performance creative children *should* drop out of school— but that is another paper), but the evidence suggests that the majority are. Similarly, of course, all dropouts are not lower-status children. But again, the majority are, and I would postulate that with middle-class children there is a higher incidence among dropouts of psychological malfunctioning, while with lower-status children, it is more likely to be associated with sociocognitive dissonance and general problems of communication.

as the term has been characteristically used in educational circles but, rather, to the sociocognitive preparations and anticipations of the child for this new experience. Next, are the parents helped to become aware of the school's purpose, the nature of its demands on the child, and how they—even if uneducated—can play a meaningful role in the education of their child? Is the school accessible to these parents? In other words, is it a place which stimulates embarrassment for their ignorance and fear of its power, or is it a center for comfortable relationships and a sharing of their interest in their child?

In this interaction among three elements, what about the school itself—the third element? Is it a structure that the community can be proud of and where the staff can share this pride? Does it have teachers and administrators who see a challenge, or are they interested only in securing discipline and in surviving the day? Do they have some understanding of the social backgrounds of their children and the temporary educational limitations that may have been imposed by these backgrounds? Is there a reasonable amount of staff stability, particularly in the early years? And is there some attempt to adjust the curriculum and primers to current life realities?

The answers to these questions we all really know. The experiences of the child from the disadvantaged background simply do not prepare him for successful school performance. The teacher has, more often than not, *not* been trained in the sociology of learning; and also, more often than not, her training fails to give her a sense of challenge in teaching children, particularly those who start out with handicaps. Usually, she prefers, both by training and personal inclination, the immediately bright, responsive child who also most likely places a type of demand on her professional skills which is more congruent with the orientation of her training. The schools are likely to be underequipped, closed to the children for after-school experimentation with extra-curricular books and arts and crafts, and closed to the community as evening centers for learning and socializing. More likely than not, nobody explains to the parents how they can help or be important factors in the education of their child, and the whole process of their child's education—even for the few who become active in the PTA—remains foreign and alien to them. Often, their contact with the school carries a condescending quality. The early curriculum is likely to be unfamiliar and experientially discontinuous, while the primer, despite all criticism, is still most likely to be boring, repetitious, suburban, and altogether too white.

What have been stated here, of course, are some of the major problems of getting a grip on children from social and cultural backgrounds which do not participate in the middle-class values of the school. These problems are raised not because it is now fashionable to identify them as the source of all of our current social difficulties but because they define human realities we are just beginning to face in relation to our educational ideals. We cannot avoid the necessary focus on the early relationship among the child, the family, and the school, and on the transition between the preschool environment and the school. These factors are crucial if we mean what we say about universal education and educational opportunity.

Considering all these combinations, factors, and circumstances, it is amazing that as many children as do still find sufficient relevance in the school experience to remain. In this context it might be noted, parenthetically, that the real occupational expectations of lower-class children are more congruent with their homes and their community experiences than they are with the school setting. It may be that only as school is perceived as more functionally relevant to adult occupations that early negative experiences can become decreasingly influential in the decision to leave school. Here is not meant the Conant solution of simply more vocational high schools but, rather, the *same opportunity distribution for all populations,* regardless of subgroup membership.

IMPORTANCE OF A PRESCHOOL TRAINING PROGRAM

There are many possible avenues through which solutions for these problems could be evolved. But none of them exists independently, and any successful solution must involve a confluence of institutional changes on the level of the child, of the curriculum, of teacher preparation, adequate economic support for schools, and community-school bridges with two-way traffic. Nevertheless, there are certain possibilities for social intervention on the child-focused level that may open individual escape hatches and that may require only minimal changes in the structures and processes of current school operation. The most important of these areas of social intervention, and one that comes least into conflict with existing institutionalized barricades to change, is that of an intensive, highly focused preschool training program.

From present data it cannot be said definitely that there is any direct relationship between early school experience and the school dropout; but I hypothesize a very strong relationship between the first school experiences of the child and academic success or failure, and that the more invariant the school experience is, the more important is the early experience to the academic success of the child. I would also hypothesize that children who have had preschool and kindergarten experience are more likely to cope appropriately with the kinds of things the school demands intellectually than are children who have not had this kind of previous experience. This hypothesis would be particularly true for children from lower socioeconomic groups, and it would be most true for children who come from the most peripheral groups in our society.

For example, what happens when a child from these groups comes to school for the first time in the first grade? If he has not had experience with books, with the kinds of perceptual and developmental demands that are made by the school, and with the kinds of language skills implicit in the nature of the communication that comes from the teacher to the child, then that child's chances of starting to fail within the school situation are greatly enhanced. It is common in the first grade for a teacher to talk to the class for a period of ten minutes or so. Yet very often these children have never before experienced a ten-minute-long speech sequence coming from an adult to a child. So in school, at the very beginning, the child experiences "foreign" information coming in at a rapid rate, requiring complex auditory differentiations for which life has not suitably programmed him. What is likely to happen in this process, and fairly immediately, is that the youngster will start to look upon school as a place where he does not understand and where he experiences debilitating failure. Perhaps more important, the teacher often starts to build in expectations of the child's failing. It is probable that, at a very early age, the child perceives this expectation of failure. And the children who are most likely to have these expectations directed toward them are children who come with the fewest aptitudes for fulfilling a middle-class set of values. These children tend to be the most poorly dressed, to have a dialect, to come to school somewhat late, and, in general, not to fit naturally into the kinds of middle-class constraints and constrictions that are established within the school system.

The child who comes to school with very few of the kinds of intellectual cognitive structures that it demands will be basically the most susceptible to this process of failing, and he will be the least likely to start communicating with the teacher. The critical question, then, is whether a child can at least begin the educational process by learning the basic skills. In order to accomplish this for children from socially marginal backgrounds, some kind of antecedent experience to compensate for the inadequacies within their homes and in their intimate social environments would be highly likely to help them achieve a positive adjustment to the demands of the school. (The use of the term "adjustment" here is not meant to imply adjustment to the social aspects of the school process, or to the conformity pressures of the school. Such questions are beyond the scope of this paper.)

A good preschool program would attempt to bring the lower-class child to a kind of parity with the preparation for school that the home, community, and at least relative affluence characteristically give to the middle-class child. Such programs could only be set up after intensive training of teachers and staff to work on the problems of communicating with parents as well as developing methods and techniques for compensating the youngsters for a narrowness of experiential variation. The attempt would be to enrich those developmental areas most functional and operative in the school situation, thereby establishing both cognitive and attitudinal continuity between the preschool and school years. Hopefully, because the child is most responsive to acquiring basic skills at pre- and early-school ages, these skills can be fostered with reasonable readiness, and their acquisition can thus help lay the basis for a reduction in school failure experiences and for an increase in school success. The skills involved include, for example, the visual and auditory perception which underlies reading, language abilities, spatial and temporal orientation, general information, familiarity with books, toys, and games, and the development of a sustained curiosity. In addition, the attempt must be made to engage the child as an active participant in the learning process rather than as a passive recipient of a school experience.

SCHOOL VERSUS HOME?

In facilitating the learning process in underprivileged youngsters, the school must expect frequently to do a portion of the job traditionally assigned to the home, and the curriculum must be reorganized to provide for establishing a solid base for the special learnings that are necessary.

It is important to emphasize that the early training recommended here is not a matter of inculcating middle-class values but, rather, of reinforcing the development of those underlying skills that are operationally appropriate and necessary for both successful and psychologically pleasant school learning experiences. The fact that these skills are almost routinely stimulated in middle-class homes does not mean that in content they are middle class. For instance, there is nothing fundamentally culturally loaded in a good or poor memory, but it can be awfully important in preparing for an examination.

Another question must also be considered: How are the child's first anticipations developed toward the school? It is often stated that among Negro parents there is low motivation toward school accomplishment. I have not found this to be so. I have found a great degree of motivation, but a lack of understanding of how instrumentally to make these aspirations operative for the child. The problem, then, is to interpret for the child the kind of behavior that will make it possible for him to function well and to cope with the school's mechanisms. One way this could be handled is through a direct relationship between the teacher and the community. For example, there are some communities where the school is seen as a major and central resource center. Where it is kept open in the evening, there are library books that can be taken out, and the school can be favorably perceived as a place of social transition. When the school is a real part of his life and of his community, the child can more normally have the opportunity some day to decide if he wishes to move toward a learning experience consistent with the demands of the school, if he wants to stop with a lower level of education, or if he wants to seek advancement in some type of vocation with skills less closely related to the requirements of formal schooling.

To return more directly to the problem of anticipations toward the school, there is reason to believe that the sense of failure that often develops at an early stage projects itself through the total experiences of the child—not only temporally, in terms of his reaction to the demands of the school, but also in terms of his whole concept of self-identification, of a positive self-concept, of the development of a sense of dignity. This sense of dignity, I think, is closely related to how much money, how much concern, and how much institutional modification we are willing to invest in education. In neighborhoods where most schools have practically every window broken, there are some protected schools which are beautifully kept. There is a reciprocal feedback, as if the institution and the children were working with and cooperating with one another, and there is a sense of mutual respect that goes along with it. Here too, of course, is where teacher training in community sociology and mental health becomes a very important issue.

Horizons and goals are stimulated early in life; and if the parents have had low ceilings because of impoverished experiences, having known job insecurity, humiliating negotiations with welfare agencies and landlords, and the like, there is not much left to give the child a sense of identifying the self with goals that take individual impetus and disciplining. This problem, in a larger context, is societal and has its analogous aspects in the routinized existence of much of the middle-class, rigid schedules, automated work, and cities and suburbs that share an ugly sameness and drabness. Sometimes the excitement to be sparked in a child must reach his subjective self, his imagination and individual poetry. After this, he might make discriminations and differentiations not seen by his peers in the external world. This development of the inner self, which can certainly start soon after the development of language, can be an intrinsic part of the preschool experience and, possibly, a basis for much later motivation.

FEMALE DROPOUTS

It is often in school that another element of the dropout problem, related to a different type of discrimination, takes form—and is regularly ignored. There is a special complex of difficulties associated with the female dropout. Typically, discussions of dropouts deal with all eases as an undifferentiated totality or concentrate on males without recognizing that many of the factors responsible for high dropout rates among Indian Americans, Negro Americans, etc., are similar to those operating on girls. At some undefined point, our social expectations as reflected through our teachers become differentiated with respect to intellectual behavior in boys and girls. This distinction is probably not always a conscious distinction, but males of any social class are more or less expected to have to use their intellects in the business of preparing to make a living. For females, this assumption is less likely to be made, and the antecedent attitudes are probably manifested in the preschool and kindergarten. I know of no data here, but there is no other known area of strongly ingrained social attitudes and expectations which is completely discontinuous with earlier, though not necessarily discernible, orientations. It seems improbable that these sex-related expectations would develop only in the later school years. A high proportion of female school dropouts, then, are apt to be intellectually average girls who enjoy, proportionate to the boys, more academic success but still feel that intellectual development and their personal futures go along divergent paths. With society increasingly needing skilled people, the distinction between male and female intellectual roles must be explicitly eliminated early in the learning process if the later effects are to be minimized and if school is to offer the same potential to children regardless of sex.

PROSPECTS FOR A PRESCHOOL PROGRAM

The emphasis voiced here on the preschool program as a means of accommodation between the school, the child, and his family represents, it is felt, a necessary approach to the dropout problem. It is beyond our present scope to examine it from the other end of the continuum: the problem of the motivation of the high school student to join the labor force when the opportunities available to him may not be numerous or productive. Further, the high incidence of minority-group dropouts makes necessary a consideration of prejudice in employment patterns. But these are broad societal problems, to be attacked and solved in the social arena. And even if they were solved, the individual problems of the unprepared child coming into the unpreparing school would assume even greater importance. Developmentally, it would seem that preschool experience is one of the first areas in which to approach the problem, and one in which there may be less resistance.

There seems to be a great need currently to discuss all problems thoroughly, to investigate their causes, and to delineate all possible solutions; and then to implement only those solutions that have been rendered sufficiently sanitary that they represent no threat to the status quo. The danger to the approach discussed here is that it will be put into the context of the stress-free, allegedly supportive, "mom"-istically-oriented, deintellectualized enclosures where much of early childhood education is both considered and carried out. If such takes place, social experimentation would be sterilized and useless. But if social scientists and educators undertake relevant projects jointly, in a spirit of experimentation and with bovicidal collaboration against the accumulated sacred cows, the possibilities of humane success are greatly enhanced.

PART II

Cognitive and Language Factors in the Education of the Disadvantaged Child

8 /

Learning in the Disadvantaged

CYNTHIA P. DEUTSCH

In some respects, a title such as "Learning in the Disadvantaged" is reminiscent of the "Honeybunch" series of children's books: the differing titles such as "Honeybunch in the Country" and "Honeybunch in New York" served only to identify different locales in which the saccharine little girl had the same experiences with the same kinds of people. Honeybunch herself always exhibited the same reactions and never changed. Similarly, in the title suggested for this paper, "learning" could be regarded as a stable given, while the samples or populations or topics could be referred to as variable factors, having no intrinsic influence on the process itself. Thus, the particular social category of the learner is quite irrelevant to understanding and discussion of the process. There is historical precedent for considering learning in this way, in that it has been extensively studied in simple situations, such as maze running, with the aim of abstracting principles to be applied to other organisms, situations, and levels of complexity. In other words, learning can be seen as a property of the organism—or, more accurately, of its nervous system—and a property which can be reduced to neurophysiological essentials. So a title such as "Learning in the Disadvantaged," like "Honeybunch in the Country," could be simply a device for altering minimally the arena of discussion rather than designating a particular content.

However, learning can be viewed in a manner which includes particular attributes of the learner, the context, and the content of the material to be learned. Despite the fact that the S–O–R paradigm offered a basis for such an emphasis, the experimental psychologists who specialized in learning theory twenty and thirty years ago eschewed it; as a result the findings from the multitude of learning studies yielded very little of relevance to human learning in a realistic social context. A variable such as the meaningfulness of what was being learned, in fact, was something that got in the way, so nonsense syllables were the content of choice for many experiments. The learning curves derived from such material find little application in the study of school learning, or in evaluating the differences in learning among differing populations.

With the current emphasis on education, and on the search for more effective teaching methods, learning theory has found its way through the maze and into the classroom. This process has brought about a focus on the learner and his specific characteristics—and in that context, a title such as "Learning in the Disadvantaged" takes on a rather specific meaning. It is in this sense that this paper has been prepared. It includes, therefore, some discussion of the characteristics of the disadvantaged with respect to some of the skills underlying learning, and some treatment of the stimulus organization consistent with the learner's characteristics and the stimuli represented by the materials to be learned.

There are different kinds of learning and different kinds of disadvantage. For the population referred to in this paper, "disadvantaged" is only the latest in a series of euphemisms, which have included "slum-dwellers" and just plain "poor people." These last two terms are concretely descriptive of the economic situation of these people, but by using the term "disadvantaged" the intention is also to convey a categorization involving social or psychological variables. Since disadvantage exists only in a relative sense, the term needs somewhat further explication. For purposes of this discussion, the designation is used relative to the demands of the school and, later, the job market: the population being referred to are disadvantaged with respect to what is demanded for educational attainment and occupational mobility and advancement. The conditions of life at home for the children in this population are not continuous with the milieu of the school, and do not prepare them well for the demands placed on them by the school and by the broader society.

There are three major assumptions upon which the discussion which follows will be based:

1. The social milieu in which the child grows up is highly influential in determining the kind and degree of his experience. This is rather obvious on the macroscopic level: the slum child has a different

milieu and therefore a different set of experiences from the middle-class child. However, in current studies at the Institute for Developmental Studies (IDS), we are finding this true on a more microscopic level as well. An instrument known as the Deprivation Index, when applied to households of ostensibly the same socioeconomic status (SES) level, yields differences between families in social experience such as trips away from the neighborhood, interaction between parent and child, organization of the home and of the family schedule, and the like. These differences are also found to be associated with scores on verbal and IQ measures given to the children.

2. The ease of acquisition of new knowledge and skills—learning —is based in large part on the prior experience and knowledge of the organism. Ample documentation for this position is to be found in Hunt's *Intelligence and Experience*,[5] which includes much work from many sources.

3. The nature of the stimulus—its organization, speed and manner of presentation, and the like—is influential in acquiring new knowledge. The relationship established between the experiential background of the organism and the nature of stimulus presentation is what Hunt refers to as the "match."

The discussion which follows concerns verbal, perceptual, and attention characteristics of children who come from disadvantaged circumstances, and how these characteristics are related to their learning.

Let us begin with the verbal area.

A large cross-sectional language study done at IDS has indicated that children from disadvantaged backgrounds enter school with a somewhat different language system than do middle-class children. These differences obtain particularly in the grammatical structure of the language used, and in language used to relate one thing to another, as contrasted with the more simple descriptive uses (see Chapters 10 and 18). These differential language findings are consistent with the reports of Bernstein,[1,2] and with data reported by Jensen.[6] In general, the language used by the disadvantaged children may be described as simpler in syntax and less rich in descriptive terms and modifiers than is the language of the middle-class child.

These differences come about apparently because the homes from which the children come are far less verbal than the average middle-class home. Verbal interaction between parent and child tends to be in brief sentences and commands rather than in extensive interchange, and a great deal of communication in the very low-income home is gestural. Labeling of objects and actions in the environment is not emphasized. There are few if any books or magazines in the home, and the child gets little exposure to the printed word as a source of information or of communication.

These differences in linguistic background between the disadvantaged and the more privileged home are too well known to belabor further here. The point to be made about them is that the verbal and linguistic experience of the child influences his learning. Not only does the child who has an impoverished verbal background have a more restricted vocabulary and especially, as indicated earlier, a narrower and simpler syntax for purposes of communicating with others, but in all probability he has what Jensen calls a "higher threshold" for verbal mediation.[7] Thus the child, as a result of his experiential background, is less able to solve problems by verbal mediation than would be true of the child with greater language experience. The potential importance of this background for learning cannot be overestimated, in view of the fact that the problems whose solutions are facilitated by verbal mediation are not limited to verbal problems, or even to problems verbally stated. In many so-called non-verbal tasks, verbalization plays an integral role, and many non-verbal problems are solved with the use of verbal mediation. Jensen[7] points out the crucial role of verbal mediation in the solution to the problems posed by the Raven Progressive Matrices. Other examples may be found in such a test as the WISC. The Picture Completion subtest, for example, presents the subject with a series of pictures in which something is missing. This is of course a visual stimulus—but the response called for is a verbal one: a label. Another example would be the Object Assembly subtest on the same scale. There is considerable evidence to show that having labels for unfamiliar objects facilitates learning about them. Therefore, in tasks such as those in the Object Assembly, it may well be that the child who thinks in verbal terms—and is therefore more likely to label the incomplete object as he is working with it—will perform better even on such highly spatial tasks.

The exact nature of the verbal skills which underlie verbal mediational processes is still obscure. Whether simple exposure to a highly verbal environment lowers the threshold for the use of verbal mediation or whether what is important is extensive practice with verbal-type problems is not really known yet. While it will take extensive longitudinal studies on large samples to make such a determination, a promising tool has been formulated in the last several years: the Illinois Test of Psycholinguistic Abilities (ITPA) (see Chapter 1, pp. 14–16). The test is a diagnostic test, in the sense that what emerges for each subject is a profile of scores along several linguistic dimensions, such as auditory decoding, visual-motor association, vocal encoding, and the like. In this way, as with any constructed scale, the components of a given overall score can be analyzed in terms of patterning of strengths and weaknesses.

In an effort to learn more about the linguistic organization and growth of young children, especially those from disadvantaged backgrounds, we have been applying this test to the children in our preschool enrichment groups and to a control group. The preliminary results are that the experimental group performs at a higher level on the test than does the control, but that the subtest patterning of the two groups is almost identical. Apparently, the language experiences which the experimental group had during the enrichment year raised their overall level, but did not alter the patterning of language skills. Our same two groups of children were also tested on the Kendler concept-formation paradigm,[8] but there was no significant difference between the experimental group and the controls in the number of subjects who could be designated "mediators" according to Kendler's system. Further investigation and retesting, it is hoped, will determine if further language training does alter the ITPA pattern, and if such patterning can be predictive of mediational behavior on the reversal shift technique. The level of performance of the experimental group on the ITPA was below the average, though on some subtests the difference was not significant; so it may also be that the overall ITPA score could predict mediation. If so, the implication would be that a language-enriched curriculum could foster the growth of verbal mediational processes in disadvantaged children, even without giving them any specific training in the use of verbal mediation.

Language was selected as one of the three areas of emphasis in this paper because it is obviously crucial to reading and to other academic performance. In the cross-sectional study previously referred to, one finding was that there were greater differences between the lower-class and middle-class children at the fifth-grade level than at the first-grade (see Chapter 18). While the data do not come from a longitudinal study, it still seems warranted to note that the disadvantaged children seem to become more disadvantaged, at least in the language area, as they go through school. What this fact indicates about the effects of the school on development is, for the moment, irrelevant. The point is that ground can be lost, relative to the development of the more privileged group. To the extent that language influences other learning, this developmental decline can be especially serious.

In evaluating possible remedies for poor progress in language development, cautious optimism seems the appropriate attitude. The ITPA results quoted above, as well as the test-retest gain of experimental enrichment groups on the Peabody Picture Vocabulary Test, indicate that such scores can increase following an experimental compensatory education program. It is not yet known if such an increase will be maintained over long periods of time, with or without a continuing enrichment program, or if language growth carries as a necessary corollary the growth in learning skills per se. As indicated above, one aspect of this question is being addressed in the ITPA study. Our longitudinal study—carrying the same groups of children through a special curriculum from the nursery year through the third grade, and continuing extensive evaluation of them through the sixth grade—will also yield some information on this question when completed.

In the meantime, Bernstein's work, the work of Bereiter and his group, that of Gray and her group, the Baltimore language study, and others, as well as our own findings, are all contributing information and hypotheses in the area of language enrichment, an area which seems to be quite universally recognized as critical in the learning— and the teaching—of disadvantaged children.

In the perceptual area, where there is somewhat less widespread interest and work at the present, a greater emphasis is justified. Historically, theorists and researchers in this area have been concerned with the mechanisms of perception, and the influence that the organization of the stimulus field—particularly the visual field—exercises on what is perceived. The work on social influences on perception (with the exception of the well-known early study by Bruner and Goodman[3] and a few scattered cross-cultural studies) has been concerned almost exclusively with the short-term influences of particular experimentally imposed or manipulated experiences. Unlike language, which is so obviously determined by social experience, perception has traditionally been regarded as a function quite independent of one's overall social milieu, an assumption which is open to serious question.

The fundamental contradiction to the assumption would be based on the proposition that experience and practice are influential in perceptual development. This does not seem so untenable when one considers the visual-deprivation experiments as examples, and it is certainly not unreasonable to view deprivation as a continuum. When so viewed, it becomes logical to assume that deprivation of varying degrees can be associated with perceptual disabilities of varying degrees. For example, as shown in the studies reported by von Senden,[11] people deprived of visual-form experience for varying periods of time will show varying degrees of impairment in form discrimination. Might it not be true also that people deprived *in varying degrees* of visual-form experience would show lesser, and perhaps more subtle, deficiency in form discrimination?

Slum homes provide few toys or other playthings for a child; neither are there picture books. Further, there is usually a paucity of household objects. Might it not be that such restrictions in the visual field inhibit the development of form perception? How can a child learn to differentiate the forms of a square and a triangle if the differences are not explicitly pointed out to him, even if his visual sensory apparatus is intact? What is the role of familiarity in accurate perception? Is it possible that new forms will be more easily differentiated if their components are more familiar, or if the child has a wider range of familiar forms against which to compare the novel? Fantz's work[4] indicates that preference develops in accord with early exposure. Why shouldn't accuracy and ease of discrimination similarly relate to experience?

These questions have no definite answers at the present time. Posing them in this way places perceptual discrimination in a developmental and social context which is open to intensive experimentation, and, hopefully, removes the issue from the now sterile "nativism-empiricism" controversy.

The suggested questions for investigation have related to visual perception primarily, but the inference should not be drawn that they are applicable only to vision. For further explication, let me briefly mention the hypothesis about auditory discrimination which is discussed in Chapter 12 at some length: that the noisy background and the weak signal conditions under which slum children live predispose them to learn early to tune out auditory stimuli. Both the signal-to-noise ratio itself and the inattention which it promotes operate to reduce the amount of auditory discrimination experience to which the child is exposed, and this eventuates in his later poorer performance on auditory discrimination tasks. While we do not as yet have sufficient data either to confirm or disconfirm this hypothesis definitively, so far our investigations in the area have supported the assumptions.

It is pertinent here to mention some recent specific analyses of auditory discrimination data which relate both to perceptual and to linguistic development. One of the primary tests used to evaluate auditory discrimination is the Wepman.[12] Item analysis of Wepman protocols done by my colleagues has shown that the most frequent items missed are those pairs which differ in the final phoneme, and that whenever in our samples groups of children with learning disabilities are compared with control groups, there are significant differences in final-phoneme discrimination whether or not the differences in initial-phoneme discrimination are significant. It seems fairly certain that the differences in performance by placement of phoneme are real ones. The implications for grammar and syntax are obvious, since most grammatical inflections in English are carried at the end of the word. There are also conceptual implications, in that accurate definition of number and tense can be very important in both stating and solving problems. Here it is relevant to note that, in the ITPA study, the subtest patterns show for both the experimental and the control groups the poorest performance in those which involve auditory stimuli and call for knowledge of grammar and of function. Perhaps even more interesting is the fact that these are also the two subtests on which the experimental group is farthest above the control group. Unfortunately, data on the Wepman for these groups are not yet analyzed.

That discrimination can be successfully taught to young children can be implied from the experimental-control group differences in the ITPA data. Whether it can be trained in older children, especially those who already show considerable deficiency, is less clear. A study recently concluded at the Institute involved the testing and training of auditory discrimination in a group of third-grade reading retardates. The purpose of the study was to determine if training in auditory discrimination would enable retarded readers (who, we have found, are deficient in this skill, with respect to average or good readers) better to profit from reading instruction. Four groups were defined: one which received regular auditory discrimination training and also remedial reading, one which received only auditory training, one which received only remedial reading, and a control group which received neither. The second two groups also had a play period (during which the activities were neither auditory nor book-or-reading-related) in order to equalize the time spent with the tutor. A battery of eleven auditory discrimination tests was administered before, immediately after, and twice more at spaced intervals after, the training period, which was one school semester's length for each group. The special work given the children was in addition to their regular schoolwork. Overall analyses indicate no differential auditory discrimination improvement for those children who had specific auditory training. The more microscopic analyses are still underway, and it is not yet known whether some differential performance or patterning of performance will be defined.

Attentional processes are, in essential respects, a part of both perceptual and linguistic development, and are being considered separately here only for convenience. It is obvious that experience will mean little unless the input channels are sufficiently open and attuned to the stimuli being presented. Both the state of the organism and the organization of the stimuli and the field in which they are presented influence attention. The state of the organism can be considered to include both the neural state and the motivational state. While the former may not be too directly influenced by the social environment (though the possibility of a somewhat indirect influence must not be negated), certainly the latter is; and here the social environment quite directly influences the selection of stimuli which are perceived.

The educators of the thirties were quick to point out that, if children lose interest, they do not attend and therefore do not learn. Therefore, much effort was expended to attract the children's attention. Unfortunately, almost all of this effort was directed toward making the stimuli compelling. Virtually no care was taken to insure the kinds of experience that would influence the motivational state of the child. A child who feels lost in school because demands and materials are unfamiliar and discontinuous with what he previously experienced at home will not attend properly to the stimuli presented. A child who has not previously been exposed to as much as ten minutes of uninterrupted speech will have great difficulty in listening all the way through so long a statement. Furthermore, a child who has not previously learned to respond to rather elaborate spoken directions will not be able even to attend to, let alone follow, all the directions. Such difficulties have strong negative effects on motivation and as a result negatively affect the child's attentiveness and therefore his learning. Once the attentiveness has been, as it were, tuned out on the inside, it is difficult to reinstate it, no matter how attractively and seemingly effective attention has been engineered by organization of the stimulus field. Further, the stimulus organization, to be effective, must relate to the child's background of experience.

Very early a child learns to be selective in what he perceives: this is a prime necessity, inasmuch as one is always assailed by many more stimuli than it is possible to respond to. Hierarchies of attentional and response systems are established, apparently on a neural as well as an experiential level, related to sensory modality preference and efficiency as well as to the "compellingness" of individual stimuli. A stimulus-field organization, to be effective in channeling a child's attention to the aspects most relevant to the learning task, should be consistent with a child's already learned hierarchies. What these are for different children at different ages are far from clear, and many experimenters and teachers have found a child relating to what was conceived of as a nonessential part of the stimulus material. It is probable that a child's background yields not only particular amounts and kinds of stimuli, but also some *channeling* of his attention to particular aspects of the stimuli present. Here it may well be that the middle-class background gives a child not only a great amount and variability of stimuli, but also an attentional channeling which is consistent with his response to aspects of stimuli which are most relevant for his school performance.

Apart from these built-in hierarchies and proclivities, however, one must address the question of the manner in which attention is engineered by stimulus-field manipulation, and how often the original purpose is overwhelmingly defeated. The best example is the modern primer. Because color attracts attention, it is used quite lavishly. Because children like pictures—or are thought to like pictures—they are included multitudinously. But by these measures, the children's attention, of course, is attracted to the colored pictures, rather than to the print, which is the stimulus to be learned. The child is confronted with the task of attending to a relatively small black-and-white stimulus in the face of a strong, competing, large colored one. It is good to note that some of the new experimental reading series have abandoned this format, whether or not for conscious reasons of better visual and attentional coordination. Another example of self-defeating stimulus organization may be found in many elementary school classrooms. The rooms are often a riot of color: posters all over the walls, pictures the entire length of the room, etc., etc.—all distractions from the teacher's voice and from whatever content is placed on the blackboard or the bulletin board, or in the pupil's notebook in front of him. These comments do not reflect support for a movement back to the austere, dull, and undecorated classroom, but simply for a movement toward a judicious use of attention-getting aids. A stimulus analysis of the classroom and the learning materials presented would yield considerable information about the objects to which attention is really being called. Then, a redesigning of the placement of the stimuli and of the stimuli themselves should enable the creation of attractive classrooms and materials without the danger of engineering the child's attention to the nonessential stimuli.

With regard to other correlates of attention, I would like to cite a series of studies at the Institute involving the use of our modification of the Continuous Performance Test (see Chapter 11). Our version uses colored dots, inasmuch as the subjects for whom it was adapted were young children and retarded readers. Briefly, the task is a vigilance one, which involves attending continuously to a series of stimuli and pressing a button when the one previously designated as correct is presented. The visual form of our test uses a memory drum, on which colored dots are presented at the rate of one per second. Each dot appears in the aperture for 0.6 second, and there is 0.4 second between stimuli. This is subjectively rather a rapid rate, and it is necessary to pay close attention in order not to miss a stimulus. Subjects are told to press the button every time the red dot appears. An auditory analogue uses the naming of the colors in the same order and at the same rate, with the same stimulus—red—being the correct one. In all our studies using this device, the clinical-type sample has always done more poorly than its control group. For example, retarded readers perform more poorly than good readers. The original scoring of the technique involved a simple tabulation of incorrect and correct presses, and missed presses (i.e., when the correct stimulus appeared and the button was not depressed). However, more recently we have connected the device to an electronic clock, so it is possible to record the elapsed time between stimulus presentation and button press. When these results are analyzed, what is found is that many of the responses labeled incorrect by the old scoring method are really simply late responses to the correct stimulus. That is, the retarded readers, for instance, are responding correctly to the stimuli, but their responses are made too late to be recorded as correct. (They occur too soon to be real responses to the stimulus following the correct one, so it is obvious that they are slow but correct.) Since the Rosvold, Mirsky, and Kornetsky[10] studies with the CPT indicate that the test is sensitive to central changes in arousal or attention, it seems most reasonable to view the children with learning disabilities as having faulty or slow attentional processes.

Recent drug studies by Kornetsky and his colleagues[9] indicate that there are differential effects of various substances, depending on whether the timing of a task like the CPT is experimenter- or subject-controlled. While the drug studies as drug studies are irrelevant for this discussion, the fact that the two types of stimulus presentation control can be differentiated is highly relevant—and relevant to understanding the role of attention in performance.

Even before the implications of all these CPT findings for children's learning have been investigated experimentally, their relevance for the classroom seems obvious. What is needed is a well-engineered stimulus field and a speed of presentation adjusted to the children's actual rate of response. This latter may be harder to accomplish than it looks. Some classroom observational data collected by some of my colleagues show that, without being at all aware of it, many if not most teachers tend to give less response time to the child whom they see as a poorer student than they give to the child who they are more sure knows the answer. This practice results in less time being given to the child who in reality takes longer to respond, than is given to the child who actually needs less time. This kind of teacher behavior also influences directly the number of success experiences of the slower responding child, and also influences his performance indirectly, by conveying subtly that the teacher does not expect him to know the answer. For the children are aware of the differential time allotment and of its implications even though the teachers in the sample are not.

What are the implications for "learning in the disadvantaged" from these brief discussions of the verbal, perceptual, and attentional processes? Many of the studies referred to drew samples from lower-class and middle-class groups in order to make direct comparisons between them. Other data, gathered for other purposes, also yielded information on such comparisons. For example, in the studies of retarded versus normal readers, we are dealing with populations which are biased on SES lines. That is, the prevalence of reading retardation is much higher (estimates range from four to ten times higher) in disadvantaged groups than in middle-class groups. Hence, whatever characteristics are found in retarded readers will be found in a larger proportion of disadvantaged children than in middle-class children.

The burden of the data and hypotheses presented is that disadvantaged children suffer in the three areas mentioned, and that these areas represent crucial underlying skills in school learning. Further, the implication is that these children are deficient in these skills as a result of the deficits they experience in their home backgrounds. Data are adduced to show that skills in these areas can improve, though there is not yet concrete evidence to indicate that such improvement will result in overall academic or conceptual improvement. There are no data to the contrary; it is simply that the whole approach to the specific areas is too new to have permitted as yet the gathering of definitive data.

Another fairly clear point is that children from more privileged backgrounds are superior in most of these skills, and that groups of such children show a lower rate of reading and other learning disabilities. Therefore, it does seem reasonable to conclude that improvement in these skills could result in better progress in school learning, and a lower rate of learning disabilities.

Evidence may be adduced from the fact that many of the disadvantaged children who have difficulty with school learning learn many other things most adequately, when their experiential background is appropriate for such learning. For example, large numbers of five-year-old children are quite capable caretakers for their infant and toddler siblings. These children can be quite independent in personal care from a very early age, dressing themselves and then helping younger siblings to dress at ages when middle-class children do not do so. More examples could be cited, but the point is made: These children do not show the same disabilities in learning when the behavior called for is consistent with their experience. Perhaps this is an instance in which the old concept of cultural relativism is appropriate: The middle-class children learn well those tasks which are consistent with their training and experiences, and so do the lower-class slum children. The problem is that it is the school-type learning which is related to the values of the broader society—and to the later job needs of the children—and this is the type for which the middle-class child's background best equips him. The implication is, therefore, that it is not the learning ability per se of the slum child which is deficient, but only his background of experiences. It is on this basis that compensatory education programs have been established by us at the IDS and by various other groups around the country. As both our measuring instruments and our curricula are sharpened, the answers to many of the questions posed in this paper should be forthcoming.

Two words of caution are in order before concluding.

One is that, despite the cultural-relativism hypothesis put forth above, it must be recognized that the deficiencies which seem to exist in the slum child have to do in part with cognitive and concept-formation behavior, and these are skills which underlie many problem-solving abilities, even in non-verbal areas. If, as is hypothesized, it is impoverishment of experience which negatively affects the development of these skills, then that impoverishment is associated with a debilitation at the center of the growth of basic learning skills, and not with more superficial, and presumably more easily compensated, skills.

The second word of caution applies especially to the area of training and curriculum. It is highly likely that experience alone is not enough to enable the disadvantaged child to overcome the poverty of his background. That is, what is probably necessary is experience that is engineered, labeled, verbalized, and repeated in such a way that it is made relevant both to the child's previous experience and to his later activities. In other words, a trip to the zoo will not in itself make up the child's lack of previous trips, acquaintance with animals, with the use of transportation to get there, and the like. What is necessary is the organizing of the trip in such a way that it reinforces knowledge the child already has, and imparts specific labels and procedures that he can make use of in the future. For example, a trip to the zoo can contribute to an understanding of the concepts "larger" and "smaller" by making obvious for the child the sizes of the various animals and comparing one to the other in the words of the concept: the elephant is *larger* than the monkey; the ostrich is *smaller* than the horse. Simply taking the child to the zoo and expecting him to acquire this concept himself is unrealistic.

That this is true can be seen in unplanned real-life examples as well as in pedagogical theorizing and evaluation of enrichment curriculum experiences. I recently had occasion to meet a number of children of migrant workers. These children are disadvantaged not only by their impoverished home backgrounds, but by their irregular school attendance as a result of the family's travel from one crop harvest to another. But the children, in contrast to city slum children, are not disadvantaged by a geographical narrowness: by the age of ten, those to whom I spoke had traveled thousands of miles, usually in cars or small trucks. When some of the children from city slums who have never been more than ten blocks in any direction from their homes show little concept of distance, geography, or mileage, it is easy to attribute their deficit to simple lack of experience. But when migrant children show the same type of deficit, it becomes apparent that experience alone is not enough. The migrant children, who were interviewed informally and with no sampling procedure, had a very poor concept of distance and time. These children gave for the width of the continent estimates which varied from ten to one hundred miles, even though they themselves had traveled from Oregon to Texas and back several times, with a trip or two from Texas to Florida in between. It seems clear that their deficient knowledge and unrealistic estimates were due to the lack of any attempt to specify and make meaningful their extensive geographical experience. Apparently, a child can travel thousands of miles, but if the time, the mileage, and the geography are not pointed out to him in some meaningful manner, little specific learning about distance is gained.

Curricula which simply present a cafeteria of experience, and experiences which do not include some direction, cannot be expected to succeed—or to accomplish much—in ameliorating the school learning disabilities manifested by the disadvantaged child. Therefore, the evaluation of the specific skills and deficits of children from varying backgrounds should continue, and the attempt should be made to devise curricula and experiences which will be consistent with the current skills of the child and which will be effectively directed toward his growth in the areas of deficit.

REFERENCES

1. Bernstein, B. Social class, linguistic codes and grammatical elements. *Lang. & Speech*, 1962, **5** (4), 221–240.
2. Bernstein, B. Social structure, language and learning. *Educ. Res.*, 1961, **3**, 163–176.
3. Bruner, J. S., & Goodman, C. C. Value and need as organizing factors in perception. *J. abnorm. soc. Psychol.*, 1947, **42**, 33–44.
4. Fantz, R. L. The origins of form perception. In P. H. Mussen, J. J. Conger, & J. Kagan (Eds.), *Readings in child development and personality*. New York: Harper, 1965. Pp. 72–84.
5. Hunt, J. McV. *Intelligence and experience*. New York: Ronald, 1961.
6. Jensen, A. R. Learning in the preschool years. *J. Nursery Educ.*, 1963, **18** (2), 133–138.
7. Jensen, A. R. Verbal mediation and educational potential. Unpublished manuscript, 1965.

8. Kendler, Tracy S. Development of mediating responses in children. In S. C. Wright & J. Kagan (Eds.), Basic cognitive processes in children. *Soc. Res. Child Develpm. Monogr.*, 1963, **28**, 33–48.

9. Kornetsky, C., & Orzack, Maressa Hecht. A research note on some of the critical factors on the dissimilar effects of chlorpromazine and secobarbital on the digit symbol substitution and continuous performance tests. *Psychopharmacologia*, 1964, **6**, 79–86.

10. Rosvold, H. E., Mirsky, A. F., Sarason, E., Bransome, E. D., Jr., & Beck, L. H. A continuous performance test of brain damage. *J. Consult. Psychol.*, 1956, **20**, 343, 350.

11. Senden, M. von. *Raum- und Gestaltauffassung bei operierten Blindgeborener vor und nach der Operation.* Leipzig: Barth, 1932. Cited by D. O. Hebb, *The organization of behavior.* New York: Wiley, 1949. Pp. 28–31.

12. Wepman, J. Manual of directions: Auditory Discrimination Test. Chicago: Author, 1958.

9 /

The Social Context of Language Acquisition

VERA P. JOHN AND

LEO S. GOLDSTEIN

The child, surrounded by a sea of words, sequentially and selectively acquires the nouns, verbs, and phrases of his language as well as the gestures, intonations, and dialect of those with whom he interacts. The rate and breadth of this complex acquisition are proportional to the scope of his verbal interactions with those charged with his care.

Language is so pervasive in human behavior that the process of language acquisition is often taken for granted. A comprehensive treatment of this process is obviously beyond the scope of this paper. There are too many gaps in our current knowledge to make such an attempt feasible.

In consideration of such limitations, therefore, this paper will focus upon social conditions that affect language acquisition. More specifically, it will focus upon the gradual shift in the child's use of words from labeling specific and often single referents to the use of words for signifying categories of objects, actions, or attributes. The hypothesis advanced here is that the rate and breadth of this shift vary from one social context to another, and that it has differential consequences for cognitive development dependent on the social context in which it occurs. This hypothesis will be examined and discussed chiefly in terms of the pertinent literature, with occasional reference to empirical studies.

The need to modify the cognitive growth patterns of young children—particularly of those children who live in the slum areas of our major cities—has added new impetus to the search for a clarification of the relationship between language and thought. It is our intention to examine aspects of word acquisition as related to conceptual development, particularly the development of verbal mediation.

The literature on the development of language, structured largely in terms of maturational theory and based on the congruent findings of careful investigators, specifies an approximate sequence and timetable of children's verbal development. The focus of many of these studies has been on the rate of language acquisition, the unit studied being the number of different words elicited from the young child in a standard setting. Here, the social environment is viewed either as a hampering or enhancing medium in which the development of speech occurs, and the basic process of growth is considered to be neurophysiologically determined.

Although these studies have given us more facts about the increase of the child's active vocabulary, they have failed to deal with language development within the context of modern psychological theories such as those of Hebb and Hunt. Similarities in the quantitative features of overt behavior (i.e., the size of spoken vocabulary) are assumed, by normatively oriented researchers, to be behaviors functionally equivalent for groups of children differing in background. However, studies limited to word counting afford little insight into the dynamic relationship between social experience and language. While many of these investigators (e.g., Gesell, Templin) may be aware that the content of speech is culturally determined, too often their writings have not reflected this awareness.

In contradistinction to the maturational approach to language development as exemplified by the investigators mentioned above, Osgood's model of language conceptualizes words as abbreviated motor behavior. While his approach permits a simplified description of the complex behavior of language, it focuses on variables which would appear to be tangential to language acquisition. More importantly, motor learning requires little social interaction, but language cannot be acquired in an interpersonal vacuum.

On the other hand, the theoretical writings of Bernstein,[1,2] and the recently translated book of Vygotsky,[16] present approaches which are useful in the study of language acquisition in a social context. In his writings, Bernstein emphasized status as a major social determinant of speech patterns within social groups. More centrally related to the approach taken in this paper are hypotheses advanced by Vygotsky three decades ago. He proposed that the conditions which influence the development of speech (overt language) are also related to the development of verbal mediation (covert language). Further, he suggested that a socially determined learning condition of central importance in the acquisition of language is the availability of adults for engaging the child in dialogue.*

Consequently, the central theme of this discussion, partially based on Vygotsky's thinking, is that children *develop* and *test* their tentative notions (hypotheses) about the meanings of words and the structure of sentences chiefly through verbal interaction with more verbally mature speakers.

LABEL AND CATEGORIES

• *The Acquisition of Labels*

Social interaction with verbally mature individuals, which affects language acquisition, begins with the occurrence of the infant's earliest vocal responses. Some findings have illustrated the effects of social environment on vocalization in children as young as six months.[3,14] The child's language development in the first two years of life is primarily in the nature of increasing comprehension of the speech of those around him. By age two, he has developed a speaking vocabulary which may range from 3 to 300 words. In the next two years, the child shifts from using words exclusively as labels with single referents to the use of words which have multiple referents (rudimentary categories).

This process of acquiring and enlarging the use of labels can be sketched in general terms. At an elementary stage of language acquisition, before his first birthday, the child perceives a word as being one of a multitude of attributes of an object (shape, weight, color, name). By the repeated association of seeing and touching the object, and hearing the name of the object, the child acquires a bond between word and referent. Usually, the source of auditory stimulation is the mother. In addition, children engage in communicative interaction with siblings, relatives, other children, teachers and neighbors. The role of more impersonal sources of communication, e.g., television and radio, has become increasingly important in children's acquisition of words.†

* The relationship between children's verbal skills and parental availability has been stressed by McCarthy.[12] She postulates a gradient of verbal proficiency as a function of the amount and kind of contact the child experiences with his mother.

† Novel but simple learning is well understood by advertisers. The highly predictable association between the picture of the Coca-Cola bottle and its name from the TV sound track is a fact of great utility in label acquisition.

Put on a more technical level, in describing language acquisition, some researchers rely on the conditioning paradigm. However, such a model presents certain difficulties in that it emphasizes a one-to-one relationship between stimulus and response. In reality, the word to be learned is usually embedded in a sentence (the verbal context) and its referent (the object which is to be paired with the word) is surrounded by a multitude of extraneous features in the environment. Learning labels requires selective attention—the inhibition of irrelevant aspects of the learning environment.

This learning of new verbal responses, particularly by young children, can be facilitated by a relative invariance in the environment. One of the major characteristics of the home, a natural setting for language acquisition, is its intrinsic variability. This is particularly true of lower-class homes, which have been described as lacking in scheduling or predictability for children, and as more crowded, and more transient in their inhabitants than middle-class homes. Children raised in such lower-class homes participated in the studies reported below.

In spite of the complexities and difficulties involved in the process of label acquisition, children do acquire words in the midst of the "noise" of the natural environment. Some accomplish this more readily than others. The abundance of opportunities for hearing the names of objects while seeing and touching them is such that most two-year-olds can understand and use effectively a number of labels.

• Receptive Labeling

Children from different social classes vary in their knowledge of words. Some studies of social-class differences have recorded systematic variations in verbal indices of children grouped according to father's occupation and/or education. Children from high-income, high-status families have been found to speak in longer sentences, more articulately, and with a more varied vocabulary than do their lower-class peers.[15] Thus, in order to understand better the implications of such findings, it is necessary to examine *qualitative* as well as quantitative differences in children's verbal behavior.

One example of qualitative differences in children's verbal behavior emerged from an item analysis of the responses of young Negro children to a receptive verbal task, the Peabody Picture Vocabulary Test (PPVT). Briefly described, the PPVT consists of a series of increasingly difficult items which require the child to display his com-

prehension of labels, when confronted with four drawings, by pointing to the correct picture-referent. The standardization group for this
test consisted solely of white children residing in and around Nash-
ville, Tennessee.

As part of a larger investigation, the PPVT was administered to
four-year-old lower-class Negro children who had been selected to
participate in a preschool enrichment program. Of the first thirty-five
words of the test, clusters of items which the children had failed were
identified. Three clusters of words were found to be particularly difficult: action words (*digging, tying, pouring, building, picking*); words
related to rural living (*leaf, bee, bush, nest*); and words whose referents may be rare in low-income homes (*kangaroo, caboose, accident*).
(Other studies, such as that by Eells,[5] have shown similar trends in
that older lower-class children failed to identify words such as "harp,"
the referents of which are not usually available in lower-class environments.)

These results raised a question of great interest to us: Why did
these lower-class children have such a high percentage of failure with
action words? If the environment provides abundant opportunity for
the child to hear simple labels, then action words are as likely to be
heard by lower-class children as by middle-class children. Perhaps the
explanation lies in the learning environment. Children from low-
income homes have relatively little opportunity to engage in active
dialogue when learning labels. Milner[13] has described the paucity of
verbal interaction of children with adults in the low-income as contrasted with the high-income Negro home.

It is our contention, therefore, partially supported by Bernstein's
research, that the crucial difference between middle-class and lower-
class individuals is not in the quality of language, but in its *use*. The
functional diversity in language may be a direct result of the occupational and educational experiences of the speaker. Middle-class occupations generally require and permit verbal interaction with a variety
of people. The individual must continually adjust his speech in terms
of rate, intonation, vocabulary, and grammatical complexity, in an attempt to provide optimal communication. In contrast to this, the verbal interaction required in lower-class occupations is of a more routine, highly conventionalized nature. The middle-class individual,
then, develops a more *flexible* use of language than that found in
persons from lower-class backgrounds. The gap between the speaker's
verbal skill and the listener's potential for comprehension is greatest in

adult-child verbal interactions. Here, the ability to use language flexibly is most important—it permits the adult to adjust his speech to fit the child's level of comprehension.

But if the lower-class child has to rely upon the frequency of co-occurrence of label and referent to a greater extent than the middle-class child, then, for him, the invariance between word and referent must also be greater. Yet, the learning of verbs and gerunds by frequency of occurrence instead of by active dialogue is more difficult than is the learning of labels for specific objects. Gerunds such as "tying" were failed, not because the children were deficient in experience with the referent but rather because they had difficulty in fitting the label to the *varying forms of action observed and experienced*. This fitting process, which consists of selecting the specific connection between word and referent, occurs more easily when there is a variety of *verbal interaction* with adults. The middle-class child learns by feedback: by being heard, corrected, and modified—by gaining "operant control" over his social environment by using words that he hears. The child learns by interacting with an adult teacher who plays an active role in simplifying the various components of word-referent relationships.

In this discussion, the acquisition of labels has been conceptualized as the result of the interaction of two major variables. One, the stability of the word-referent relationship, refers to the specificity of the features of the referent and the degree of its invariance within the learning context in the natural environment. The second variable, derived from the frequency and type of verbal interaction during language acquisition, refers to the amount of corrective feedback the child receives while learning a new label, i.e., the consistency with which his speech is listened to, corrected, and modified.

Figure 9–1 illustrates the postulated relation of these two variables, in the acquisition of specific labels (A) and of action words (B). Words such as "Coca Cola" and "ball" have characteristics of high stability and physical constancy and occur within relatively few learning contexts. Such words are easily learned by the mere frequency of co-occurrence of word and referent, and require little corrective feedback. Because of the relatively lower stability of the word-referent relationship for words such as "key" and "teacher," a somewhat greater amount of corrective feedback is necessary for their acquisition (line A).

Most action words occur in contexts of moderate to high variance.

As the stability of the word-referent relationship decreases, the amount of corrective feedback required for acquisition increases (line *B*).

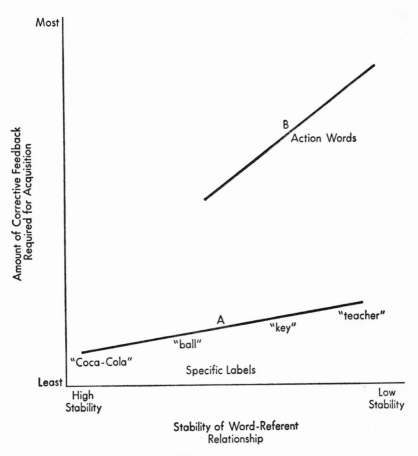

Figure 9–1

This relationship is postulated for words which are abundant in the natural environment of lower-class as well as middle-class children —but not for words such as "caboose," "accident," and "kangaroo," which may occur infrequently in the lower-class setting. Therefore, the postulated interaction rather than experiential rarity may explain more simply the slower rate of acquisition of labels and action words by lower-class children.

Briefly, our analysis indicates that the child's acquisition of words with shifting and complex referents will be impeded if the required adult-child verbal interaction is insufficient or lacking.

• *The Acquisition of Categories*

While the child is acquiring new labels he also is gaining additional referents for those labels already in his repertoire. Young children, unskilled in the use of words, often reveal their understanding of the nuances of a label, i.e., the multiplicity of their referents, through nonverbal behavior. Long before the two-year-old can correctly pronounce the word "horse," he indicates that he knows several referents for the word when he hears it spoken by pointing to his rocking horse or reaching for his stuffed animal. By the quality and amount of corrective feedback he gives, the actively participating adult determines the breadth of the generalization and the precision of the discrimination the child relies upon while learning multiple referents.

The PPVT data discussed earlier indicate that lower-class children, because of insufficient corrective feedback, have great difficulty in acquiring words which appear in a number of different contexts. The specific context in which a label is first acquired, one characterized by low "noise" or one in which there is frequent reoccurrence of label and referent, is limiting and restrictive. Generalizing a word from one setting to another requires the discovery of the irrelevant variations which accompany the essential constancy. As Brown[4] has said: ". . . a speech invariance is a signal to form some *hypothesis* about the corresponding invariance of referent" (italics ours).

This process of discovering invariance common to multiple instances of a label is fundamental for the *conceptual* as well as the verbal development of the young child. However, little is known about the mechanics of this process, beyond the recognition that *both* generalizations and discriminations have to be made by the child learning multiple meanings of words.*

As part of a larger study designed to gather information about the verbal skills, intellectual performance, and motivational approaches of white and Negro, first- and fifth-grade, lower- and middle-class children in New York City, the Concept Sorting Test, developed by the senior author and her co-workers, was used to investigate category formation in young children. The test consists of sixteen simple

---

* By means of corrective feedback, the child learns that a "dog" is not a horse or cat or some other grossly similar object in his environment (discrimination). He also learns that "dog" is not only that white thing with black spots, but it is also that big brown thing that makes a loud noise, and that other thing with the long floppy ears (generalization).

drawings which can be grouped into functional pairs (e.g., *sailor* and *boat*) or into logically consistent piles (e.g., *means of transportation* or *animals*). After the child has finished sorting the cards into piles, the examiner elicits from the child a verbal rationale for each sort. Some examples of the verbalizations of lower-class and middle-class Negro children are given below. (The concept was represented by pictures of four men at work: a policeman, a doctor, a farmer, and a sailor.)

Lower-class first-graders	*Middle-class first-graders*
a. "because doctor nurses these other people"	a. "because they all men"
b. "because the man and big Bill (policeman) like each other."	b. "all the same, all of them are men"
c. "because they look the same"	c. "They are both people."

Two hypotheses which were formulated in the major study are relevant here. Verbally less-experienced children were expected to sort the stimulus cards into a larger number of piles. It was also anticipated that middle-class children (as a group, considered to be verbally more experienced) would offer an explicit statement of a concept, e.g., "they are all animals," while the verbal rationale of lower-class children would reflect a specific aspect of communality, e.g., "they all have legs." These hypotheses were partially substantiated.[8]

The examples given above illustrate the general tenor of responses given by the children. The middle-class (Negro) children tended to produce category labels more often than their lower-class peers, who were instead inclined to focus on nonessential attributes. We may say that those children who were successful on this task were those who had developed skills for discovering the crucial, invariant features of objects having the same name.

WORDS AS MEDIATORS

The individual's ability to solve complex problems is related to the use he makes of language in verbal mediation. Jensen[7] defines verbal mediation as ". . . verbal behavior which facilitates further learning, which controls behavior, and which permits the development of conceptual thinking." In some of their research, the Kendlers[9,10] have found an increase with age in children's reliance on words as mediators while solving a reversal shift problem. Antecedent conditions necessary for the development of verbal mediation have not yet been explored.

In this paper we posit that, while the child gains practice in correctly identifying objects having the same name and while he develops his knowledge about the hierarchy of category names, he also develops skills of use in verbal mediation. Again, we ascribe a crucial role in the development of verbal mediation to the availability of adults, who serve as language models and participate in an ongoing dialogue with the child.

Evidence currently available suggests that some children who can be described as proficient in *overt* verbal skills also rely upon *covert* language—or verbal mediational processes—when approaching complex problems. Luria's studies of speech-delayed twins[11] exemplify the parallel development of verbal skills and verbal mediation.

Children from backgrounds of educational retardation have been shown to perform poorly on verbal and conceptual tasks. Jensen[6] taught a group of educationally retarded adolescents to use verbal mediation in a task which required the learning of a list of paired associates. These subjects learned to construct a sentence around each pair of meaningful words. A control group of subjects from similar background, who were not instructed in this use of verbal mediation, took five times as long to learn the task. It appears that children who receive insufficient verbal stimulation in early childhood develop deficiencies not only in overt verbal skills but also in verbal mediational behavior.

In our stress on the importance of variety in stimulation, our position is in basic agreement with that of Hebb and other developmental theorists concerned with cognitive processes. However, we have also attempted to specify the demands on the child as he learns. The child, confronted with several disparate objects having a label in common, has to identify those critical and invariant features common to the objects. Similarly, when confronted with two or more non-verbal tasks, the child identifies the common critical features by invoking mediating responses. In both of these learning situations the child is actively searching for invariance among features of his environment. The tools he uses in this search have been sharpened in his verbal communication with others.

Communication and cognition, traditionally treated as separate aspects of language, are posited here as fundamentally interrelated in the early stages of language acquisition. Language is seen as func-

tional behavior for the young child. While he uses his slowly developing communicative skills to inform those who care for him about his
needs, he is also organizing his perceptual and social worlds through
language. The social environment in which these functions develop
are highly complex. Of particular importance is the amount of attention paid to the child's own attempts at early verbalizations: the opportunity made available to the child to learn by feedback, by being
heard, corrected and modified—by gaining "operant control" over his
social environment as he uses words that he has heard.

In our analysis, the child from a lower socioeconomic background
may experience a deficient amount of verbal interaction. He learns
most of his language by means of *receptive* exposure—by hearing,
rather than by the correction of his own active speech. Words acquired with little corrective feedback in a stable learning environment
will be of minimum use as mediators, at a later stage of development.
In contrast, the child whose language acquisition is characterized by
active participation with a more verbally mature individual not only
develops greater verbal proficiency—as a result of being listened to
and corrected—but also is more likely to rely on, and use effectively,
words as mediators.

Language is a socially conditioned relationship between the
child's internal and external worlds. Once able to use words as mediators, the child can effectively change his own social and material reality.

A NOTE ON ENRICHMENT

Can educational implications for preschool programs be drawn from a
theoretical statement on language acquisition? Though some of the
ideas presented in this paper may be utilized by the early childhood
educator, primarily, this treatment of verbal behavior is presented as a
model of label acquisition. Ideas developed within the context of a
simplified and abstract treatment of language may have to undergo
substantial modification in order to be applied in the classroom. However, some general points related to enrichment can be made, based
upon the above discussion.

Certainly, the crucial importance of actively stimulating language
growth in the classroom is recognized by teachers of the socially disadvantaged. But the feeling of urgency they bring to the task of in-

creasing the verbal repertoire of children sometimes results in a stress on *quantitative* growth only. This emphasis on vocabulary expansion is not surprising in light of the maturational approach to language.

If the communicative and cognitive functions are significantly related at the beginning of language acquisition, it becomes important to discover ways for these aspects of language to be maintained interrelatedly in enrichment programs. A mechanical approach to vocabulary building will not produce the desired end of developing useful verbal skills. Sylvia Ashton-Warner has vividly described her way of teaching reading to young Maori children. She utilized their deeply personal experiences as basic *content* while imparting the *mechanics* of letters. Similarly, the teacher in the enrichment classroom can discover the interests and concerns of her children by being sensitive to their products.*

As was our purpose, this paper has stressed the acquisition of highly developed linguistic patterns as being crucial to young children. Because language is both a highly personal and an objectively necessary tool, however, the educator must be wary lest children learn to resent the acquisition of verbal skills. The teaching of words must be carried out with originality, flexibility, and restraint.

In becoming aware of some of the features underlying label acquisition, the classroom teacher can create a variety of learning contexts built around experiences of significance to the children. The teacher who is aware of the importance of verbal dialogue in the shift from labeling to categorizing can direct learning not only by her own interactions, but, also, by helping children in the classroom to be effective speakers as well as active listeners.

* In a summer enrichment program combining instruction and research, the senior author and her teacher-colleagues worked with kindergarten children. Each child was asked to retell a standard story in front of a tape recorder. In studying the modifications of the story made by each child, much was learned about sequential language as well as about the themes of particular interest to young children raised in low-income areas. These children also told a "made-up" story, and in these fantasy products they often related events of concern. Though some of the children spoke with poor articulation and others could not think up their "own" story, many children in this group displayed forcefulness of style and communication strength in their descriptions.

REFERENCES

1. Bernstein, B. Language and social class. *Brit. J. Sociol.*, 1960, **11**, 271–276.
2. Bernstein, B. Linguistic codes, hesitation phenomena and intelligence, *Lang. & Speech*, 1962, **5** (1), 31–46.
3. Brodbeck, A. J., & Irwin, O. C. The speech behavior of infants without families. *Child Develpm.*, 1946, **17**, 145–156.
4. Brown, R. *Words and things.* New York: Free Press, 1958.
5. Eells, K., Davis, A., Havighurst, R. J., Merrick, V. E., & Tyler, R. *Intelligence and cultural differences.* Chicago: Univer. Chicago Press, 1952.
6. Jensen, A. R. Learning ability in retarded, average, and gifted children. *Merrill-Palmer Quart.*, 1963, **9**, 124–140.
7. Jensen, A. R. Learning in the preschool years. *J. Nursery Educ.*, 1963, 133–139.
8. John, Vera P. The intellectual development of slum children: some preliminary findings. *Amer. J. Orthopsychiat.*, 1963, **33**, 813–822.
9. Kendler, H., & Kendler, Tracy S. Inferential behavior in preschool children. *J. exp. Psychol.*, 1956, 311–314.
10. Kendler, Tracy S. Development of mediating responses in children. In J. Wright & J. Kagan (Eds.), Basic cognitive processes in children. *Soc. Res. Child Develpm. Monogr.*, 1963, **28**, 33–53.
11. Luria, A. R., & Yudovitch, S. Y. *Speech and the development of mental processes in children.* London: Staples Press, 1961.
12. McCarthy, Dorothea A. Affective aspects of language learning. Presidential Address, Division of Developmental Psychol., APA, 1961 (mimeo).
13. Milner, Esther. A study of the relationship between reading readiness in grade I school children and patterns of parent-child interaction. *Child Develpm.*, 1951, **22**, 95–112.
14. Rheingold, H., & Bayley, Nancy. The later effects of an experimental modification of mothering. *Child Develpm.*, 1959, **30**, 363–372.
15. Templin, Mildred C. *Certain language skills in children.* Minneapolis: Univer. Minnesota Press, 1957.
16. Vygotsky, L. *Thought and language.* Ed. and transl. by E. Hanfmann & G. Vakar. New York: Wiley, 1962.

10 /

Communication of Information in the Elementary School Classroom[*]

MARTIN DEUTSCH, ALMA LEVINSON,
BERT R. BROWN, AND
ESTELLE CHERRY PEISACH

BACKGROUND

Language is a central factor in school performance, both in the major interpersonal communication function and in its mediational function in problem solving. Nearly all children in a given city go to a school system reflecting the orientation of the dominant sociocultural group; even though various subcultures use language differently with respect to children. Whether the different language atmospheres are based on cultural or socioeconomic factors, they result for children in both differential acquisition of language facility and in variations in performance on language-related tasks. Primary here are the language requirements of the school as they relate to communication and comprehension and, eventually, to such specific skills as reading. For example, the influence of the teachers obviously will be dependent on the child's prior experience in handling "lengthy" verbal statements. This experience would include both the child's receptive understanding and his expressive ability.

The work of investigators such as Young,[30] Irwin,[12] Anastasi,[1] and Templin[26] has shown that the structure of the language system which an individual acquires is related to background features associated with social class, such as occupation, education, and the like. Bernstein[4] has further emphasized these relationships in his discussion of the existence of different language systems in middle- and in lower-class groups. He refers to the former as an *elaborated* system, in which

[*] For a description of related literature, more detailed results, procedures, and discussion, see the original report.[8] A brief summary[9] has also been published.

the probability of predicting the pattern of organizing elements in a language sample is reduced, as the speaker will select from a relatively extensive range of alternatives. Lower-class speech, he says, is characterized by a *restricted* code, in which the number of alternatives for the speaker is limited, and, consequently, the probability of predicting the pattern is greatly increased.

Recognizing that there are socially determined differences in children's language patterns raises the question of what their influence is on the learning process. It would seem desirable to know more about the structure of children's language. It might be that the child has two simultaneous systems, one reflecting the larger mass-media influences, and the other reflecting the culture of his specific subgroup. In addition, it would be relevant to explore the relationship of speech patterns to intelligence test and achievement scores, and to investigate the interrelationships among some of the components of children's language patterns. One way of accomplishing this would be to reduce to a minimum the inhibiting or facilitating influence of the teacher or the tester in the situation in which expressive language samples are obtained. Another method would be to use the dialect of each child's own group as the stimulus material to measure his language performance. Both of these methods were used in the present study, in which the purpose was to evaluate children's abilities to express themselves meaningfully and to comprehend the language of their teachers and peers. More specifically, this study was intended to evaluate (*a*) the expressive linguistic skills and speech content of children of different ages, races, and social-class backgrounds and (*b*) the extent to which information is successfully communicated from teachers to pupils of these different backgrounds and among such pupils.

It is not yet known how the extent of language differences between lower-class children and teachers with middle-class training and, for the most part, middle-class backgrounds, influences classroom communication. The tendency of the lower-class child to be inattentive in school is often seen as an example of poor motivation. Instead, it may be that comprehension is severely limited by the demands of a situation in which instruction is geared to the listening habits and patterns of middle-class speech. The lower-class child does not have the same background, in range or intensity, of verbal interaction with adults as does the middle-class child. It is not known what effect this may have on the basic channel of communication in the classroom, namely, the teacher's verbalizations to her pupils.

Because of the redundancies inherent in any language, parts of a speech sequence can be anticipated even if the listener's attention level has fluctuated considerably. Rarely does each word in a sequence of speech prove necessary for the transmission of new information. A child's comprehension and learning depend, in large part, on his abilities to substitute, from context, meaningful words for those not heard or unfamiliar to him. The ability to make these tacit predictions is related to a series of language variables: active vocabulary, grasp of the complexities of language structure, and familiarity with the general context of the material and the like.

The present study represented, in part, an effort to survey the language skills of the intellectually normal but socially disadvantaged child. Particular emphasis was placed on the range of his oral vocabulary, his linguistic skills, and his ability to understand others' communications. Groups of Negro and white boys and girls of differing social class and age levels were included in the study in order to evaluate the relationship between background and developmental characteristics and particular language abilities. While special emphasis was placed on expressive language, the study included an evaluation of receptive language skills through the assessment of the child's ability to comprehend language.

EXPRESSIVE LANGUAGE STUDY

This study of expressive language, that is, relatively spontaneous verbalizations, was designed to evaluate specific aspects of both the linguistic skills and the speech content of children from three different socioeconomic groups. In addition to using a social-class variable, subgroups of first- and fifth-grade Negro and white boys and girls were used in order to explore certain developmental, race, and sex influences.

• The Subjects

The subjects who participated in the study were first- and fifth-grade pupils from twelve New York City public schools. In order to evaluate selected aspects of expressive speech of school children, subjects were chosen to represent various combinations of the two school grades, three socioeconomic (SES) levels, race (Negro and white), and sex.

The original design of the research called for a minimum of five subjects within each cell. Limitations of time and availability of pupils resulted in some variation from the desired cell size. The final sample consisted of a total of 167 children.

The social-class level of each subject was determined by means of an Index of Socioeconomic Status.* The cooperation of the schools made it possible to gather the necessary background data on each child, although the primary source of information was a mail questionnaire sent to each subject's parent or guardian. The Index has a 10-point range, and on the basis of the education and occupation of the family breadwinner, each subject is assigned a rating on the continuum. The Index was developed on data from public school children, and the range does not cover the highest social strata in society.

Three social-class groupings were evolved and categorized as lower class (SES I), intermediate (or lower-middle) class (SES II), and middle class (SES III). The SES I household is characterized by a main wage earner whose educational attainment ranges between elementary school and the ninth grade, and who is unemployed or holds an unskilled or semiskilled job. The main wage earner at the SES II level is likely to have an education ranging between the seventh grade and high school graduation, and holds a clerical, sales, or skilled job. The SES III household is characterized by a main wage earner whose education ranges between high school graduation and college graduate training, and who is employed in a skilled job or in a professional or managerial capacity.

• *Procedures*

The subjects of the research were selected from schools located within neighborhoods serving the various social-class and racial groups required by the design of the study. Each subject was tested by a trained examiner on the school premises in rooms set aside for the purpose. Information on the general intellectual, reading, auditory-discrimination, and language abilities of the subjects was obtained as described below.

* The Index of Socioeconomic Status was developed at the Institute for Developmental Studies. The specific procedures for assigning SES ratings to subjects and a description of the method used to develop the Index can be found in Appendix 1 of the original report.[8]

INTELLIGENCE MEASURE

The Lorge-Thorndike Tests, Form A, Level 1[16] for the first-graders and Level 3, Nonverbal, for the fifth-graders, were used to measure intelligence. The test was presented to groups of fifteen children.

READING MEASURE

The Gates Advanced Paragraph Reading Test, Form I,[10] was administered to all fifth-graders. The subjects were tested in groups of no more than fifteen children at one time.

AUDITORY-DISCRIMINATION MEASURE

The Wepman Auditory Discrimination Test,[27] designed to measure the accuracy of the child's ability to perceive differences between similar stimuli (i.e., words), was administered individually to each first- and fifth-grader by means of prerecorded tapes.

LANGUAGE MEASURE

In order to assess aspects of the verbal skills available to the child, a technique for obtaining continuous speech samples was required. Descriptions of the methods used with the first- and fifth-graders follow.

THE CLOWN AND ROCKET TECHNIQUES*

The Clown and Rocket tasks, for the first- and fifth-grader, respectively, of the expressive language study, were designed to elicit relatively spontaneous speech on any topic selected by the child. The first-grade child was read a story about Happy the Clown and was then introduced to Happy, a papier-mâché head of a clown, and asked to play a game with the clown. A microphone was hidden in the clown's neckpiece. The child was seated directly in front of the clown, who spoke to the child by means of a hidden tape recording and asked to play a game with him. The child was told he would receive a prize if he played the game well and that when the clown was happy his nose would light up. The clown's nose was lighted by the examiner,' by means of apparatus out of the child's sight, only when the child spoke, thus providing immediate reinforcement for the desired response. The Rocket technique was, in effect, an "upward extension" of the Clown test for the older children. The motivating principle was that a rocket

---

* The Clown technique was adapted from that designed by Dr. Kurt Salzinger.[22]

was designed to move closer and closer to a moon as the child spoke. For both age groups, five minutes of the child's response to the speech task was recorded.

The linguistic analysis of the Clown and Rocket data consisted of measures of total verbal output, the four major parts of speech, sentence length, number of sentences formed, number of dependent clauses, number of all clauses, maze words, extraneous words, and type-token ratios (measure of range of vocabulary).

TRANSCRIBING THE DATA

The tapes of the speech samples elicited by the Clown and Rocket techniques were transcribed according to the following rules:

1. The child's speech was transcribed without punctuation, yielding protocols uncluttered by breaks which would interfere with a structural analysis.

2. The transcriptions did not take into account the child's pronunciation or articulation, since the research was not focused on phonemic patterns or dialect. Everything the child said, including such fillers as "uh" and "er," was transcribed.

3. Protocols were timed, and a note was made of the one-minute and five-minute intervals in each child's speech sample.

4. Pauses longer than ten seconds were noted by a series of dots; incomprehensible words were indicated by dashes.

EXCERPTS OF CLOWN AND ROCKET PROTOCOLS

The eight excerpts below represent selected speech samples obtained from the Clown and Rocket procedures for first- and fifth-graders, respectively. Within each grade, the protocols represent Negro and white subjects from the extremes of the social class subgroups employed in the research, i.e., SES Group I (lowest) and SES Group III (highest).

No effort was made to select protocols according to sex, but male and female subjects are represented equally. Each excerpt consists of approximately 100 words selected so that the subject's meaning was retained.

At the first-grade level, it can be seen that the protocols of the lower social-class children differ markedly from those of the middle-class children. Compared to the middle-class boy (protocol 3), the lower-class boy (protocol 1) used more self-referent pronouns, fewer different verbs, and less-complex verb stems, and the speech was organized at a much simpler level. The middle-class subject told a story well known to him which immediately aided him in producing well-organized speech, since a familiar story represents habituated speech. While the middle-class child may have a larger repertoire of stories, the lower-class child was not constrained from story telling despite the possibility of his having fewer at his disposal. Protocols 2 and 4 show similar differences in variety of verbs, complexity of verb stems, and speech organization.

At the fifth-grade level, the speech content and range of vocabulary and verbs tend to identify the social-class membership of the subjects.

First Grade
1. SES I, White Male, IQ 102
I play in school and I and I color and I write and I read and then after I read I get my coat and go home that's all and when I go home I gets off and then I play with friends and then I go somewhere to skates with the skates and then I go upstairs and then I eat supper and then I go down again and then I buy something and then I go upstairs I watch television and then I go to bed and then in the morning I eat breakfast and then in the afternoon I go to school and I do the same things what I did then I sit in the auditorium and sometimes I play records.
2. SES I, Negro Female, IQ 102
What make you so happy all the time how can you talk with your nose you're a nice fellow you ever been in in the circus you ever been a clown in the circus how'd you get them rosy red cheeks and your lips are red and your eyes are blue and your eyebrows are brown what's that little thing you got down there like here like presents you like everybody to play with you.
3. SES III, White Male, IQ 107
Once upon a time there was a little boy and his name was Jack and they were poor and his mother told Jack to go sell the cow for some money and then Jack sold the cow for some beans and on his way home he dropped the beans into a hole and then a big beanstalk grew and he climbed up and he came to a big big castle where the giant lived and he found a chi- a chicken that lay golden eggs and he wanted to try to get it so they be rich so then he tried knocking on the door and see who would answer.
4. SES III, Negro Female, IQ 110
Well I in school I know a little girl and she went to school with me in kindergarten and I used to know her since I was in kindergarten and we used to be so good friends then one day I went to see Pinocchio with her and we met another one of my school friends and she had one of her friends and so then her friend came with her

and her brother and then her friend's brother so then she won a prize and at the end of the show they give everybody something to color and then one Saturday I went to Palisades.

Fifth Grade
5. SES I, White Female, IQ 92
When we're bad in the classroom we have to put our hands on our heads and when Mr. P goes out of the room all the boys start making noises the whole class rather makes noises and he comes back and he doesn't say nothing well when Mr. P knows that we're being bad or something and he doesn't know he doesn't say anything about it he puts people out of the room for doing nothing like he put two girls out of the room last week for um for tying their shoelaces and plenty of things happen in the class.

6. SES I, Negro Female, IQ 90
I come to school in the mornings then I go in the yard to get ready go up go in the classroom and by eight-thirty I come to school and eight-thirty is over 'bout quarter till nine we start going upstairs and at nine we get upstairs then we get in the room we take off our coats we first we see which class which one goes which line goes in first so the first line that goes in gets in first the girls or the boys then after that we hang up our coats or some kids run to the water fountain to get some water.

7. SES III, White Male, IQ 97
Discover what things there are there and all see what happens in the universe my friends and I were playing ball last Monday and the team won 23 to 10 I was on the team that lost which had 10 I made a home run some a couple of singles and double today we might have a game which are the sides I don't know which it's gonna be say there the moon is neuter we might reach the moon after a while when scientists discover what possibilities might happen on the moon the moon will be probably be interesting to see if man will reach the moon if he does I would like to go on the moon and see what things there would be up there.

8. SES III, Negro Male, IQ 96
I like to uh uh learn about space and rockets and stuff like this and the moon doesn't look that way it has craters and stuff scientists say that Mars is the only planet in the solar system that would support life besides the earth and I think they're right because they think that there's vegetation on Mars it has uh two magnetic poles it has uh things that are similar to earth.

The speech samples which follow were taken from Negro and white, SES II, first- and fifth-grade subjects. The protocols were given by children who obtained Lorge-Thorndike Intelligence Test scores at the extremes of the continuum representing the total research sample.

At the first-grade level the age group, in general, gave repetitious material and took a relatively concrete approach with an expected awareness of the Clown. The children with higher-tested IQ scores tended to give more elaborate productions and demonstrated a better grasp of cause and effect than did the lower-measured IQ group. The fifth-graders' Rocket productions often dealt with the same content given by the younger children. However, the children with higher IQ test scores tended to give a wider range of vocabulary and content, more detail, more complex sentence structure, and more original content rather than mere repetition of familiar material, compared to the children with lower IQ test scores.

First Grade
9. White Male, IQ 81

Well one day my friend was by the beach and I was by the beach and my friends Jim and Joe they wanted to find me by the beach so Joe found me but Jane was looking in a different place they went one of them went that way and that way and then Joe found me and then me and my father and Joe not my father me and my cousin Janet went into the water alone and then we were in the water and then we went out of the water and then their mother Beebe was finding Joe first and think they found Jane first and then they found Joe and then we went someplace by the police and then Beebe came and found Joe.

10. Negro Male, IQ 80

You make funny noise you make funny mouth and you make funny tears and you make funny house and you make funny eyebrows and you make funny things like a eye you a good clown you or you you went be the happy happy clown you so happy today he is big clown you so big you almost turn to a funny little baby clown you is so happy you might jump out the big window you look funny funny funny to me you is very and funny you is funny funny funny clown.

11. Negro Female, IQ 119

A little girl came along and her name was Goldilocks she knocked on the door but no one didn't answer so she opened the door and on the table was three bowls papa's and mama's and baby's sister first she tried all of them but all of them was too hot she tried two but they was just right so those two she ate all up then she went to sit down one chair was too high one was too soft one well both of them was nice so she only set in one and soon it just crashed so she was getting setting too dead sleepy so then there was a bed upstairs.

12. White Male, IQ 130

Sometimes when there was a little boy he always used to go out and play with some children and then when he always used to go back in his house he wanted to go to the bathroom so when sometimes when he does that his mother got mad because she didn't want him to keep on walking in and out of the house and then finally she saw him one day foolin with some matches so she took 'em away and she spanked him then she put it so then that day his mother said you couldn't get it so then that day his mother said you couldn't go out you were a bad boy yesterday.

Fifth Grade
13. Negro Male, IQ 64

I go to this school P.S. 144 and I'm in 5–4 my teacher's Miss S I have a lot of friends in this school and in other schools this is a nice game I am playing and I'm glad to be playing it and I hope I'll get promoted to the sixth grade this year my mother's name is Karen my father's name is Skip I name it after me my name is Skippy I have a little brother named Current he is almost four weeks old be glad when he get big enough and I can play with him this is a very big school I go to this is a nice room in it it also has a bathroom in the side and it is a few bathrooms on this floor and some on the other one my cousin go to this school too he is a little boy in the second his name is Gregory and plus I have a little friend in the kindergarten his name is Billy he live around my block.

14. White Male, IQ 79

I have a friend in my class his name is James how high is the rocket how high is the rocket going I would like how far is the moon from the earth how big is the rocket we do spelling and arithmetic and science in my classroom I have two teachers I go to the library my sister she wanna be a nurse I would like to know how tall how high is the moon how far is Venus from the earth I like to do chemistry and work with germs with a telescope and I work with microscope, toy rockets, and I play ball and I have a friend in my class.

15. White Male, IQ 131

My mother's name is Edith my father's name is Lou my sister's name is Richard my mother's name is my sister's name is Barbara and my name is Michael my sister is 13 my brother is 3–4 in school we usually have math in the morning and social studies spelling language and then it's about lunchtime and sometimes on Tuesday we have gym in the afternoon and we also have it on Thursday that's today and we beat the other class all the time and then in the afternoon we usually work on our puppets and I put on it's made of clay.

16. Negro Female, IQ 122

Yes I'd like to tell you about my little sister Gail her name is Gail Maria she's only six months old but she's a lot of fun anyway every day when I come out when I come home from school she sits in her crib waiting for me first thing she does she starts calling name at least she tries to say dada and she hardly can sit up yet yesterday she was trying to crawl in her bed she almost fell out she fell the day the same day she almost she was sitting on my bed and she tried to crawl off to follow me the first time I ever took care of Gail she fell off the bed.

The following measures were selected: the sheer number of words spoken by each child during the testing period (TVO, total verbal output); the use of the four major parts of speech, i.e., nouns, verbs, adjectives, adverbs; type-token ratios (TTRs, the ratio of the number of different words in a speech sample to the total number of words used); the number of sentence units spoken by each child; the mean length of sentence units characteristic of the child's speech pattern; and the use of dependent and independent clauses. The TVO yielded a measure of verbosity; the TTRs gave a measure of verbal richness; the distribution of parts of speech and the various measures of sentence complexity were indicators of the children's mastery of language structure.

The language data were scored by two trained research assistants. Each rater checked the results of the other. Since the scoring procedures were specific, any differences in scoring were found to be errors rather than differences in subjective judgments.

Table 10–1 shows the specific language measures for which the Clown and Rocket data were analyzed. Also listed in Table 10–1 are certain demographic variables and additional test devices which were major aspects of the data analysis.

An analysis of syntax constitutes an exploration into the child's grasp of the implicit rules underlying the structure of English. Since the basic unit of expression of a single idea is the sentence, the Clown and Rocket protocols were coded for sentence units, a task that presented the problems characteristic of attempts to punctuate transcribed speech samples.

The first measure of syntactic ability was the total number of complete sentences spoken by the child during the five-minute testing period.

The second measure was the mean length of each child's sentences. Total number of works spoken (TVO) was also a measure used in this analysis, but many words did not fall into a sentence structure, e.g., the repetitions, false starts, and language tangles that Loban[15] conceptualized as "mazes," and these were excluded from the length of sentence word count. The mean sentence-length measure is highly sensitive, as a result, and a relatively short protocol can show a high degree of syntactic organization, while a long protocol can show poor syntactic organization.

The third measure of syntactic ability was that of dependent clauses. The dependent and independent clauses were evaluated separately at each grade level.

Table 10–1

LINGUISTIC ANALYSIS OF CLOWN AND ROCKET DATA: LANGUAGE, DEMOGRAPHIC, AND OTHER TEST MEASURES

VARIABLE NUMBER		
Grade 1	*Grade 5*	*Variable Measured*
1.	1.	tvo: Total verbal output in first minute.
2.	2.	TVO: Total verbal output in five minutes.
3.	3.	TTR (initial): Number of different words in first 100 words.
4.	4.	TTR (final): Number of different words in final 100 words.
5.	5.	Nouns: Number used in five minutes.
6.	6.	Verbs: Number used in five minutes.
7.	7.	Adjectives: Number used in five minutes.
8.	8.	Adverbs: Number used in five minutes.
9.	9.	Sentence Units: Number used in five minutes.
10.	10.	Extraneous Words: Number used within sentence units.
11.	11.	Maze Words: Number used between sentence units.
12.	12.	Mean Sentence Length: Within five minutes.
13.	13.	Wepman Error Score on "Different" Items.
14.	14.	Sex: Male coded as 1; female coded as 2.
—	15.	Reading Score: Fifth-graders—Gates Advanced Paragraph Reading Test
15.	16.	IQ Score: Lorge-Thorndike Test.
16.	17.	Race: White coded as 1; Negro coded as 2.
17.	18.	Dependent Clauses: Number used in five minutes.
18.	19.	All Clauses: Total of all clauses used in five minutes.
19.	20.	SES: Socioeconomic status, decimal rating.

ANALYZING THE DATA

The data obtained from the Clown and Rocket protocols were analyzed to determine the influence of school grade (developmental level), social-class status, race, and sex on language performance.

The first- and fifth-grade data were analyzed separately except where tests of interaction effects between grade level and other measures were desired. Correlation analysis was used to establish the interrelationships among the various linguistic variables, intelligence, reading, auditory discrimination, and demographic characteristics. To reduce the correlation matrices to their basic factorial components, factor analysis was used. This procedure resulted in the isolation of three definable factors for each grade level. Certain major defining variables within the factors were selected for further statistical treatment.*

• *Results*

INTELLIGENCE-TEST RESULTS

The results of the Lorge-Thorndike, Form A, Level 1, administered to the first-graders, and Level 3, Nonverbal, administered to the fifth-graders, are shown in Tables 10–2 and 10–3. Two-tailed t-test comparisons were made of the subgroup differences in mean IQ test scores.

As shown in Table 10–2, at the first-grade level SES I subjects obtained a mean IQ score significantly lower than either the SES II subjects or the SES III subjects. The difference in mean IQ score between the SES II group and the SES III group was not significant. In addition, there were no significant differences in mean IQ scores between the Negro and white subjects or between the male and female groups, where both comparisons were computed across the social-class subgroups.

Table 10–3 shows that at the fifth-grade level significant differences in mean IQ scores, in the expected direction, were obtained between SES groups I and II, and I and III. As at the first-grade level, there were no significant differences between the SES II and SES III groups. Also, as at the first grade, there were no significant differences between the measured intelligence of male and female subjects. However, a significant difference in mean IQ was obtained for the Negro and white comparison, with the 10-point difference in score favoring the white subjects.

The data clearly establish an association between measured intelligence and SES level and also reflect associations among IQ score, race, and age.†

---

* Although various language measures have been found to correlate highly with each other, only vocabulary measures are known to correlate significantly with IQ score.[20, 26] Therefore sampling methods designed to form subgroups equated for IQ score were rejected. Instead, analyses of variance and covariance were used on the selected defining variables of the factors. These analyses permitted evaluations of the language data both as separate from and as influenced by measured intelligence. The harmonic mean was used as an approximation for missing cases, in order to adjust for inequalities in cell size.

† These findings are in agreement with those of previous studies showing that on standard group and individual intelligence tests, middle-class children score higher than do lower-class children. For discussion of this phenomenon and that of cumulative deficit, whereby disadvantaged children show increasing IQ decrements with age see Chapter 14 and Chapters 13 and 18. The reader is cautioned against inferring inherent social class and racial differences from these data. These findings will be discussed later.

Table 10-2

MEANS, STANDARD DEVIATIONS, AND SIGNIFICANCE TESTS OF LORGE-THORNDIKE IQ SCORES BY SES, RACE, AND SEX FOR 62 FIRST-GRADE SUBJECTS

	SES I			SES II			SES III			Total		
	N	X̄	SD	N	X̄	SD	N	X̄	SD	N	X̄	SD
Male	13	91.7	12.7	17	103.6	14.0	10	113.3	13.0	40	102.2[b]	15.4
Female	9	94.4	9.7	5	105.4	14.7	8	105.6	17.0	22	101.0	14.3
Negro	10	92.1	5.7	12	99.9	12.8	6	105.8	13.8	28	98.4[c]	11.9
White	12	93.4	14.8	10	108.9	13.9	12	111.9	15.6	34	104.5	16.7
Total	22	92.8[a]	11.4	22	104.0	13.8	18	109.9	14.9	62	101.73	14.81

Note.—The following two-tailed t-test comparisons are based on the subgroup mean scores given above.

[a] SES I vs. SES II: $t = 2.87$; $p < .01$
SES I vs. SES III: $t = 4.06$; $p < .01$
SES II vs. SES III: $t = 1.26$; N.S.
[b] Male vs. female: $t = .29$; N.S.
[c] Negro vs. white: $t = 1.65$; N.S.

Table 10-3
MEANS, STANDARD DEVIATIONS, AND SIGNIFICANCE TESTS OF LORGE-THORNDIKE IQ SCORES BY SES, RACE, AND SEX FOR 105 FIFTH-GRADE SUBJECTS

	SES I			SES II			SES III			Total		
	N	$\overline{X}$	SD	N	$\overline{X}$	SD	N	$\overline{X}$	SD	N	$\overline{X}$	SD
Male	15	92.9	18.4	17	102.0	18.8	17	105.1	13.8	49	100.3[b]	17.5
Female	27	91.3	13.1	15	101.9	12.5	14	113.6	8.4	56	99.7	14.9
Negro	23	89.6	14.7	18	98.1	13.7	13	101.2	11.6	54	95.2[c]	14.4
White	19	94.7	15.3	14	107.0	17.6	18	114.5	9.5	51	105.1	16.4
Total	42	91.9[a]	15.0	32	102.0	15.9	31	108.9	12.3	105	99.74	15.88

Note.—The following two-tailed *t*-test comparisons are based on the subgroup mean scores given above.

[a] SES I vs. SES II: $t = 2.75$; $p < .01$
SES I vs. SES III: $t = 5.10$; $p < .01$
SES II vs. SES III: $t = 1.91$; N.S.
[b] Male vs. female: $t = .18$; N.S.
[c] Negro vs. white: $t = 3.24$; $p < .01$

LANGUAGE RESULTS

Tables 10–4 and 10–5 show the intercorrelation matrices for the first- and fifth-grade data, respectively. Each matrix was subjected to a standard centroid factor analysis for the purpose of identifying common dimensions among the many variables. The first 10 centroids, accounting for the largest proportion of the common variance, were rotated to an orthogonal simple-structure solution using the varimax analytic method.

Table 10–6 shows the group means and standard deviations for each variable, by grade level. Table 10–7 shows the ratio of each language measure to the total speech output (TVO). Tables 10–8, 10–9, and 10–10 show the loadings on three factors extracted from each matrix.

It can be seen from Table 10–6 that the fifth-grade group was more productive than the first-grade group on each language variable of the research. Table 10–7 shows that despite the grade-level differences in mean absolute scores, the proportion of the mean language scores to the total output of speech was, in general, the same for the two groups. The exceptions to this occurred on the type-token ratio, nouns, and sentence-length measures.

Although the fifth-graders had a higher type-token ratio score than the first-graders did, when the number of words compared was held constant for two groups, the first-graders used more different words than the fifth-graders when the score was proportionate to the total speech output. In other words, although the fifth-graders talked more than the younger children, their speech vocabulary was not proportionately more varied. However, the fifth-graders used proportionately more nouns than the first-graders did, and the older group used longer sentences than the younger children did.

The ratios also reveal that first-graders did not maintain their initial flow of words whereas fifth-graders increased their flow of words after a relatively slower start.

INTERCORRELATIONS OF THE VARIABLES

Factor analysis uncovered three definable factors for each grade.

Factor 1, *verbal output*, the dominant factor which accounted for 67 per cent and 69 per cent of the common variance for grades one and five, respectively, showed appreciable loadings on nine variables. Table 10–8 indicates that the variables load at an extremely high level

Table 10-4

INTERCORRELATIONS AMONG LANGUAGE AND OTHER MEASURES, GRADE 1

(N = 62)

Variable	No.	2	3	4	5	6	7	8	9	10	11	12	13	14	15	16	17	18	19
tvo	1	85	18	40	79	82	62	73	73	41	20	43	−12	16	20	01	81	80	26
TVO	2		25	39	93	95	75	87	86	45	30	46	−04	19	14	−04	86	91	27
TTR (initial)	3			65	36	15	27	35	15	−04	−13	23	−36	19	36	−30	23	18	33
TTR (final)	4				48	29	37	38	25	02	01	26	−27	32	21	−17	38	30	30
Nouns	5					86	70	81	80	39	23	44	−04	25	15	−13	77	84	27
Verbs	6						68	80	89	37	32	34	02	15	14	01	83	92	24
Adjectives	7							71	70	34	17	23	11	17	08	03	71	74	10
Adverbs	8								82	38	29	30	00	07	10	−08	82	87	17
Sentence Units	9									19	19	04	02	14	11	04	72	98	19
Extraneous Words	10										13	57	15	−02	02	−12	48	28	25
Maze Words	11											−02	00	−13	−12	25	14	18	−07
Sentence Length	12												−07	19	02	−21	47	16	21
Wepman Error Score	13													−17	−35	20	03	02	−11
Sex	14														−04	12	13	15	18
IQ	15															−21	10	11	43
Race	16																−05	02	−13
Dependent Clauses	17																	84	19
All Clauses	18																		20
SES	19																		

Legend: $r > .25, p < .05; r > .32, p < .01.$

Table 10–5

INTERCORRELATIONS AMONG LANGUAGE AND OTHER MEASURES, GRADE 5

(N = 105)

Variable	No.	2	3	4	5	6	7	8	9	10	11	12	13	14	15	16	17	18	19	20
tvo	1	85	−09	−13	79	81	61	59	70	37	28	29	−11	07	08	24	−12	59	77	08
TVO	2		−12	−21	88	96	67	73	82	46	35	30	−03	07	05	19	−06	74	94	04
TTR (initial)	3			46	02	−17	11	−16	−11	−33	−36	04	−16	−04	10	18	02	−01	−07	24
TTR (final)	4				−06	−24	15	−18	−11	−34	−18	−11	03	−01	14	22	−01	−12	−14	30
Nouns	5					80	67	49	75	33	31	31	−06	03	10	18	−05	56	80	03
Verbs	6						58	72	83	47	32	21	00	09	03	14	−04	74	95	01
Adjectives	7							40	54	21	23	26	10	07	11	17	−04	54	65	17
Adverbs	8								65	39	32	08	09	08	−11	11	09	49	69	−01
Sentence Units	9									23	26	−02	01	11	−02	12	04	38	88	−01
Extraneous Words	10										39	16	−02	−25	−06	−08	−01	37	34	−01
Maze Words	11											03	13	−12	07	−17	07	09	22	−19
Sentence Length	12												−11	−09	−05	19	−06	37	17	12
Wepman Error Score	13													02	−04	−35	09	05	03	05
Sex	14														04	−03	−07	09	11	−11
Reading	15															25	−36	06	01	−07
IQ	16																−37	13	15	33
Race	17																	−13	−03	−10
Dependent Clauses	18																		77	08
All Clauses	19																			04
SES	20																			

Legend: $r > .19$, $p < .05$; $r > .25$, $p < .01$.

Table 10–6

MEANS AND STANDARD DEVIATIONS OF LANGUAGE AND OTHER MEASURES, BY
SCHOOL GRADE

Variable	FIRST GRADE ($N = 62$)		FIFTH GRADE ($N = 105$)	
	Mean	SD	Mean	SD
tvo (1 minute)	69.79	42.48	102.10	41.80
TVO (5 minutes)	322.94	176.81	524.03	197.49
TTR (initial)	50.77	7.85	55.96	8.72
TTR (final)	49.85	8.46	55.55	7.50
Nouns	53.40	34.14	93.33	31.90
Verbs	64.16	33.30	97.90	38.96
Adjectives	20.16	16.19	29.47	15.64
Adverbs	27.84	21.78	37.85	21.42
Sentence Units	42.76	21.08	52.91	19.58
Extraneous Words	4.31	5.06	13.05	11.58
Maze Words	21.40	20.67	31.26	23.17
Sentence Length	6.35	2.04	8.95	3.80
Wepman Error Score	8.39	5.50	4.53	2.74
Dependent Clauses	9.61	7.72	17.84	14.04
All Clauses	52.37	27.18	71.00	28.33
Reading	—	—	38.43	19.44

Table 10–7

RATIO OF MEAN LANGUAGE VARIABLE SCORES TO MEAN TOTAL VERBAL-OUTPUT
SCORE, BY SCHOOL GRADE

Mean Language Score:TVO	Grade 1	Grade 5
tvo:TVO	.22	.19
TTR (average):TVO	.15	.10
Nouns:TVO	.13	.18
Verbs:TVO	.20	.19
Adjectives:TVO	.06	.06
Adverbs:TVO	.09	.07
Sentence Units:TVO	.13	.10
Extraneous Words:TVO	.01	.02
Maze Words:TVO	.07	.06
Sentence Length:TVO	.02	.10
Dependent Clauses:TVO	.03	.03
All Clauses:TVO	.16	.14

along a very restricted range, which was somewhat narrower at grade
one than at grade five. The factor components were identical at both
grade levels except for some variations in the order of the loadings.

Verbal output appeared to represent quantitative and qualitative
aspects of children's speech. Although the components of the factor
are largely measures of productivity (e.g., total number of clauses, sen-

Table 10–8

FACTOR 1, FIRST- AND FIFTH-GRADE DATA, ROTATED FACTOR LOADINGS

FIRST GRADE		FIFTH GRADE	
Variable	*Loading*	*Variable*	*Loading*
All Clauses	.96	All Clauses	.97
TVO	.94	TVO	.97
Verbs	.92	Verbs	.95
Sentence Units	.92	Sentence Units	.86
Adverbs	.89	Nouns	.84
Nouns	.86	tvo	.84
Dependent Clauses	.83	Adverbs	.73
tvo	.80	Dependent Clauses	.72
Adjectives	.78	Adjectives	.71

Table 10–9

FACTOR 2, FIRST- AND FIFTH-GRADE DATA, ROTATED FACTOR LOADINGS

FIRST GRADE		FIFTH GRADE	
Variable	*Loading*	*Variable*	*Loading*
TTR (initial)	.80	TTR (initial)	—.66
TTR (final)	.71	TTR (final)	—.62
Wepman Error Score	.51	Extraneous Words	.52
IQ	.39	Maze Words	.46
Sex	.35	SES	—.33
SES	.35	IQ	—.23

Table 10–10

FACTOR 3, FIRST- AND FIFTH-GRADE DATA, ROTATED FACTOR LOADINGS

FIRST GRADE		FIFTH GRADE	
Variable	*Loading*	*Variable*	*Loading*
Sentence Length	—.61	Race	—.55
Extraneous Words	—.56	IQ Score	.55
SES	—.43	Reading Score	.40
tvo	—.34	Wepman Error Score	—.37
IQ Score	—.33	Sentence Length	.35
Dependent Clauses	—.33	tvo	.27
Race	.31		
TVO	—.27		

tences, words, and parts of speech), other measures appeared to meas-ure more qualitative aspects (e.g., sentence complexity or dependent clauses). Moreover, since it is possible to use many words merely to form short, simple sentences, the fact that "all clauses" (the sum of dependent and independent clauses) was the variable which loaded most heavily in the factor is significant. This measure superseded the TVO and parts-of-speech measures, indicating that factor 1 involved more than a sheer word count.

Inspection of the factor components in Table 10–8 revealed associations (see Tables 10–4 and 10–5) among sentence complexity (dependent clauses), productivity and words and sentences (TVO), and the parts-of-speech measures (nouns, verbs, etc.)

Table 10–11 presents the means of the variables included in factor 1 for each grade level. Speech productivity, as measured by the language variables indicated, increased significantly with age. Three-way analyses of variance and covariance on TVO, the variable selected to represent the verbal output factor, revealed no significant SES or race differences, as shown in Table 10–12. It is likely that background characteristics are more apt to influence variables related to speech quality alone.

The factor loadings among the defining variables obtained for factor 2, named *variety of output,* for the first- and fifth-grades, are presented in Table 10–9. The means, by grade level, for each defining variable of this factor are given in Table 10–6.

Table 10–11

MEAN TOTAL VERBAL OUTPUT (TVO) BY SES, RACE, AND SCHOOL GRADE

Subgroups	N	$\overline{X}$	SD
Grade 1, White			
SES I	11	281.09	163.29
II	10	396.60	196.63
III	12	318.42	197.47
Grade 1, Negro			
SES I	11	275.09	173.23
II	12	287.42	104.12
III	6	444.67	145.57
Grade 5, White			
SES I	15	504.80	259.71
II	13	549.62	158.48
III	19	551.68	178.96
Grade 5, Negro			
SES I	23	531.70	221.77
II	18	498.50	149.62
III	17	507.18	182.76

Table 10–12

ANALYSIS OF VARIANCE AND ANALYSIS OF COVARIANCE (CONTROLLING FOR IQ) ON TOTAL VERBAL OUTPUT (TVO)

Source	ANALYSIS OF VARIANCE			ANALYSIS OF COVARIANCE		
	df	Mean Square	F	df	Mean Square	F
SES	2	41,306	1.11	2	3,490	<1
Race	1	3,428	<1	1	3,917	<1
Grade	1	1,341,251	35.94*	1	1,403,306	38.68*
SES × Race	2	49,074	1.32	2	46,491	1.29
SES × Grade	2	26,939	<1	2	23,604	<1
Race × Grade	1	6,571	<1	1	1,508	<1
SES × Race × Grade	2	48,730	1.31	2	44,352	1.22
Within	155	37,315		154	36,044	

* $p < .01$.

Variety of output accounted for only 19 and 17 per cent of the common variance for grades one and five, respectively. The two variables which loaded most heavily on this factor, initial and final type-token ratios, did so for both grades one and five, though the loadings were higher at the first-grade level.

Among first-grade children, the most varied speech tended to be produced by girls and was associated with higher scores on an intelligence test, greater sensitivity to auditory stimuli, and higher socioeconomic levels. Fifth-grade children employed a significantly wider range of oral vocabulary than did first-graders. At the fifth-grade level, the most diversified vocabulary was associated with higher intelligence, with higher SES status and, logically enough, with a smooth flow of speech (e.g., less extraneous words).

Table 10–13 presents the mean TTR scores and standard deviations of each subgroup.

The TTR (final) measure was selected to represent the variety of output factor for three-way analyses of variance and covariance by SES, race, and grade (see Table 10–14). Analysis of variance showed a significant main effect for SES level. However, this effect disappeared when the effect of intelligence was controlled by the covariance analysis. This finding can be understood by considering that while higher TTR scores tended to be significantly associated with the higher IQ test scores* there were highly significant differences among

* Grade 1: TTR (initial) and IQ, $r = .36$, $p < .01$; Grade 5: TTR (final) and IQ, $r = .22$, $p < .05$.

the mean IQ test scores of most of the SES groups of the research sample.

Table 10–13

MEAN TYPE-TOKEN RATIO (FINAL TTR) BY SES, RACE, AND SCHOOL GRADE

Subgroups		N	$\overline{X}$	SD
Grade 1, White				
SES	I	11	.50	.08
	II	10	.55	.05
	III	12	.54	.05
Grade 1, Negro				
SES	I	11	.46	.06
	II	12	.47	.08
	III	6	.54	.10
Grade 5, White				
SES	I	15	.55	.08
	II	13	.57	.06
	III	19	.55	.09
Grade 5, Negro				
SES	I	23	.52	.10
	II	18	.58	.08
	III	17	.60	.07

Table 10–14

ANALYSIS OF VARIANCE AND ANALYSIS OF COVARIANCE (CONTROLLING FOR IQ) ON TYPE-TOKEN RATIO (FINAL TTR)

Source	ANALYSIS OF VARIANCE			ANALYSIS OF COVARIANCE		
	df	Mean Square	F	df	Mean Square	F
SES	2	3	4.56*	2	115	1.80
Race	1	1	1.50	1	25	<1
Grade	1	9	14.86**	1	1,063	16.61**
SES × Race	2	1	2.17	2	165	2.58
SES × Grade	2	<1	<1	2	36	<1
Race × Grade	1	1	2.87	1	246	3.84
SES × Race × Grade	2	<1	<1	2	38	<1
Within	155	.66		154	64	

* $p < .05$.
** $p < .01$.

The third factor accounted for only 14 and 13 per cent of the variance at grades one and five, respectively. Moreover, curious differences in linguistic behavior between the two grade samples were indicated by the factor structures. Whereas grade differences between the first two factors were of degree, factor 3 was different in type.

For the first grade, factor 3 was named the *sentence length* factor. The defining variables of this factor are shown in Table 10–10. It can be seen that factor 3 was one of verbal quality as represented by mean sentence length, with SES, intelligence, and race contributing moderately. However, the interaction between SES and race was not powerful enough to reach the .05 level of statistical significance. Table 10–15 shows the mean sentence-length scores and standard deviations of each subgroup.

For the fifth grade, factor 3 was labeled *intellectual efficiency*. As can be seen in Table 10–10, the main defining variables were race and intelligence with reading, Wepman error score, mean sentence length, and verbal output (first minute) loading moderately, in contrast to the findings for the first-grade data.

Table 10–15

GRADE 1 MEAN SENTENCE LENGTH BY SES AND RACE

Subgroups		N	$\overline{X}$	SD
White				
SES	I	11	7.33	2.02
	II	10	6.43	1.78
	III	12	6.47	2.21
Negro				
SES	I	11	5.12	1.60
	II	12	5.84	2.03
	III	6	7.43	1.17

• *Scoring the Speech Content*

Data from the Clown and Rocket techniques were analyzed for content to determine if first- and fifth-graders from different social-class levels characteristically talk about different experiences. At the same time, the data permitted an evaluation of certain effects of age, grade, race, and sex differences on speech content.

Of special interest was whether middle-class children would reflect the academic orientation of their group by having spoken more about school than did lower-class children. To test this, it was important to know not merely how much verbiage was devoted to school as an area of social experience but also the character of the child's verbalization about school. What aspects of school did he talk about?

Studies? Play activities? The teacher's personality? Subcategories established for each major content heading made it possible to evaluate differences and to generate additional lines of inquiry. For example, are middle-class children particularly involved in school experience, and is this reflected in their preoccupation with scholastic performance and achievement? Or, perhaps, do lower-class children have a tendency to focus on the non-academic aspects of school life in a verbal situation such as described here?

Working empirically with the Clown and Rocket protocols, a list of topics and the criteria for content categories were established. To provide a more detailed content analysis, subcategories were delineated within each general topic. Coding of the content was done by sentence units. Each sentence unit was assigned to one of the content categories. No sentence unit was scored more than once. A tally was kept of the number of times each category was referred to by the subjects.

The content categories represented those experiences spoken about most frequently by the children in the test situation. In evaluating the protocols, efforts were made to characterize the children's references to various aspects of their social experience. It was noted, for example, that in speaking about school or family life, the children dealt with the following areas: descriptions of the physical environment; descriptions of activities; descriptions of people according to their physical appearance, activities, behavior, social roles, and relationship to the subject; and descriptions of interaction between other people and the subject, including the child's feelings and opinions about others. The major topics included, among others, references to "school," "family," "friends," "leisure-time activities," and "fantasy." Typical subtopics were "school studies," "school activities," "family members—identification" (e.g., "I went shopping with my mother.").

The content of the Clown and Rocket protocols was analyzed according to the chi-square (χ^2) method. Since categories were established for almost every topic referred to by the children, the data analysis capitalized on chance. To compensate for this, it is necessary to interpret significant findings cautiously. A technique for three-way χ^2 analysis which partitions the χ^2 in a manner analogous to the partitioning of the variance in analysis of variance was utilized for examination of the topical and subtopical categories.* The method yielded

* See Winer[29] for a description of chi-square analysis for a mixed model when sampling is restricted with regard to variables A and B but random with respect to C (pp. 629–632).

the effects due to the main classifying variables as well as the effects due to various combinations (interactions) of the variables. The topical and subtopical categories were systematically analyzed as follows whenever cell frequencies permitted:*

Grade × SES × content category
Grade × race × content category
Grade × sex × content category

Significant grade effects were obtained for 90 per cent of the analyses. Consequently, the grades were treated separately in pursuing further analyses involving SES × race × content category. In actual practice, most of these analyses were focused on the fifth grade, wherein theoretical cell frequencies were large enough to permit χ^2 analysis.

SUMMARY OF CHI-SQUARE RESULTS

Comparisons of the speech content of first- and fifth-grade subjects, further divided into subgroups according to socioeconomic level, race, and sex in Table 10–16, revealed that the most striking and consistent differences were obtained in relation to grade level. These include, among others, greater proportions of fifth- than first-graders talking about such topics as identification and interaction with teachers and with peers, participation in hobbies, activities pursued alone, and discussion of the future. Proportionately more first- than fifth-graders entered into direct conversation with the examiner.

The influence on speech content of SES level, race, and sex, including the interaction of these with grade level, yielded fewer but still a substantial number of significant differences. Examples of these results include proportionately more subjects emphasizing topics as follows: SES III, both grade levels, "family identification"; SES III, first grade, "references to family members"; SES II, fifth grade, "school activities"; SES III, first grade, SES I, fifth grade, "independent activities"; white subjects, both grade levels, "school studies"; Negro subjects, both grade levels, "immediate test situation"; white subjects, first grade, Negro subjects, fifth grade, "home routines" and

---

* Five categories omitted from the analysis because the cell frequencies were too low to meet chi-square requirements were: A_1—Physical Description of School, A_5—Teacher Description, B_1—Physical Description of Home, F_2—Other Fantasy, H—Geographical Description. Three "miscellaneous" categories were not evaluated.

203 / M. Deutsch, A. Levinson, B. R. Brown, E. Cherry Peisach

Table 10–16

FREQUENCIES AND χ^2s FOR GRADE DIFFERENCES IN CONTENT RESPONSES

Content		Grade 1 (N = 62)	Grade 5 (N = 105)	χ^2
A_3—Studies	(yes)	20	50	3.94*
	(no)	42	55	
A_4—Teacher Identification	(yes)	1	15	7.23**
	(no)	61	90	
A_6—Teacher Interaction	(yes)	4	38	18.31**
	(no)	58	67	
B_3—Family Identification	(yes)	7	26	4.46*
	(no)	55	79	
B_5—Family Interaction	(yes)	16	43	3.85*
	(no)	46	62	
C_1—Friends' Identification	(yes)	5	34	12.88**
	(no)	57	71	
C_2—Friends' Description	(yes)	3	23	8.65**
	(no)	59	82	
C_3—Friends: General Interaction	(yes)	15	63	20.08**
	(no)	47	42	
C_4—Friends: Group Interaction	(yes)	2	24	11.44**
	(no)	60	81	
D_1—Independent Activities	(yes)	11	36	5.28*
	(no)	51	69	
D_2—Reading	(yes)	2	13	4.00*
	(no)	60	92	
D_3—Hobbies	(yes)	3	18	5.37*
	(no)	59	87	
F_1—Fantasy: Future	(yes)	16	46	5.41*
	(no)	46	59	
G_2—Interaction with Examiner	(yes)	44	57	4.53*
	(no)	18	48	
I—Self-Identification	(yes)	7	27	5.00*
	(no)	55	78	

* $p < .05$.
** $p < .01$.

"entertainment"; girls, both grade levels, "teacher interaction" and "friends' description"; boys, fifth grade, girls, first grade, "school activities" and "home routines."

RECEPTIVE LANGUAGE STUDY

The two main objectives of this aspect of the study were the evaluation of (a) the extent to which information is successfully communicated from teachers to pupils of various social backgrounds and (b) the degree of effective communication among children from different social backgrounds.

• The Subjects

The research sample consisted of 64 first-grade children and 127 fifth-graders. As in the first study, on expressive language, subgroups were defined by social-class level, race (Negro and white), and sex. The fifth-grade subjects were further divided into two groups to permit varying the mode of presentation of the experimental technique (the Cloze procedure). All subjects, pupils in the New York City public schools, were tested on the school premises.

SOCIOECONOMIC LEVEL

For this experiment, children coming from the intermediate social class level (SES II) were excluded; only SES I and SES III children were used. Except for some underrepresentation of middle-class Negro males who received the visual presentation of the test material, cell frequencies were approximately equal.

INTELLIGENCE

The Lorge-Thorndike Tests, Levels 1 and 3, Nonverbal, Form A,[16] were administered to all the subjects of the study. Means and standard deviations of Lorge-Thorndike IQ scores for the various cells are reported in Tables 10–17, 10–18, and 10–19.

Analysis of variance of the IQ test data indicates, for the first-grade sample, that SES I children obtained a significantly lower mean IQ than did SES III children ($F_{1,56} = 30.68$, $p < .01$), and Negro children earned a significantly lower mean IQ than white children did ($F_{1,56} = 6.44$, $p < .05$). For the fifth-grade samples, analysis of variance also indicated a significant difference by social class in the same direction as reported above ($F_{1,111} = 59.77$, $p < .01$). There were no significant racial differences in the fifth-grade sample. There were no significant sex differences at either grade level. These findings are related to the receptive language results, as will be shown later.

Although the two samples of fifth-grade subjects were matched on the basis of SES, race, and sex, the mean IQ test score of those subjects receiving the visual mode of presentation was significantly higher than the mean IQ of those receiving the auditory presentation ($F_{1,111} = 5.41$, $p < .05$). These mean IQ differences between the experimental groups appeared to be a chance outcome of the random sampling procedures used, rather than the result of any bias in assigning subjects to groups.

Table 10–17

MEANS AND STANDARD DEVIATIONS OF LORGE-THORNDIKE IQ SCORES BY SES, RACE, AND SEX FOR FIRST-GRADE SUBJECTS, CLOZE AUDITORY PRESENTATION

($N = 64$; N per subgroup $= 8$)

Group	NEGRO $\overline{X}$	SD	WHITE $\overline{X}$	SD	TOTAL $\overline{X}$	SD
			SES I			
Male	89.3	11.2	99.3	17.8	94.3	14.5
Female	86.4	7.0	95.1	11.0	90.8	9.0
Total	87.9	9.1	97.2	14.8	92.5	12.8
			SES III			
Male	108.6	10.4	113.4	12.5	110.0	11.5
Female	103.6	14.4	110.4	7.4	107.0	10.9
Total	106.1	12.4	111.9	10.0	109.0	11.2
			Totals			
Male	98.4	14.5	106.3	10.6	102.6	14.2
Female	95.0	14.1	102.8	12.0	98.9	14.4
Total	97.0	14.2	104.5	14.4	100.8	14.3

Table 10–18

MEANS AND STANDARD DEVIATIONS OF LORGE-THORNDIKE IQ SCORES BY SES, RACE, AND SEX FOR FIFTH-GRADE SUBJECTS, CLOZE AUDITORY PRESENTATION

($N = 62$)

Group	NEGRO N	$\overline{X}$	SD	WHITE N	$\overline{X}$	SD	TOTAL N	$\overline{X}$	SD
				SES I					
Male	7	97.7	7.5	8	87.8	15.4	15	92.4	11.7
Female	8	94.8	8.6	8	85.9	12.3	16	90.4	10.5
Total	15	96.1	7.9	16	86.8	13.5	31	91.3	11.9
				SES III					
Male	10	98.9	12.6	6	125.0	14.6	16	108.7	13.4
Female	8	108.9	8.0	7	113.3	22.8	15	111.1	14.9
Total	18	103.3	11.9	13	118.7	19.6	31	109.8	15.1
				Totals					
Male	17	98.4	10.5	14	103.7	24.0	31	100.8	17.8
Female	16	101.8	11.1	15	98.7	23.3	31	100.3	17.2
Total	33	100.1	10.8	29	101.1	22.9	62	100.6	17.5

Table 10–19

MEANS AND STANDARD DEVIATIONS OF LORGE-THORNDIKE IQ SCORES BY SES, RACE, AND SEX FOR FIFTH-GRADE SUBJECTS, CLOZE AUDITORY PRESENTATION

$(N = 65)$

	NEGRO			WHITE			TOTAL		
Group	N	$\overline{X}$	SD	N	$\overline{X}$	SD	N	$\overline{X}$	SD
				SES I					
Male	10	101.9	12.6	8	101.6	15.0	18	101.8	13.7
Female	14	91.7	9.4	8	96.3	10.6	22	93.4	9.8
Total	24	96.0	11.6	16	98.9	12.9	40	97.2	12.1
				SES III					
Male	3	103.7	3.5	8	120.3	14.0	11	115.8	11.1
Female	6	110.8	7.1	8	114.3	10.5	14	112.8	9.0
Total	9	103.4	17.7	16	117.3	12.3	25	114.1	11.8
				Totals					
Male	13	102.3	11.8	16	110.9	17.0	29	107.1	12.7
Female	20	97.5	12.4	16	105.3	13.8	36	100.9	9.5
Total	33	99.4	12.2	22	108.1	15.5	65	103.7	12.0

• *Procedures*

The Cloze procedure, a simple word-deletion technique, was developed by Taylor[25] to study the comprehensibility of written communication. The more stereotyped the message in terms of its lexical, grammatical, and syntactical structure, the better are subjects able to replace omitted items. This technique provided a flexible means of using the ability to predict words deleted from speech samples as a measure of children's understanding of teachers' language and the language of fifth-grade children from various social backgrounds.

Restriction of the presentation of the Cloze material to the usual written method makes the task dependent on reading skill. An auditory form more closely approximates verbal communication, since the listener must rely on his auditory perception and his recall of the prior speech sequence. The Cloze material used in this research was selected to represent speech of different social groups. Variations in intonation and inflection were, of course, more easily captured in an auditory than in a visual presentation.

FIRST-GRADE CLOZE

The first-graders, who in any case would not be expected to have reading skills, received only an auditory presentation. Usually a Cloze passage is constructed by deleting every nth word. The mutilated passage is then presented to the subject, who supplies the deleted word. On the basis of pretesting, it became evident that a Cloze passage presented this way would be much too difficult for first-graders. A simpler modification was therefore prepared.

Verbatim samples of first-grade teachers' continuous speech were taped in classrooms during typical lessons. From these samples three paragraphs, each containing six sentences, were selected. Instead of deleting every fifth word of the continuous speech samples, the final word in each sentence was omitted. Sentences were read to each first-grade child by the examiner, who instructed the child to say the missing word whenever the examiner signaled by clapping hands.

FIFTH-GRADE CLOZE

Paragraphs representing the speech of fifth-grade teachers were prepared for the fifth-grade children. Two paragraphs of approximately fifty words each were selected from taped fifth-grade teachers' speech and prepared by deleting every fifth word. The paragraphs were then re-recorded by Institute personnel with the appropriate words deleted for auditory administration and presented to sixty-two of the fifth-grade children. The subjects listened to the taped presentation of the entire selection, including the periods of silence which indicated that something had been deleted. Immediately after this presentation the tape was replayed, and each child was required to write the word he thought had been deleted.

The same paragraphs also were prepared for visual presentation, i.e., in written form, and presented to the remaining sixty-five fifth-graders. These subjects read each selection in which the deleted words were indicated by lines and then reread the selection, filling in each deleted word seriatim. This form provided more cues than the auditory form because, while he was writing, the subject was able to see what preceded and followed the deletion; on the other hand, the subjects receiving the auditory presentation could depend only on recall.

Speech samples of fifth-grade children of varying social background were obtained from the Rocket protocols, described previously. Four paragraphs of approximately fifty words each, two representing the speech of children of SES I and two representing the speech of children of SES III, were selected. In order to balance the effects of race and sex as well as those of social class, each paragraph represented a different SES level-race-sex combination: a middle-class Negro girl; a middle-class white boy; a lower-class white girl; and a lower-class Negro boy. Criteria for selection of paragraphs were clarity of original tapes and continuity of thought sequences.

The paragraphs of children's speech were then prepared in the same way as had been the teachers' speech for the fifth-grade samples. Children having the same demographic characteristics as the children on the original tapes re-recorded the paragraphs with the appropriate words deleted for the auditory presentation. In addition, a visual form of the children's paragraphs was prepared. The two forms of the children's speech were then administered together with the paragraphs of teachers' speech. For the auditory task, children were tested in groups of approximately six subjects; for the visual task, groups consisted of approximately thirteen subjects. Two examiners were present at each test session.

• Scoring the Cloze Data

Three scores were developed for both the first- and fifth-grade Clozes: two are measures of a child's ability to predict a word which maintains the meaning of the paragraph; the third score measures a child's ability to predict the correct grammatical form required by the gap. Specifically, the criteria for the three scores are:

1. Absolute score. The insertion is identical with the deletion, or the same word with altered or incorrect grammatical structure, e.g., "childs" for "children."

2. Contextual score. The insertion is either the original deletion or one which maintains the meaning of the original paragraph, e.g., "doctor" for "nurse."

3. Grammatical score. The insertion has the same grammatical construction even if the meaning differs from that of the original word, e.g., "alone" for "outside."

For the first-grade presentation and the fifth-grade visual presentation, all three scores were used and analyzed. For the fifth-grade auditory presentation, only one measure, the absolute score, was used in the analyses. The children who received the auditory presentation recorded their responses on answer sheets. Since it was extremely difficult to determine which answer referred to which deletion, it was almost impossible to score an answer for its contextual or grammatical correctness.

Reliabilities for the three measures by grade and mode of presentation are reported in Table 10–20. Table 10–21 reports the reliabilities for the various types of fifth-grade children's speech according to mode of presentation. The absolute score consistently proved to be less reliable than either of the other two measures. The fifth-grade speech samples were more reliable than the first-grade measures. This was due to the fact that the first-grade task was quite easy; consequently, test scores showed very little variability.

Table 10–20

CORRECTED SPLIT HALF RELIABILITIES (*r*) OF CLOZE SCORES FOR TEACHERS' AND CHILDREN'S SPEECH BY SCHOOL GRADE AND MODE OF PRESENTATION

		TEACHERS' SPEECH SAMPLES			CHILDREN'S SPEECH SAMPLES
	GRADE 1 ($N=64$)	GRADE 5 ($N=127$)			
Score		Auditory ($N=62$)	Visual ($N=65$)	Auditory ($N=62$)	Visual ($N=65$)
Absolute	.52	.66	.55	.69	.59
Contextual	.55	—	.75	—	.72
Grammatical	.60	—	.80	—	.84

Note: The fifth-grade auditory presentation was not scored for contextual and grammatical measures (see text).

Table 10–21

CORRECTED SPLIT HALF RELIABILITIES (*r*) OF FIFTH-GRADE CLOZE SCORES, CHILDREN'S SPEECH SAMPLES

Score	SES I Speech	SES III Speech	Negro Speech	White Speech	Boys' Speech	Girls' Speech
Auditory Presentation ($N=65$)						
Absolute	.33	.41	.58	.46	.62	.50
Visual Presentation ($N=62$)						
Absolute	.28	.68	.47	.47	.37	.45
Contextual	.66	.65	.62	.77	.63	.70
Grammatical	.75	.72	.78	.79	.63	.64

• *Results*

RELATIONSHIP BETWEEN CLOZE DATA AND IQ TEST
SCORES

All the Cloze measures were found to be significantly correlated with
IQ (see Table 10–22). Since the SES III groups obtained higher mean
IQ test scores than the SES I samples, an analysis of variance and an
analysis of covariance was computed for each of the Cloze measures.*
These data were analyzed separately for the first and the fifth grades
and for the teachers' and the children's speech samples.

Table 10–22

PEARSON CORRELATION COEFFICIENTS (r), LORGE-THORNDIKE IQ SCORES AND
CLOZE SCORES BY SCHOOL GRADE, SPEECH SAMPLE, AND MODE OF PRESENTATION

Score	FIRST GRADE ($N = 64$)	FIFTH GRADE ($N = 127$)				
		AUDITORY MODE ($N = 62$)		VISUAL MODE ($N = 65$)	
	Teachers' Speech	Teachers' Speech	Children's Speech	Teachers' Speech	Children's Speech
Absolute	.23	.53	.39	.44	.38
Contextual	.41	—	—	.46	.32
Grammatical	.23	—	—	.45	.37

Note: The fifth-grade auditory presentation was not scored for the contextual and
grammatical measures.
Note: For $N = 60$: $r = .21$, $p = .05$; $r = .30$, $p = .01$.

• *Summary of Receptive Language Results* †

The data derived in this study were treated by analysis of variance
and covariance, using SES level, race, and sex as the variates.

---

* These analyses were made possible through the assistance of Bernard
Carol, Department of Preventive Medicine, New York Medical College, and Jay
Siegel, N.Y.U. Data Processing Center, with a computer program for analysis of
covariance design with disproportionate N's. Since the interactions for higher-
order interactions were still in the experimental stage, only the main effects and
first-order interactions obtained with this program are reported. Higher-order
interactions were examined by a method of contrasts which gives a final F
without preliminary sums of squares.
† The receptive language results have been published in more detail by
Cherry Peisach,[5] as well as in the final project report.[8] Numbers in parentheses
refer to the mean scores of the group referred to.

TEACHERS' SPEECH SAMPLES

Analysis of the data revealed an increase in SES differences from first to fifth grade. The SES III sample was superior to the SES I sample on the Cloze contextual score only, at the first-grade level, but the SES III group was superior to the SES I group on all three scores of the Cloze at the fifth-grade level (see Table 10–23). These differences were not upheld when IQ variations were controlled through analysis of covariance.

There were no significant Negro-white differences at the first-grade level. Fifth-grade Negro children were less accurate (6.82) than white children (7.97) in replacing the identical word (absolute score) deleted from samples of teachers' speech. But no Negro-white differences appeared in the ability to replace words that maintained the meaning of the passage (contextual score) or that met the syntactical requirements (grammatical score) of the gap produced by deletion. The poorer performance of Negro children on the absolute measure was the consequence of the Negro SES III subgroup's low mean score (6.33) as compared with that of the white SES III group (9.52). Negro SES I children obtained a higher mean absolute score (7.15) than white SES I children (6.56). Again Negro-white differences were not upheld when IQ was controlled through analysis of covariance.

Generally speaking, the fifth-grade girls obtained higher mean scores than the boys did on the Cloze tasks. Since the boys had obtained higher mean IQ scores (Lorge-Thorndike Nonverbal IQ Test),

Table 10–23

MEANS AND STANDARD DEVIATIONS FOR SIGNIFICANT SES DIFFERENCES, FIRST-AND FIFTH-GRADE CLOZE, TEACHERS' SPEECH

Group	N	$\bar{X}$	SD
First grade			
Contextual score:			
SES I	32	14.91	1.85
SES III	32	16.00	1.50
Fifth grade:			
Absolute score:			
SES I	71	6.89	3.09
SES III	56	7.98	3.10
Contextual score:			
SES I	40	13.18	3.22
SES III	25	15.72	2.41
Grammatical score:			
SES I	40	14.45	3.26
SES III	25	16.72	2.75

analysis of covariance sharpened and revealed the fifth-grade female superiority on the absolute and grammatical scores of the teachers' speech items. The fifth-grade sex difference on the grammatical score was identified as a function of social class. SES I girls (15.54) were superior to SES I boys (13.11) on this measure of the Cloze task, but no significant difference was apparent between SES III boys (16.91) and girls (16.57).

CHILDREN'S SPEECH SAMPLES

The children's speech paragraphs were administered only to the fifth-grade sample. Comparison of the auditory and visual modes of presentation revealed that the auditory form was considerably more difficult. However, the absence of significant interactions between mode of presentation and any other classifying variable, e.g., SES level, indicated that no subgroup was penalized by the more difficult auditory Cloze.

Significant SES differences were obtained for all three Cloze measures of the children's speech paragraphs (see Table 10–24). In contrast to the results on the fifth-grade teachers' speech paragraphs, the SES differences obtained for the absolute and grammatical scores of the children's speech paragraphs were maintained even when IQ was controlled through analysis of covariance. No Negro-white differences were obtained with respect to samples of children's speech.

SES I children (9.77) did as well as SES III children (9.98) did in replacing the identical deletion from samples of lower-class children's speech. However, SES III children obtained a higher mean absolute score (11.45) than did SES I children (9.39) on the middle-class children's speech items. Further, the mean grammatical score of the SES I children (18.12) was approximately equal to that of SES III children (18.96) on the Negro passages, but the SES I mean grammatical score (15.90) was considerably lower than the SES III mean grammatical score (18.20) on the white selections. In other words, unrelated to the difficulty level of the items, SES I subjects did as well as SES III subjects on lower-class and Negro children's speech passages. However, SES I subjects did more poorly than SES III subjects on white children's passages and SES III subjects were considerably superior to SES I subjects on middle-class children's speech.

The Negro (18.36) and white (18.47) subgroups obtained approximately equal mean grammatical scores on the Negro children's

Table 10–24

MEANS AND STANDARD DEVIATIONS FOR SIGNIFICANT SES DIFFERENCES, FIFTH-GRADE CLOZE, CHILDREN'S SPEECH SAMPLES

Group	N	$\overline{X}$	SD
	Absolute Score		
SES I	71	19.17	6.91
SES III	56	21.43	6.83
	Contextual Score		
SES I	40	33.75	4.16
SES III	25	36.56	3.12
	Grammatical Score		
SES I	40	33.98	3.85
SES III	25	37.16	2.67

speech samples, but white subjects obtained a higher mean grammatical score (17.59) than Negro subjects (16.00) did on the white children's selections. In addition, despite the lower difficulty level of the girls' speech, Negro subjects (9.27) were superior to white subjects (9.00) on boys' speech items, whereas the performance of the Negro subjects (10.61) was inferior to that of white subjects (11.48) on girls' speech items. The quality of the Negro middle-class girl's recorded speech was not different from that of the middle-class white girl's recorded speech, and only the lower-class Negro boy's speech could be classified as regional (Southern) speech. This finding suggests greater efficiency in performance when responding to familiar speech subpatterns.

These findings, plus the finding mentioned above regarding teachers' speech samples (Negro SES I subjects' superior mean absolute score, compared to Negro SES III subjects' mean absolute score), indicate that the discrepancy between Negro and white performance is least, or nonexistent, under two conditions: when the selection is Negro speech, and when the subjects are of the Negro lower-class subgroup.

Again, as with the teachers' speech items, the superiority of fifth-grade girls compared to fifth-grade boys was shown most clearly through the analysis of covariance. Girls earned higher mean absolute and contextual scores than the boys did. Significant SES by-sex interactions for all three Cloze measures revealed that, in all cases, SES I girls were superior to SES I boys, but SES III boys and girls were approximately equal in performance (see Table 10–25).

Table 10–25

MEANS AND STANDARD DEVIATIONS FOR SIGNIFICANT SES BY SEX INTERACTION, FIFTH-GRADE CLOZE, CHILDREN'S SPEECH SAMPLES

	MALE			FEMALE		
Group	N	$\bar{X}$	SD	N	$\bar{X}$	SD
Absolute Score						
SES I	33	16.82	6.88	38	21.18	6.33
SES III	27	21.18	4.70	29	21.66	7.09
Contextual Score						
SES I	18	32.00	4.76	22	35.18	3.00
SES III	11	37.09	2.07	14	36.14	3.78
Grammatical Score						
SES I	18	33.28	4.52	22	34.50	3.25
SES III	11	37.73	1.79	14	36.71	3.20

CONCLUSIONS AND IMPLICATIONS

• Measured Intelligence and the Language Measures

With regard to the relationship between measured intelligence and language, the expressive language study confirms and extends the findings of previous work by H. M. Williams[28] and Templin.[26] The first-grade data of the present study revealed the positive relationship of range of vocabulary (final TTR measure) and sound discrimination ability (Wepman Error Score) to intelligence reported by both Williams and Templin. As in these earlier studies, the first-grade data revealed no other significant intercorrelations of language measures with IQ scores. At the fifth-grade level, however, in addition to the continued association of vocabulary range and sound discrimination ability with intelligence test performance, the absolute number of words spoken (TVO) and mean sentence length were found to be significantly associated with IQ score. It appears that among older children greater fluency can be expected from children with higher IQ scores. That the fluency consisted of meaningful combinations of words was indicated by its positive association with the mean sentence length measure in which repetitions have been subtracted from the word count.

The children with higher measured intelligence, at both grade levels, were more adept at dealing with the receptive language task, the Cloze, than were the children with lower IQ scores. While it is possible that the visual Cloze task was essentially a reading comprehension test, the higher IQ subjects were also more successful on the auditory Cloze items.

• Expressive Language Skills

The use of the intercorrelation technique on language data obtained from the same subjects has been rare. Studies using the procedure include those by Williams,[28] Schneiderman,[23] and Templin.[26] Of these, Templin's was the most comprehensive and the most similar to the present study. Factor analysis was used with data of this nature for the first time in the current study.

Williams'[28] data on preschoolers' spontaneous conversation included scores on correctness and completeness of word usage, mean length of expression unit, sentence completeness, and complexity of organization. He reported moderate correlations among all these measures except vocabulary, which proved to have a high degree of independence. The present findings were quite consistent with those of Williams, including the appearance of the vocabulary measure, the type-token ratio, as the major defining variable of the variety of output factor (factor 2).

Templin found that of 189 correlations obtained across age level, 76 per cent were significant at the .01 level, and only 12 per cent did not reach the .05 level of confidence. The data of the present study differed from Templin's in showing fewer significant intercorrelations between language variables. At grade 1 it was found that 39 per cent of the correlations were significant at the .01 level, and 45 per cent did not reach the .05 level of confidence; at grade 5, 35 per cent of the correlations were significant at .01 level, and 59 per cent did not reach the .05 level of confidence. Although Templin did not present the separate computations by age level, inspection of the correlation matrices of her study reveals that in Templin's data, too, changes in the magnitude and direction of the various intercorrelations often occurred with increased age. The direction of the changes apparently depends upon the particular language measure evaluated.

Templin's results showing a higher percentage of significant correlations between language measures than was obtained in this study seems related to several differences between the two studies. These include differences in scoring procedures used, in the test situation in which the language samples were obtained, and differences in the specific procedures used for testing language skills. The similarities between the present data and Templin's findings are discussed later.

In comparing the language behavior of children of different age levels Templin found that the correlations among vocabulary and length and complexity of response decreased with age during the early school years. This same pattern was obtained when the first- and fifth-graders of this research sample were compared. Templin[26] speculated that ". . . at the older ages . . . the samples of language obtained in spontaneous utterances in a child-adult setting are not long enough for the complexities of sentence structure and the larger vocabulary of use to become apparent" (p. 127). However, the issue is probably more related to the quality, rather than to the quantity, of speech older children offer in adult-child test situations. Even though the fifth-graders produced significantly longer sentences than the first-graders did, the proportion of complex sentences to the total speech output was the same at both grade levels.

In the current study it was found that among first-graders repetitions of words within sentences were significantly related to sentence length ($r = .57$) and complexity ($r = .48$); among fifth-graders the correlation of repetitious words with sentence length ($r = .16$) dropped below the significance level and the correlation with sentence complexity ($r = .37$) also dropped in magnitude. The extraneous repetitions appear to have served as "bridges" between words connected in meaning for the first-grade child, as he mentally prepared a relatively complex, lengthy sentence or thought. However, in the case of the older children the repetitions did not appear to improve speech quality in any way.

At the first-grade level, the significant correlations of expressive language skills with SES level included the measures of verbal output (tvo; TVO), the type-token ratios, total number of nouns and verbs used, and the number of repetitious words within sentences (extraneous words). These measures were all positively associated with higher social-class status.

217 / M. Deutsch, A. Levinson, B. R. Brown, E. Cherry Peisach

At the fifth-grade level, the type-token ratios were significantly and positively associated with social-class status, and the lower-class children used significantly more repetitious words between sentences (maze words) than the middle-class children did.

That diversified vocabulary, represented by the type-token ratio, proved to be related to social-class level was in accordance with expectations. The differences in range of vocabulary, comparing SES groups, were far more evident than the differences in general productivity. These results suggest that children of different social-class levels vary more in *how* they express themselves than in *how much* they express. It is, after all, experience that largely determines the child's language development, including his skill in using language for different purposes. The extent to which the child can manipulate ideas, even those ideas which he possesses the language skills to consider, is a function of his background. Since the child's culture, including his social-class membership, provides him with the basic model from which to learn, differences in culture can be expected to produce differences in behavior, including language behavior. A major distinction between the language experiences of middle- and lower-class children is the difference in training which their respective cultures offer them in dealing with abstract ideas.

Bernstein[2,3] has described the process whereby the language of lower-class children is such that it leads to deficiencies in conceptualizing. One consequence of this process is that the more a test device evaluates conceptual abilities, the more likely are differences related to antecedent, i.e., background, characteristics to appear. Evidence for this view was seen in the results of present research, which showed that by the time children reached the fifth grade, intelligence tests, which at this age level rely so heavily on conceptual problems, penalized children in relation to their social-class status.

The consistent finding of significant developmental differences occurred as expected. A more provocative approach to the data was the examination of the various ratios of the mean scores of each language measure to the mean total verbal output scores at each grade level. Considering the particular age groups involved, it is not difficult to understand that the younger children were not able to maintain their initial pace of speech over the five-minute testing period and that the fifth-graders, at a more self-conscious stage of social behavior, "warmed up" more slowly. It was also possible that the initial flow of speech was more rapid among the younger than among the older children owing to a motivational factor: it may have been that the first-graders were more stimulated to keep the clown's nose lighted than the fifth-graders were to move the rocket toward the moon. A higher proportion of different words to the total output, and proportionately fewer nouns, would have been expected of the older group, as compared to the first-graders. The reverse findings in this research are probably explained by the fifth-graders' reactions to a relatively unusual conversational task.

Of the many language variables showing significant grade level differences, the sentence-length measure appears to be the most useful, showing, as it does, such marked grade-level differences in both absolute quantity and proportion to total speech output.

The considerable number of variables which showed no significant grade-level differences in *proportion* to total speech output suggests further evidence for Menyuk's[19] conclusion that children learn the basic structures of adult language at a very early age. Apparently, this conclusion holds not only with regard to familiarity with the various syntactical structures of language, as her data reveal, but also in the extent to which use is made of complex sentence structure. The most striking evidence for this view was the results of this study showing that the fifth-graders produced a greater number of complex sentences, as compared with first-graders; yet they did not produce *proportionately* more complex sentences than did the first-graders.

At the first-grade level, white children produced more varied vocabulary and yielded fewer redundancies, or falterings, between sentences. At the fifth-grade level, however, there were no significant relationships between any measured language skill and racial group. Young Negro children, then, appear to be most in need of language experiences which will increase both general fluency and range of vocabulary, though it may be that this conclusion overlooks the possibility that the performance of the young Negro child was adversely influenced by the presence of white examiners.

More striking than the few positive findings referred to above is the relative absence of Negro-white differences on the language measures of this study. This is important evidence that the cognitive repertoire of Negro and white children can be similar as well as different, as it tends to be on IQ and certain other tests. Further, when the number of significant correlations of language measures with SES level are considered, it becomes clear that SES is a more powerful determinant of language behavior than is racial membership.

In general, this study bears out the findings of previous recent studies which show relatively few differences between boys and girls on certain language skills. Among the differences obtained in this research were: first-grade girls employed a wider range of oral vocabulary and used more nouns than boys did; fifth-grade boys faltered and repeated themselves more within sentences than girls did. The appearance of sex differences in language skills is seen to depend on which language measures are evaluated and the conditions under which the language samples are obtained.

- *Interrelationships of Language, Demographic, and Other Test Measures*

The major contribution of the factor-analytic approach to the language variables of the research was its specification of three relatively independent clusters of interrelated language variables at each grade level. While previous child language studies have shown that, except for vocabulary range, most language measures are highly associated with each other, there has been no clear indication of the dependence or independence of the different language measures beyond the absolute magnitude of the intercorrelations.

The verbal output factor (factor 1) shows the strong degree of interrelationships among language measures dependent on the comparative length of the speech sample given by a subject within a specified period of time.

The variety of output factor (factor 2) specifically corroborates previous findings showing the relative independence of vocabulary scores from other language measures. Factor 2 confirmed the association of vocabulary with measured intelligence and with SES level, related as the latter is to IQ score. Factor 2 also indicated that among first-graders good auditory discrimination ability was positively associated with IQ and SES. Templin's concern that her sound-discrimination test not act as an intelligence or vocabulary test led her to formulate a special procedure almost certain to insure that each subject would recognize the stimulus words. Nevertheless, she obtained exceedingly high correlations between the discrimination measure and vocabulary scores in the three- to five-year-olds, and there were significant correlations between sound-discrimination scores and IQ scores in the six- to eight-year olds. It is not clear from the data of this study, or from Templin's, why such associations exist, though various explanations are possible. It may be that the general mental competence leading to high IQ and vocabulary scores encompasses heightened sound discrimination. Or, it may be that what is operating is a more specific underlying ability to respond to the auditory test directions. Or, perhaps, good sound-discrimination skills may promote vocabulary development and other language skills necessary for efficiency on intelligence tests.

The variety of output factor for the fifth-grade sample revealed that at this developmental age the boys had, more or less, reached the girls' level in range of oral vocabulary. Conclusions about vocabulary and sex differences apparently require special attention to the specific age level being considered, as well as to the specific language measure. In the older group, the auditory-discrimination task did not emerge in association with the vocabulary–IQ–SES cluster, and the use of repetitious words appeared, indicating lack of fluency. The strength of the repetitions-*within*-sentences measure (extraneous words) was particularly evident. This finding may reflect a higher degree of self-consciousness in the fifth-grade group, compared to the first-graders. If so, the lack of ease may be characteristic of the age level in general, or it may reflect the group's self-consciousness with the particular task.

The components of factor 3, first-grade sentence length, raise an interesting point. The mean sentence-length measure has long been relied on as a major qualitative measure of language development. At the first-grade level, the data indicated the appropriateness of this, as the sentence-length measure was joined by the fluency, complexity, productivity, SES, IQ, and race variables. At the fifth-grade level, however, the third factor was different in that the sentence-length variable was superseded by IQ and by other measures strongly associated with IQ score. This outcome was in spite of the evidence that the fifth-graders in this sample appear to have performed in accordance with expectations for their age group.[6] It seems that Templin was correct to doubt the usefulness of the mean sentence-length measure for evaluating the verbalizations of older children tested in an adult-child situation. By the age of nine or ten, the artificiality of such test situations may delimit the quality of the speech productions to a significant extent. This view is supported by data showing that in written compositions this age group produces longer sentences than those obtained from any adult-child test situation.[11]

At the fifth-grade level, the third definable factor in verbal behavior proved to be primarily one of intellectual efficiency or achievement, in contrast to the language-quality content of the third factor in the first-grade data. It appears that, as Negro children get older, the discrepancy between their IQ scores and those of white children increases, while the discrepancy between the two groups' scores on the language measures of this research decreases. At the first-grade level, the disadvantaged child's experiences seem to have been relatively sufficient to provide him with certain language skills. By the fifth grade, however, he does not seem to have had the background of experiences in the use of the more complex language necessary both for success on intelligence tests and for expressing himself meaningfully in complex sentence structure.

A significant decrement in mean performance level on verbal tests and on tests of general intellectual ability during the school years was hypothesized by Klineberg[13] and substantiated by Deutsch and Brown (see Chapter 14). These investigators have attributed the drop in performance among lower social-class children to limited environmental stimulation. Deutsch and Brown have demonstrated that the deficit is very pronounced by the time a child reaches the fifth grade. This "cumulative deficit" phenomenon occurs with striking regularity among lower social-class Negro youngsters in homes broken by absence of father.

Since it was found that language differences between social classes were not maintained when IQ was controlled, how much leeway remains for the educator to improve children's language skills? Dawe's[7] study showed that, when she trained preschoolers in language, she obtained an increase in IQ score as well. It is now more clearly specified in which areas of language disadvantaged children require special attention and that the training should commence at as early a school age as possible. However, it should be noted that Dawe's study did not employ control groups in which subjects received attention, interest, etc., without the specific language training. It is therefore unclear whether improvements in language and IQ test scores were due to special training, to the child's positive response to the focus on him, or to some combination of the two

• The Content of Expressive Language

The analysis of the content of protocols from the Clown and Rocket situations was striking in the evidence for differences in amount and variety of verbal behavior between grade levels and the relative absence of these differences between social-class levels, races, or sexes.

The results did not reveal significant differences in focus on academic activities according to social class membership, although non-academic school activities received some emphasis from subjects of the highest social class level assessed in the study. While there were several instances where the content was influenced by the variables of race and sex, there was no consistent trend or pattern in the findings.

As would be anticipated for older children, fifth-graders were more likely than first-graders to refer to school, teacher, etc. Also consistently with expected differences by age, the older group indicated more involvement with such topics as friends, career, and activities undertaken independently. While the younger children might have been expected to emphasize family topics, the reverse proved to be the case. However, the older group did indicate greater involvement with friends than with family, a finding consistent with peer interests typical for their age level.

That social situations have greater interest for girls than for boys appeared in the data of the first-grade group. By the fifth-grade level, however, this expected trend was overshadowed by the boys' marked interest in peer-group activities.

The greater frequency of first-graders' verbalizations about the examiner, as compared to fifth-graders', may have been a reflection either of the younger child's tendency toward greater openness of expression, or spontaneity, at least in certain situations, or a reflection of his greater dependence on adults.

The evaluation of interactions among social-class level, grade, and race revealed several significant findings. Among these, higher social status and a focus on routines and family relationships were found to be associated. This result can be interpreted as an outcome of the emphasis on planning and organization of activities within the family constellation itself, which tends to be more characteristic of upper- than of lower-class groups.

More Negro than white children, at both grade levels, discussed the immediate test situation. The Negro subjects may have been able to verbalize their reactions to the test situation more freely than the white subjects were. Or, the reverse might be true: more frequent references may suggest discomfort due to the presence of the white examiner. It is apparent that the possible examiner effect warrants further controlled exploration, although the use of the Clown and

Rocket mechanical devices as the recipients of the child's speech was an effort to minimize the interpersonal factor in the test situation as much as possible.

The basis for an expectation that social-class membership would influence speech content has been established by previous authors. Bernstein's[4] discussion of the "restricted" language used mainly by the lower working class and the "elaborated" language characteristic of the higher social class covers both structural and topical aspects of British speech. Landreth,[14] too, has pointed out that "environmental differences are reflected in differences in the form and content of children's speech in different situations and in the level of speech development in children whose environments offer different kinds and amounts of speech stimulation" (p. 152).

The Clown and Rocket task attempted to encourage the production of continuous spontaneous speech samples; however, the general tendency toward similarity of content raises the question of whether the test situation served to obscure differences among groups. It has been found that children use more socialized speech in the presence of adults than with peers.[24] Landreth, too, has pointed out that the particular situation in which the speech samples are obtained has marked influence on the content. Testing the children in the school setting and in the presence of an adult may have had the effect of evoking responses the children considered acceptable to the examiners.

Several factors suggest that the Clown and Rocket tasks may have been more suitable for eliciting relatively spontaneous speech from first- than from fifth-graders. Whereas the younger group is still relatively close to the monologue stage of speech behavior, fifth-graders are at a developmental period of lessened spontaneity. The test protocols of some fifth-grade subjects contained critical, or otherwise self-conscious, remarks about the task. In contrast, the greater frequency and quality of the younger children's references to the immediate situation and to the examiner suggested greater spontaneity on the part of first- as compared to fifth-graders, even though, unexpectedly, the first-graders rarely entered into direct "conversation" with the clown.

• *Receptive Language Skills*

Social-class differences in certain receptive language skills are considerably more apparent at fifth grade than at first grade. At first-grade level, middle-class children gave significantly more meaningful responses (contextual score) to the teachers' speech Cloze items than the lower-class subjects did. At the fifth grade, lower-class children did less well than their middle-class peers on all the Cloze measures of teachers' speech: they less often replaced the exact missing word, less often filled the deletion with a contextually meaningful response, and less often were able to substitute for the deleted word a word correct in grammatical form. While these effects were not maintained when intelligence was controlled statistically, nevertheless, the data support the point of view that there is a language barrier between the middle-class teacher and the lower-class child, particularly the child in the higher elementary school grades. This finding is consistent with data showing that IQ differences due to social class increase with age.[16]

In all cases it was the measures that correlated .40 or above with IQ that showed SES differences. Again the interrelationship between language skills and performance on an intelligence test is demonstrated, even when the test is a so-called non-verbal one, as was the case in this study.

However, that there is an influential variable other than measured intelligence was demonstrated by the results with the children's speech samples. Lower-class children's ability to fill in the deletion with the exact word omitted was as good as middle-class children's performance when both groups were responding to lower-class speech samples. The performance of the middle-class child was significantly superior to that of the lower-class child when the speech passage was a middle-class one, and it was this effect which produced the significant social-class difference.

One of the most striking results of the present study was the relative absence of Negro-white differences, particularly in light of the relationship of both the task and race to IQ. There was only one significant result with respect to racial subgroups: Fifth-grade Negro children were less able than white children to replace the identical deletion. However, no difference was found between Negro and white children in the ability to replace words that maintained the meaning (context) of the passage or that fulfilled the grammatical requirements of the gap. This study was relatively unique in that effort was made to balance the sample for both SES and race. The results indicated that social class appears to be a more relevant factor than race in effecting performance on the type of language comprehension task represented by the Cloze technique.

One fact regarding Negro performance became salient from this study. It was the Negro SES III subjects whose performance, relative to their social class, was most inadequate. The absolute score Negro-white difference for teachers' speech was revealed to be due to the SES III subjects' poor performance. This finding could be interpreted in relation to IQ scores, since the difference between SES I white and Negro children's mean IQ scores was minimal, but the difference between SES III white and Negro children's mean IQ scores was 14 points. However, Negro SES III subjects' mean IQ was higher (7 points) than Negro SES I subjects' mean IQ score. Nevertheless, SES I Negro subjects did as well as SES I white subjects and SES III Negro subjects on the Negro children's speech samples, with respect to the absolute score. It may be that Negro SES III children can be considered to speak two dialects with subsequent diminished efficiency in each dialect.* Diminished efficiency due to conflicting dialects might also explain the relatively poorer IQ achievement of the Negro SES III children.

The importance of dialect as a factor in Negro-white communication was further evidenced by the differential grammatical score performance of Negro and white children on passages of Negro and white speech. Negro subjects did as well as white subjects on Negro passages, but obtained lower scores than white children did on white selections. Although the girls' passages were generally easier than the boys' paragraphs, Negro subjects did as well as, or better than, white children in replacing the identical deletions in the boys' paragraphs. This finding can be attributed to the fact that the only characteristically regional passage was that of the lower-class Negro boy, since the Negro group obtained a lower absolute score for the girls' paragraph.

* This interpretation is similar to a theoretical position described by Dr. Susan Ervin in an address to the Institute staff. Ervin reported on studies showing that children who speak two dialects show the same diminished efficiency in each as is seen in children who speak two languages.

• Receptive Language and Sex Differences

Again, the data suggested a relationship between grade level and performance. At the first-grade level, there were no differences between girls and boys in the ability to comprehend teachers' speech. By the fifth-grade level, girls surpassed boys in their ability to cope with grammatical structure and in the preciseness with which they understood the speech sample, irrespective of IQ score. This finding is particularly interesting in the light of the conflicting evidence related to sex differences in language abilities. The fact that the boys did as well as the girls in gaining *general* understanding of the speech passage (contextual score) indicates that conclusions about sex differences must be very precise in identifying the language variable under consideration.

The evidence that lower-class girls earned higher grammatical scores on the teachers' speech items than did lower-class boys was consistent with the findings of other studies showing that within the lower social-class group, girls show an advantage over boys on various test measures.[18] Similar findings appeared with regard to the children's speech Cloze task on which, in general, lower-class girls performed better than did lower-class boys, while there were no differences in performance when middle-class boys and girls were compared. It should be noted that, in all cases, sex differences were a function of social-class level.

The superior ability in the area of receptive language on the part of the girls can be interpreted as an outcome of the girl's identification with and time spent with the mother, whereas in the lower-class home there is often not a father present with whom the boy can identify.

• Evaluation of the Test Devices

The method used to elicit relatively spontaneous expressive speech samples, the Clown and Rocket techniques, appears to have been as satisfactory a method as any used in previous studies of children's language where the speech was obtained in a child-adult situation. The evidence for this is the general similarity of the findings to those of earlier studies. However, this is not to say that the method is ideal. That the fifth-graders seem ill at ease in the Rocket situation has previously been indicated. Further, the results suggest that for the fifth-graders the task did not reach the limits of that age group's ability. Higher correlations between the type-token ratios and IQ score, at both grade levels, had been anticipated, since vocabulary measures generally do associate highly with measures of intelligence. At the fifth-grade level, the correlations of type-token ratios with IQ did not reach the acceptable .05 level of significance. The differences between the two grade levels in mean TTR score, while highly significant, were numerically very slight, though it is certain that the older group possesses a wider vocabulary range than indicated. The results showed that the two grade levels, though so far apart in age, yielded proportionately the same productivity on many of the language measures. It may be that by the time children reach the first grade, the basic organization of language has already been established. Or it might be that the fifth-graders' abilities were not fully measured. In general, although the same language variables tended to cluster together at each grade level, the first-grade data showed more stable, uniform patterns than were seen in the fifth-grade data. For the fifth-graders, a more naturalistic setting than the Rocket task might result in even more representative speech samples.

The Cloze technique, through which an effort was made to evaluate the ability of children to comprehend the speech of their teachers and of their peers, requires further refinement for this purpose. For example, instead of deleting every nth word, it might be more productive to delete words specifically selected in order to evaluate comprehension of the syntactical requirements of the passage.

It is clear that the auditory mode of presentation was qualitatively more difficult for the children than the visual form was. Nevertheless, the auditory form deserves emphasis since it so much more closely approximates verbal interaction. The extra time required for individual administration of the auditory mode of presentation appears to be warranted.

• Implications for Education

The findings of this broad study of expressive and receptive language in children have the following implications for the educator:

1. Children disadvantaged by conditions related to social-class status and/or minority group membership require special training in such language areas as vocabulary development, general ease in self-expression leading to lengthy but meaningful verbalization, greater

exactness in sound discrimination, and precision in the use of language.

2. This research shows the close relationship between intelligence, as measured by standardized IQ tests, and language skills. Previous studies suggest that improving language skills can raise IQ scores.

3. Different subgroups of first-grade children tend to be more similar in their general language functioning than are fifth-grade children. It is therefore important to emphasize language development at as early an age as possible.

• Implications for Further Research

Suggestions for further research arising from the current study include the following:

1. The children who participated in the present investigation of expressive language were included in the research project of a larger study, and parent interview data have been collected for each child. To gain further insights into the conditions related to higher IQ and language scores, it would be valuable to investigate these data from pupils of the lowest social-class group who scored highest and lowest on the language variables.

2. Longitudinal studies utilizing the Clown technique with the same children at different levels of their development, comparing the results to their general classroom and academic functioning, would serve to clarify the functions measured by the device.

3. Since the content of the expressive language samples of all the children was strikingly similar, it would be desirable to devise test situations which simultaneously maximize idiosyncratic content and lend themselves to standardized procedures.

4. Further analysis of the current expressive language samples might include the measurement of speech pauses defined by Bernstein[4] as "hesitation phenomena." Bernstein has found that hesitations between speech sequences are related to levels of verbal planning, or speech complexity. His research, based on British working-class adolescents, has shown provocative relationships between social-class level and hesitation phenomena.

5. Further studies of expressive language behavior should include assessments of the influence of the examiner's sex, race, and social-class characteristics on the children's responses.

SUMMARY

The major findings of the expressive and receptive language studies may be summarized as follows:

1. While fifth-grade children were found to be more productive on every language measure than first-graders were, in general the proportion of any language score to the total output of speech was the same at both grade levels.

2. Three relatively discrete factors of interrelated language and/or demographic variables were obtained for each of the two age groups studied. These clusters indicated the following: (a) Many of the traditional language measures yielded overlapping results owing to their high degree of dependence on total speech productivity. (b) Range of oral vocabulary tended to be relatively independent of other language measures and showed a positive relationship to social-class level. While the higher social-class group demonstrated a wider range of oral vocabulary than did the lower-class group, this relationship was not maintained when differences in IQ score were controlled. (c) The mean sentence-length measure was related to social-class level among younger children but not among the older group. Lower-class first-graders tended to use shorter sentences than a comparable age group of higher social-class subjects. (d) At the fifth-grade level the race variable was related to intelligence, reading skill, and sound discrimination test scores but not to the language measures of this research. At the first-grade level, the race variable was related to neither the language nor the other test measures.

3. The content of children's speech obtained in a relatively unstructured adult-child testing situation was, in general, not significantly influenced by variables of sex, race, or social class level. Older children, who talked considerably more than the younger children did within a specified period of time, were found to cover a wider range of topics rather than to discuss any one topic more fully than did the younger group.

4. The results of this research, compared with those of previous studies, suggest that the appearance of sex differences in language performance is highly dependent on the age and social-class level of the subject and on the specific linguistic skill measured.

5. Where social class or racial differences in language performance

appeared, they were usually found in conjunction with significant differences in performance on the Lorge-Thorndike IQ Tests. The language performance of fifth-grade children, compared with first-grade subjects, was somewhat more sensitive to the influence of social class and race variables.

REFERENCES

1. Anastasi, Anne. *Differential psychology*. New York: Macmillan, 1958.
2. Bernstein, B. Social class and linguistic development: A theory of social learning. In A. H. Halsey, J. Floud, & C. A. Anderson (Eds.), *Education, economy, and society*. New York: Free Press, 1961. Pp. 288–314.
3. Bernstein, B. Social structure, language and learning. *Educ. Res.*, 1961, 3, 163–176.
4. Bernstein, B. Linguistic codes, hesitation phenomena and intelligence. *Lang. & Speech*, 1962, 5, 31–46.
5. Cherry Peisach, Estelle. Children's comprehension of teacher and peer speech. *Child Develpm.*, 1965, 30 (2), 467–480.
6. Davis, E. A. Mean sentence length compared with long and short sentences as a reliable measure of language development. *Child Develpm.*, 1937, 8, 67–79.
7. Dawe, Helen C. A study of the effects of and educational program upon language development and related mental functions in young children. *J. exp. Psychol.*, 1942, 2, 200–209.
8. Deutsch, M., Maliver, Alma, Brown, B. R., & Cherry, Estelle, *Communication of information in the elementary school classroom.* Cooperative Research Project No. 908 of the Office of Education, U.S. Department of Health, Education, and Welfare, April, 1964.
9. Deutsch, M., Maliver, Alma, Brown, B. R., & Cherry, Estelle. *Communication of information in the elementary school classroom.* Moravia, N.Y.: Chronicle Guidance Publications, April, 1965. (Abstract)
10. Gates, J. *Gates Advanced Paragraph Reading Tests, Form 1.* New York: Bureau of Publications, Teachers Coll., Columbia Univer., 1958.
11. Heider, F. K., & Heider, Grace M. A comparison of sentence structure of deaf and hearing children. *Psychol. Monogr.*, 1940, 52, 42–103.
12. Irwin, O. C. Infant speech: The effect of family occupational status and of age on use of sound types. *J. Speech Hear. Disord.*, 1948, 13, 224–226.
13. Klineberg, O. Negro-white differences in intelligence test performance: A new look at an old problem. *Amer. Psychol.*, 1963, 18 (4), 198–203.

14. Landreth, Catherine. *The psychology of early childhood.* New York: Knopf, 1960.
15. Loban, W. Language ability in the middle grades of the elementary school. Unpublished post-doctoral study, Univer. Calif., 1961.
16. Lorge, I., & Thorndike, R. L. *Lorge-Thorndike Intelligence Tests, Levels 1 and 3 (Nonverbal), Form A.* New York: Houghton-Mifflin, 1954.
17. Lorge, I., & Thorndike, R. L. *Lorge-Thorndike Intelligence Tests, technical manual.* New York: Houghton-Mifflin, 1954.
18. McCarthy, Dorothea A. Language development in children. In L. Carmichael (Ed.), *A manual of child psychology.* New York: Wiley, 1954. Pp. 492–630.
19. Menyuk, Paula. Syntactic structures in the language of children. *Child Develpm.,* 1963, 34 (2), 407–422.
20. Miller, G. *Language and communication.* New York: McGraw-Hill, 1951.
21. Riessman, F. *The culturally deprived child.* New York: Harper, 1962.
22. Salzinger, Suzanne, Salzinger, K., Portnoy, Stephanie, Eckman, Judith, Bacon, Pauline, Deutsch, M., & Zubin, J. Operant conditioning of continuous speech in young children. *Child Develpm.,* 1962, **33,** 683–695.
23. Schneiderman, Norma. A study of the relationship between articulation ability and language ability. *J. Speech Hear. Disord.,* 1955, **20,** 359–364.
24. Smith, Madorah E. A study of some factors in influencing the development of the sentence in preschool children. *J. genet. Psychol.,* 1935, **46,** 182–212.
25. Taylor, W. L. "Cloze procedure," a new tool for measuring readability. *Journalism Quart.,* 1953, 30, 415–433.
26. Templin, Mildred C. Certain language skills in children, their development and interrelationships. *Inst. Child Welf. Monogr.,* 1957, No. 26.
27. Wepman, J. *Manual of direction: Auditory Discrimination Test.* Chicago: Author, 1958.
28. Williams, H. M. An analytic study of language achievement in preschool children. *Univer. Iowa Stud. Child Welf.,* 1937, **13** (2), 9–18.
29. Winer, B. J. *Statistical principles in experimental design.* New York: McGraw-Hill, 1962.
30. Young, F. M. An analysis of certain variables in a developmental study of language. *Genet. Psychol. Monogr.,* 1941, **23,** 3–141.

11 /

The Relationship of Auditory and Visual Functioning to Reading Achievement in Disadvantaged Children*

PHYLLIS A. KATZ
AND MARTIN DEUTSCH

One of the most serious problems facing educators today is the high percentage of children who are retarded in reading. This issue has recently been attracting a great deal of attention, and numerous rehabilitative efforts are currently being conducted in the schools. Although remediation is clearly necessary, a more comprehensive approach to the reduction of reading disabilities requires the delineation of causal variables. Under optimal conditions, such an approach would lead to the early diagnosis and correction of learning problems, thereby preventing both the failure experiences and the negative attitudes toward education which many poor readers subsequently develop.

Reading is an enormously complex process which encompasses numerous sensory, motoric, conceptual, and communication skills. The teaching of reading is, in fact, predicated on the possession of minimal levels of certain of these skills. In early reading instruction, for example, the child is required to learn to associate a specific oral-language response (the teacher's voice) to a novel visual cue (a printed word). This process presupposes that the child is capable of attending to, discriminating, recognizing, and remembering both auditory and visual stimuli. It is further assumed by most educators that the beginning reader is equally proficient with regard to both the auditory and visual channels of communication. In many cases such assumptions may not be at all warranted. Difficulties might arise with

---

* For other discussions of the study, see the original report,[15] and papers by Katz[11] and Katz and Deutsch.[13, 14, 16] A brief summary[17] has also been published.

respect to any one or more of such perceptual skills, and deficiencies may be more pronounced in one modality than another. Furthermore, it is conceivable that the child may be perfectly capable of responding to and retaining auditory or visual information when presented alone, and may experience difficulty only when both kinds are presented together.

The present research attempted to obtain information about possible interrelationships among some of the visual and auditory functions which underlie reading behavior. If inadequacies in these underlying skills could be found to be related to early reading difficulty, such information would have many practical implications. It might be possible, for example, to avoid reading difficulties in some children by administering training in these auditory and visual skills at an early stage.

The notion that defective auditory or visual functioning, or both, may play a role in producing reading retardation has been suggested by numerous investigators, and in recent years there has been increased interest in studying the perceptual behavior of children who are retarded in reading. One of the difficulties with much of the research in this area, however, has been its somewhat restricted emphasis. Studies have typically focused on only one specific auditory or visual skill (usually acuity) with one particular age group. There are virtually no studies which have employed a multivariate approach to investigating both auditory and visual skills in the same population. As a result, insufficient attention has been devoted to two issues of major theoretical importance: (a) the relation between various auditory and visual skills in children, and (b) the developmental aspects of such modality functioning.

Because of the relative lack of empirical evidence in these areas, a host of questions of obvious importance to the educator remain unanswered. For example, do auditory and visual materials elicit equivalent performance in all subskills underlying reading? Might certain perceptual deficiencies persist for longer periods of time than others? Are some of these deficiencies more susceptible to improvement than others? Is the relative importance of certain perceptual skills to reading constant at all developmental levels, or do complicated interactions exist between modality functioning and age? Answers to such questions are currently unavailable both because of the paucity of data and because of the lack of a comprehensive theory relating perceptual development to reading achievement. Prior to the construction of such a theory, however, what is needed is considerably more basic information about the modality functioning of children.

The research reported herein was designed to explore the relationships between auditory and visual functioning and reading achievement. An additional objective of the present design was to investigate the influence of developmental factors on these variables.

Toward this end, a wide variety of perceptual responses was sampled in poor and normal readers at three different age levels, including such responses as: (a) reaction times to lights and tones presented sequentially, (b) ability to continuously attend to and track auditory, visual, and combined auditory-visual stimulation, (c) capacity to discriminate auditory and visual material varying in meaningfulness, (d) capacity to memorize aurally and visually presented words and digits, and (e) ability to learn lists of auditory and visual meaningful material.

Wherever possible, the same type of response was obtained on the same group of children with auditory and visual stimuli matched in difficulty level. In addition to the variation of stimulus modality, the response tasks were also varied according to the complexity of the component skills.

The data were obtained on lower-class Negro males, a population which has typically been characterized by a relatively high incidence of reading retardation. It was hoped that the results of this study would aid in the early diagnosis of reading problems and the construction of more effective remedial techniques with such children.

PROCEDURE

• Subjects

Subjects were chosen from the first-, third-, and fifth-grade classes of two elementary schools in the Harlem area of New York City. The Gates Advanced Primary Reading Test was administered on a group basis to all male pupils in the third and fifth grades in both schools at the beginning of the school year (total $N = 385$). In order to assess potential reading ability on the first-grade level, the Reading Prognosis Test of the Institute for Developmental Studies was administered to all first-grade males at the two schools at the beginning of the year (total $N = 178$). This Reading Prognosis Test (RPT) has been described in detail elsewhere.[35] The test's reliability and predictive validity on a similar sample appeared sufficiently high (i.e., $r = .82$) to warrant its use as a prognostic indicator.

Frequency distributions of reading scores were obtained for each grade level, and the final sample was selected from the upper and lower 30 per cent of these scores. The children whose scores fell in these categories constitute the "high" and "low" readers. The resultant sample numbered 168 children. There were 28 children at each reading and grade level (i.e., first grade low, first grade high, etc.). The mean Reading Prognosis and Gates APR score for each grade are presented in Table 11–1.

Table 11–1

MEAN READING PROGNOSIS AND GATES APR SCORES (IN GRADE LEVEL) OF SAMPLE
CHILDREN ($N = 28$ IN EACH GROUP)

| Grade | READING GROUP | |
	Low	High
First	29.8	83.2
Third	2.2	3.9
Fifth	2.8	5.0

In addition to reading tests, Lorge-Thorndike Intelligence Tests were administered at the beginning of the school year to all sample children. Also, information relevant to the socioeconomic status of 75 per cent of the children was obtained from mail questionnaires sent to the parents. The results indicate that most of the children in the sample come from families where the parents work at unskilled factory jobs and have received little education beyond elementary school.

It should be noted that the final group of 168 children does not constitute a completely random sample. Children were selected for the final sample if, in addition to the reading scores, they met the following criteria:

a. Ss were Negro and male (approximately 95 per cent of the children in the two schools were Negro).

b. English was the dominant language spoken at home.

c. Lorge-Thorndike IQ was 70 or above.

d. No severe emotional, visual, or auditory problems were noted on the school record cards.

Thirty-five children with reading scores in the upper and lower 30 per cent of the distribution were eliminated because they did not meet one or several of the above criteria. The final sample of 168 was, however, selected randomly from the remaining pool of 300 children.

Because of both time limitations and the undesirability of repeatedly testing the same children, not all Ss received all techniques. Instead, children were randomly selected from the sample of 168 to receive one or two measures.

• Background and Description of Techniques Employed

BIMODAL REACTION-TIME APPARATUS

This apparatus, previously described in detail by Sutton et al.,[33] is capable of automatically presenting four separate stimuli: a red light, a green light, a high tone of 1,200 cycles per second, and a low tone of 400 cycles per second. The specific design used was somewhat modified for greater portability. In the present study, S's task was to lift his finger from a button every time a stimulus was perceived. Reaction time to each stimulus was automatically recorded. The stimulus program was designed so as to appear random to Ss. However, each stimulus was preceded by every other one an equal number of times. The interval between stimuli was varied randomly, lasting for either 1.5, 2.0, or 3.0 seconds. There was a one-minute delay at the end of each block of 33 trials.

Investigations of reaction-time performance on tasks requiring rapid attentional shifts between the auditory and visual modalities have demonstrated that longer latencies are associated with schizophrenics[33] and neurological patients.[1] In the only study employing children, Raab, Deutsch, and Freedman[28] obtained a relationship between modality-shifting efficiency and reading achievement in sixth-graders.

In the present study, a group of 48 Ss was chosen from the total pool of 168. There was an equal number of children from each grade and reading level. All Ss were tested individually in the school. Upon entering the experimental room, S was seated in front of the apparatus and instructed as follows: "We're going to play a game with lights and sounds. See this window. Well, every now and then you will see some lights here: a red light or a green light. Other times you will hear some sounds, a high sound or a low sound. Now, I would like you to put your finger down on this button. Every time you see a light or hear a sound, pick up your finger as fast as you can. Then put your finger right down again and wait for another light or sound. When another one comes, pick up your finger again as fast as you can. Then put it right down and wait for another light or sound. When another one comes, pick up your finger again as fast as you can. Then put it right down again and wait for another."

The presentation of the stimuli automatically terminated if S did not re-press the button. When this occurred, S was told to press the button again, which began the sequence. Each S received 198 trials.

CONTINUOUS PERFORMANCE TEST

The Continuous Performance Test (CPT) is a measure-of-vigilance performance. Vigilance has been operationally defined as a situation in which a subject must respond to a sporadically presented stimulus.[23] This behavior has also been called "monitoring" and "watch-keeping." What is required of the subject is a period of sustained attention, and efficiency in detecting signals (usually visual) is measured.

There have been no studies exploring this type of behavior in children, although, in adults, this task has been useful in diagnosing patients with brain damage[31] and subcortical abormalities.[24]

The technique used in the present investigation was an adaptation of the test described by Rosvold *et al.*[31] Colors were employed as stimuli with the children, however, rather than letters, which were used in the earlier study. There were three forms of the test: visual, auditory, and combined auditory-visual. In the visual version, the stimuli were dots of different colors on a memory drum. S was exposed to one stimulus per second. His task was to press a button as soon as he saw the color red. In the auditory form, the stimuli were tape-recorded names of colors. Again, S was exposed to one stimulus per second. Analogously, S was instructed to press a button as soon as he heard the word "red." On each version of the tasks, 80 "red" stimuli were randomly interspersed among a total of 560 stimuli. S's performance was automatically recorded on tape and reaction times to the correct stimuli were obtained from those tapes. In order to be correct, S had to press the button within a period of 100 milliseconds to 1 second after the stimulus presentation.

A total of 48 Ss were tested on the combination form of the Continuous Performance Test. In this technique 280 auditory and 280 visual stimuli were randomly interspersed. There were 40 red visual stimuli and 40 auditory "reds." S was instructed to press the button as soon as he either saw the color red or heard the word "red."

Due to equipment problems on the single auditory and visual versions of the test, the initial protocols obtained could not be used. The equipment was rebuilt and Ss were tested the following year on these techniques. Thus the results on the auditory and visual forms of the test are not directly comparable to the combination form, since the auditory and visual CPTs were administered to second-, fourth-, and sixth-grade Ss, whereas the combined form was given to first-third-, and fifth-grade Ss. A total of 66 Ss received the single auditory and visual versions, counterbalanced for order of administration.

DISCRIMINATION TASKS

Although it might be expected that any deficit in either visual or auditory discrimination would contribute to reading difficulty, the research literature to date seems somewhat contradictory regarding the role that such skills play in producing reading retardation.[11] With regard to discrimination of visual stimuli, several earlier studies have obtained positive findings[7, 8, 27, 30] whereas more recent studies have failed to obtain a positive relationship.[6, 9, 18] Most of the studies on auditory discrimination have demonstrated a positive relationship to reading achievement,[2, 36, 37, 39] although there has not been complete consistency here.[29]

A difficulty with much of the earlier research has been the inadequate control of stimulus presentation. Thus, in the typical case where the experimenter reads the words to be discriminated aloud to each subject, the pronunciation would not be constant, and the subject could obtain visual cues by observing the tester's lip movements.

In the present study, four discrimination tests were administered to 72 children in the second year of testing; thus the Ss were in the second, fourth, and sixth grades. In order to keep the stimulus presentation as constant as possible, the auditory stimuli were presented on tape, and the visual discriminanda were presented on slides.

The four tests differed according to both the stimulus modality and the level of meaningfulness. One auditory and visual test was composed of twenty-four English word pairs. Sixteen pairs were different; eight were identical. Twenty-four Hebrew words were employed as visual and auditory nonmeaningful stimuli. Again, sixteen items were different and eight were the same. The rationale for the inclusion of Hebrew words was to assess whether anticipated differences between children were due to differing discrimination ability or merely to differences in familiarity with the materials. The Hebrew words were unfamiliar to all the children.

For the auditory tasks, S was instructed as follows: "Some words will be read to you—two words at a time. I want you to tell me whether you hear the same word twice or two different words. Remember: if the two words are exactly the same, you say 'yes' or 'same.' If they are not exactly the same, you say 'no' or 'different.' " Time between word pairs was one second.

The visual stimuli were presented on slides, with one word above the other. A tachistoscopic shutter was used and the word pairs were exposed for a 1-second duration. Instructions analogous to those of the auditory task were employed.

Each S was seen twice and given an auditory and visual discrimination test at each sitting. The order was counterbalanced across Ss.

MEMORY SPAN

Investigators have long been interested in the relative efficiency of auditory and visual stimulus presentation in the area of immediate memory and the learning of lists. Most of the older studies, conducted with adults, have not demonstrated agreement as to whether auditory or visual presentation is superior. In adults, differences appear to be in part a function of the type of material to be retained, so that colors and meaningful word lists might be memorized more efficiently when presented visually[20, 21, 25, 26, 38] whereas auditory presentation might be superior for nonsense syllables, digits, and prose.[3, 4, 10] Studies employing elementary school children, however, have all tended to indicate that auditory presentation is superior,[19, 31, 40, 41] and a recent study by Friedman[5] concluded that the advantage of auditory presentation was even more pronounced for fifth-grade retarded readers than for normal readers.

A most serious limitation of all the previously cited studies employing children, however, has been the use of printed words as visual stimuli. Because of this, these earlier results could be explained more parsimoniously as being related to the young subject's unfamiliarity with reading material, rather than to any intrinsic inferiority of visual memory and learning.

The present investigation attempted to control for this familiarity variable by employing pictures of common objects rather than common nouns as meaningful visual stimuli.

Auditory and visual memory span were tested using both verbal material and digits.

With the auditory test, S was instructed as follows: "I'm going to say some numbers (or words) and when I'm through I want you to tell me just what you heard."

For the visual tests, the instructions were: "I'm going to show you some numbers (or pictures), and when I'm through I want you to tell me just what you saw."

The digit span test was administered both auditorily and visually. The items ranged from two to eight digits, and testing was discontinued if S missed two consecutive items at any level. The meaningful stimuli were eight items (either pictures or words), presented either visually or auditorily, and S's score was the number of items S could repeat after one trial. There were 72 Ss who received these tests.

SERIAL LEARNING TASKS

Serial learning was measured by the number of correct responses made to fifteen trials of the same words and pictures employed to assess memory span. In addition to the single auditory and single visual presentation, a combined auditory-visual test was also administered to 48 Ss. The combined version consisted of four words and four pictures employed in alternating sequence. S was instructed to repeat everything he saw and heard. The particular items which were presented visually or auditorily were counterbalanced across Ss.

Testing was discontinued after one perfect repetition of the eight items or at the end of fifteen trials. Pretesting revealed that the task was too difficult for first-grade Ss if the correct order was required in the repetition. Accordingly, the order of repeated items was disregarded in the analysis although E always presented the stimuli in the same order.

RESULTS

• *Bimodal Reaction Time*

Two measures of reaction time were employed in the analysis of the data: (a) mean reaction time to stimuli which were preceded by stimulation in a different modality, and (b) mean reaction time to stimuli preceded by same-modality stimuli. These measures will subsequently be referred to as *cross-modal* and *ipsi-modal* reaction times, respectively. Both of these conditions occurred with equal frequency. The mean reaction times of each group are presented in Table 11–2.

Table 11–2

MEAN REACTION TIMES (IN MILLISECONDS)

	TYPE OF REACTION TIME	
Group	Ipsi-Modal	Cross-Modal
First Grade—low	772	862
First Grade—high	612	644
Third Grade—low	501	586
Third Grade—high	507	559
Fifth Grade—low	449	491
Fifth Grade—high	397	418

A mixed type III analysis of variance[22] was conducted on the scores. The analysis indicated that, as expected, all Ss took longer to respond to stimuli which were preceded by a stimulus in a different modality ($F_{1,42} = 50.93$, $p < .001$). The main effect of age was statistically significant ($F_{2,42} = 14.44$, $p < .001$), indicating that older children have faster overall reaction times. The mean total reaction times for the first-, third-, and fifth-grade groups were 726, 541, and 438 milliseconds, respectively. Although the poor readers responded more slowly, the main effect of reading level was not significant at the generally accepted level ($F_{1,42} = 3.87$, $p < .10$).

The result of major interest to the purpose of this study is the interaction between type of reaction time (i.e., ipsi- and cross-modal) and reading level. This interaction was significant at the .01 level ($F_{1,42} = 7.37$), indicating that retarded readers exhibited greater difficulty than normal readers in shifting from one modality to another. The mean increase from the ipsi- to the cross-modal condition for the retarded readers was approximately twice that for the high-reader groups. Thus, this interaction supports the hypothesis that poor readers cannot shift attention between modalities as rapidly as normal readers.

Although the difference between good and poor readers was somewhat greater at the earlier age levels, the interaction of age by reading level did not reach the generally accepted level of significance. Neither were the other interaction effects statistically significant.

Since the two reading groups differed with respect to IQ scores, the question can be raised as to whether intellectual factors played a role in the differences in modality shifting behavior. In order to obtain information on this question, difference scores between cross- and ipsi-modal reaction times were computed for each S, and these were corre-lated with Lorge-Thorndike IQ scores. The resulting correlation co-efficient was $-.21$ which was not significantly different from zero ($Z = 1.46$). In addition, the correlation obtained between IQ and total reaction time was not significant ($r = .22$). Thus, it may be concluded that performance on this bimodal reaction time task is not significantly related to intelligence.

• *Continuous Performance Tests*

VISUAL AND AUDITORY FORMS

The number of correct responses was obtained on the auditory and visual form for each S. A correct response was classified as one in which the S pressed the button from 100 milliseconds to 1 second after the onset of a red stimulus. Responses occurring sooner than 100 milli-seconds after stimulus onset were considered to be anticipatory re-sponses, and these were analyzed separately. The upper limit of 1 sec-ond was chosen because after that time the succeeding stimulus was automatically presented. The mean percentage of correct responses on these tasks is presented in Table 11–3.

Table 11–3

MEAN PERCENTAGE OF CORRECT RESPONSES ON CONTINUOUS PERFORMANCE TEST IN SINGLE MODALITY ($N = 11$ IN EACH GROUP)

	MODALITY	
Group	Auditory	Visual
Second—Low	65.0	46.2
Second—High	85.0	50.0
Fourth—Low	77.8	65.5
Fourth—High	88.1	66.5
Sixth—Low	92.6	76.6
Sixth—High	91.8	81.6
Total	500.3	386.4

An analysis of variance of these scores revealed that the three main effects of age, reading level, and modality were all statistically significant. These differences indicate that older children performed more efficiently ($F_{2,60} = 29.93$, $p < .001$), that poorer readers exhib-ited poorer performance ($F_{1,60} = 4.85$, $p < .05$), and that all children did better on the auditory form of this task than on the visual ($F_{1,60}$ = 88.37, $p < .001$). None of the interactions was statistically significant.

An analysis subsequently conducted on the number of anticipatory responses revealed trends which paralleled the above analysis. More anticipatory responses were made by younger children ($F_{2,60} = 3.98$, $p < .05$), by poorer readers ($F_{1,60} = 9.25, p < .01$), and in response to visual stimuli ($F_{1,60} = 26.76$, $p < .01$). In addition, the reading level by modality interaction was significant ($F_{1,60} = 5.68$, $p < .05$) indicating that the differences between the good and poor readers were largely attributable to performance on the auditory form.

The significant difference between good and poor readers on the number of anticipatory responses is of interest because it shows that the poor readers were responding, i.e., were pressing the button as often as the good readers, but were responding incorrectly.

Correlations obtained between IQ scores and visual CPT performance were not significant. Intelligence scores were, however, related to auditory performance at the second- and fourth-grade levels ($r = .59$ and $r = .62$, respectively), but not at the sixth-grade ($r = -.27$). In an additional analysis, difference scores between auditory and visual performance were obtained from each S and these were correlated with Lorge-Thorndike IQ scores. The resultant correlations were not statistically significant at any grade level.

COMBINED AUDITORY-VISUAL FORM OF CPT

Correct responses on this technique were defined in the same manner as on the single-channel vigilance task. The mean percentage of correct responses on the combination form are presented in Table 11–4.

Table 11–4

MEAN PER CENT CORRECT RESPONSES ON COMBINED AUDITORY-VISUAL FORM OF CPT

| Group | MODALITY | | |
	Auditory	Visual	Total
First—low	80.0	45.5	62.8
First—high	62.7	54.1	58.4
Third—low	83.5	43.4	63.4
Third—high	78.7	75.5	77.1
Fifth—low	87.5	85.9	86.7
Fifth—high	86.5	87.0	86.7
Total	478.9	391.4	

Analysis of these data showed that poor and good readers did not differ significantly on the overall number of correct responses. The differences between age groups and between modalities were significant at the .01 level, indicating that older children made more correct responses, and that the visual stimuli were most difficult for all Ss. This latter finding corroborates the results obtained with the single-channel forms. In addition, the reading level by modality interaction was significant ($F_{1,36} = 6.49, p < .05$), indicating that the poor readers exhibit a greater discrepancy between auditory and visual vigilance performance than do the good readers.

Some differences in the pattern of results of the single-channel and combination forms of the CPT should be noted. Although visual performance was inferior on all forms of the CPT, performance of the various reading groups with respect to the auditory form deserves some comment. On the single-channel auditory form, the second- and fourth-grade poor readers performed poorly compared to the normal readers. On the combination form, the auditory performance of the first- and third-grade poor readers was somewhat superior to the normal readers. Unfortunately, the age groups on these tasks are not directly comparable. The results do suggest, however, that vigilance performance on two channel tasks may not be predictable from single-channel ones. Apparently, having to attend to auditory and visual stimuli at the same time may require different skills than attending to either modality in isolation.

• Discrimination Tasks

The mean number of errors made on the various discrimination tests are presented in Table 11–5. These errors represent the number of times the children responded "same" to the 16 pairs of stimuli in each test which were actually different.

An analysis of variance was performed on these error scores. This analysis indicates that the main effects of age and of reading level were statistically significant, as was the age by reading level interaction. Differences attributable to age and reading level were in the expected direction, i.e., older children and good readers exhibit better discrimination skills than do younger children and poor readers. The significant interaction indicates that the discrimination tests differentiated best between the good and poor readers, at the second grade level.

The effects of modality and meaningfulness were also statistically

Table 11–5

TOTAL NUMBER OF ERRORS TO DIFFERENT PAIRS ON DISCRIMINATION TESTS

Group	ENGLISH		HEBREW	
	Auditory	*Visual*	*Auditory*	*Visual*
Second—low	88	91	102	132
Second—high	38	27	50	92
Fourth—low	36	37	59	103
Fourth—high	18	22	39	96
Sixth—low	33	22	53	93
Sixth—high	10	9	20	71
Total	220	208	323	587

significant at the .001 level. As expected, all children performed better on the English than on the Hebrew word pairs. Furthermore, overall performance was poorer with the visual stimuli than it was with the auditory. This modality difference, however, was largely attributable to the difficulty the children had with the Hebrew visual stimuli, as was evidenced in a significant modality by meaningfulness interaction. This interaction revealed that visual performance was poorer than auditory performance with non-meaningful stimuli, whereas auditory presentation of familiar English words elicited somewhat more difficulty than did normal presentation. Neither modality nor meaningfulness significantly interacted with age or reading level, thus suggesting that underlying discrimination skill, rather than familiarity with the material, is differentiating the groups.

In summary, these findings may be taken as evidence for the fact that poor and good readers differ in their ability to discriminate between pairs of linguistic stimuli presented in two modalities with two degrees of meaningfulness. The differences were most pronounced at the younger age levels.

Intelligence appears to be related to both auditory and visual discrimination at the three grade levels. Pearson product-moment correlations between IQ and number of auditory errors for the second, fourth and sixth grades were −.53, −.61, and −.40, respectively; corresponding correlation coefficients involving visual discrimination errors and IQ were −.68, −.39, and −.56. All were statistically significant. Thus, it may be concluded that discrimination performance is related to age, reading ability, and Lorge-Thorndike scores.

• *Memory Span*

DIGITS

On the digit span tests, the measure employed was the maximum number of digits the child could repeat correctly. Table 11–6 presents the mean correct responses for each group.

Table 11–6

MEAN CORRECT RESPONSES ON DIGIT SPAN

Group	MODALITY		
	Auditory	Visual	Total
First—low	4.0	1.4	2.7
First—high	4.5	3.4	4.0
Third—low	4.1	3.6	3.8
Third—high	5.4	4.6	5.0
Fifth—low	5.2	4.6	4.9
Fifth—high	5.2	5.4	5.3
Total	28.4	23.0	

An analysis performed on this measure revealed that the main effects of age, reading level, and modality were all statistically significant at the .001 level. Thus, the older children and the good readers remembered more digits and, in general, better performance was evident on the auditory form of this test. A significant age by modality interaction ($F_{2,42} = 7.69, p < .01$) revealed that the younger children had greatest difficulty with visually presented digits. It should be noted, however, that this finding may be somewhat of an artifact since several of the first-grade children used in the study were rather inaccurate in reading visual digits. This was somewhat surprising since pretesting with a similar group of Ss had revealed that they had been able to read visually presented numbers. In view of this, therefore, these findings should be accepted with caution.

Correlations between digit span (auditory and visual) and IQ were performed at each grade level. The only significant correlation ($r = .48, p < .05$) was found between visual digit span and IQ on the third-grade level. All the other correlations did not reach the generally accepted level of confidence. The general absence of relationship was somewhat surprising since the Digit Span is actually used as a subtest of the Wechsler Intelligence Scale for Children. The Lorge-Thorndike Test, however, contains tasks of a different nature which do not involve immediate memory.

VERBAL MATERIAL

The mean number of correct responses made by each group is presented in Table 11–7.

Table 11–7

MEAN NUMBER OF CORRECT RESPONSES ON WORD AND PICTURE MEMORY SPAN

(*Maximum* = 8)

	MODALITY		
Group	*Auditory*	*Visual*	*Combined Auditory and Visual*
First—low	3.4	3.4	3.4
First—high	3.9	4.4	4.2
Third—low	2.6	4.1	4.2
Third—high	3.8	4.2	4.2
Fifth—low	2.8	4.0	4.2
Fifth—high	4.0	4.1	5.1
Total	3.4	4.0	4.2

An analysis of variance on these scores revealed that the effects of reading level and modality were statistically significant at the .01 level. Thus, on memory for verbal material, poor readers had shorter memory spans than did good readers. Additionally, all children exhibited poorest performance on auditorially-presented stimuli. Interestingly enough, no age differences were noted on this task.

• *Serial Learning*

The primary measure employed in analyzing the children's serial learning was the total number of correct repetitions made by S in 15 trials of an 8-item test. It should be recalled that three forms of a serial learning task were administered: an auditory, a visual, and a combined auditory-visual presentation. The mean number correct on each of these forms is presented in Table 11–8.

Table 11–8

MEAN NUMBER CORRECT ON SERIAL LEARNING

(*Maximum* = 120)

Group	MODALITY		
	Auditory	Visual	Combined Auditory and Visual
First—low	83.2	96.9	78.0
First—high	109.5	106.8	110.6
Third—low	94.1	105.1	100.6
Third—high	108.4	112.0	113.2
Fifth—low	102.5	111.0	109.4
Fifth—high	109.0	110.4	116.1
Total	101.2	107.0	104.0

The analysis of this measure revealed significant differences associated with age, reading level, and type of presentation. Older children learned more easily than did younger children, and good readers showed better learning scores than did poor readers. For the sample as a whole, visual presentation was easiest, whereas the auditory modality evoked the greatest difficulty. The one exception to this occurred in the first-grade potentially poor reader group, which had the lowest scores on the combination form.

As was true with the discrimination skills, the interaction between age and reading level was significant, indicating that this task differentiates reading level best with younger children.

The finding which is perhaps of greatest interest is the significant reading level by modality interaction ($F_{2,84} = 7.08$, $p < .01$). This indicates that although the poor readers learned more slowly on all tasks, they had particular difficulty with auditory stimuli. The average discrepancy between the auditory and visual forms was 10.9 for the retarded group as compared with .7 for the normal readers. Thus, the poorer readers exhibited a more uneven pattern of modality functioning.

Inspection of the data revealed that, contrary to expectation, the retarded readers gave as many verbal responses as did the good readers. Many of these responses, however, were extraneous and appeared to represent associations to the stimulus material such as substituting the response "spoon" for the stimulus "cup" or "cat" for "dog." The mean numbers of such associational responses for the retarded and normal groups were 10.0 and 2.9, respectively. This difference was statistically significant at the .05 level ($F_{1,42} = 4.17$). Furthermore, there was a greater tendency for such association errors to occur under conditions of auditory presentation. In the total sample, the average number of extraneous responses was 10.5 on the auditory form as compared with 2.5 on the visual, a difference significant at the .01 level ($F_{1,42} = 6.06$). This finding thus corroborates the results presented above, indicating that these children had their greatest difficulty focusing on auditory stimuli in serial learning.

Once again the question may be raised concerning the role of intelligence. The correlation between composite learning score (all serial learning tasks) and IQ was statistically significant in the first-grade group ($r = .56$), but not significant on the third- or fifth-grade level. Correlations obtained between auditory-visual discrepancy scores and IQ were not significant. Thus, it may be concluded that IQ is related to serial learning performance only at the first-grade level.

DISCUSSION

The most significant finding to emerge from this project was the consistency with which the various auditory and visual measures differentiated good from poor readers. Since many of these techniques have a long psychological history, the results of the individual measures will first be discussed in the light of previous work done in the area.

On what might be considered the least complex of the response measures used, poor readers exhibited greater difficulty in switching from one modality to another than did good readers of the same chronological age. This result suggests that one variable which may underlie reading performance is the capacity to respond quickly to two sequentially presented stimulus modalities. This finding is in accordance with an earlier study of Raab, Deutsch, and Freedman,[28] which also found such differences. In the present investigation, however, the trend was observed in younger children as well as older ones.

In general, children retarded in reading revealed poorer performance in vigilance situations. The low reading group made fewer correct responses and more incorrect responses, thus suggesting a deficiency in their capacity to sustain attention to a specific stimulus. This deficiency was especially pronounced on visually presented stimuli. One possible reason for this finding may be that the visual stimuli, which were dots of color, were more similar to one another than the color names. (It should, of course, be noted that none of the Ss were color-blind.) Results on the combined auditory-visual presentation revealed another trend. Here it was noted that poor readers exhibited a greater discrepancy between auditory and visual performance than did good readers. Some of the younger poor readers, in fact, got all responses correct in one modality while ignoring the other completely. This finding may be interpreted as corroborating the results on the Bimodal Reaction Time apparatus, i.e., that poorer readers experience difficulty responding appropriately to two stimulus modalities at the same time. It should be noted that these interpretations cannot be adequately verified at the present time, since no previous work has been done relating vigilance performance to reading achievement. The findings of this study, however, suggest that this may be a fruitful area for investigation.

The results relating discrimination performance to reading achievement are in agreement with earlier studies. It was clear in this study that poor readers differed from good readers in both auditory and visual discrimination skills, and the difference in auditory discrimination could not be attributed to visual cues since the stimulus presentation was taped. With respect to English words, auditory presentation was somewhat more difficult than was visual presentation. The level of stimulus meaningfulness appeared to affect general discrimination performance; however, this variable did not interact significantly with reading level. It can be concluded, therefore, that differences in the performance of good and poor readers were due to discrimination-skill variability and not to increased familarity or meaning of the stimuli.

On the more complex tasks, the good readers exhibited longer memory spans and superior learning efficiency. Although this general finding is in accordance with previous results,[11] the specific modality pattern observed in the present investigation differed from that obtained in earlier studies. In the memory and learning of words, auditory presentation elicited poorer performance in the present study. This trend was especially pronounced in retarded readers as evidenced by the significant reading level by modality interaction. Earlier investigations of children's auditory and visual learning reported that auditory presentation was superior in children. As was noted, however, a difficulty of these earlier studies was that the visual stimuli were printed words. Thus, the visual presentation differed from the auditory not only in modality, but also in familiarity for the young children. One possible reason for the discrepant results obtained in this study is that the visual stimuli were pictures of objects which were familiar to all the children. Under such conditions it would appear that visual presentation elicits better performance.

Investigation of developmental trends in the present study revealed that age differences paralleled the differences in reading achievement. This suggests that good readers may be operating on a higher developmental level, perceptually, than their retarded-reader counterparts. Differences associated with age were obtained with reaction times, vigilance performance, discrimination skills, digit span, and serial learning. The only task which failed to differentiate among first-, third-, and fifth-grade children was memory for words. Why this should be the case is somewhat puzzling. Since there did not seem to be very much variability on this measure, the possibility suggests itself that the age range tested was too restricted with respect to word memory. It may be that if older children were included in the sample, developmental trends might be observed.

An issue initially raised was whether perceptual skills showed similar patterns of development for poor and good readers. With regard to this issue, it is of interest to note that certain of the measures differentiated good and poor readers equally well at all age levels studied, whereas others discriminated children of differing reading ability best at the younger age levels. Reaction time to shifting modalities and vigilance performance significantly differentiated good and retarded readers at the fifth- and sixth- as well as at the first- and second-grade level. With regard to discrimination and serial learning performance, however, significant age by reading level interactions was obtained. This suggests that there are some skills in which poor readers "catch up" developmentally, whereas there are others in which they continue to function at a lower level. It is of course impossible to say whether this "catching up" is mainly due to maturational or experiential variables, since these were not controlled for in the present study. Future study of the determinants of perceptual patterns might yield some valuable information in this regard.

The specific direction of these age by reading-level interactions deserves some comment since in most instances the differences were greatest at the first-grade level. This finding lends additional support to the notion that perceptual factors may play a causative role in producing reading retardation.

Since one of the primary interests of the present investigation was the study of modality functioning in children, the obtained patterns of performance with respect to the auditory and visual modalities warrant some discussion. It is evident from the findings that children are not equally proficient with regard to both auditorially and visually presented stimuli in all perceptual skills. The actual patterning of modality functioning appears to be a complex issue. Children's visual performance was inferior on tasks involving vigilance, discrimination, and memory for digits. The reverse was true for memory and serial learning of words, where a distinct disadvantage was evident on auditorially presented stimuli. If the responses sampled herein can be taken to reflect an underlying continuum of complexity, ranging from simple button pressing to the learning of meaningful material, then the possibility suggests itself that auditory stimulation creates greater difficulties for children as the task becomes increasingly complex and meaningful. Further study is indicated to substantiate this possibility.

Although differences were observed between the auditory and visual functioning of all children on a few of the tasks (e.g., vigilance and serial learning), significant reading level by modality interactions was obtained on others, thus suggesting that with poor readers, the discrepancy in modality functioning is even greater than that which would be normally expected. This more uneven pattern of performance by the retarded readers revealed itself not only with respect to the single-channel tasks, but on those requiring attention to both modalities as well. Since the fifth- and sixth-grade children tended to show the least discrepancy between modalities, it is possible that the poor readers' performance is indicative of a developmental lag in perceptual functioning. It would be useful in this regard to obtain similar data from adults.

The relationship of intelligence test scores to the tasks employed in the present study deserves some comment. Since it has so frequently been demonstrated that standardized IQ scores of various kinds are related to scholastic achievement, educators often tend to "explain" any differences obtained between high and low achievers as a function of IQ. The present investigators do not, of course, take the position that intellectual status as measured by IQ tests does not play a rather obvious role in learning how to read. The correlations typically obtained between reading performance and IQ test scores range from .50 to .60.[11] The magnitude of these correlations indicate that knowing IQ scores of children still leaves a great deal of the variability in reading skills unaccounted for (i.e., from 64 per cent to 75 per cent, to be specific). Thus, there are clearly other factors besides intelligence which contribute to achievement in reading. Many of the skills measured in the present study, such as modality shifting, vigilance, memory, and serial learning efficiency, were shown to be significantly related to reading ability but not primarily to IQ scores. It should be noted that the primary concern of the present study was not to ferret out the intellective and non-intellective components underlying reading skill, a complex problem worthy of studying in its own right, and one which would require a different kind of experimental design than that used herein. The results of the present study, however, do suggest that many perceptual measures may contribute to the prediction of reading achievement in a way that does not overlap with intelligence test scores.

Pragmatically, the findings of the present study suggest that what is needed is both more careful and detailed analyses of the various skills involved in reading than has been done heretofore, plus a better assessment of children's functioning with regard to these skills. Such an analysis should be undertaken with a view toward developing more precise and experimentally determined teaching techniques which would counteract the varied deficiencies children bring with them to the classroom. For such a program, the educator would, of course, need to obtain information about a child's perceptual skills. It is interesting to note that although a great deal of attention has been devoted to the measurement of intellectual factors in children, not very much diagnostic consideration has been given to the perceptual factors which may underlie reading performance. Thus, although early assessments of children's capabilities usually include intelligence tests, they do not typically include measurement of reaction time or attention. The findings in the present investigation that many perceptual measures were related to reading ability but were not highly related to standardized IQ scores suggest that non-intellective factors contribute independently toward the prediction of reading achievement. Thus, such perceptual measures might profitably be obtained from children entering school in order to arrive at more accurate diagnosis and remediation of potential scholastic problems.

A final word of caution should perhaps be interjected at this point concerning the present findings. It should be noted that these results were obtained on what might be considered a homogeneous group of children. They were all Negro males and tended, as a group, to fall into the lower socioeconomic stratum, as measured by parental occupation and education. This fact certainly limits the generalizability of the findings to "average" middle-class white children, and future investigations should be performed to extend the sample. Pragmatically, however, the present urban sample is one which produces an exceedingly high percentage of scholastic failure. Thus, while the results may not hold true for all children, they can be generalized to the group that may benefit most from improved teaching techniques.

SUMMARY

The present study assessed some aspects of the perceptual and cognitive performances of 168 Negro, male, lower-class children. Good and poor readers were tested at three grade levels on a variety of tasks which involved simple reaction time, vigilance performance, discrimination, memory, and learning. The stimuli employed varied in modality (i.e., auditory, visual, or both channels together) as well as complexity.

The major finding was that retarded readers differed from normal readers on all perceptual measures obtained. On a reaction-time task, the poor readers exhibited longer latencies in shifting from one sensory modality to another than did good readers. In their monitoring of stimuli, the poor readers had greater difficulty inhibiting responses to inappropriate stimuli. Their ability to differentiate between similar auditory and visual stimuli was decidedly inferior to their normal reader counterparts. Furthermore, the poor readers recalled and retained sequentially presented material less efficiently than the more skillful readers.

In addition to these gross perceptual differences, certain patterns of modality functioning appeared to be related to reading retardation in this group of children. Depending upon the nature of the task, difficulties were more pronounced with regard to one modality rather than another. Thus, with relatively simple stimuli, the poor readers appeared more prone to attentional lapses when the presentation was visual rather than auditory. On the more complex tasks involving memory and serial learning, however, the poor readers exhibited greater difficulty handling auditory rather than visual material. In general, the children who were retarded in reading exhibited more discrepant modality functioning than normal readers.

The developmental patterns that emerged from this investigation suggest that the various perceptual skills may differentially relate to reading achievement at different maturational stages. Deficiencies in serial learning performance and discrimination between perceptually similar stimuli were particularly pronounced in the youngest children tested, and seemed to decrease somewhat with age, even in the retarded-reader group. Vigilance performance and memory, however, differentiated poor from good readers equally well at all age levels tested. These findings suggest that poor readers may "catch up" in some skills with development, whereas others may require specific intervention for correction. It was further suggested that more comprehensive assessment of children's skills (both intellective and perceptual) be undertaken prior to reading instruction in order to construct more effective training techniques.

References

1. Benton, A. L., Sutton, S., Kennedy, J. A., & Brokaw, J. R. The cross-modal retardation in reaction time of patients with cerebral disease. *J. nerv. ment. Dis.*, 1962, **135**, 413–418.
2. Bond, G. L. *The auditory and speech characteristics of poor readers.* Teachers Coll. Contr. Educ., 1935, No. 657.
3. Cantril, H. & Allport, G. W. *The psychology of radio.* New York: Harper, 1935.
4. Elliot, F. R. Memory for visual, auditory, and visual-auditory material. *Arch. Psychol.*, 1936, **29**, No. 199.
5. Friedman, R. M. A comparative study of the retention level of verbal material presented visually and orally to fifth-grade students. Unpublished master's thesis, 1959, Adelphi College.
6. Galifrent-Granjon, N. *Enfance*, 1951, **5**. Cited in M. D. Vernon, *Backwardness in reading.* Cambridge: Cambridge Univer. Press, 1957.
7. Gates, A. I. *The psychology of reading and spelling.* New York: Teachers Coll., Columbia Univer., 1922.
8. Gates, A. I. A study of the role of visual perception, intelligence and certain associative processes in reading and spelling. *J. educ. Psychol.*, 1926, **17**, 433–445.
9. Goins, J. T. Visual perceptual abilities and early reading progress. *Suppl. educ. Monogr.*, 1958, No. 87.
10. Henmon, V. A. G. Modes of presentation and retention. *Psychol. Rev.*, 1912, **19**, 79–96.
11. Johnson, Marjorie S. Factors related to disability in reading. *J. exp. Educ.*, 1957, **26**, 1–26.

12. Katz, Phyllis A. Verbal discrimination performance of disadvantaged children: subject and stimulus variables. *Child Develpm.*, 1967, 38 (1), 233–241.
13. Katz, Phyllis A., & Deutsch, M. The effects of varying modality of stimulus presentation in serial learning on retarded and normal readers. Paper presented at Eastern Psychol. Ass., April, 1963.
14. Katz, Phyllis A., & Deutsch, M. The relationship of auditory-visual shifting to reading achievement. *Percept. mot Skills*, 1963, 17, 327–332.
15. Katz, Phyllis A., & Deutsch, M. *Visual and auditory efficiency and its relationship to reading in children.* Cooperative Research Project No. 1099 of the Office of Education, U.S. Department of Health, Education, and Welfare, 1963.
16. Katz, Phyllis A., & Deutsch, M. Modality of stimulus presentation in serial learning for retarded and normal readers. *Percept. mot. Skills*, 1964, 19, 627–633.
17. Katz, Phyllis A., & Deutsch, M. *Visual and auditory efficiency and its relationship to reading in children.* Moravia, N.Y.: Chronicle Guidance Publications, April, 1965. (Abstract)
18. Kendall, B. S. *J. educ. Psychol.*, 1948, 39. Cited in M. D. Vernon, *Backwardness in reading.* Cambridge: Cambridge Univer. Press, 1957.
19. Kirkpatrick, E. A. An experimental study of memory. *Psychol. Rev.*, 1894, 1, 602–609.
20. Koch, H. L. Some factors affecting the relative efficiency of certain modes of presenting material for memorizing. *Amer. J. Psychol.*, 1930, 43, 370–388.
21. Krawiec, T. S. A comparison of learning and retention of materials presented visually and auditorially. *J. gen. Psychol.*, 1946, 34, 179–195.
22. Lindquist, E. F. *Design and analysis of experiments in psychology and education.* Boston: Houghton Mifflin, 1953.
23. McCormack, P. D. Performance in a vigilance task as a function of length of inter-stimulus interval. *Canad. J. Psychol.*, 1960, 14, 265–268.
24. Mirsky, A. F., & Rosvold, H. E. The use of psychoactive drugs as a neuropsychological tool in studies of attention in man. In L. Uhr and J. G. Miller (Eds.), *Drugs and behavior.* New York: Wiley, 1960. Pp. 375–392.
25. Munsterberg, H. & Bigham, J. Memory. *Psychol Rev.*, 1894, 1, 34–38.
26. O'Brien, F. J. A qualitative investigation of the effect of mode of presentation upon the process of learning. *Amer. J. Psychol.*, 1921, 32, 249–283.
27. Phelan, M. B. Visual perception in relation to variance in reading and spelling. *Catholic Univer. America Educ. Res. Monogr.*, 1940, 12, No. 3.
28. Raab, Shirley, Deutsch, M., & Freedman, A. Perceptual shifting and

set in normal school children of different reading achievement levels. *Percept. mot. Skills,* 1960, **10,** 187–192.

29. Reynolds, M. C. A study of the relationships between auditory characteristics and specific silent reading abilities. *J. educ. Res.,* 1953, **46,** 43–49.

30. Riley, Sister Mary. Visual perception in reading and spelling: a statistical analysis. *Catholic Univer. America Educ. Res. Bull.,* 1929, **4** (1).

31. Rosvold, H. E., Mirsky, A. F., Sarason, E., Bransome, E. D., Jr., & Beck, L. H. A continuous performance test of brain damage. *J. consult. Psychol.,* 1956, **20,** 343–350.

32. Russell, R. D. A comparison of two methods of learning. *J. Educ. Res.,* 1938, **18,** 235–239.

33. Sutton, S., Hakerem, G., Zubin, J., & Portnoy, M. The effect of shift of sensory modality on serial reaction time: A comparison of schizophrenics and normals. *Amer. J. Psychol.,* 1961, **74,** 224–232.

34. Vernon, M. D. *Backwardness in reading.* Cambridge: Cambridge Univer. Press, 1957.

35. Weiner, M., & Feldmann, Shirley. Validation studies of a Reading Prognosis Test for children of lower and middle socioeconomic status. *Educ. psychol. Measmt.,* 1963, **23,** 807–814.

36. Wepman, J. M. Auditory discrimination, speech, and reading. *Elem. School J.,* 1960, 325–334.

37. Wheeler, L. R., & Wheeler, V. D. A study of the relationship of auditory discrimination to silent reading abilities, *J. educ. Res.,* 1954, **48,** 103.

38. Whitehead, L. G. A study of visual and aural memory processes. *Psychol. Rev.,* 1896, **3,** 258–268.

39. Wolfe, L. S. *J. genet. Psychol.,* 1941, **58.** Cited in M. D. Vernon, *Backwardness in reading.* Cambridge: Cambridge Univer. Press, 1957.

40. Worcester, D. A. Memory by visual and by auditory presentation. *J. educ. Psychol.,* 1925, **16,** 18–27.

41. Young, W. E. The relation of reading comprehension and retention to hearing comprehension and retention. *J. exp. Educ.,* 1936, **5,** 30–39.

12 /

Auditory Discrimination and Learning: Social Factors

This paper will deal with events in only one of the various modalities through which stimuli are received, processed, and responded to: that is, audition. Further, the paper will not be concerned primarily with hearing per se, and its adequacies and limits, but rather with the discrimination of one sound from another, and with the recognition of sounds and their referents. Discussion of these latter functions presupposes a normal receptive sensory apparatus. Omission here of other modalities and of abnormalities in sensory sensitivity does not mean ignoring these other variables, but limitations of space. It must be added, though, that the data gathered early in our research pointed to auditory discrimination as an exceedingly important factor in verbal behavior, and as a result, further studies have supplied much more information about auditory discrimination than about similar functions related to other modalities.

The importance of accurate input to appropriateness of response does not need belaboring: It is well illustrated in the visual trials of Mr. Magoo, of the animated cartoons. And we have such stories as that of the three deaf ladies on the train, in which the first says to the second, "What time is it?"; the second replies "Thursday"; and the third says, "So am I—let's go get something to drink." Both Mr. Magoo and the three ladies had misperceptions because of the inadequate sensitivity of the basic receptors, and presumably all would come to appropriate conclusions if their receptors were sensitive enough to be activated by the stimuli with which they were presented. Thus, one cause of inaccurate input is insensitivity of the receptor itself, so that the information which reaches the analyzing or interpreting areas of the brain is inaccurate or incomplete. This same result can occur, of course, if the stimulus intensity is below the threshold value for a normally sensitive receptor. When this happens, the tendency is for the missing stimuli to be supplied internally, as was shown in the experiments on subliminal stimulation, and as can be seen in the children's game of "telephone" as well as in the examples given above.

In all the examples given, the sensory input which reaches the analyzing centers is faulty, whether through abnormal insensitivity of the receptor or because of subthreshold values of the stimulus. The analyzer, so to speak, does the best it can with what it gets, the percept is formed, and the response is faulty or inappropriate because of this inaccurate feedback.

After simple sensitivity, the next level of sensory response which can be considered is discrimination, a function which corresponds to the stimulus property of frequency. Discrimination is, of course, impaired by inadequate receptor processes. Yet it is also possible to have intact end organs and still be unable to discriminate differences in tone or between particular sounds. This kind of disability blends into a third level of function, defined by Hardy[5] as recognition—the ability to name or reproduce a particular sound or word. These functions apparently are subsumed by the higher nervous centers, and in the case of auditory stimulation, presumably by the temporal lobes and the temporal-parietal regions of the brain. It is possible, thus, to have fully intact end organs—i.e., to have vibrations received and transmitted by the ear—and still not to discriminate or to understand or recognize sounds, if there are lesions in the crucial cerebral areas.

However, for discrimination and recognition, another set of variables is as crucial as the intactness of the brain. These variables have to do with experience and exposure to the adequate stimuli. Thus, one might have fully adequate auditory sensory apparatus, both peripheral and central, and yet, on being exposed to a spoken foreign language for the first time, be unable to recognize any referents to or meanings of the words heard—perhaps also finding it difficult or even impossible to discriminate sounds or words from each other. These discriminations come only with experience and practice in responding to the stimuli. A better example for purposes of the following discussion would be the infant who hears but who does not discriminate or recognize. It is only through experience which involves consistent exposure to particular auditory stimuli that the baby comes to discriminate sounds, to recognize words and relate them to their referents, and ultimately to use words himself. The gross link between hearing and speech is thus an obvious and well-established one. But there is no reason to suppose that the relationship is a unitary one, unaffected by the quality or consistency of the speech which the child hears, or by the circumstances under which the stimulation occurs. People speak consistently with the local dialect which surrounds them. These facts are well known, and most school systems, for example, require speech tests as part of the teacher-licensing procedure to insure that the children in school will be exposed to standard, correct speech.

This perhaps already obvious point has been somewhat belabored in the interests of underlining the importance of experience and exposure in the development of speech and of language. Thus far, only the gross aspects of stimulation have been dealt with. But other facts and current theories of sensation and perception are here pertinent. For example, the reticular system, which seems to be responsible for a general, overall activating function in the nervous system, without which no stimulus is effective, is able to influence transmission of sensory messages within the central nervous system. Animal experiments show that when the reticular system is directly activated, sensory transmission is inhibited or facilitated, depending on where the activating stimulus is applied. Experiments by Hernández-Peón and others indicate that activation of the brain-stem reticular formation inhibits auditory transmission very early in the path of that transmission. In addition, it has been found in cats that auditory-evoked potentials are reduced when the animal is attentive to stimuli in other modalities.[6] Similarly, the potentials in other modalities are reduced when the animal's attention is on an auditory stimulus. It was also found that afferent messages elicited by stimuli which are attended to are facilitated.

It is not planned here to make the sometimes tempting but always erroneous direct transition from animal experimentation to human functioning or behavior. Nevertheless, the animal experiments do provide hypotheses about functioning in the human nervous system, and these hypotheses can be viewed in the light of behavioral data which are available or which can be gathered. In these terms, the findings from these animal experiments on the reticular system are consistent with the information-theory findings that the signal-to-noise ratio is influential in the stimulus perceived and in the response evoked. The higher the ratio—i.e., the greater the amount of "signal" as compared with "noise"—the more likely will be the accurate perception of the signal. This formulation is, of course, consistent with the Gestalt formulations regarding figure-ground relationships in visual perception. The theoretical as well as actual importance of the environment also has roots in Gestalt perceptual theory.

To return, though, to the postulated relationship between the reticular system and the signal-to-noise ratio, one could hypothesize that with a low ratio—i.e., with a lot of noise in the system—the excess activation of the reticular system is interfering with travel of the signal up the neural paths. There are some human learning experiments which show that some "noise" in the system is beneficial for learning, while too much "noise" is disorganizing. One could hypothesize, again, that this finding has to do with reaching a level of activation which prepares the organism to accept and respond to a stimulus, but not exceeding that optimal level and thereby producing a blocking out of the desired stimulus. Similarly, human learning experiments on repetitiousness of stimulation and animal studies on habituation to consistent stimulation are in agreement: i.e., perception of the stimulus can be dulled or abolished by continued identical presentation. This last assumption can be further verified by the casual observation that continued stimuli to which we become accustomed (i.e., to which we adapt) are blocked out, as in the case of random street noises outside a home or office, or the noise of machinery with which one works. Myklebust's[9] differentiation of modalities is pertinent here. He classifies vision and hearing as distance senses, but points out that hearing is largely a background sense, since auditory stimuli are always present: we are unable to avoid the impingement of the physical properties of sound. Therefore, we might postulate that auditory stimuli are particularly prone to a "tuning-out" process, to a learned inattention.

Granting, for the moment, the accuracy of these hypotheses, one could expect that a child raised in a very noisy environment with little directed and sustained speech stimulation might well be deficient in his discrimination and recognition of speech sounds. He could also be expected to be relatively inattentive to auditory stimuli, and further, to have difficulty with any other skill which is primarily or importantly dependent on good auditory discrimination. The slum child does indeed live in a very noisy environment, and he gets little connected and concentrated speech directed to him. If he does show poor auditory discrimination, and if for the most part the sensitivity of the end organ is normal, then the hypothesized process by which the poor discrimination is produced would point to methods of alleviation. Since the data presented in the previous chapter and the data which will be discussed here seem to indicate the importance for reading skill of accurate auditory discrimination, and since lower-class children show a much greater incidence of reading retardation than do the children from more privileged backgrounds, alleviation of difficulties in auditory discrimination would appear to be potentially highly important.

This reasoning implies certain desirable conditions for children's auditory learning. Certainly one would try to place the child in a quiet environment and minimize stimuli to other modalities while maximizing the particular auditory stimuli being presented (i.e., maximize the signal-to-noise ratio). Further, one would want to avoid too much repetition of the same stimulus, while at the same time avoiding presentation of too many different stimuli which might in themselves be distracting. This is virtually an operational definition of good and approved teaching technique, and it is indeed illuminating to discover the experimental and theoretical path by which it was arrived at!

But all the foregoing was neither just a pleasant exercise on an unfamiliar path with the goal of arriving at a familiar courtyard, nor simply a fancy justification for educational desiderata. Rather, the path can be a principle against which educational innovations can be evaluated. More important, this path can open up wide areas of research in fields peripheral to education and can perhaps point the way to the objective measurement of "distraction" or "quiet" for particular children and particular learning situations. By discovering ways in which knowledge in seemingly disparate areas can be brought to bear on common problems, new knowledge and new techniques for obtaining more knowledge can also be found. But further, and possibly most important, other variables, perhaps previously not considered, can be evaluated for potential import to the problem at hand.

If we correctly place the problem of auditory discrimination (in the absence of serious disability in the nervous system) in the environmental organization of auditory stimuli, then we must also consider the developmental level of the child when he is exposed to the various auditory organizations. It is known that there are certain optimal times for various kinds of stimulation, and that, in fact, in some areas there are also critical times—times within which a given type of stimulation will be effective and outside of which it will not. Such concepts of optimal and critical times are well established in biology, and are becoming so in biopsychology and in theories of animal behavior. Again, from this work, certain principles can be adduced which can be tested against the phenomena of human behavior. It is already known that foreign languages, for example, can be most easily learned by normal children relatively early in life, but after their basic language is established. Similarly, it is known that, for the most part, the complex type of motor coordination necessary for riding a bicycle, for example, is most easily acquired in childhood rather than in adulthood. (Whether this advantage is largely because of the greater plasticity of the motor patterns or because of the poorer cognizing of events connected with falling off and the simultaneous greater resiliency of the physical structures in the event of falling is, for purposes of this discussion, immaterial. What matters is the fact that it is more possible to learn to ride a bicycle earlier in life than it is later in life.) It was shown in the studies of persons who gained vision after being blind for all their lives up until surgery that, after a certain age, pattern vision could never be acquired if there had been no earlier visual stimulation. (These findings are consistent with those on chimpanzees reared in the dark for varying lengths of time.) Thus, concepts of optimal time are not new to human behavior theory.

In educational circles, the concept has been most often transformed to the idea of "readiness," and the most frequent use of this concept has been to delay certain kinds of teaching. That is, the emphasis in "readiness" is on *waiting* for a more optimal time. In biology and in animal psychology, on the other hand, the most frequent emphasis has been on providing particular stimulation *early enough*. Only in theories of personality, in discussions of psychopathology, and in some orientation to some motor skills have theorists of human behavior emphasized the importance of early correct stimulation or treatment.

In a recent article bearing on this issue, Scott[12] points out that ". . . organization inhibits reorganization. Further, organization can be strongly modified only when active processes of organization are going on." He states, further, that it is this fact that "accounts for critical periods in development." He hypothesizes, on the basis of data which he presents, that the "critical period for any sort of learning is that time when maximum capacities—sensory, motor, and motivational as well as psychological ones—are first present." This places the emphasis squarely on earlier, rather than later, stimulation and teaching, and places the evaluation burden on discovering the developmental progress of the particular capacities which are to be stimulated. Scott's position here, though largely theoretical and not based on data on children, is very similar to Fowler's[4] argument for the efficacy of preschool training.

While we do not at present know precisely the time at which the maximum capacity to develop auditory discrimination is reached, nor the exact maturational sequence in discrimination difficulty of various types of sounds, we do know that by the time children come to the first grade many of them already have poor discrimination abilities organized. Following Scott's dictum that "organization inhibits reorganization," we can thus assume that a better time to train good auditory discrimination would be before first-grade entrance. From here it is not, I hope, too unwarranted a leap to the hypothesis that the optimal time for such learning must be before the age at which children enter the first grade.

In considering the slum child from this point of view, then, we must conclude that at his optimal time for learning auditory discrimination—some time in his preschool years—he is confronted with a very poor situation for this learning: a very noisy environment, and one with many distractors and low signal-to-noise ratio. Thus, at a time when he might most easily learn discriminations, he is encouraged by the stimulus properties of his environment to become inattentive to the appropriate stimuli, and, in fact, perhaps to block out many of them altogether. Further, there is some evidence for a kind of Gresham's Law in auditory stimuli. Cherry[1] reports that when a "noisy" noise is fed into one ear at the same time that a "purer" noise is fed into the other, the "noisy" noise blocks out the purer one. Another factor may serve as an impediment to the development of good auditory discrimination skills. In New York City, at least, the child from the overcrowded living area is assailed by numerous dialect patterns, so even the relatively weak signal in the environment of noise is not a consistent one.

Now, from the fact that foreign languages can be learned at almost any age (albeit with more effort and often more slowly) and from similar related data, we can hypothesize that such learning has optimal times but not critical times—that is, that there is no cut-off time beyond which such learning cannot take place. While it does not therefore follow that auditory discrimination per se does not have critical time limits for its learning, there is circumstantial justification for an at least heuristic and optimistic view. But whereas during an optimal period for such learning the directed teaching necessary might be minimal, as the best period passes, more and more direction and more and more optimal stimulus conditions will be necessary. This chain of hypotheses would lead, then, to a directed emphasis on the teaching of auditory discrimination to any child who shows poor skill in this area. The degree of direction and of emphasis on this skill would vary, of course, depending on the age of the child, pending the discovery of the actual optimal times involved. But from the above reasoning, one could certainly say that such emphasis should be present in any teaching done before the child reaches the first grade. This hypothesis is further supported by the data to be presented below relevant to the relationship between auditory discrimination and verbal and reading ability.

Before proceeding to consideration of the data and their implications, however, let me make one other point. While the kind of training indicated is highly consistent with good teaching practice, typically, in preschool installations such as nursery schools, the curriculum is a much freer one, oriented mainly toward the child's interpersonal relationships and containing therefore many more distractions which would create "noise" in the auditory system. The reasoning on auditory discrimination and its potential optimal period would imply a more school-like organization for the nursery school—at least for such functions as auditory training. If the hypotheses to be presented below about the importance of this function for many other verbal skills are borne out by further research, then the introduction of more structured periods into an unstructured program will be amply justified.

Now let us proceed to the data relating to auditory discrimination. These data were gathered in connection with several different projects. As a result, there is inconsistency of measures employed from one sample to the next, and there is also some inconsistency of statistical treatment. But all samples have in common data on auditory discrimination gathered on the Wepman Auditory Discrimination Test.[13]

This individually administered test consists of 40 pairs of words, 30 pairs of which differ from each other only in either the initial or final sound. Ten pairs are the same. The subject's task is to listen carefully to each pair of words and say whether they are the "same" or "different." The method exemplified by this test has been long in use as a measure of auditory discrimination. One advantage of the Wepman test is that it is long enough to provide an adequate behavior sample. Another is that it is highly systematized. (The word pairs chosen by Wepman were matched for familiarity by selecting words as close together as possible from the Lorge-Thorndike Word Book, and every possible match of phonemes used in English was made within phonetic categories, with no cross-phonetic category matching being included.) Also, Wepman has rough norms for the test.

The test yields two scores for each subject. The "same" scores refer to the number of same pairs which the child correctly identified as same, and the "different" scores refer to the number of different pairs which the child correctly identified as different. In practice, only the "different" scores are used or interpreted. Wepman points out in the test manual that the "same" items are included mainly for purposes of testing the validity of the test; he does not use them in interpreting the test findings. The "same" scores are, further, not comparable to the "different" scores, inasmuch as there are considerably fewer same than different pairs (10 as opposed to 30). Thus, too, the actual scores obtained on the same items have a very narrow range, and the correlations between these scores and the other variables would be accordingly attenuated. It is our practice to administer the test by means of a tape recording, playing the tape through earphones, with an examiner in the room with the child and the tape recorder. The examiner was thus able to determine, at least behaviorally, if the child was attending to the stimuli.

All the other test data also were gathered according to the procedures outlined in the respective manuals. However, where the Digit Span test appears as a variable, this was administered at a time different from the administration of the WISC, and the WISC administration did not include this subtest.

Table 12–1 presents correlational data on the Wepman test and various other measures, including the subtests of the WISC, the Gates reading tests, the Roswell-Chall word-parts test, and the Institute Orientation Scale. The correlations in the first column were obtained on a sample of 26 fifth-grade children, all of whom were retarded in reading by one to three years. In the second column are correlations of the same variables for a sample of 30 fifth-grade children who were not retarded in reading. All the children in the two groups are Negro; socioeconomic status does not differ significantly between the two groups. Column 3 shows correlations for a sample of 98 fifth-grade children, and the last column refers to a sample of 72 first-grade children. The samples represented in columns 3 and 4 were balanced on both race and socioeconomic status: 25 per cent of them are lower-class white, 25 per cent are lower-class Negro. These children were unselected with regard to the reading variable.

Among the correlations reported for the samples selected on reading ability there are few high values, but all which are significant relate the Wepman score to some verbal ability. For the subjects who were retarded in reading (column 1), the highest correlations are with the WISC Vocabulary Score and the WISC Verbal Score (but this includes the Vocabulary subtest). Other significant correlations are with the Comprehension subtest of the WISC and the Gates Advanced Paragraph Reading Test. The average correlation between the Wepman and the subtests which comprise the primary verbal factor on the WISC (Information, Comprehension, Similarities, and Vocabulary)[2] is .43 ($p < .05$). For the normal reading group (column 2), however, the only significant correlation is between the Wepman score and the WISC Comprehension subtest. It is to be noted that in neither group was a significant correlation obtained between the Wepman and a non-verbal or performance measure, or between the Wepman and the two information measures—the WISC Information subtest and the Institute Orientation Scale.

On examining column 3 of Table 12–1, which reports results on a fifth-grade sample unselected for reading level, we find a significant relationship between the Wepman score and the Orientation Scale. Some of this difference may be simply a statistical function of the difference in sample size (i.e., this correlation is smaller than the corresponding one for the average readers, but attains significance because of the larger N). Another possible explanation of this difference, occurring as it does in two groups of the same age, is that it is produced because of the greater heterogeneity of the larger group with regard to socioeconomic and racial variables, as well as reading level. The contribution to the obtained result of the greater range in background and ability will have to be determined by further data analysis. For the first-grade sample, which is also heterogeneous and large, the correlation between Wepman and Orientation Scale is also significant.

For the nonselected fifth-grade sample, there is one other significant Wepman correlation, and that is with Lorge-Thorndike score, which is an intelligence measure. For the first-grade sample however, the corresponding correlation is not significant, while the correlation between the Wepman and the Peabody Picture Vocabulary Test (PPVT) is significant. The PPVT is also an intelligence measure, but one which uses verbal behavior, while the Lorge-Thorndike form at this level is non-verbal. Here, then, we may be confirming what was previously noted: the Wepman correlates with verbal measures, but not with non-verbal or performance ones.

Let us turn for a minute from the relational data to the description of the performance of the children on the Wepman test itself. For

269 / Cynthia P. Deutsch

Table 12–1

CORRELATIONS BETWEEN WEPMAN AUDITORY DISCRIMINATION TEST AND OTHER MEASURES

	Grade 5 Retarded Readers (N = 26)	Grade 5 Average Readers (N = 30)	Grade 5 Nonselected Sample (N = 98)	Grade 1 Nonselected Sample (N = 72)
Lorge-Thorndike			.24*	.14
PPVT				.50**
Institute Orientation Scale	.04	.31	.21*	.39**
Gates Adv. Reading	.45*	−.09	.14	
Gates Oral Diagnostic	.20	.23		
Roswell-Chall Sounds	.22	.23		
Roswell-Chall Words	.24	.23		
Roswell-Chall Syllab.	.32	.14		
WISC Info.	.36	.17		
WISC Comp.	.45*	.39*		
WISC Arith.	.00	.07		
WISC Simil.	.29	.08		
WISC Vocab.	.61**	.31		
WISC Verbal Scale	.52**	.30		
WISC Pict. Comp.	.20	.13		
WISC Pict. Arr.	.18	.29		
WISC Block Des.	−.02	−.06		
WISC Obj. Assem.	.00	.16		
WISC Coding	−.23	−.29		
WISC Perf. Scale	.07	.06		
WISC Full Scale	.27	.04		
Digit Span	.15			

* $p < .05$
** $p < .01$

the two samples selected on reading ability, mean different scores of 23.15 and 25.83, with standard deviations of 3.5 and 1.9, respectively, are obtained. These mean scores at this age level would both fall into Wepman's category of "inadequate development." (For children age eight and older, this category comprises all scores below 27.) The greater variability of the retarded reader group is a consistent finding for many measures. The Wepman means and standard deviations for the samples unselected on reading ability are 25.49, with a sigma of 2.77 for the fifth-grade sample, and 21.40 with a sigma of 6.0 for the first-grade sample. These scores also fall into the "inadequate development" category. However, the exact meaning of these scores, especially for the fifth-grade sample, must remain in doubt in the absence of specific statistical breakdowns along socioeconomic and reading ability parameters.

To sum up the significant relational findings in Table 12–1, it is possible to say that the Wepman correlates with few other measures, but that these measures include only those which relate to verbal skills. More significant relationships are found between Wepman scores and verbal measures for retarded readers than for normal readers among fifth-grade children, and for first-graders as opposed to fifth-graders when the subjects are unselected in terms of reading ability.

One other kind of Wepman-verbal relationship is worthy of mention.

For one of the studies which yielded the data reported in Table 12–1, five-minute expressive speech samples were elicited from 120 of the children in the samples which were unselected on reading ability. These 120 included 60 fifth-grade children, and 60 from the first grade. The speech protocols were scored for 18 verbal measures, such as the Type-Token Ratio, and the percentages of various parts of speech in a sample of a given length. These scores were correlated with each other, and with the Wepman; it is only the latter results which are of concern here. The overwhelming majority of the correlations between these measures and the Wepman was not significant, and the figures are therefore not reported in tables here. However, it is well to note that our inference from the few significant relationships which were obtained is that good Wepman performance may relate to lack of redundancy in speech in first-grade children—an interesting finding in the light of the pathological speech entity known as "cluttering." Redundancy in speech may well be a less severe form of cluttering, and if so, as with many speech disorders, one would expect to find reduced auditory discrimination ability associated with it. This finding may or may not have import for the hypotheses relating environmental circumstances to perceptual development. But the fact that Wepman scores are related to the speech measures, as might be predicted that they would be, does lend some substantiation to the validity of the Wepman as an auditory discrimination measure for the samples used here.

Another series of studies emphasized the relationship to learning —particularly reading—of perceptual rather than language skills. Specifically, the studies related visual and auditory efficiency to reading ability and to such tasks as serial learning. Let us now consider these data, which were treated by analysis of variance.[*]

The data are reported by technique, with a separate tabular pres-

* Some of this data has been reported in the previous chapter. The reader may want to refer to Chapter 11 for other related findings.

entation for each one. The number of subjects included for each technique is indicated on the appropriate table. The subjects represented in successive tables are in most cases different children, so performance on one of the tasks cannot be related to performance on the others. All the groups had in common lower socioeconomic status, and they were all Negro males. Half of them represent the upper third in reading ability in their school group ("Good readers"), and half represent the lowest third ("Poor readers").

Table 12–2 shows the Wepman data. From it can be seen that the Wepman differentiates good from poor readers at the .001 level of confidence. This would tend to confirm the finding, reported in Table 12–1, of a significant relationship between Wepman score and score on the Gates Reading Test for the fifth-grade retarded readers. Table 12–2 also shows that the Wepman differentiated among the age groups, with older children having significantly better scores. The interaction between age and reading is also significant. Inspection of the data underlying this finding reveals that the differentiation between reading groups is less for the older children than it is for the younger ones.

Table 12–2

WEPMAN AUDITORY DISCRIMINATION TEST: COMPARISON OF GOOD AND POOR READERS IN THE THREE GRADE LEVELS

($N = 8$ in each group)

	GRADE 1		GRADE 3		GRADE 5	
	Poor Readers	*Good Readers*	*Poor Readers*	*Good Readers*	*Poor Readers*	*Good Readers*
Mean Number of Errors	18.1	7.8	10.0	5.5	7.8	6.9

Result of analysis of variance:
  Age level: $p < .01$
  Reading level: $p < .001$
  Age x reading level: $p < .01$

Data obtained on the bimodal reaction time apparatus show that older children have significantly faster reaction times to stimuli, irrespective of modality or of sequence of stimuli. It is also apparent that, for all the children, the cross-modal reaction time is longer than the ipsi-modal. But the significant interaction between reading level and modality shift indicates that poorer readers are disproportionately slower in cross-modal reaction time than are good readers. This substantiates a finding reported on the basis of initial studies done earlier. These data, then, would indicate that poorer readers have poorer auditory discrimination and that they have greater difficulty in shifting from one modality to another.

Table 12–3 reports the data on the combined form of the Continuous Performance Test (CPT)—that is, the form in which auditory and visual stimuli are interlaced. Here we see a reversal in the trend of the findings: the response to the auditory stimuli was more correct than to the visual, and the interaction between reading level and modality indicates that the auditory functioning was disproportionately superior for the retarded readers. Katz[7] has explained this finding in

Table 12–3

Continuous Performance Test—Combination Form (Mean Percentage of Correct Responses): Comparison of Good and Poor Readers in Three Grade Levels

($N = 8$ in each group)

| | MODALITY | | |
Sample	Auditory	Visual	Auditory and Visual
Grade 1			
Poor Readers	80.0	45.5	62.8
Good Readers	62.7	54.1	58.4
All Grade 1	71.4	49.8	60.4
Grade 3			
Poor Readers	83.5	43.4	63.4
Good Readers	78.7	75.5	77.1
All Grade 3	81.1	59.4	70.3
Grade 5			
Poor Readers	87.5	85.9	86.7
Good Readers	86.5	87.0	86.5
All Grade 5	87.0	86.4	85.6
All Subjects	79.8	65.2	72.5

Significant results of analysis of variance:
   Age level: $p < .01$
   Modality: $p < .01$
   Reading level x modality: $p < .05$

terms of different strategies of approach on the part of the good and the poor readers. She believes that the poor readers attend only to stimuli in one modality and block out the other. Such a theory, which seems eminently plausible in view of the data, would emphasize again the difficulty for the retarded readers of shifting from one modality to the other. It must be pointed out here that the auditory task for the subject on the CPT is quite different from the one presented by the Wepman. On the CPT, discrimination is called for—but it is between names of colors, none of which sounds very similar to the "correct" color (i.e., the one in response to which the subject is to press the button) which is "red." On the Wepman, of course, the pairs of words presented differ minutely, and only at either the beginning or the end of the words. Further, the stimuli on the CPT are presented serially, and a judgment is required for each one, while the Wepman stimuli are pairs of words.

When we consider data pertaining to the use of the two modalities for learning, we find once again (see Table 11–8, page 249) slightly poorer performance with auditory presentation. The discrepancy here between the visual and the auditory modalities is enhanced in the case of the poorer readers, and the poorer readers are also slower in serial learning generally. The older children learn more quickly than the younger ones, and this is also true for the data on Digit Span performance (see Table 11–6, page 247).

Here too the poorer readers are poorer. The differences in favor of auditory presentation found here are suspect, as Katz[7] reports that several of the first-grade children did not recognize the numbers when they were presented visually (see Table 11–6). If, on further study of only older children who recognize the printed numbers, the auditory difference is confirmed, that might be related to the similar finding on the CPT. Here, however, it would be necessary to evaluate the results in terms of the relative verbalness of the stimulus material. As Milner[8] points out, even the effects of brain lesions can differ, depending on the content of the stimulus material used to test the function. She says that the degree to which the material is verbal is the crucial parameter.

The data presented so far can be summed up in terms of the characteristics of poor readers: they have more difficulty with auditory discrimination; they have greater difficulty in shifting from one modality to another and back again; and they are more inefficient at a serial learning task when the stimuli are auditory than when they are visual. In all these findings, the performance of poorer readers as related to better readers parallels the performance of younger children as compared with older ones. It will also be remembered that in the data presented earlier the poor readers showed higher correlations between auditory discrimination and verbal and intelligence measures, and that the younger children showed also a greater relationship between the auditory measure and the verbal measures. Further, the retarded readers showed a significant relationship between auditory discrimination and reading score, while this was not true of the normal readers of the same age and socioeconomic background.

There are two discrepancies in this picture. The poorer, as well as the better, readers make better scores on the auditory presentations on the CPT, and likewise on the auditory presentation on the Digit Span. The importance of this discrepancy will have to be evaluated in the light of further data analysis. Such analysis will have to consider the relative scores on the all-auditory and the all-visual forms of the CPT (the scores reported are for the combined form only) and further evaluation of the Digit Span, excluding children who do not recognize the numbers visually.

In returning to the main body of the results, however, one is struck by the apparent importance of auditory discrimination and general auditory responsiveness for verbal performance and reading ability, specifically. Such a finding would have support in Hardy's[5] analysis of reading disabilities in terms of disorders of communication. Further, if one uses his three-function analysis of auditory mechanisms, involving tracking of the acoustic stimuli, it is necessary to regard auditory discrimination and recognition as basic to the more advanced processes. These processes are: (1) *processing* (ability to perceive rapidly successive bits of information, as in perceiving speech); (2) *pattern-making* (capacity to relate this information in terms of significance to past and present behavior); and (3) *retention*. In these terms, discrimination between sounds presented successively and recognition of sounds singly or in patterns would be basic to both receptive and expressive communication skills. Further, these receptive and expressive skills cannot be separated into two distinct functions, but must be seen as aspects of the same basic language process. If reading does belong in that category, then it is highly likely that a skill which underlies other aspects of communication processes would also be strongly related to, and influential in, the development of reading ability.

The similarity between the retarded readers and the younger children leads to an hypothesis of immaturity in these basic functions on the part of the retarded readers. This would support deHirsch's[3] hypothesis of "neurophysiological immaturity" in many children with reading and with language defects. Since in the absence of irreversible brain lesions (or of a critical-time postulate which would indicate that the critical time was past) immature skills can mature, it is possible to construe the age by reading skill interactions as evidence for the maturation of the functions under consideration.

Most reading-readiness tests in current use emphasize readiness in terms of visual perceptual skills, rather than auditory ones. Most of these tests have been constructed with middle-class subjects in mind. Most of the subjects who contributed to the data presented here were lower-class children. If the hypotheses presented in the first part of this paper can be accepted, it may well be that lower-class children, who live in very noisy environments, do not develop the requisite auditory discrimination abilities to learn to read well—or adequately— early in their school careers. In contrast, middle-class children from quieter and more speech-directed environments would not have this problem. It is not meant here to imply that all children from disadvantaged environments are going to be poor in auditory discrimination, while all middle-class children are going to have adequate skill in this area. Rather, the implication is that the conditions under which children live, particularly early in life, are going to affect auditory skill in a predictable way. Within this framework, large individual differences are possible among children who live in close proximity to one another, depending, for example, on the amount of speech and other meaningful auditory "signals" which are directed toward them. Middle-class children do live in a more speech-directed environment and at the same time in a less noisy and crowded one (i.e., there is both more signal and less noise in the system), and this could have a direct effect on their auditory skills.

Thus it might be that reading research which includes mainly middle-class subjects would not discover auditory discrimination problems to be as widespread as would research directed mainly to the child from deprived areas. This is not to say that reading experts have not known all along that auditory functioning was involved in reading, but only that it has been the visual which has been stressed— and successfully so with middle-class children. But the discrepancy in incidence of reading retardation between middle-class and lower-class children is very large, and it is possible that at least a portion of this discrepancy is attributable to differential difficulties in auditory discrimination. This hypothesis is, of course, a testable one.

This reasoning leads me to postulate that a particular minimum level of auditory discrimination skill is necessary for the acquisiton of reading and of general verbal skills. Once that minimum level is reached, perhaps, auditory discrimination is no longer highly correlated with these abilities. If true, this would account for the decreasing differentiating ability of auditory tasks as children—retarded and normal readers—get older. Of course, even if the auditory skills should mature simply as a result of time and the children's exposure to the school situation, without specific recognition of the problem and training in the area, it would be possible for children with such deficiencies—or immaturities—to fall far behind in many aspects of their school work and thus be unable to catch up, even when the deficiency is overcome. This would, of course, underline the importance of training in auditory discrimination early in the school career. And certainly it would emphasize the importance of such training in any pre-school program directed to lower-status children, a population in which the base rate of reading retardation is extremely high.

In one sense, this whole paper has been concerned with the interaction and interpenetration between the more social and the more biological factors in human development. Auditory discrimination is clearly a function mediated by the nervous system; yet it can be profoundly influenced by the conditions of life of the individual, and, in turn, can affect his relationship to his environment and the people in it. According to data reported by Pasamanick[10] and others, the nervous system of the developing embryo is very susceptible to influences from the mother's nutritional state, which in turn is strongly influenced by the socioeconomic status of the mother. Thus, not only does man's environment influence him, but it may be that it plays a role in molding his very reactive processes to it. This holds out great promise for the potential effects of programs such as our preschool enrichment which are designed to vitiate the deleterious effects of deprived environments. Such programs might really effect lasting changes.

REFERENCES

1. Cherry, C. Two ears—but one world. In W. Rosenblith (Ed.), *Sensory communication.* Cambridge: MIT Press and New York: Wiley, 1961. Pp. 99–117.
2. Cohen, J. The factorial structure of the WISC at ages 7–6, 10–6, and 13–6. *J. consult. Psychol.,* 1959, 23, 285–299.

3. DeHirsch, Katrina. Tests designed to discover potential reading difficulties at the six-year-old level. *Amer. J. Orthopsychiat.*, 1957, **27**, 566–576.

4. Fowler, W. Cognitive learning in infancy and early childhood. *Psychol. Bull.*, 1962, **59**, 116–152.

5. Hardy, W. G. Dyslexia in relation to diagnostic methodology in hearing and speech disorders. In J. Money (Ed.), *Reading disability: Progress and research needs in dyslexia.* Baltimore: Johns Hopkins Press, 1962. Pp. 171–177.

6. Hernández-Peón, R. Reticular mechanisms of sensory control. In W. Rosenblith (Ed.), *Sensory communication.* Cambridge: MIT Press and New York: Wiley, 1961. Pp. 497–520.

7. Katz, Phyllis A. Visual and auditory efficiency and its relationship to reading in children. Progress Report, 7/1/62–12/31/62, Cooperative Research Project No. 1099 of the Office of Education, U.S. Department of Health, Education, and Welfare.

8. Milner, Brenda. Laterality effects in audition. In V. Mountcastle (Ed.), *Inter-hemispheric relations and cerebral dominance.* Baltimore: Johns Hopkins Press, 1962. Pp. 177–195.

9. Myklebust, H. R. *The psychology of deafness.* New York: Grune & Stratton, 1960.

10. Pasamanick, B., & Knobloch, Hilda. Epidemiologic studies on the complications of pregnancy and the birth process. In G. Caplan (Ed.), *Prevention of mental disorders in children.* New York: Basic Books, 1961. Pp. 74–94.

11. Raab, Shirley, Deutsch, M., & Freedman, A. Perceptual shifting and set in normal school children of different reading achievement levels. *Percept. mot. Skills*, 1960, **10**, 187–192.

12. Scott, J. P. Critical periods in behavioral development. *Science*, 1962, **138**, 949–958.

13. Wepman, J. *Manual of directions: Auditory Discrimination Test.* Chicago: Author, 1958.

PART III

Aspects of Race and Social Class
in the Education and Integration
of the Disadvantaged Child

13 /

Dimensions of the School's Role in the Problems of Integration

MARTIN DEUTSCH

We often move from the social to the psychological to the educational level with a great ease, maybe with too much ease. Often we lose thereby a real appreciation of what some of the transitional determinants might be. Particularly is this so when we are concerned with the education of all children and with the kinds of major changes in social structure that are required by the Supreme Court decisions and by the changes in American life in the last decade. We now ask, what can a school system accomplish? What can we accomplish to make integration meaningful, and what are some of the antecedents required in order to produce a social basis for work toward a truly integrated experience for the child?

The role of the school here carries with it certain very special responsibilities. The school has become a pivotal point of a very real social struggle: the struggle for the full realization of our social potential, the struggle for the kinds of social equality that will result in the maximizing of opportunities for all children. It is also—and I feel it is only—through education that disproportionate subgroup concentration in the lower socioeconomic groups can be influenced so that at least social-class barriers to true integration will be minimized. Many of the barriers we talk about are social-class barriers, but they have become caste as well as class barriers because of the particular history surrounding the institution of slavery and the period after the Emancipation Proclamation.

There is no longer any question of the critical role of the environment in the growth of the child. The major questions that remain here relate to the specifics of the interaction between environment and development and the differentials which may exist in the potency of various influences at different stages of development. Segregation is an aspect of experience in the growing up of both Negro and white children, and this experience plays a crucial role in determining their developing attitudes toward the self and toward the human condition. It must be obvious, further, that an essentially nondemocratic experience does not foster the growth of a democratic value system.

Now, it should be recognized that, with the kinds of inadequate environment that have been described in many places, and that I also have talked about in other chapters, many children will not be offered an opportunity to reach their full potential. As long as institutionalized forms of discrimination are maintained, as long as Negro and white children do not have a chance to touch the future in the present through integrated experiences that are meaningful, neither group is being adequately prepared for the future. I think this point is vital because it is now clear to all but the Neanderthals that the future will see an integrated America. Social change, though we might not see it from our particular vantage point, is moving quite rapidly, and the momentum is likely to increase considerably as time goes on. Certainly what is now termed the social revolution of 1963 has underlined this.

Segregated conditions play a particularly invidious role in the child's growing up. These conditions create an incorrect picture of America and an incorrect picture of what kinds and types and forms of human relations are possible. But, in a more specific psychological sense, they do not give the Negro, Puerto Rican, or most other minority-group children the tools for handling daily intergroup, interpersonal relationships or the strategies that are instrumental for handling the kinds of problems that must be overcome to achieve individual success in our society. An example of this would be the role vicissitudes involved in locating and negotiating for a job.

If the school is to play a major part in at least partially compensating for the unhealthy kinds of environments associated with poverty and segregation, one has first to assume that this function is a desirable one. My assumption is that this part is, in fact, a necessary one; I can identify no other institution that is in the position of the school to influence significantly the development of all children.

The school must be a vital institution in the whole process of social change. The struggles around questions of strategies and goals of integration could lead to a real revitalization of education. The problems surrounding the integration question go to the core of the guiding philosophies in American education and place the educator in the role of an engineer of social change. There are many other social forces that we would like to see play a part, but one cannot sit back and wait and hope that social change will take place simultaneously on every level. One has to identify the influential elements that can be introduced from one's own daily activities; for us here this means dealing with the problem of the child and the school.

As the school gets oriented toward this role—sometimes on its own volition, sometimes with much external pushing and shoving—certain limitations emerge which are inherent in its own structure, history, and organization, and in the social context in which it finds itself.

To digress for a moment: It is interesting to note a particular confluence of events. At the time of the first Sputnik, great anxiety was expressed as to inadequacies in the American educational system. Many suggestions were made for major alterations and most especially for more status and prestige for the educational system and its personnel in a general recognition of their role in the overall development of the child's intellectual, creative, and general psychological capabilities. Aside, however, from some content changes in curricula and a generally healthy focusing on problems of intellectual development, relatively little change accrued from discussion of this so-called "crisis." However, the then-recognized need for major institutional modifications emerges most dramatically in the present very real crisis surrounding, generally, the integration problem and, specifically, the issue of facilitating the development of the individual potential in America's underprivileged. This crisis situation not only alters the consciousness of educators in regard to a section of the population, but of necessity improves the possibilities for real basic alterations in both structure and philosophy that will have positive influence on the development of all youth, i.e., privileged and underprivileged. In this sense, the struggle for an integrated America offers an opportunity for a most critical evaluation of present inadequacies in the educational system and accomplishes what the external competitive condition—i.e., Sputnik—could not.

Let us return, though, to a consideration of the obstacles in the way of the school's assumption of major new roles.

Some of the limitations come from the larger social community. The ambivalence of much of the community to allow complete integration must be recognized; for example, there are advantages for the status quo in having a large, low-paid, marginal population. Such economic factors and the attendant psychological conditions of a pecking hierarchy yield to some the facade of automatic status and superiority, and here we find a source of some of the ambivalence and much of the hostility toward integration.

I would hypothesize that the corruption of human potential that is inherent in all situations where there exist caste and class symbols for superior and inferior status is virulent in a classroom which reflects these conditions. Too often rewards are based not on individual accomplishment, but on things like tested intelligence levels, race, and father's occupation. A major obstacle, then, which must be overcome is the intrusion of these values into the classroom. To do so, preservice and in-service training must assist the teacher to perceive social relationships from a broader perspective than her own class position. In a sense, not to prepare the teacher to be able to do this could effectively sabotage meaningful integration.

Another obstacle is the historical drag of the actual behavior systems which are at variance with the explicit value system. This obstacle makes it difficult for teachers and administrators—who are often under pressure—to recognize that much must be altered in terms of the new matrix of our social system, in terms of the demand for equality, and in terms of what equality really means. This recognition carries with it the conviction that social contradiction can, to some extent, be handled through the processes of the school. To accomplish this objective, the school, with reference to other institutions, should demand an unequally large amount of funds, educationally qualified individuals, institutional structures, experimental programs, and what have you, in order to create maximally fostering conditions for the realization of individual potential for the child from a deprived environment. This is, I think, one of the basic principles with which we have to concern ourselves. *If society takes away, if society has maintained a hundred years of second-class citizenship for the Negro, if society always insists that new migrants—regardless of what ethnic group—maintain some kind of secondary citizenship for a few generations, then it becomes society's role to compensate for this loss*—and it is a tremendous loss of potential. This is especially true now as so many of the traditional steps on the occupational ladder are disappearing with increasing technology. More and more America is confronted with a large mass of unskilled, unemployed people, a disproportionately high percentage of whom come from minority groups, while there are many skilled, relatively highly specialized and paid, occupational categories searching for workers.

As was previously pointed out, the school has an important role in society's compensation for the situation. But there will always be some lag, some segment where the child has not caught up, as long as we have a society that allows discriminatory conditions and, most important, is not actively engaged in giving behavioral reality to its explicit democratic value system. That means an active, intense, frontal struggle for meaningful integration. Further, if the schools are to be successful in their efforts, the first demand must be for the support and enrichment of the school system itself by the community.

Related to problems of compensation is another obstacle; it arises from the failure to plan for social change, so that occupational and economic necessities change faster than either static institutional situations or human beings can accommodate. This is again a rather crucial element in the school situation. So much development and modification have taken place, and there has been such very real change in urban America, that the school has had created for it much more than its previous passive educational role. The school can no longer simply receive children and test, grade, and categorize them without reference to their individual social backgrounds, their latent and manifest cognitive strengths, their attitudes toward learning, and their aspirations. Instead, the school is becoming a very active participant in preventing certain forms of mental illness and in preventing juvenile delinquency, and on a more positive side, in really developing human potential to the maximum level of which the individual is capable.

Now, if we do not become discouraged by more social microscopic conditions that inhibit change, and we, instead, look especially at the school and what the possibilities might be there, the school—as the most sensitive, and as one of the most significant points for social change—has a problem in itself. It has, so often, and certainly in all large urban areas, become a bureaucratic dinosaur, and now it is being asked to funnel, digest, and utilize the work of the human sciences and of education in a creative manner to handle social problems. A degree of social engineering is called for that I don't think is asked of any other institution. The magnitude of the task does not mean that one has to be patient while these obstacles are worked with, but it does mean that the system has to plan, to re-think the fundamental issues, and to come out of it with some kinds of systematic formats for operations and changes in the educational structure and in educational curricula.

There are a few points here that relate to what the school can do on an everyday basis in order to accomplish some of the objectives discussed here. One is in terms of the educational apparatus itself, another is in terms of the enrichment of the child, and a third relates to the larger community.

Let us consider first an aspect of the educational apparatus.

In response to challenge, education has the disadvantage of a long and encumbering history. In a sense, the institution of education —the school—*is* the status quo. It often operates through huge, politically oriented bureaucracies that continually inhibit its potential for change and for developing strategies for meeting social crises such as those inherent in the new urban America. These bureaucracies are often so large that introduction of meaningful change, even when agreed on by the higher echelons, is limited by the clogging of communication channels with paper, red tape, and assorted other artifacts, and by the constraints under which the average classroom teacher operates. A chasm is created between policy and implementation, and as a result many inconsistencies are produced. For example, well thought-out and efficient systems are instituted for bussing children across districts to accomplish physical integration, but, too often, once the children are in the new school a laissez-faire attitude prevails. There are too many children who sit in a segregated island in a so-called integrated classroom, with there being no real attempt to help the children establish some intergroup, interpersonal knowledge and relationship. One possible technique, for example, in a newly integrated classroom would be to use a simple autobiographical method, where each child tells something about himself and his interests and aspirations, so that through the formal structure of the classroom children will have a basis for accumulating a little personal knowledge of each other as individuals.

While, of course, the school cannot assure that children in the same classroom will relate to each other well, particularly when there are large social class differences, it can be aware of the problem and devise techniques, such as the one suggested above, within the formal curriculum, to increase the probability of interpersonal relationships. Here is where it is necessary for specialists in disciplines such as anthropology, sociology, and social psychology to be actively involved in evaluating and guiding this process. These specialists can not only help to devise specific methods and techniques, but they can give in-service training to teachers and administrators aimed at helping them to understand the problems of sociocultural dissonance. The social scientists should have considerable independence, so that they do not become cannibalized and digested by the bureaucracy; at the same time they should function as an indigenous part of the school system.

The suggestion of social science contributions to school integration within the context of discussing the activities of the school system with regard to its own organization stems from the understanding that physical integration can be considered only a first step in the process. Physical integration is a necessary step, but it must not be confused with the goal of compensating the child for experiential deprivation which interferes with his receptivity to the learning process, and prevents him from participating and competing on the basis of his own abilities. Successful participation involves a whole complex of social and psychological factors, including self-image, achievement motivation, sensory and linguistic development, and the like. The effects of discrimination and impoverishment on these attributes have been discussed extensively in the recent literature. However, in the context of the school's role in integration, the nullification of these detrimental consequences is the major goal. It is here that the active participation of school personnel is so necessary, and it is here that education has the opportunity both structurally and functionally to reorient itself to changing social realities.

Simple mechanical implementation of physical integration can make a farce of real integration. I have seen too many administrators and teachers who see integration as an unwelcome threat to the *status quo* and their "power prerogatives," and these people can nullify real implementation. It is necessary for the system to have the flexibility to reeducate or remove such personnel. It must be stated that many of the people who thus impede real progress do so through a dedication to the bureaucratic forms in which education has so often immobilized itself, rather than through any active desire to frustrate the goals, though in many instances such activities may be accompanied by highly internalized social class prejudices based on a different orientation toward life and differing expectations of children's behavior and performance. For example, I have noted in in-service courses the tendency on the part of some teachers to engage in extremely tenuous psychologizing of the children's behavior and reactions. This tendency is manifest particularly around the interpretation of hyperactivity, attentional shifting, and inhibited communication with the teacher. Actually, non-middle-class children do not, for the most part, conform to middle-class classroom behavior mores, and the teacher interprets the apparent withdrawal of the child in psychological—or pseudo-psychological—terms. It is true that the teacher does not receive from these children the kinds of reinforcement that come from an actively expressed curiosity and from an uninhibited verbal rapport. This places on the teacher an extra responsibility to delay her gratification until she has won the trust of the children and successfully interpreted to them the demands of the school situation. Standard teacher training as yet does not equip the teacher with the understanding and techniques necessary to accomplish this. So it becomes the responsibility of the school itself—and particularly the urban school—to provide the appropriate in-service training to both new and experienced teachers and administrators. In the absence of such training, it is hard to know how effective school personnel can be in fostering the true goals of integration.

A much-discussed major issue in the organization of integrated schools is that of heterogeneous versus homogeneous ability groupings. Within the normal intellectual range there may be strong arguments for homogeneous grouping, but at the same time there are also sound arguments for the heterogeneous organization. When we consider the classroom which contains children of widely differing backgrounds, the issue becomes more than simply one for educational argument. In a general sense, this problem is becoming more important than bussing of children and redefining of neighborhood boundaries. Most important, it should influence the composition of school populations and the locating of many new schools in border areas. These actions have the effect of insuring heterogeneity of background of children in each classroom. Under these conditions, homogeneous grouping creates *de facto* segregation in the classroom. Therefore, if there are to be integrated experiences there must be heterogeneous groupings.

Though this is not the place to go into it, there are also strong arguments as to possible advantages in the homogeneous learning situation. However, with the overlap between deprived circumstances and minority group membership, there will be a bunching up of minority group scores at the lower end of the continuum. Homogeneous grouping serves to underline the racial category with a derivative of it, which is secondary status in the classroom. It is true that this is often disguised by assigning noninvidious identifications to the ability groupings, but I have yet to meet a child who cannot identify his ascribed status. If heterogeneous grouping makes for some unfairness to the majority group child, that is simply the price that must now be paid for a hundred years of segregation and lack of attention to the special educational problems of the minority child. The better and the faster the school can adjust to and formulate curricula consistent with our changed urban society, the lower the price will be. In other words, the school should not extract a further price from the minority-group child for integration, but instead tax itself to develop techniques that are appropriate for groups of diversified ability. This issue is essentially a moral one, and the learning situation has enough inherent strength to encompass the forms that will be demanded. Basically, the track system is an example of the unwillingness of the community to pay the price. The use of the track system can easily become extremely rigidified, and despite efforts to the contrary, it can lock many children within early-determined expectation and accomplishment boundaries.

Another problem of homogeneous groupings, and most specifically of an all-pervasive track system, is the determination of the teacher's expectations of the child and her inevitable, even if unintentional, communication of these expectations to the child. As so often happens in the development of any system, the doors of each compartment become locked, and what is created is an intellectual ghetto. The fact that some administrators point to cracks in the wall—and a few children do squeeze through these cracks—does not reduce the reality of the closed doors. It is objectively very difficult to get away from differing sets of expectations for the children in different tracks or groups. These expectations seep into the teacher-child interaction and into the learning process. A tendency develops to reduce the level of the stimuli presented to conform with the expectations of the child's performance. When a particular child answers a question correctly, instead of consciously raising the demand level for him, the tendency is to keep this level constant for a period of time and thus adjust to the performance expectations for the group. So what is developed is a kind of compression system. While the argument is often advanced that heterogeneous groupings can be unfair to the child who is farthest from the group norm, the same can be said of the homogeneous group, especially as regards the child who is starting to move intellectually and reaching in the direction of his potential.

Another overriding consideration that relates to the total school experience and to all aspects of integration is the development of the child's self-image and the need to help him to build a sense of respect for himself and his intellectual capabilities, whatever they may be. The lower-class child experiences the middle-class oriented school as discontinuous with his home environment and comes relatively poorly prepared in the basic skills on which the curriculum is founded. The school becomes a place which makes puzzling demands and where failure is frequent and feelings of competence are subsequently not generated. The best theoretical model relating to this process, I think, is White's theory of competence motivation.[1] He points out that experiences of success and accomplishment engender feelings of competence which in turn generate primary motivation. As was indicated, the school experiences of the socially deprived child do not easily yield success, and special effort and programming are required to build motivation.

So often the school experience is an intellectually frustrating one as the child is always being compared and graded, if not any longer on a racial basis, on an intellectual and personality one. He is being compared with his teacher's model-image of middle-class children, with his classmates, with national norms, with the highest achieving youngster in his class, etc. We could have a much more motivating and a much more democratic educational system if each child were instead, in effect, used as his own control by having each successive performance compared with the previous performance. In this way, a child's performance could be evaluated not on the cross-sectional aspects of achievement, but on the longitudinal axis. The child's failures would be in terms of his own antecedent scores rather than competitively determined by the performance of others. He would be able to achieve real gratification from accomplishments that compare favorably to other children in terms of magnitude of improvement rather than placement on the achievement hierarchy. This procedure would be one way of nullifying the accumulated frustrations so often for these children associated with intellectual activities, and particularly with early school experience. When we talk about the school compensating a child for life inequalities, much of that compensation must be in the area of building motivation and finding ways of creating more positive concepts in regard to both the self and the intellective activities.

It is again in this area that the mechanical application of integration could have additional harmful implications. In order to get away from prejudice, many school systems have dropped all reference to really crucial life variables like race. In essence, I think this represents a most invidious form of prejudice. Children cannot grow up with a consistent and positive concept of the self if the fact of being Indian or Negro becomes a source of embarrassment or something that for some reason the environment insists on not mentioning. The fact of being Negro or white can no more be ignored than can that of being boy or girl, as it carries with it certain on-going personal, social, and cultural connotations. Teachers, both white and Negro, must be helped to deal with questions of race and intergroup relations on an objective, frank, professional basis, or their embarrassment and circumventing of the issue will somehow always be communicated to the child, and to the Negro child the connotation attached will be a negative one and will have a depressing influence on his motivation and social integration in mixed groups.

This discussion has consistently returned to the vital role of the adult, most particularly the teacher, in influencing the child's developing self and social perceptions through her interaction with him. Another aspect of the child's performance around which this process takes place is intelligence test scores. I do not here want to go into the question of the validity of the IQ, beyond observing that with increasing massive social intervention it should increasingly become a much poorer predictor of school success for the child from marginal circumstances. Rather, I want to point out that the child's IQ score—no matter how valid or invalid as a predictor of later achievement—can become the basis for the teacher's expectations of his performance, and through a variant of the process delineated earlier, can come to have a large and negative influence on his school progress. Again, in terms of the whole question of self-image and building a psychology of competence, it might be worthwhile to use the intelligence test only as a clinical diagnostic instrument. In this way, another potential source of negative feedback could be eliminated.

If, though, the schools insist on the maintenance of the IQ, there is potentially a way of working it out, though much investigation is still required. In a symposium at the American Psychological Association meetings in 1960, Otto Klineberg pointed out that one can anticipate that children from underprivileged areas will have lower IQ's along certain dimensions, and that these dimensions can potentially be identified and perhaps some formula can be constructed to allow for the effects of background inequities. Data collected at the Institute for Developmental Studies demonstrate that, when controlling for social class, fifth-grade Negro children without fathers in the home tested significantly lower than similar children with fathers in the home. Concomitantly, Negro lower-class children with preschool experience tested significantly higher than those without such experience. What the intervening variables might be is not relevant here, though one could speculate that they might have something to do with the presence or absence of opportunities for increased adult-child interaction. The point is that there are environmental circumstances that play a direct role in lowering IQ's and that the result of these circumstances should not be codified in the school records and form a basis for the child's curriculum or for the teacher's interpretations. Hopefully, we will some day come to the point where we can have a whole series of multiple equations by which one can recognize that a certain set of circumstances will yield a particular set of consequences. For example, the absence of a preschool experience would perhaps be worth three or four IQ points; certain specific levels of poverty and deprivation, the existence of discrimination or experience of certain types of discrimination, the existence or the nonexistence of a father in the home, and the like, could also be judged as to their value in IQ points, and a score could be calculated for each child on the basis of such formulas.

No matter what the circumstances, children cannot be helped to develop their potential intellectual strengths if the community and society do not supply the school system with the funds to create the therapeutic tools to do the job. One of the keys to successful integration is the facilitation of intellectual and psychological growth so that the detrimental influences associated with poverty can be overcome by the focused efforts of reoriented school curricula. Of course, there are other interrelated roads: housing, jobs—the whole social macrocosm. But our job here is to concentrate on that area in which we hopefully have some small influence.

In other papers I have emphasized the importance of utilizing behavioral science knowledge in programming learning sequences, in training teachers in the social aspects of the learning process, and, most particularly, in the development of specialized, systematic enrichment programs, with low teacher-pupil ratios, full-time kindergartens, intensive preschool experiences, and ungraded early grade sequences. If society will not supply the money for these things, the schools will fail to accomplish what the current social situation requires. In this rich, abundant economy of ours the funds must be there. And when human need and our need as a society for the potential contributions from all people are strongly enough recognized, the funds will be made available, especially when social survival may be dependent on the development of these human resources. But even with the funds, the schools could fail if they are not ready for the metamorphosis to the active role previously discussed. Programs to reverse the effects of deprivation cannot be put together in a day, and people can't be trained in a month to carry them through. This hasty preparation has been a consistent weakness of many programs which have been established. The children, society, and the problem deserve teachers and administrators who have been extensively trained and selected to do the job. Also, programs to raise the horizons of children must not be allowed to be dominated by public relations needs, or by an urgent requirement to get results. It is necessary for programs to be rigorously evaluated, carefully researched, to be conducted on an interdisciplinary basis—for all the human sciences have a lot to contribute—and it must be recognized that it is better to get results a year later and for these results to have depth and a temporal stability, than for ephemeral changes to be registered quickly.

A note of caution must be sounded as to the choice of methods best to insure the goals of integration. We must be concerned that even with open enrollment and bussing, the location of neighborhood schools be consciously planned wherever possible in such a way as to draw on a heterogeneous population. The point here is that open enrollment, bussing, etc., place an extra burden on the minority group child and his parents, and wherever this can be eliminated through rezoning, new construction, and the like, it should be done, thereby not placing the burden of change on the child.

There may be certain circumstances where the physical conditions of integration may be of less immediate importance than establishing the most fostering environment for cognitive growth. For example, one or two hours daily spent in the whole bussing operation might be too much to require of a child in order just to sit with white children in some distant neighborhood. It might be better if we keep in mind the eventual aims and goals, and have the child spend three hours in a type of all-day neighborhood school, fully equipped to offer the most fostering and most highly developed educational experience for him. I would also be somewhat concerned about bussing middle-class white or Negro children into slum areas. It is not that this would necessarily be bad for the children, but that it could do great damage to the potential for integrating schools by provoking irrational fears on the part of parents, resulting in the massive withdrawal of middle-class children—both white and Negro—from the public schools, and creating a completely class- and caste-segregated public school system. The danger here is particularly apparent in regard to people of newly arrived middle-class status, as one of the major sources of inter-group conflict is the perceived threat to newly achieved but insecurely held social status. I am not suggesting that insistence on middle-class or lower-class children having to travel to boundary areas should be relaxed, nor that children should not be bussed from one district to another. Rather, what I am saying is that bussing, for example, which at best is one of many possible steps in the right direction, should not be confused with the goals of eventual indigenous integration. Neither should the use of bussing be seen as an end in itself and permit the schools to relax after they have worked out bussing arrangements. There is always the danger that a bureaucratic system will for all practical purposes rest content with the form and mechanics of integration. As previously pointed out, what goes on in the classroom is the real issue. It is only through a massive improvement of his educational experience that the child will develop the abilities to achieve more secure social status. Thereby a basis will also be established for full social integration.

It can be noted that the bulk of this discussion relates to counter-acting the effects of poverty, segregation, and attendant deprivation and reflects areas needing special attention if the integrated experience is to be interpreted meaningfully by the school for the child. Of course, in the broadest sense, the objective is to assist children in the realization of individual potential leading to the jumping of social class boundaries. The eventual aim of school integration, thought of in this social context, is to eliminate the largely ethnic basis of social-class membership and to create conditions in which basic ability will be the determinant of social mobility, and of individual self-realization.

REFERENCE

1. White, R. Motivation reconsidered: The concept of competence. *Psychol. Rev.*, 1959, 66, 297–333.

14 /

Social Influences in Negro-White Intelligence Differences

MARTIN DEUTSCH AND
BERT R. BROWN

This paper reports on some aspects of experience that influence the development of intellective functions in children. The social experiential variable is often treated in the psychological literature in a most macroscopic manner. It has been one of our purposes to break down the attributes of social experience along what might be called social environmental and developmental dimensions.

As regards the social environmental, the attempt has been to analyze racial-group membership by some of its psychological properties, to determine some of the components of social class, and to determine something of the interaction of the two, particularly as it impinges on intellectual achievement and growth.

On what we are calling the developmental dimension, the focus has been on identifying "experience groups" in terms of language, perception, learning, general intellective functioning, and to a lesser extent, self, attitudinal, and motivational variables. These variables, in turn, have been broken down into more specific components for measurement and for evaluation of interrelationships.

The data have been collected on cross-sectional samples, but the work is closely associated with a large-scale longitudinal study which attempts to manipulate mediating environmental variables and to measure any subsequent behavioral modification or facilitation in intellectual growth. The cross-sectional study referred to is a large social-class and race analysis, involving first- and fifth-grade children, which we colloquially refer to as the "Verbal Survey"—a term which is something of a misnomer, as the range goes beyond verbal measures.

This report is concerned with the intellectual test differences between Negro and white first- and fifth-graders of different social classes—though the focus in this report is largely on the lower class. Two more specific independent variables of special significance are presence or absence of father in the home, and whether the child had an organized preschool experience.

The data reported in this paper are from a sample of 543 urban public school children stratified by race, grade level (first- and fifth-graders), and social class, as measured by the Institute's twelve point SES scale. This scale is derived both from prestige ratings of occupation as well as education of main breadwinners and yields a weighted index of these factors for each subject in the sample. The distribution of index scores is broken down into twelve levels and subsequently trichotomized into three socioeconomic strata. SES comparisons reported in this paper are made among three distinguishable social-class levels, I, II, and III, where level I represents the lowest group on the continuum and III the highest. Housing condition for these S's was evaluated along a six-point continuum from "Sound, with all plumbing facilities" to "Dilapidated" following from the technique suggested by the U. S. Census of Housing.[9] The weighted SES index score correlates .27 with the housing-condition index for a sample of 292 children within the larger group of 543. The magnitude of this correlation is low but significant for the sample size on which it was obtained.

The intelligence test used was the Lorge-Thorndike, Level 1, Primary Battery for first-graders, and Level 3 for fifth-graders. Both forms, as described by the authors, are essentially non-verbal.[8] Level 1 uses pictorial items only to measure abstract thinking, pictorial classification, and pictorial pairing. Level 3 uses picture classification, pictorial analogies, and numerical relationships. This test was selected because of the inclusion in its standardization population of a much better than usual representation of the lower social-class categories. The test was given in small groups, during school hours, by trained examiners on the Institute's research staff.

The SES data were gathered by mailed questionnaires and home interviews. The SES items were only a part of the interview schedule. The rest of the items had to do with home conditions, daily routine, and aspirations of both parents and children. The appropriate items here are now being collated into a "Deprivation Index" for purposes of identifying the sources of inter- and intra-class variation.

Table 14–1 presents results of a three-way analysis of variance using Lorge-Thorndike IQ scores as the dependent variable. It can readily be seen that fifth-grade IQ scores do not differ significantly

Table 14–1

ANALYSIS OF VARIANCE[a] AND CELL MEANS ON LORGE-THORNDIKE INTELLIGENCE TEST PERFORMANCE BY GRADE, RACE, AND SOCIAL CLASS

($N = 543$)

Source	Sum of Squares	df	F	Significance
Grade	634.429	1	3.153	N.S.
Race	10,119.416	1	50.296	p < .0001
SES	14,429.344	2	35.859	p < .0001
Within	106,834.966	531		
Total	137,656.866	542		

[a] Interaction terms have been omitted from the table, as none reached significance.

MEAN LORGE-THORNDIKE IQ SCORES FOR SES GROUPS, RACE GROUPS WITHIN SES GROUPS, AND TOTAL RACE GROUPS[b]

Group	$\bar{X}$	SD	N
SES I			
White	97.24	15.35	104
Negro	91.24	13.25	157
Total	93.63	14.43	261
SES II			
White	105.59	14.88	68
Negro	94.87	14.70	111
Total	98.94	15.67	179
SES III			
White	114.92	12.05	52
Negro	102.57	14.53	51
Total	108.81	14.70	103
Total Race Groups			
White	103.88	16.12	224
Negro	94.32	14.53	319

[b] Two-tailed t-tests for differences between total race groups and SES levels significant at $p < .01$.

from scores achieved by first-grade children. Differences between scores of Negro and white children can be seen to be highly significant ($p < .0001$) and are equally strong between SES levels. Examination of the secondary tables of means and sigma's for subgroups within each of these variables indicates the direction and magnitude of these differences. Clearly, the means for white children are significantly higher than are mean IQ scores for their Negro counterparts and the relationship is documented by t-test differences between race groups reaching significance at $p < .01$. Similarly, inter-level differences are significant for SES groups at $p < .01$. While the analysis of variance does not indicate a significant race by SES interaction, inspection of the means shows: (1) that Negro children at each SES level score lower than white children, and (2) that Negro-white differences increase at each higher SES level. While children in each racial group show gain in IQ with ascending SES level, gains for the white group appear to be considerably greater.

These results are consistent with other data[1, 4, 6] and could reflect the ascending isomorphism between social class and the item content of intelligence tests. Nevertheless, such results are usually predictive of school achievement, although their meaning with regard to individual potential may be questionable.

It is extremely interesting to note this more sharply defined escalation of the white majority group child's IQ through the three social-class steps. In the lowest class, where social deprivation is most homogeneous and the influence of race is attenuated by the pervasiveness of poor living conditions, there is somewhat less difference, as has been mentioned, between Negro and white.

To summarize: (1) a linear relationship exists between SES and performance level for both Negro and white groups, and (2) within this linear relationship the absolute increase in IQ is greater for the white group than it is for the Negro.

The interpretation put forth here for these data is that the influence of racial membership tends to become increasingly manifest and crucial as the social-class level increases. The hypothesis we would advance has to do with increased participation in the cultural mainstream, and the differing conditions under which Negroes and whites participate (see Chapter 3). The weight of color and resulting minority status, it is postulated here, results in much less participation by the Negro, while the lowest class status operates similarly for the white as well as for the Negro. In other words, it is much more difficult for the Negro to attain identical middle or upper-middle-class status with whites, and the social-class gradations are less marked for Negroes because Negro life in a caste society is considerably more homogeneous than is life for the majority group This difference makes it extremely difficult ever really to match racial groups meaningfully on class status as the context and history of social experience are so different.

There is support for the "participation" hypothesis in some social-background data. These data indicate that there are fewer variegated

Table 14–2

INCIDENCE OF FATHER'S PRESENCE IN THE HOME BY RACE WITHIN SES GROUP

($N = 543$)

Condition	SES I WHITE		SES I NEGRO		SES II WHITE		SES II NEGRO		SES III WHITE		SES III NEGRO	
	N	%	N	%	N	%	N	%	N	%	N	%
Father present in home	(88)	84.6	(88)	56.1	(61)	89.7	(80)	72.1	(52)	100.0	(44)	86.3
Father *not* present in home	(16)	15.4	(69)	43.9	(7)	10.3	(31)	27.9	—	0.0	(7)	13.7
N =	(104)		(157)		(68)		(111)		(52)		(51)	

Note: χ^2 for SES × father condition = 28.01, 2 *df*, $p =$ <.001
χ^2 for Race × father condition = 39.152, 1 *df*, $p =$ <.001

family activities, such as eating together or taking trips, in the Negro as opposed to the white group. These differences are especially apparent at the lower SES levels. It may well be that such family experiences operate differently at the higher SES levels, but our data for the SES III group are incomplete and there is no indication that the differences would reach statistical significance.

This information demands that we probe even more carefully into background variables as possible sources of some of the variation in intelligence scores found in different population groups.

One of the most striking differences between the Negro and white groups is the consistently higher frequency of broken homes and resulting family disorganization in the Negro group. Indeed, Table 14–2 indicates that this phenomenon varies directly with social class and with race, both at $p < .001$ by χ^2 test.

We are *not* here considering the very real historical, social, and economic antecedents of this condition, but are instead simply making an empirical observation. Since in the vast majority of cases the home is broken by the absence of the father, this is used as a rough indicator of family cohesiveness. The absence or presence of the father has been shown in other studies to relate to need achievement and aspiration levels, especially of boys[2] (see also Chapter 6).

Table 14–3 presents the results of a four-way analysis of variance of Lorge-Thorndike scores, using sex, grade, race, and presence of father as independent variables.

As can be seen, significant differences are obtained on the race and presence of father variables, with white children scoring higher than Negro, and children coming from homes where fathers are present having significantly higher scores than children from fatherless homes. None of the interaction terms was statistically significant (SES could not be included in the analysis of variance because in our Class III sample there were no white fatherless families. Thus, by dropping SES III's from this analysis, the N here becomes 440).

To get at the influence of father's presence on intelligence score within groups, several additional comparisons were made. Because the absence of significant interactions in the data might relate to the strong pull exerted on the scores by race differences, the data from the Negro sample were subjected to specific analysis within grade and SES. Special attention was paid to lower SES, as the number of homes without fathers was largest in this group, and the comparisons, thus, were more meaningful.

Table 14–4 presents the comparisons for first- and fifth-grade Negro children in the lowest two SES groups.

As is seen from Table 14–4, a consistent trend within both grades at the lower SES level appears, and in no case is there a reversal of this trend: for males, females, and the combined group, the IQ's of children with fathers in the home are always higher than those who have no father in the home. In addition, a constricted range of performance, as reflected in standard deviation units, is found among fifth-graders without fathers in the home, as opposed to both first- and fifth-graders in homes where fathers are present.

Differences between first- and fifth-grade children, controlling for father in home, are not significant, and they are not reported here in tabular form. Within the Negro lower-class there is a consistent dec-

Table 14–3

ANALYSIS OF VARIANCE[a] ON LORGE-THORNDIKE INTELLIGENCE SCORES BY SEX, GRADE, RACE, AND PRESENCE OF FATHER IN THE HOME

(*SES Groups I and II only, N = 440*)

Source	Sum of Squares	df	F	Significance
Sex	8.726	1	<1.000	N.S.
Grade	404.317	1	1.882	N.S.
Race	2,580.069	1	12.013	<.01
Father in Home	954.073	1	4.442	<.05
Within	91,490.127	424		
Total	101,313.415	439		

[a] Interaction terms have been omitted from the table, as none reached significance. The obtained *F* value in each case was less than 1.00.

MEANS FOR RACE GROUPS[b]

Group	$\overline{X}$	SD	N
Negro	92.75	14.02	268
White	100.72	15.91	172

MEANS FOR FATHER CONDITION[b]
(*Combined Race Groups*)

Condition	$\overline{X}$	SD	N
Father in Home	97.83	15.25	317
No Father in Home	90.79	14.18	123

[b] *Note:* *t*-tests for differences between race groups and father condition significant at $p < .01$.

rement in IQ level from the first to fifth grade, there again being no reversals in direction in sex or father-in-home categories. (In comparisons made between first- and fifth-graders in the white lower-class sample there is a nonsignificant increment in score from first to fifth grade.)

While the specific interaction term for this break in the previous four-way analysis of variance did not reach statistical significance, the data in Table 14–4 are presented for the purpose of identifying cells in which IQ differences, as predicted by family stability, are greatest. Also the specific descriptive data are revealing in that there is no reversal of trend even though the analysis of variance did not yield statistically significant results.

Further analysis will reveal if the Negro score decrement from first to fifth grade is accounted for by the greater proportion of broken Negro homes. This also might account for some of the differences between Negro and white intelligence scores.

A weakness in these cross-sectional data is that there is no reliable way of knowing how long the fifth-grade children have lived in homes without fathers, or whether this has been a recurrent or a consistent condition. But it is reasonable to assume that on the average the fifth-graders have had more fatherless years than the first-graders. If this assumption is tenable, then what we might be tapping is the cumulative effect of fatherless years, and if so, might explain why the first-grade differences are not significant: they are simply not significant *yet*. This hypothesis is supported by the limited variance reported in Table 14–4 for fifth-grade children from fatherless homes in contrast to the greater variance shown among children on the same grade level but coming from homes in which fathers are present.

A second, and perhaps more parsimonious, explanation for this finding is that IQ tests at the fifth-grade level may tap more responses which directly relate to the role of the father in the family structure for both boys and girls. This finding might have particular reference to the cohesiveness of the family and the variety of activities in which the family participates, and most specifically may simply reflect the quantity of verbal interaction engendered through the medium of family organization and activity.

Another background variable which might relate to intelligence test performance is the amount and timing of schooling the child has had. As with the father variable, it was thought that the more opportunity the child has for adult-child contact, conversation, and experi·

Table 14–4

PERFORMANCE ON THE LORGE-THORNDIKE INTELLIGENCE TEST AMONG LOWER AND LOWER MIDDLE CLASS (SES I AND II) NEGRO CHILDREN WITH AND WITHOUT FATHERS PRESENT IN THE HOME

Group	FATHER PRESENT			FATHER ABSENT		
	$\bar{X}$	SD	N	$\bar{X}$	SD	N
Grade 1						
Male	95.55	15.74	31	87.71	21.70	28
Female	94.50	10.39	10	88.20	12.19	5
Total	95.24	14.51	41	87.78	20.40	33
SES I						
Grade 5						
Male	90.81	13.14	26	83.41	9.65	17
Female	95.19	14.73	21	87.70	9.75	20
Total	92.77	13.89	47	85.73	9.81	37
Grade 1						
Male	98.35	12.18	26	92.80	18.64	10
Female	99.27	12.99	15	—	—	—
Total	98.68	12.33	41	92.80	18.64	10
SES II						
Grade 5						
Male	94.78	15.12	23	91.75	15.67	16
Female	90.25	17.19	16	93.00	12.27	5
Total	92.92	15.89	39	92.05	14.65	21

ential variety, the more positive the influence on his performance. Also Fowler's analysis[5] pointed out the importance for the child of cognitive stimulation and practice in the early years. As was seen in Lee's study[7] of IQ differences between Negro children born in Philadelphia and those who migrated there from the South, consistently higher IQ test scores were obtained by children who had the longest residence in the presumably more fostering northern environment. Lee's data also show a consistent difference in favor of Negro children who had a kindergarten experience, as compared with those who did not. Therefore, an experiential variable selected for analysis in the present study was whether or not the child had any formal preschool educational experience. Because of the variety of types of preschool experience—some children had nursery and no kindergarten, others reversed—the variable was treated dichotomously as "some preschool experience" or "no preschool experience."

Table 14–5 reports results of a three-way analysis of variance of Lorge-Thorndike scores for fifth-grade children by sex, race, and preschool experience.

Table 14-5

ANALYSIS OF VARIANCE[a] ON LORGE-THORNDIKE INTELLIGENCE SCORES BY SEX, RACE, AND PRESCHOOL EXPERIENCE

(Grades 5, SES I and II only, $N = 246$)

Source	Sum of Squares	df	F	Significance
Sex	128.204	1	<1.000	N.S.
Race	1,785.477	1	7.873	<.01
Preschool Experience	1,619.750	1	7.143	<.01
Within	43,083.956	238		
Total	50,027.132	245		

[a] Interaction terms have been omitted from the table, as none were significant. The F value in each case was less than 1.00.

MEANS FOR RACE GROUPS

Group	$\overline{X}$	SD	N
Negro	90.90	13.89	144
White	99.82	16.40	102

MEANS FOR PRESCHOOL CONDITION[b]

Condition	$\overline{X}$	SD	N
Preschool Experience	97.42	15.72	152
No Preschool Experience	90.65	14.32	53

[b] N's for Preschool Condition reduced from total N for fifth grade due to missing data.

As can be seen, race differences are significant at the $p < .01$ level, and so are preschool experience differences. Those children who have had preschool experience score significantly higher than those without. Again the interaction terms were not significant.

Table 14-6 presents the same analysis for the first-grade group. Here, while the significant race difference in test performance prevails ($p < .05$), the difference as predicted by preschool experience is not significant, although *directionality* is still apparent. In other words, presence or lack of preschool experience at grade 5 more highly differentiates intelligence test scores than it does at grade 1. Nevertheless, at grade 1 this variable still differentiates between the two groups ($p. < .10$), though not within the convention limits of statistical significance.

This finding is consistent with those for the father-in-home vari-

Table 14–6

ANALYSIS OF VARIANCE[a] ON LORGE-THORNDIKE INTELLIGENCE SCORES BY SEX, RACE, AND PRESCHOOL EXPERIENCE

(Grade 1, SES I and II only, $N = 194$)

Source	Sum of Squares	df	F	Significance
Sex	17.283	1	<1.000	N.S.
Race	1,152.579	1	5.817	<.05
Preschool Experience	609.235	1	3.074	<.10
Within	25,162.214	186		
Total	27,148.326	193		

[a] Interaction terms have been omitted from the table as none reached significance.

MEANS FOR RACE GROUPS

Group	$\bar{X}$	SD	N
Negro	94.90	13.92	124
White	102.01	15.27	70

MEANS FOR PRESCHOOL CONDITION[b]

Condition	$\bar{X}$	SD	N
Preschool Experience	100.03	13.99	112
No Preschool Experience	94.48	16.24	23

[b] N's for Preschool Condition reduced from total N due to missing data.

able, and, therefore, lends support to the cumulative deficit hypothesis previously advanced: that deprivational influences have a greater impact at later developmental stages than at earlier ones.

The effect of the father-in-home variable on IQ for this sample has been shown in the data presented here. What is less easily measurable, but may nonetheless exist, is the potential systematic lowering of Negro children's IQ by the greater prevalence of broken homes in Negro SES groups I and II. In our samples, for example, there is a significantly greater frequency of broken homes among the Negro group, as compared with the white, and it is hard to estimate what the overall effect may be of this family instability in the development of the Negro child. From these data, it is quite conceivable, if not probable, that one effect would be the systematic lowering with age of IQ scores of the children where markedly unfavorable social conditions exist.

The data presented here represent only a small portion of those we have collected on the children in the various samples. When one surveys the entire mass of data, what is striking is the fact that on most of the *social* variables the Negro group shows greater deprivation. This fact is true within social-class categories, with the possible exception of Social Class II, though even there the factors associated with racial discrimination and caste are still quite operative. The class and caste discussion of Dreger and Miller[3] shows adequate recognition of this problem. The conclusion is inescapable that the Negro group is a socially deprived one, and that whatever other measures and functions are sensitive to social effects will also reflect this deprivation.

We are attempting to measure the ingredients of deprivation with the aim of developing a typology of deprivation which organizes experience in developmentally relevant groupings that can be related to sources of socially determined group variation in IQ performance. It would seem probable that when behavioral scientists have been able to classify and measure the elements and variables in social deprivation, the observed differential in intelligence test scores between Negro and white samples will be accounted for.

The present data on family cohesion and preschool experience represent two possible environmental modifiers of intelligence test performance that would seem to account for a portion of differences found between ethnic, class, or experiential groups. If these are influential variables, a positive implication is that they are amenable to social intervention and change.

References

1. Anderson, W. F. Relation of Lorge-Thorndike Intelligence Test scores of public school pupils to the socioeconomic status of their parents. *J. exp. Educ.*, 1962, 31 (1), 73–76.
2. Ausubel, D. P., & Ausubel, Pearl. Ego development among segregated Negro children. In A. H. Passow (Ed.), *Education in depressed areas.* New York: Teachers Coll. Bureau of Publications, Columbia Univer., 1963, 109–141.
3. Dreger, R. M., & Miller, K. S. Comparative psychological studies of Negroes and whites in the United States. *Psychol Bull.*, 1960, **57**, 361–402.
4. Eells, K., Davis, A., Havighurst, R. J., Merrick, V. E., & Tyler, R. *Intel-*

ligence and cultural differences. Chicago: Univer. Chicago Press, 1951.

5. Fowler, W. Cognitive learning in infancy and early childhood. *Psychol. Bull.*, 1962, **59**, 116–152.

6. Kennedy, W. A., Van De Riet, V., & White, J. C., Jr. A normative sample of intelligence and achievement of Negro elementary school children in the southeastern United States. Monogr. Soc. Res. Child Develpm., 1963, **20**, No. 6.

7. Lee, E. S. Negro intelligence and selective migration: A Philadelphia test of the Klineberg hypothesis. *Amer. sociol. Rev.*, 1951, **16**, 227–233.

8. Lorge, I., & Thorndike, R. L. *Lorge-Thorndike Tests of Intelligence,* Specimen Test Booklet. New York: Houghton Mifflin, 1959.

9. U. S. Bureau of the Census. *U.S. census of housing,* 1960, **3**, City Blocks, Series HC(3), Nos. 274–276.

15 /

Race and Social Class as Separate Factors Related to Social Environment

RICHARD D. BLOOM, MARTIN WHITEMAN, AND MARTIN DEUTSCH

There have been numerous studies in which some measure of social class has been used to identify and classify the backgrounds of a sample of respondents. Myrdal,[2] however, has pointed out that race also plays a significant part in defining the social condition of individuals. Thus, regardless of his class level, a Negro may experience less access to such societal features as good housing, educational facilities, and job opportunities than does his white counterpart. It would seem relevant, therefore, to evaluate *both* race and social class as separate factors determining social environment. Unfortunately, many previous studies have not been able to carry out such an evaluation satisfactorily because their sample designs have often confounded race and class. This problem arises from the difficulties in finding Negro and white respondents distributed in similar proportions in each social class.

The present study made an effort to overcome this problem by means of a sample in which race and social class are empirically independent of each other. It is hoped that the data in this study will clarify the following issues: (1) the similarities and differences in the patterns of association which race and social class hold with a number of attitudinal and environmental variables; and (2) the extent to which race and social class jointly interact in defining and influencing environmental conditions and attitudes. For the latter problem, interest is not centered upon the simple associations between race or social class and the dependent variables. Rather, the concern is with the extent to which the associations between class and the dependent variables show differential patterns from race to race. Fourteen dependent variables were studied, but only those which showed statistically significant associations will be reported. Those variables not showing significant relationships dealt with the respondents' exposure to mass media.

RESEARCH PROCEDURES

The sample consisted of children and parents who were involved in an on-going research project on cognitive processes. The group of children consisted of approximately equal numbers of Negro and white boys and girls in the first and fifth grades. The sampling procedures aimed at securing a study group in which the social-class level would be adequately represented within each race. Therefore, in selecting the sample, schools located within census tracts with known socioeconomic characteristics were used to identify likely areas containing families of certain social and racial groups. The school records then were examined to provide a list of students from which the sample was randomly selected.

A total of 340 pairs of parents and children was originally chosen. This N was reduced to 292 as a result of the inability to complete interviews with either the parent or the child. Chi-square analyses of this sample indicated that the lack of an association between race and social class was maintained.

The social-class standing of the sampled households was measured by an index consisting of two equally weighted components: the educational level of the main support of the family and a prestige rating of his (her) occupation based on the North-Hatt study.[3] The distributions of the scores for these components were totaled for a combined index value. The distribution of these totaled scores was then trichotomized into the following levels.

Level I. A typical family in this group has as a main wage earner a person who is unemployed, or who has an unskilled or semiskilled job. The educational level is likely to range from elementary schooling to completion of the eighth grade.

Level II. The typical family at this level is headed by a wage earner with a semiskilled, clerical, or sales job whose education ranged from about nine grades to high school graduation.

Level III. The typical household is headed by a professional or managerial wage earner whose education would be high school graduation, college, or graduate work.

The data were based primarily on personal interviews with the children and responses by parents to a questionnaire which was mailed to them. An effort was made to interview as many as possible of the parents who did not return the forms. For these interviews, the same questions were used as those in the mailed questionnaire. No differences in the distributions of responses were noted between parents answering the questions by mail or in the home interview.

The format for both the parental and child questionnaires consisted primarily of questions requiring the respondent to supply specific information; there were also some open-ended questions. Most of the data were obtained from a parent. In a few instances, children supplied the data. Each table indicates which source was used. The adequacy of coding responses to the open-ended questions was determined by having independent coders recode a 20-per cent random sample of the questionnaires. The reliability check showed an agreement of at least 90 per cent between coders.

RESULTS AND DISCUSSION*

Table 15–1 presents the percentages for each dependent variable found to be significantly associated with either or both social class and race. Table 15–2 lists the significance of these associations.

There are two characteristics in which Negroes (regardless of class) and the Level I group (regardless of race) show the same direction of association. Thus the housing of Negroes and Level I respondents is rated as more dilapidated than is the housing of others (Table 15–1, B). Similarly, there is a higher incidence of the father being absent from the home in the Negro and Level I samples (Table 15–1, A). As race and class are empirically independent of each other in the sample, it is possible to suggest explanations for these results. The quality of housing may be determined by patterns of segregation in the case of the Negro, or by poverty for the Level I group. The absence of the father may reflect a historically based matriarchal tradition in the Negro family[1] or an unstable family organization resulting from the stress of adverse economic conditions in the lowest social group.

* The results are analyzed by a χ^2 model appropriate for complex contingency tables. In essence, this model allows for the partition of the total χ^2 and degrees of freedom into components analogous to factorial analysis of variance designs. In this study, the total χ^2 is partitioned into separate tests of association of race and social class with a given dependent variable. In addition, there is also a test of the combined association of race, social class, and the dependent variable. A thorough discussion of the use of χ^2 for multiple classification designs is provided by Suttcliffe.[4]

Table 15–1

PERCENTAGE (AND NUMBER) FOR THE DEPENDENT VARIABLES FOUND SIGNIFI-
CANTLY ASSOCIATED WITH RACE OR SOCIAL CLASS

A. FATHER PRESENT IN THE HOME [a]

| | CLASS LEVEL | | | |
	All %	I %	II %	III %
All	85	72	90	97
	(281)	(106)	(102)	(73)
Negro	78	62	85	93
	(143)	(55)	(55)	(33)
White	92	82	96	100
	(138)	(51)	(47)	(40)

[a] Data source: parental response.

B. DILAPIDATED HOUSING [b]

| | CLASS LEVEL | | | |
	All %	I %	II %	III %
All	63	77	54	55
	(292)	(109)	(106)	(77)
Negro	70	78	64	68
	(153)	(58)	(58)	(37)
White	56	76	44	45
	(139)	(51)	(48)	(40)

[b] The data were derived from the 1960 Census tracts' rating of housing adequacy. Inasmuch as the housing ratings were available for blocks within Census tracts but not for specific household units, a mean weighted index was computed from the distribution of housing units rated as falling into the categories of sound versus varying degrees of dilapidation. A household having an index of three or above was classified as dilapidated.

C. PARENTAL EDUCATIONAL ASPIRATIONS FOR CHILD; DESIRES SOME DEGREE OF COLLEGE TRAINING [c]

| | CLASS LEVEL | | | |
	All %	I %	II %	III %
All	94	88	96	98
	(288)	(108)	(106)	(74)
Negro	97	96	97	100
	(150)	(57)	(58)	(35)
White	89	79	95	97
	(138)	(51)	(48)	(39)

[c] Responses were dichotomized between parents who desire their children to have a high-school education versus those who desire college training (including college graduation and post-graduate work). No one in the parental sample indicated aspirations below high school.

D. PARENTS DESIRING HIGH STATUS OCCUPATIONS FOR THEIR CHILDREN [d]

| | CLASS LEVEL | | | |
	All %	I %	II %	III %
All	88	75	94	97
	(244)	(95)	(88)	(61)
Negro	93	86	96	100
	(129)	(51)	(50)	(28)
White	82	64	92	94
	(115)	(44)	(38)	(33)

[d] The occupations were rated on a ten-point scale as derived from the research of North and Hatt.[3] Occupations rated seven and above were categorized as high-status positions.

E. CHILD'S OWN OCCUPATIONAL ASPIRATIONS; DESIRES A HIGH-STATUS OCCUPATION

	CLASS LEVEL			
	All %	*I* %	*II* %	*III* %
All	70 (229)	55 (73)	72 (84)	81 (72)
Negro	78 (96)	65 (26)	84 (37)	82 (33)
White	64 (133)	49 (47)	66 (47)	80 (39)

F. PARENTAL PERCEPTION OF OWN STATUS AND CONDITIONS IN SOCIETY: THOSE PERCEIVING THEIR STATUS AS IMPROVING [e]

	CLASS LEVEL			
	All %	*I* %	*II* %	*III* %
All	65 (283)	53 (107)	68 (103)	79 (73)
Negro	76 (149)	68 (57)	72 (57)	94 (35)
White	54 (134)	36 (50)	63 (46)	66 (38)

[e] Parental responses were dichotomized between those who perceived their status in society as improving versus those who perceived their status as remaining the same or going down.

G. CROWDEDNESS IN THE HOUSEHOLD [f]

	CLASS LEVEL			
	All %	*I* %	*II* %	*III* %
All	36 (292)	47 (109)	37 (106)	20 (77)
Negro	35 (153)	57 (58)	33 (58)	5 (37)
White	37 (139)	35 (51)	42 (48)	33 (40)

[f] Based on a person-to-room ratio as obtained from information provided by the parent. A household with a ratio of 1.5 or greater was classified as crowded.

H. ADULT RESPONDENTS HAVING UPWARD OCCUPATIONAL MOBILITY [g]

	CLASS LEVEL			
	All %	*I* %	*II* %	*III* %
All	17 (243)	9 (82)	20 (97)	23 (64)
Negro	15 (130)	11 (44)	13 (54)	22 (32)
White	20 (113)	5 (38)	28 (43)	25 (32)

[g] The main breadwinner in a household was classified as upwardly mobile if his current job was rated as more prestigeful (by the North-Hatt scale) than his first permanent job. The table represents a dichotomy between respondents having upward occupational mobility versus those whose status has remained the same or has gone downward.

I. CHILDREN WHO HAVE A NUTRITIONALLY ADEQUATE BREAKFAST [h]

	All %	I %	II %	III %
		CLASS LEVEL		
All	25	17	27	34
	(287)	(106)	(105)	(76)
Negro	25	19	30	28
	(151)	(58)	(57)	(36)
White	25	15	23	40
	(136)	(48)	(48)	(40)

[h] Data were obtained from reports by the children of the kinds of foods they had for breakfast on the day they were interviewed. A nutritionally adequate breakfast was defined as consisting of juice or fruit, milk, cocoa, or tea, and one or more of the following —cereal, eggs, cheese, meat, and bread.

J. MOTHER'S PRESENCE WITH THE CHILD AT BREAKFAST [i]

	All %	I %	II %	III %
		CLASS LEVEL		
All	32	28	34	36
	(287)	(107)	(104)	(76)
Negro	25	23	26	25
	(150)	(56)	(58)	(36)
White	40	33	43	45
	(137)	(51)	(46)	(40)

[i] Each child was asked to recall whether or not he had breakfast with his mother on the day preceding the interview.

K. PARENTS PERCEIVING THEIR CHILD AS READING ADEQUATELY FOR HIS AGE [j]

	All %	I %	II %	III %
		CLASS LEVEL		
All	79	71	81	86
	(256)	(94)	(90)	(72)
Negro	73	66	78	77
	(131)	(50)	(46)	(35)
White	85	68	84	95
	(125)	(44)	(44)	(37)

[j] Each parent was asked whether child was reading satisfactorily for his age.

A second group of findings concerns the similarity of patterns of association between Negroes and the Level III respondents. The results contradict the stereotype of the Negro parent being intrinsically less motivated for his child than his white counterpart. As shown in Table 15–1, C and D, Negro parents, regardless of class level, and Level III parents, regardless of race, show similar aspirational patterns. Thus Negro parents express significantly higher occupational and educational aspirations for their children than does the white group as a whole. This trend is also reflected by the Negro children themselves (Table 15–1, E) whose occupational aspirations are significantly higher than those of the white children. Somewhat related to the above pattern, Table 15–1 F, indicates that, in comparison to the Level I respondents and to all white respondents, Negroes show a significantly higher tendency to perceive their condition in society as improving.

These findings may be one manifestation of the current push by Negroes for equal rights, self-improvement, and greater integration into American society. The higher aspirations may also reflect an understanding by the Negro that in a "white world" he must aim higher and be better in order to get as far as his white counterpart.

A third set of relationships points to aspects of family life which are class-linked rather than associated with race. G, H, and I of Table 15–1 show that there are more crowded housing conditions in Levels I and II than in Level III; that there is less actual occupational mobility in Level I than in Level III; and that children in Level I households are less likely to have nutritionally adequate breakfasts than are children in Levels II and III. Such characteristics as these seem to be a product of educational and economic disadvantage rather than anything related to either race. Negro-white differences in these characteristics are not significant. This conclusion would be qualified somewhat with respect to crowdedness of housing (Table 15–1, G). Here the picture is complicated by the significant interaction between class and race. The greater crowdedness in Level I is especially striking among the Negro respondents. Negroes in Level I have even less living space than would be predicted from knowledge of race and class taken as separate rather than as interacting attributes.*

A fourth group of findings (Table 15–1, I, J, and K) refers to characteristics which are linked to race and not to class. One interesting finding is the significantly greater tendency for Negro than for white mothers not to be present in the home with their children at breakfast.† Such an absence is not clearly related to poverty, for the mother's absence is not prevalent in the lower levels. This measure

* Conversely, Negroes in Level III tend to live in less crowded conditions than their white counterparts.

† No significant associations were noted for the presence of the mother at dinner time. In addition, in those cases where the father was living in the home, no significant associations were found in relation to his presence at either breakfast or dinner.

may reflect a stronger tendency for Negro mothers than for white mothers to work and therefore to have less time for the child. This

Table 15–2

SIGNIFICANCE LEVEL OF χ^2 TESTS OF ASSOCIATION

Dependent Variable	Negro-White	Class Level	Race and Class Level (Interaction)
Father present in the home	.01	.001	N.S.
Dilapidated housing	.02	.001	N.S.
Parental educational aspirations for the child	.01	.001	.05
Parent's choice of child's future occupation	.01	.001	N.S.
Child's own occupational aspiration	.02	.005	N.S.
Parental perception of own status in society	.001	.01	N.S.
Crowdedness in the household	N.S.	.001	.01
Occupational mobility	N.S.	.05	N.S.
Nutritional adequacy of child's breakfast		.01	N.S.
Mother's presence with child at breakfast	.01	N.S.	N.S.
Parental estimation of child's reading ability	.05	N.S.	N.S.

trend may also be symptomatic of family instability as reflected in the higher incidence of the Negro father not living in the home. A further finding is that proportionately fewer Negro than white parents perceive their children as reading adequately. One interpretation of this result is that because Negro parents have high aspirations for their children (as suggested by some results described above) they are likely to be especially critical of their children's achievement.

A fifth point refers to the paucity of statistically significant interactions between race and social class. Thus, the relationships between social class and various environmental conditions are generally similar in the white and Negro samples. However, the social effects of race and class may combine in defining and influencing social conditions. To use a more familiar example, intelligence and motivation probably contribute to much of the variance in scholastic achievement. Although intelligence and motivation do not necessarily interact, they might combine so that the lowest achievers are those with the least ability and lowest motivation. In a similar way, the cumulative social effects of race and class may be reflected in some of the observed

Negro-white differences—for example, housing dilapidation. In this case, a Negro rated in a lower social class is likely to live in highly dilapidated areas not only because of his poverty, but also because of the patterns of housing segregation which exist for Negroes in general.

The relative effectiveness of race and social class in predicting environmental correlates comprises the sixth and final point. The results indicate that the association of environmental conditions with social class tends to be stronger than with race. Of the eleven dependent variables evaluated in this study, eight showed stronger relationships with class than with race. Although it is risky to generalize from magnitude of statistical *significance* to magnitude of statistical *association,* one may tentatively conclude that social class may be a more potent variable than race in predicting environmental and attitudinal factors.

CONCLUSION

The results of this study suggest the complexity of the interrelationship between race, social class, and the specific dependent variables. Reflecting this complexity is the fact that Negroes share some characteristics with Level I individuals, but overlap with Level III in others. In addition, some environmental conditions were found to be associated solely with either race *or* class, but not with both. Further research, using sample designs similar to the one used in this study, is needed to clarify these complexities. Thus, it would be useful to delineate clusters of variables which are unique to either race or social class, as well as specific areas in which these parameters interact, if indeed they do.

REFERENCES

1. Frazier, E. F. *The Negro family in the United States.* (Rev. ed.) New York: Dryden, 1942.
2. Myrdal, G. *An American dilemma.* New York: Harper, 1944.
3. Reiss, A. J. *Occupations and social status.* New York: Free Press, 1962.
4. Suttcliffe, J. P. A general method of analysis of frequency data for multiple classification designs. *Psychol. Bull.,* 1957, **54,** 134–137.

16 /

Some Effects of Social Class and Race on Children's Language and Intellectual Abilities

MARTIN WHITEMAN, BERT R. BROWN, AND MARTIN DEUTSCH

There is a frequently replicated finding that socioeconomic status (SES) and racial-group membership are important correlates of children's performance across a variety of measures of ability. Numerous investigations have demonstrated that on the average: (a) lower SES children tend to perform less well than upper SES children; (b) Negroes perform less well than whites; and (c) within SES groups there is a tendency for white children to score at higher mean levels than Negro children.[2,3,5] As Klineberg[5] has noted, the outstanding, and as yet uncontrolled, factor in this research is the existence of considerable intraclass variance and intergroup overlap in the score distributions of measured abilities among these children. Perhaps the most prominent sources of this variability in performance are important differences in environmental conditions which may be experienced by children within the same SES levels or racial groupings.

For purposes of empirical study, SES levels, as well as racial groups, have traditionally been treated as homogeneous entities. This treatment has permitted classification of subjects into groups for comparative analysis, but almost inevitably yields sizable error variance.

The assumption of relative homogeneity has been empirically useful; however, its latent function has been to limit investigators to demonstrating that differences in IQ or in other more specifically defined abilities exist between: (a) children coming from lower- as opposed to middle-class environments, or (b) Negro as compared to white children.

It is of significance that while the replication of these normative differences has been highly consistent, investigators have largely failed to pursue the matter further, and have, thereby, neglected to pose an important question. This question is concerned with the identification of specific features of the lower-class environment which are associated with cognitive and verbal development. Beyond demonstrating that differences between groups exist, we must identify environmental factors which, when present or absent, can be related to performance on measures of these abilities. It is also important to determine whether deficiencies in environmental stimulation, or, more appropriately, environmental "deprivations," have any greater effect on younger as opposed to older children in terms of their developing cognitive and verbal abilities. Presumably, the longer a child has experienced deprivation, the more pronounced should be its effects on the development of these abilities. Related to this question is the problem of the kinds of abilities being studied. Though by no means definitive, there is a body of evidence suggesting that language measures are particularly responsive to the effects of social disadvantage.[1, 6] It would be important, therefore, to compare the environmental correlates of measures varying in the language component.

The purposes of the present study are:

1. To explore whether relations between specific environmental factors and performance on tests of cognitive and verbal abilities are independent of SES and race.

2. To investigate differences between younger and older children in cognitive and verbal abilities in an effort to determine whether the adverse effects of a socially deprived background become more pronounced with the passage of time.

3. To explore whether some specific environmental factors reflecting social disadvantage interact jointly with SES and race to affect children's performance on some cognitive and verbal tasks.

4. To investigate whether the deprivational aspects associated with lower socioeconomic status, Negro status, or some specific environmental factors have greater effect upon more verbal as compared to less verbal tests.

Let us examine the concept of "deprivation" and its use here. Environmental factors can be viewed as socially depriving when at least two conditions are met: (a) when they are predominantly found within certain social groupings such as those defined by SES or race, and (b) when they are associated with impaired performance, e.g., lowered academic achievement.

An environmental condition may be associated with a particular psychological deficit, but it would not be considered socially depriving if the condition were not socially patterned. Thus, a particular mode of child rearing may be associated with cognitive deficits, but we would not consider this as a social deprivation unless the mode of child rearing were more prevalent in one specific segment of the culture than in another. Nor would it be considered as a deprivation unless it also entailed a functional or behavioral deficit.

Social deprivation implies further that the association between social grouping and specific environmental factor is not strictly causal, e.g., not genetically determined, but mediated by more basic societal conditions such as unemployment, poverty, and inequality of opportunity in various areas. With the removal of such conditions, the association between social grouping and the socially depriving factor may vanish. Social deprivation also implies that the association between environmental condition and performance decrement *is* causal, at least insofar as the deprivational factor hampers the learning of the performance in question. From this discussion, it can also be seen that "social deprivation" is a relative term. It is relative in two senses. First, a given environmental factor may be deprivational relative to one social group, e.g., low SES, but not deprivational relative to another social group, e.g., Negro. Second, the environmental factor may be deprivational with respect to one ability or performance, but neutral or even advantageous with respect to other behaviors or functions.

From the above, it follows that the investigation of social deprivations involves both conceptual and empirical steps. The conceptual step implies the delineation of environmental conditions which on an a priori basis might qualify as social deprivations. In our study we have selected fifteen of these conditions from a broader array of over thirty background variables. These fifteen factors include motivational variables, e.g., schooling that parents desire for the child; factors related to the family, e.g., whether or not there is a father in the home; and variables related to parental interaction, activities with adults, and school experiences.

The empirical step stems directly from our conception of social deprivation. Each of these fifteen factors is studied from two vantage points: (*a*) whether it is related to an important psychological function such as reading, and (*b*) whether it is related to an important social grouping such as SES. The environmental conditions which meet these dual criteria might then be viewed as social deprivations. Six factors met these criteria and have been combined into a composite score, the Deprivation Index. The particular items of the Index and the mode of combination will be discussed below.

At this point, it would be well to summarize some of the functions which such an index can serve. The Deprivation Index can play the role of *specifier*, i.e., it contains specific environmental features meeting criteria of social deprivation that we have set down above. It can play the role of *mediator*, i.e., it can help account, at least partially, for the relation between SES and scores on ability tests. It can also play the role of *independent contributor*, i.e., as a set of environmental conditions which accounts for aspects of performance not accounted for by SES or race. Finally, it can serve as an *interactive* variable. Thus, it may, in combination with other background factors, serve to account for performance over and beyond the contribution of the background variables taken singly.

METHOD

A sample of 292 first- and fifth-grade Negro and white children was obtained from 12 elementary schools located in three boroughs of New York City. The schools were selected to maximize the possibility of obtaining samples of Negro and white children with comparable SES distributions. The first and fifth grades were sampled to obtain approximately equal numbers of white and Negro subjects coming from both lower and middle SES backgrounds. The sample was also stratified by sex. Non-English-speaking children were eliminated from this group. This is, of course, a cross-sectional study of first- and fifth-grade children, rather than a longitudinal study in which the same children would have been followed from the first through fifth grade.

An objective estimate of socioeconomic status was obtained for each S by ratings of the occupational prestige and educational attainment of the main support in each S's family. This estimate was used to distinguish three SES levels within our sample: SES I, lower; SES II, lower middle; and SES III, middle.

The Deprivation Index was formed by obtaining a composite score for each S across six background variables. Each variable included in the Index was dichotomized to yield a score of one or two. The summed score was operationally defined as an Index of Deprivation. These variables, and the manner in which they were dichotomized, are identified in Table 16–1.

With the exception of housing information, data on each of these items were obtained either from parents or from S's themselves. An estimate of housing conditions was made for the dwelling unit of each S by obtaining data from the U.S. Census of Housing, by block, for New York City.[7]

The correlations between each of the six environmental variables given above and fifth-grade Gates Reading Score ranged between .20 and .32, all relatively small correlations, but each exceeding chance expectation for a sample of this Size ($N = 167$). The multiple correlation between the six environmental variables and reading grade level scores was .49. In addition, the multiple correlation between these six variables and SES was .48. This overall correlation is significant ($p < .01$), but since it accounts for not more than 25 per cent of the total variance within the sample on these variables, we may conclude that it is not sufficiently redundant with the SES measure to render it useless.

Table 16–1

DESCRIPTION OF VARIABLES IN DEPRIVATION INDEX

Variable	Dichotomized
1. Housing Dilapidation index for block on which S resides, and assigned to him, computed from census data.	1 = Anything less than sound with complete plumbing (either dilapidated or deteriorating). 2 = Sound with complete plumbing
2. The educational aspirational level of the parent for the child.	1 = College or less 2 = Graduate or professional training
3. The number of children under 18 in the home.	1 = 3 or more 2 = 2 or less
4. Dinner conversation.	1 = Did not engage in conversation because: Not allowed to Others participated but child did not No conversation, no indication why Ate alone 2 = Engaged in conversation
5. Total number of cultural experiences anticipated by child for coming weekend—i.e., visiting relatives, family, museums, library, zoo, travel outside New York City, school or lesson work.	1 = None 2 = One or more experiences
6. Attendance of child in kindergarten.	1 = No attendance at kindergarten 2 = Attendance at kindergarten

Each of the six variables may be viewed as an indicator of a specific type of sociocultural deprivation which may occur in varying degree within any SES level, although we would generally suppose high deprivation to be more severe and more frequent within lower as opposed to middle or upper SES groups.

A more "deprived" score on the Index was obtained by those children with a cumulation of the following conditions, each of which is significantly associated with lower SES and with lowered reading achievement at the fifth-grade level. These children tend to have missed kindergarten; their families are larger, more crowded, and located in the more dilapidated neighborhoods; the parents have lower educational aspirations for the children; and the latter report relatively limited conversation at dinner and limited "cultural activities" (as defined in Table 16–1) with parents or relatives. The decision to use a composite index reflects the belief that cumulations of these variables are more significant (and more reliable) than each variable taken singly. The multiple correlations reported above attest to the enhanced effect of the joint action of these variables.

Another problem deals with the cumulative deficit. We have been concerned with the question of whether the adverse effects of a socially deprived background become more pronounced with time. The nature of the performance in which such environment-associated impairments appear also deserves close attention. Though by no means definitive, there is a body of evidence suggesting that language measures are particularly responsive to the effects of social disadvantage

Accordingly, we have analyzed the Deprivation Index simultaneously with two other background variables, SES and race, to determine whether differences on the Index appear independently of SES and race. The analysis has also incorporated age-group differences to see whether obtained decrements in performance are significantly greater among fifth-graders as compared to first-graders—as suggested by the cumulative deficit hypothesis. Finally, a comparison has been made between two measures varying in the language component. These are: (a) a non-language test of general intellectual ability, the Lorge-Thorndike Intelligence Test, and (b) a test of vocabulary knowledge, the Vocabulary subtest of the Wechsler Intelligence Scale for Children. Forms of the Lorge-Thorndike test appropriate for each age level were used. Both forms, as reported by the authors, are designed to measure non-verbal aspects of intelligence. The first-grade form used pictorial items only to measure abstract thinking, pictorial classification, and picture-reading ability. The items found in the fifth-grade form involved picture classification, pictorial analogies, and items requiring distinction between numerical relationships. Both forms are designed for group administration.

• *Statistical Treatment*

Analysis of variance was used to determine the extent to which systematic variation in performance on the two tests occurs as a function of SES, race, age, and Deprivation Index. Since the cell Ns within this analysis are unequal, and in some cases disproportionate, analyses of variance using harmonic mean approximations were carried out on the data. For a full discussion of this procedure, the reader is referred to Winer.[8]

Since simultaneous classification of Ss by four independent variables would have resulted in cell Ns of zero, we have done three analyses in which SES, race, and Deprivation Index were varied, two at a time, together with grade level which was used in each analysis.

RESULTS AND DISCUSSION

• *Analysis of Lorge-Thorndike Test (Non-verbal form)*

Table 16–2 reveals that there were no significant differences between the two age groups on IQ scores. This was to be expected since the IQ, by definition, is adjusted for age. There were, however, significant differences between SES groups and between Negro and white Ss; and a significant interaction between grade and race.

Table 16–3 shows that these differences were in the expected directions with the means for lower SES Ss being smaller than the means for the higher SES groups. In addition to the significant differences between SES groups, the Negro Ss scored significantly lower than did the white Ss.

Table 16–4 reveals that the significant interaction between grade and race was attributable to the stronger Negro-white differences at the fifth-grade level than at the first-grade level. Whereas the Negro children averaged 5 IQ points less than the white children at the first-grade level, this difference increased to 12 points at the fifth-grade level. (The difference between Negro and white Ss reached statistical

Table 16–2

RESULTS OF THREE-WAY ANALYSIS OF VARIANCE ON LORGE-THORNDIKE IQ SCORES BY GRADE, SES, AND RACE

$(N = 292)$

Source	df	MS	f	p
Grade (A)	1	<1.000	0.00	N.S.
SES (B)	2	4362.31	21.61	$<.01$
Race (C)	1	4856.56	24.06	$<.01$
A × B	2	3.24	<1.00	N.S.
A × C	1	883.32	4.38	$<.05$
B × C	2	299.88	1.48	N.S.
A × B × C	2	130.77	<1.00	N.S.
Error	280	201.82		
Total	291			

Table 16–3

MEANS FOR SES GROUPS AND FOR RACE GROUPS ON LORGE-THORNDIKE IQ SCORES

Group	$\overline{X}$	SD	N
SES I	94.31	14.89	110
SES II	102.67	14.83	99
SES III	109.16	14.69	83
Negro	97.01	14.30	152
White	106.08	16.36	140

Table 16–4

MEANS ON LORGE-THORNDIKE IQ SCORES FOR NEGRO AS COMPARED TO WHITE Ss WITHIN EACH GRADE LEVEL

Group	$\overline{X}$	SD	N
Grade 1			
Negro Ss	99.01	13.87	68
White Ss	103.86	14.72	59
Grade 5			
Negro Ss	95.39	14.52	84
White Ss	107.70	17.37	81

significance at the fifth-grade level but not at the first-grade level, as determined by a test of simple effects.) *

Table 16–5 reveals that there were significant differences between Ss coming from more, as opposed to less, deprived background condi-

* For a complete discussion of this procedure see Winer,[8] p. 80.

tions. Lower SES ratings and scores denoting greater disadvantage on the Deprivation Index were independently associated with IQ scores. In addition, this table indicates that there was a significant interaction effect of grade by deprivation on IQ scores.

Table 16–5

RESULTS OF THREE-WAY ANALYSIS OF VARIANCE ON LORGE-THORNDIKE IQ SCORES BY GRADE, SES, AND DEPRIVATION

Source	df	MS	f	p
Grade (A)	1	0.00	0.00	N.S.
SES (B)	2	2120.95	10.06	<.01
Deprivation (C)	1	2191.07	10.40	<.01
A × B	2	45.68	<1.00	N.S.
A × C	1	1492.79	7.08	<.01
B × C	2	.44	0.00	N.S.
A × B × C	2	29.15	<1.00	N.S.
Error	277	210.77		
Total	291			

Table 16–6 reveals that regardless of grade, Ss coming from the more deprived conditions obtained significantly lower IQ scores than did Ss coming from the less-deprived background conditions. Also, the effects of deprivation on IQ scores were more pronounced among older Ss (fifth-graders) than among the younger Ss (first-graders).

Table 16–6

MEANS FOR OVERALL DEPRIVATION LEVELS AND FOR DEPRIVATION LEVELS WITHIN GRADE ON LORGE-THORNDIKE IQ SCORES

Group	$\overline{X}$	SD	N
More Deprivation	97.34	15.08	175
Less Deprivation	107.79	15.30	114
Grade 1			
More Deprivation	100.13	15.01	91
Less Deprivation	104.14	12.54	36
Grade 5			
More Deprivation	94.31	14.64	84
Less Deprivation	109.47	16.21	78

The interesting findings which emerge from Table 16–7 are: (*a*) the vanishing of the significant interaction between grade and race noted in Table 16–2, and (*b*) the maintenance of the significant grade by Deprivation Index interaction reported in Table 16–5. It appears that once disadvantage, as assessed by the Deprivation Index, is controlled, the age decrement, as assessed by the Lorge-Thorndike test, among the Negro children tends to be ameliorated. However, the converse is not true within racial groups. The age decrement associated with the Deprivation Index is still significant.

Table 16–7

RESULTS OF THREE-WAY ANALYSIS OF VARIANCE ON LORGE-THORNDIKE IQ SCORES BY GRADE, RACE, AND DEPRIVATION

Source	df	MS	f	p
Grade (A)	1	43.07	<1.00	N.S.
Race (B)	1	3131.15	14.71	$<.01$
Deprivation (C)	1	4534.89	21.30	$<.01$
A × B	1	183.24	<1.00	N.S.
A × C	1	1068.79	5.02	$<.05$
B × C	1	159.12	<1.00	N.S.
A × B × C	1	38.29	<1.00	N.S.
Error	284	212.86		
Total	291			

• Analysis of the Wechsler Vocabulary Subtest

Table 16–8 reveals that there were highly significant differences between the grades, between SES groups, and between Negro and white Ss. In addition, there were significant interaction effects of grade by SES and grade by race. The SES and race differences parallel those found on the Lorge-Thorndike test. However, in the case of the Lorge-Thorndike results, there was only a significant grade by race interaction, but not a significant grade by SES interaction.

Table 16–8

RESULTS OF THREE-WAY ANALYSIS OF VARIANCE ON WISC VOCABULARY SUBTEST SCORE BY GRADE, SES, AND RACE

Source	df	MS	f	p
Grade (A)	1	24112.03	435.29	$<.0001$
SES (B)	2	1044.82	18.86	$<.01$
Race (C)	1	52.88	9.40	$<.01$
A × B	2	262.75	4.74	$<.05$
A × C	1	463.93	8.38	$<.01$
B × C	2	24.11	1.00	N.S.
A × B × C	2	12.27	1.00	N.S.
Error	277	55.39		
Total	288			

One notes from examination of Table 16–8 that the difference between the two grade levels was a large one. Since the vocabulary subtest score is a raw score which contains no adjustment for age, it is not surprising that the differences in vocabulary, between six- as opposed to eleven-year-old children, are so large. The Negro children generally performed more poorly than did the white children, and the lower SES children performed more poorly than did higher SES children.

In Table 16–9 and 16–10 the means for the significant effects are presented. These tables indicate that differences between Negro and white Ss, as well as differences between lower and middle SES children, were in the expected direction and were sharper at the fifth-grade level than at the first-grade level. (These differences, as tested by the simple effects method, reached statistical significance within the fifth grade, but not within the first grade.)

Table 16–9

MEANS FOR GRADE LEVELS, SES GROUPS, AND RACE GROUPS ON WISC VOCABU-
LARY SUBTEST SCORES

Group	$\overline{X}$	SD	N
Grade 1	14.05	5.82	125
Grade 5	32.41	9.85	164
SES I	21.28	11.08	110
SES II	24.55	11.53	97
SES III	28.66	13.72	82
Negro	22.74	10.67	147
White	26.31	13.73	140

Table 16–11 explores the possibility of interaction between SES and the Deprivation Index. A significant interaction did not result. Interesting, however, is the loss of two significant interactions which had emerged previously in connection with the WISC vocabulary scale. These are the grade by Deprivation Index interaction (see Table 16–7) and the grade by SES interaction (see Table 16–8). The difference appears to be that the analysis reported in Table 16–11 is a simultaneous study of SES and the Deprivation Index. The analyses in Tables 16–7 and 16–8 had studied the Deprivation Index or SES simultaneously with *race*, but not with each other. Table 16–11 reveals that once there is some homogeneity in level of disadvantage, as

Table 16–10

MEANS FOR SES GROUPS AND RACE GROUPS WITHIN GRADE LEVELS ON WISC
VOCABULARY SUBTEST SCORES

Group	$\overline{X}$	SD	N
Grade 1			
SES I	12.17	5.40	46
SES II	14.72	5.81	43
SES III	15.64	5.84	36
Grade 5			
SES I	27.83	9.36	64
SES II	32.37	8.57	54
SES III	38.85	8.40	46
Grade 1			
Negro	13.97	6.19	68
White	14.14	5.49	57
Grade 5			
Negro	30.11	7.67	81
White	34.66	11.20	83

measured by the Deprivation Index, a lowered SES loses its cumulative effect. However, SES retains its cumulative effect on the vocabulary measure despite the control on race, i.e., even within the Negro and white groups. The means corresponding to the main effect of the Deprivation Index are shown in Table 16–12. The results correspond to those obtained with the Lorge-Thorndike IQ measure—the more the deprivation, the lower the vocabulary score.

Table 16–11

RESULTS OF THREE-WAY ANALYSIS OF VARIANCE ON WISC VOCABULARY SUBTEST
SCORES BY GRADE, SES, AND DEPRIVATION

Source	df	MS	f	p
Grade (A)	1	17508.48	304.11	$<.0001$
SES (B)	2	474.56	8.24	$<.01$
Deprivation (C)	1	356.45	6.19	$<.05$
A × B	2	165.09	2.87	N.S.
A × C	1	99.27	1.72	N.S.
B × C	2	53.59	1.00	N.S.
A × B × C	2	20.75	1.00	N.S.
Error	274	57.57		
Total	285			

Table 16–12

MEANS FOR MORE- AND LESS-DEPRIVED GROUPS ON WISC VOCABULARY SUBTEST
SCORES

Group	$\overline{X}$	SD	N
More deprivation	20.94	10.98	172
Less deprivation	29.53	12.60	114

Table 16–13 reveals that, in addition to the significant main effects which emerged in earlier analyses, there were significant and independent interaction effects of grade by race and grade by deprivation.

The decline in vocabulary performance in the case of the Negro children is relatively independent of the decline attributable to disadvantage, as reflected by the Deprivation Index. This independence of the Deprivation Index, in the case of the Negro children's decrement on the vocabulary scale, contrasts with what was found in the analysis of the Lorge-Thorndike test. With the latter measure, the grade by race interaction was not significant once deprivation level was controlled (see Table 16–7). There was no significant Negro decline among homogeneous deprivation groups. In the case of the vocabulary measure, however, the scores of the Negro children decline significantly despite control over deprivation level. In short, the measure which more heavily reflects language (vocabulary) is more responsive to cumulating deficits among Negroes than is the measure which draws less heavily on linguistic knowledge (Lorge-Thorndike Non-Verbal Test). Table 16–14 presents the means, indicating that among older as compared to younger children there are stronger differences on vocabulary score associated with variation on the Deprivation Index.*

* A possible confounding factor is the increased heterogeneity of variance of the vocabulary measure for the fifth-graders as compared to the first-graders. Such heterogeneity might contribute to the increased association between background factors and vocabulary among the older children, without the necessity of invoking cumulative deficit as an explanatory factor. In order to control for this differential heterogeneity of variance, the fifth-grade correlations of SES, Deprivation Index, and race with vocabulary were calculated. These Pearson product-moment coefficients were then adjusted through statistical reduction of the vocabulary variance of the fifth grade to that of the first grade, using the formula presented by Gulliksen,[4] p. 133, for predicting correlations when there are changes in the variance of a variable. Despite these adjustments there were no changes in the levels of significance for the various correlations between the three background variables and the vocabulary test.

Table 16–13

RESULTS OF THREE-WAY ANALYSIS OF VARIANCE ON WISC VOCABULARY SUBTEST
SCORES BY GRADE, RACE, AND DEPRIVATION

Source	df	MS	f	p
Grade (A)	1	19136.91	318.93	$<.0001$
Race (B)	1	322.23	5.37	$<.05$
Deprivation (C)	1	865.34	14.42	$<.01$
A × B	1	398.83	6.65	$<.05$
A × C	1	283.67	4.73	$<.05$
B × C	1	14.88	1.00	N.S.
A × B × C	1	168.86	2.81	N.S.
Error	278	60.00		
Total	285			

Table 16–14

MEANS FOR MORE- AND LESS-DEPRIVED GROUPS WITHIN GRADE LEVELS ON
WISC VOCABULARY SUBTEST SCORES

Group	$\overline{X}$	SD	N
Grade 1			
More deprivation	13.54	6.27	89
Less deprivation	15.30	4.35	36
Grade 5			
More deprivation	28.88	9.25	83
Less deprivation	36.09	9.28	78

CONCLUSIONS AND IMPLICATIONS

The findings will now be discussed in connection with the four problems posed in the introductory section.

1. The results indicate that the Deprivation Index tends to act as
a factor independent of SES and race in contributing to variation in
test performance. Thus significant main effects on both tests were related to the Deprivation Index even in groups homogeneous with respect to race or socioeconomic status. This suggests that cumulations
of specific environmental factors (e.g., low parental motivation, absence of a kindergarten experience) can have a disadvantaging effect
despite relatively high socioeconomic status, and that the diminution
of such features may have an advantageous effect despite relatively
low socioeconomic status. This latter point provides support for enrichment programs aimed at alleviating the effects of social disadvan-

tage on children of lower socioeconomic status. In a similar vein, the cumulative deficit found among Negro children on the Lorge-Thorndike test tends to be ameliorated once level of disadvantage (as assessed by the Deprivation Index) is controlled. Thus, we see that decrements in test performance associated either with Negro or lower-class status tend to be offset or mitigated in the context of cumulations of specific, advantaging environmental factors.

2. Test decrements in the more disadvantaged group (i.e., the group as determined by the Deprivation Index) were more pronounced among the older children. Thus, in the case of the Lorge-Thorndike, the older children scoring in the more disadvantaged range of the Deprivation Index tended to score relatively lower than the younger children. This progressive deficit obtained even within groups homogeneous with respect to race or socioeconomic status. On the vocabulary scale, as age increases, the disadvantaged children, whether white or Negro, tended to score relatively lower than the more advantaged children.

The findings also indicate that cumulative deficits emerge in connection with each of the three background measures studied. Not only do we find cumulative deficits emerging with respect to the Deprivation Index, but also in connection with Negro status and lower socioeconomic standing. However, socioeconomic status shows some departure from the two other background variables. Lower SES is the only one of the three variables associated with Lorge-Thorndike deficits among younger children which are as pronounced as those among older children. If we compare the role of race and SES with respect to the Lorge-Thorndike, a differentiated picture emerges—the deficit associated with lower SES begins earlier but the deficit associated with race accelerates faster. We have attempted to separate race and SES effects both by the sample design and by the statistical analysis. By these methods we have been able to study the effect of race independently of SES. In the general population, however, race and SES are by no means independent, for Negro status and lower SES are definitely associated, implying that typically the Negro child is doubly hit. Early deficit may be occasioned by disadvantaging factors associated with lower socioeconomic status; in addition, later deficit may be produced by environmental factors associated with being Negro. As the analysis has indicated, some of these later factors are related to the environmental features tapped by the Deprivation Index.

3. There was little evidence of interaction among the three main types of background variables—SES, Race, and Deprivation Index. Thus, with the test measures, performance was not significantly altered within the more complex groupings formed by any particular combination of background factors, e.g., the group which is low SES, Negro, and in the disadvantaged range on the Deprivation Index. This finding does not imply that the effect of such multiple groupings is not summative, as we have indicated above in discussing the Negro child who is more often than not of lower socioeconomic status. Indeed, the lowest scores were found among groups defined in terms of combinations of disadvantaging background factors. However, unusual decrements, not predictable from simple summation of the three main background factors, were not obtained. The suggestion here is that deprivational factors cumulating *over* time may be more important in effecting decrement than the cumulation of conditions *within* a particular time. This point, coupled with the early deprivational effect of low SES pointed out above, indicates the importance of enrichment programs which are instituted early in the child's life, i.e., before deficit sets in and before it has a chance to cumulate.

4. Our findings indicate that the effects of the background factors are a function of the kind of ability under consideration. Thus, race and SES play different roles depending upon the degree to which language is involved in test performance. In the case of the non-verbal form of the Lorge-Thorndike there was no cumulative deficit manifest when the data were analyzed by SES groups, but the same SES analysis did show a cumulative deficit in connection with the vocabulary scale. Analysis by race did yield a cumulative-deficit finding with respect to the Lorge-Thorndike. This deficit tends to vanish when some controls on level of disadvantage (as assessed by the Deprivation Index) are introduced. However, in the case of the more verbal measure, the vocabulary scale, cumulative deficits associated with race obtain even in the presence of controls on SES and Deprivation Index. The implication here is that the more linguistic measures show greater responsiveness to the cumulative effects of certain disadvantaging conditions than the measures tapping non-verbal abilities. The fact that the cumulative vocabulary deficit among the Negro children is independent of both the SES and Deprivation Index points to the importance of a close investigation of the Negro child's environment to uncover those conditions which affect his linguistic development. Such factors may include adult stimulation of the child's speech, adult re-

ward for linguistic modes of expression, the opportunity to hear new words in meaningful context, and the opportunity to discover the utility of a developing vocabulary as instrumental in satisfying one's needs and influencing the social environment.

This paper has attempted to present a differentiated picture of the environmental, temporal, and measurement conditions leading to impaired performance on psychological tests. This picture stresses the importance of specific environmental features in addition to the more global factors of race and SES; it stresses the importance of time as interacting with environmental background in producing a cumulative deficit; and, finally, it stresses the differential patterning of deficit produced by the nature of the psychological function being measured. These results, again, point to the need for comparative longitudinal studies of linguistic and cognitive growth for groups differing in social and cultural backgrounds.

References

1. Bernstein, B. Social structure, language and learning. *Educ. Res.*, 1961, 3 (3), 163–176.
2. Dreger, R. M., & Miller, K. S. Comparative psychological studies of Negroes and whites in the United States. *Psychol. Bull.*, 1960, **57**, 361–402.
3. Eells, K., Davis, A., Havighurst, R. J., Merrick, V. E., & Tyler, R. *Intelligence and cultural differences.* Chicago: Univer. Chicago Press, 1951.
4. Gulliksen, H. *Theory of mental tests.* New York: Wiley, 1950.
5. Klineberg, O. Negro-white differences in intelligence test performance: A new look at an old problem. *Amer. Psychologist*, 1963, **18**, 198–203.
6. Milner, Esther. A study of the relationship between reading readiness in grade I school children and patterns of parent-child interaction. *Child Develpm.*, 1951, **22** (2), 95–112.
7. U.S. Bureau of the Census. *U.S. census of housing*, 1960, 3, City Blocks, Series HC(3) Nos. 274–276.
8. Winer, B. J. *Statistical principles in experimental design.* New York: McGraw-Hill, 1962.

Betty

17 /

Social Disadvantage as Related to Intellective and Language Development

MARTIN WHITEMAN AND
MARTIN DEUTSCH

One of the writers often drives through East Harlem on his way to work. There is a school on 111th Street, and as he stopped for a light one morning he noticed two Negro children, about ten years old, having a bit of friendly horseplay before going to class. One was banging the other over the head playfully with a notebook. But the notebook slipped out of his hand and fell into a puddle of water. The two children stared at the notebook and then suddenly turned toward each other with gales of laughter and walked off toward school arm in arm and without the notebook. A policeman who had been standing nearby walked over to the puddle and stared at the notebook with some degree of disbelief.

This event can be understood in terms of a discontinuity between school requirements and the child's prior preparation and experiences. The child from a disadvantaged environment may have missed some of the experiences necessary for developing the verbal, conceptual, attentional, and learning skills requisite to school success. These skills play a vital role for the child in his understanding of the language of the school and the teacher, in his adapting to school routines, and in his mastery of such a fundamental tool subject as reading. In the absence of the development of these skills by the child there is a progressive alienation of teacher from child and child from teacher. In the school, the child may suffer from feelings of inferiority because he is failing; he withdraws or becomes hostile, finding gratifications elsewhere, such as in his peer group. Notebooks may be left in puddles while the camaraderie develops.

The teacher often feels inferior because she is failing too—but she can blame the child's family, or she can assign her difficulties to what she considers the child's essential unteachability. This progressive alienation contributes to the cumulative deficit observed in experientially deprived children, i.e., the decline over time in their scholastic achievements and in measures of "intellectual abilities."

This developmental conception has both research and action implications. From a research point of view, it would be important to examine very closely, on the one hand, the relation between family background and cognitive and learning skills, and, on the other hand, how these underlying abilities influence the performance of the child in the school situation. From an action point of view, it would seem reasonable to conclude that if learning sets or the level of underlying abilities are influential in a decline in performance, an improvement of these skills through an early enrichment program at the preschool and kindergarten levels may be helpful in arresting or reversing the cumulative deficit.

The Institute for Developmental Studies is engaged in both research and enrichment programs focused on the cognitive learnings and abilities of so-called disadvantaged children. The work to be discussed here is based on a conception of linguistic and cognitive factors as crucial intervening variables between environmental impact on the one hand and scholastic achievement on the other.

One of the major aims of a study of the verbal performance of first- and fifth-grade children (referred to as the "Verbal Survey") has been to identify some of the specific background variables which are related to the development of linguistic and cognitive skills. Accordingly, we have tried to obtain information about the child's social background which would go beyond the basic facts of the parent's occupation, education, and race.*

INTERCORRELATIONS AMONG MEASURES OF BACKGROUND, ABILITY, AND ACHIEVEMENT

Table 17–1 lists the background variables under several headings—social background, economic and motivational aspects, familial setting, and educational experiences, both with the parents and in more formal settings. The relation between the specific background factors and

* See the previous chapter for details concerning the development of the Deprivation Index.

reading score is also shown. It can be seen that at the fifth-grade level, the kinds of background factors which correlate significantly with reading achievement are of a varied order. There are aspects dealing with the child's physical surroundings, as housing dilapidation is associated with lowered reading scores (item 4 in Table 17–1). Of course, motivational aspects are significant, as the parent's educational aspiration for the child is related to a higher reading score. The familial composition (item 9) plays a role: the larger the family size, the lower is the reading score. Interaction and activities with parents and relatives are important. Thus higher reading levels are found among those children reporting conversations with parents during dinner (item 13) or those who have the opportunity to broaden their experiences by visits with parents to such cultural sites as zoos and museums (item 15). Finally, those children score higher in reading who have had the benefit of a kindergarten experience (item 16).

It can also be seen from Table 17–1 that each of these six variables is significantly related to the gross measure of socioeconomic status which is derived from parental education and occupation.

By contrast, there are nine background variables which are not significantly related to reading. Of these, only three are related to the SES measure. Thus there are six background variables which have an interesting dual relationship. On the one hand they show statistically significant associations with socioeconomic status, and on the other hand they are significantly associated with a scholastic achievement— reading. It is plausible to assume that the six items form a set of an interactive sort, a set which affords a specification of how the socioeconomic status of the home affects the scholastic achievement of the child. A comparison of those items which do and do not relate to reading points up the importance of the quality of the child's interaction with parents and other adults. Thus the sheer presence of mother or father at mealtimes (items 10, 11, and 12 in Table 17–1) is not significantly related to reading. However, conversation with parents during dinner is related to reading. The sheer number of activities with parents or relatives (item 14) is not associated with reading, but the number of *cultural* activities (item 13) is. A reduced family size (item 9) and kindergarten attendance (item 16) allow more opportunity for stimulating interaction between adults and children, a factor which is in all probability reflected in the efficacy of increased parental scholastic aspiration for the child (item 5).

Thus far we have been inspecting both end points of a hypothe-

Table 17–1

CORRELATIONS BETWEEN ENVIRONMENTAL CONDITIONS AND (A) GATES READING TEST AND (B) SES INDEX

(Grade 5, $N = 167$)

	Correlations with: Reading	SES Index
Social Background		
1. SES Index	.44*	—
2. Education, Main Support	.45*	—
3. Occupation, Main Support	.35*	—
Economic Aspects		
4. Housing Condition	.28*	.27*
Motivational Aspects		
5. Parental Schooling Desired for Child	.32*	.31*
6. Parent's First Choice for Child's Job	.16	.23*
7. Parent's Estimate of Child's Probable Job	.05	.22*
Familial Setting		
8. Father in Home	.12	.28*
9. Number of Children under 18	−.29*	−.20*
Educational Experiences		
Parental Interaction		
10. Presence of Mother with Child at Breakfast	.11	.09
11. Presence of Mother with Child at Dinner	.04	.09
12. Presence of Father with Child at Dinner	−.06	.09
13. Conversation during Dinner	.22*	.28*
Activities with Adults		
14. Number of Anticipated Activities with Relatives	−.05	.09
15. Number of Anticipated Cultural Activities	.25*	.28*
School Experiences		
16. Kindergarten Attendance	.20*	.20*
17. Day Care Attendance	.03	.03
18. School Utility Rating	.11	−.11

* Significant at .01 level.

sized causal sequence comprising environmental background—ability patterns—scholastic achievement. With the data we can now explore some of the abilities underlying reading and the relation of these abilities to the background conditions.

Three tests are most highly correlated with the Gates Reading Score. These are the Lorge-Thorndike IQ, the WISC Vocabulary, and the Orientation Scale, which is a verbal test tapping the child's fund of general information and conceptual understanding.

The cognitive skills underlying reading at the fifth-grade level then involve a grasp of the relationships among ideas (as tapped by the Lorge-Thorndike IQ), verbal facility and knowledge (as assessed by the Wechsler-Bellevue Vocabulary Scale), and a fund of basic factual and conceptual information (as measured by the Orientation Scale).

Table 17–2 brings together the variables related to environmental background, underlying abilities, and the reading achievement score with a view toward exploring their interrelation. If we work through the hypothesized causal sequence, we see, under bracket A of Table 17–2 that the SES Index is significantly related to each of the specific environmental conditions, as noted above. Under bracket B are listed the correlations between environmental conditions and the three underlying abilities. Of the 18 correlations, 15 are significant at the .01 level. Under bracket C, the final section of the causal sequence is shown, i.e., the correlations, all ranging above the .60 mark, between the abilities, as manifested in the three tests, and reading achievement. Several points might be noted. First, the correlations between the abilities and the achievement variable, reading, are higher than those between environmental conditions and reading (compare brackets C and F). The median correlation between abilities and reading is .64 as compared to a median correlation of .27 between environmental conditions and reading. This finding suggests that these abilities may be exerting a more direct influence on reading than the more "distant" background variables. There is consistency here with the notion that environmental conditions exert their influence on underlying skills which in turn more directly affect the development of reading skills. Second, the interrelationships among the six environmental conditions and among the three tests deserve separate attention. With respect to the former, it can be seen from the coefficients under bracket D that the interrelationships among the environmental conditions tend to be low. Thus the median of the 15 coefficients is only .17. The suggestion here is that these conditions tend to show a fair degree of independence from one another. This implies that these conditions may exert their maximum effect on abilities and on achievement by means of their cumulative interaction rather than as separate representatives of some one underlying deprivational condition. As mentioned in the previous chapter the multiple correlation coefficient expressing the relation between the cumulative effect of the six environmental conditions on reading score is .49 as compared to .32, which is the highest correlation between any specific environmental condition and reading, or as compared to .27 the median coefficient between environmental condition and reading level. If one adds the SES Index and the under- lying abilities as independent variables, i.e., brings in environmental background *and* underlying abilities as independent variables, the multiple *r* increases to .74.

By way of contrast to the relatively low intercorrelation among the environmental conditions are the correlations among the underly- ing abilities (listed under bracket E). These coefficients hover about the .70 mark. This suggests the possibility of a common factor under- lying these reading-related abilities. Indeed a factor analysis of a number of language measures at the fifth-grade level reveals that a factor can be extracted which correlates .80, .76, and .68 with the Lorge-Thornike IQ, WISC Vocabulary, and Orientation Scale, respec- tively. It is interesting, too, that this is a factor separate from one which loads .88, .85, and .71 with the Cloze Popular Score, Cloze Grammatical, and Gates Reading Test, respectively. The two factors, one identifiable as intelligence and the other as a reading or contex- tual understanding factor, are separable. However, they are not or- thogonal, i.e., they do show some interrelation. This finding would be consistent with the notion that the intellective abilities underlie and are related to reading achievement, but that the two areas—ability and achievement—represent separate functional units.

One has, then, a sense of a developmental progression. A child is born into a family with a particular social background. He has the kind of experiences which allow him to develop certain cognitive and verbal skills and these in turn contribute to the subsequent learnings (in this case, reading) expected of him in school.

It should be pointed out that there is a real problem in the inter- pretation of causal direction from these data. Thus a child's report of expected cultural activities might be attributable to his verbal respon- siveness in the test situation rather than to environmental stimulation. Militating against this interpretation, however, is the lack of signifi- cant correlation between "cultural activities" and independent meas- ures of the child's total verbal output and verbal fluency in the test situation. Also the sheer number of activities with adults as contrasted with the number of *cultural* activities does not correlate with reading achievement, contrary to the verbal-fluency hypothesis. Similarly, it may well be that some unknown portion of the association between (*a*) environmental conditions, such as the educational aspiration of

Table 17–2

INTERCORRELATIONS AMONG ENVIRONMENTAL VARIABLES RELATED TO READING, SES, AND TEST SCORES

(Fifth Grade, $N = 167$)

	SES	ENVIRONMENTAL CONDITIONS						ABILITIES			READING
	1	2	3	4	5	6	7	8	9	10	11
SES											
1	—	.27*	.31*	-.20*	.28*	.28*	.20*				.44*
Environmental Conditions											
2 Housing	.27*	—						.31*	.34*	.34*	
3 Scholastic Aspiration	.31*	.28*	—					.30*	.35*	.36*	
4 No. of Children under 18	-.20*	-.09	-.19	—				-.23*	-.24*	-.18	
5 Dinner Conversation	.28*	.17	.10	-.02	—			.20*	.27*	.24*	
6 Cultural Activities	.28*	.18	.12	-.07	.25*	—		.25*	.27*	.27*	
7 Kindergarten	.20*	.26*	.18	-.22*	.09	.05	—	.25*	.13	.12	
Abilities											
8 IQ (Lorge-Thorndike)	.37*							—			.66*
9 Vocabulary (WISC)	.49*							.67*	—		.62*
10 Orientation	.51*							.66*	.76*	—	.62*
Achievement											
11 Reading	.44*	.28*	.32*	-.29*	.22*	.25*	.20*				—

* Significant at .01 level.

the parents, and (*b*) reading achievement is due to the influence of child on parent rather than vice versa. Thus the better-achieving child may stimulate higher parental aspiration. However, one would predict from the reverse-causality hypothesis that the child would also stimulate higher occupational aspiration in the parent. The evidence does not support this view. Thus, items 6 and 7 in Table 17–1 reveal that the child's reading level is not significantly related to the parents' occupational aspiration for the child. However, it could be suggested that even this finding is in accord with the reverse causality hypothesis. One might assume that the child's scholastic achievement might affect the parents' scholastic aspiration more than their occupational aspiration—hence the obtained significant correlation between reading (a scholastic achievement) and parents' educational aspiration, but a non-significant correlation between reading and the parents' occupational aspiration for the child. However, a more direct test of the reverse causality hypothesis is at hand. One would expect, according to this view, that the parents' perceptions of the child's reading level would be a crucial variable linking the child's achievement to parental expectation. Accordingly, the correlation between parental educational aspiration and the parents' estimate of the child's reading ability was examined. The correlation between the two measures (among the fifth-graders, where reading scores were obtained) failed to reach significance ($r = .11$).

THE DEPRIVATION INDEX AND CUMULATIVE DEFICIT

Three points will be recalled from the previous chapter.

1. With respect to the independent contribution of the Deprivation Index, the results indicate that the Index is significantly related to both the Lorge-Thorndike and the WISC Vocabulary tests even within groups homogeneous in race or SES level. This result implies that, over and above the decrements associated with race and SES, the specific environmental features embodied in the Deprivation Index are capable, by themselves, of producing such disadvantaging effects.

2. On both the Vocabulary and Lorge-Thorndike measures, the Deprivation Index yielded cumulative deficits. Thus if the sample is dichotomized into those who show greater and lesser disadvantage as

assessed by the Index, the more disadvantaged group shows a decreasing IQ with age. The relatively advantaged group shows an increase with age. (See Table 16–6, page 327.) A similar pattern occurs with respect to a cumulative vocabulary deficit. Among the older fifth-grade children, those who show greater disadvantage tend to do relatively poorer than the disadvantaged children of the first grade. (See Table 16–14, page 332.)

The results also indicate that in the case of the Lorge-Thorndike the cumulative deficit is most marked among those Ss who show the specific experiential disadvantages embodied in the Deprivation Index as compared to those Ss identified more grossly as being of lower socioeconomic level. Lower SES, however, is more associated with lower Lorge-Thorndike scores among the younger children, a deficit which is as pronounced as the deficit among the low SES older children.

3. Turning to the differences between the two tests, the findings reveal that the cumulative deficits of the verbal test (Vocabulary) are associated with a broader range of background conditions than those of the more non-verbal IQ measure. Thus cumulative deficits with the vocabulary test are associated with Negro status, lower SES, and greater disadvantage as assessed by the Deprivation Index. The deficits are less pervasive in the case of the Lorge-Thorndike. There is no significant cumulative deficit associated with lower SES, as noted above. There is, however, a significant cumulative deficit related to Negro status. Thus Negro children in the fifth grade score lower relative to white children than do Negro children in the first grade. However, this deficit tends to vanish when there is control over level of disadvantage, as measured by the Deprivation Index. Within homogeneous levels of deprivation, the Negro cumulative deficit tends to be lessened; the older Negro children do not show a significant and progressive decline. However, the converse is not true. Regardless of race, the more disadvantaged older children (as assessed by the Deprivation Index) score relatively lower on the vocabulary test than the most disadvantaged younger children. The general tenor of these results points to the greater sensitivity of the language test to different patterns of disadvantage, whether these disadvantages are related to general socioeconomic level or to Negro status, or to the specific background factors implied in the Deprivation Index.

• *The Deprivation Index and Self-Concept*

The Deprivation Index is also related to self-concept. In the case of the fifth-grade children, an index dealing with favorableness of self-evaluation was constructed from two sentence-completion items. A trichotomous categorization was used—response with a favorable self-image (*a*) to both items, (*b*) to one item, and (*c*) to neither of the two items.

Table 17–3 reveals that the more deprived children tend to have the lower self-concepts. As compared to the more advantaged children, about six times as many of the more deprived children fall into the least favorable self-concept category. This finding would be consistent with our formulation above regarding the interrelation between deprivation, self-concept, and cognitive achievement. If deprivation is related to lower ability and achievement levels, and the latter in turn results in feelings of inferiority, one would expect what was found: that there would be a significant relation between increased deprivation and a more negative self-concept.

Table 17–3

DEPRIVATION INDEX AS RELATED TO SELF-CONCEPT LEVELS (FIFTH GRADE)

	SELF-CONCEPT LEVEL							
	Least Favorable		Medium		More Favorable		Total	
Deprivation Level	N	%	N	%	N	%	N	%
More	13	25	19	35	21	40	53	48
Less	2	4	21	44	25	52	48	52
							101	100

$\chi^2 = 7.88$.
$p < .05$.

A missing empirical link in this hypothetical causal chain is the relation between lowered ability level and more negative self-concept. To explore this relation the self-concept variable was related to four ability measures. The latter represented the marker variables for four factors derived from an analysis of a battery of verbal and cognitive measures administered to our fifth-grade sample. The tests are the

Lorge-Thorndike, the Word Distance (Distance Score) measure, the Cloze Popular, and the Form-Class Score of a word association test. The factors corresponding to these four marker variables were named intelligence, conceptual relatedness, conceptual understanding, and formal language. The results of a two-way analysis of variance (self-concept × type of test) are presented in Table 17–4. The main effect of self-concept is significant, and analysis of the overall trend indicates that, the more negative the self-concept, the lower are the test scores. The failure to find a significant interaction between self-concept and test indicates that the relation between more negative self-concept and lowered test score is fairly general and obtained over the various tests used in this analysis. Comparisons among the self-concept means were made to explore the locus of the significant main effect. The Newman-Keuls comparisons among means (see Table 17–4) reveal that it is the group which is most negative in self-concept which stands out as significantly lower in test performance from the other two groups. The latter two self-concept categories, defining the medium and more favorable groups, are not significantly different from one another in overall test score.

Table 17–4

MEANS AND STANDARD DEVIATIONS OF COMBINED STANDARD SCORES OF FOUR MARKER VARIABLES BROKEN DOWN BY SELF-CONCEPT

Category (Fifth Grade)

Self-Concept Levels	$\overline{X}$	SD	N
I. Least Favorable	459.32	85.51	15
II. Medium	500.63	86.56	41
III. Most Favorable	515.61	82.28	47

Note: Main effect of self-concept significant at .01 level.

NEWMAN-KEULS COMPARISONS AMONG MEANS

Self-Concept Levels	P
I vs. II	$<.01$
I vs. III	$<.01$
II vs. III	N.S.

The above analysis has related a self-concept measure to ability tests. A significant relation between self-concept and reading achievement, as measured by the Gates Reading Test, is shown by the results of an analysis of variance presented in Table 17–5. Self-concept differences are significantly related to reading scores. The more negative the self-concept, the lower the reading achievement. As was seen above in connection with the relation between self-concept and ability measures, Table 17–5 reveals that the most negative self-concept group is most demarcated from the other two groups with respect to reading level. The difference in reading score between self-concept Groups II and III (the medium and more favorable self-concept groups) is not significant.

Table 17–5

MEANS AND STANDARD DEVIATIONS OF GATES READING TEST SCORES AS RELATED TO SELF-CONCEPT LEVELS (FIFTH GRADE)

Self-Concept Levels	$\overline{X}$	SD
I. Most Unfavorable	40.01	9.61
II. Medium	46.76	10.03
III. Least Unfavorable	49.32	9.52

Note: Main effect of self-concept significant at .01 level.

NEWMAN-KEULS COMPARISONS AMONG SELF-CONCEPT MEANS

Self-Concept Levels	P
I vs. II	$<.05$
I vs. III	$<.01$
II vs. III	N.S.

Though the above presentation has highlighted a particular causal direction (from deprivation to lowered ability and achievement to lowered self-concept), an alternative interpretation can be made. It is quite probable, though difficult to explore with correlational data, that the relation between performance, whether of the ability or the achievement variety, and self-evaluation, is interactive—with the more negative self-evaluations producing as well as being produced by lower performance.

• *Deprivation Index and Interactions with Socioeconomic Status, Race, and Intelligence*

In addition to relations with cumulative deficit and self-concept, there is a third point related to deprivation. A more advantaged environment seems to counteract other conditions which tend to bring achievement levels down. Three illustrations are presented.

Among children who are relatively undeprived, as measured by the Deprivation Index, low socioeconomic status per se is much less potent as a disadvantaging factor with respect to ability tests than in the case among children who show strong deprivation on the Index. Among the latter group of children, a low socioeconomic status is most strongly related to the linguistic and intellective measures. The evidence is presented in Table 17–6, which shows the analysis of variance of the four ability measures described above. Socioeconomic status, Deprivation Index, race, and the type of test are the independent variables. It can be seen from Table 17–6 that the interaction between deprivation and socioeconomic status is significant, implying that the pattern of SES differences in test score varies from one level of deprivation to another. Table 17–7 explores further these differing patterns by listing the SES differences in overall test score separately for each deprivation level. These SES differences are more marked in the more deprived group. Table 17–8 indicates that the SES differences in test score are quite significant in this more deprived group but are not significant in the group showing lesser disadvantage. The Newman-Keuls comparisons also reported in Table 17–8 explore the locus of SES differences in the more deprived group. These comparisons indicate that the lower SES levels I and II score significantly lower on overall test score than the higher SES level III, but that the difference between the two lower levels of SES is not significant. We see, therefore, that SES differences in test score are affected by the deprivation level of the child, with lesser degrees of deprivation mitigating the effect of lower socioeconomic status.

A second illustration of the importance of deprivational background as an interactive variable is afforded by a study of the combined effects of deprivation level and intelligence on reading. Table 17–9 shows the results of an analysis of variance of Gates Reading Score among the fifth-graders with race, Lorge-Thorndike IQ (nonverbal), and Deprivation Index as the independent variables. The magnitude of differences in reading score between the higher and lower IQ groups is a function of deprivation level. It can be seen that reading differences attributable to intellectual gradations are more pronounced in the more disadvantaged group and less pronounced in the group with a lesser degree of deprivation. This implies that the effects of intellectual retardation on reading are ameliorated in the

Table 17–6

ANALYSIS OF VARIANCE OF MARKER TESTS WITH SOCIOECONOMIC STATUS, RACE, DEPRIVATION (DI), AND TYPE OF TEST AS INDEPENDENT VARIABLES (FIFTH GRADE)

Source	df	MS	F	P
Between S's				
SES	2	66,336.70	6.17	<.01
Race	1	20,099.88	1.87	N.S.
Deprivation (DI)*	1	54,431.31	5.06	<.05
SES × Race	2	7,112.40	<1	N.S.
SES × DI	2	34,916.32	3.25	<.05
Race × DI	1	1,199.61	<1	N.S.
SES × Race × DI	2	966.25	<1	N.S.
Error (between)	123	10,759.05		
Within S's				
Tests	3	1,732.16	<1	N.S.
SES × Tests	6	8,040.48	1.45	N.S.
Race × Tests	3	22,927.21	4.14	<.01
DI × Tests	3	10,351.75	1.87	N.S.
SES × Race × Tests	6	931.55	<1	N.S.
SES × DI × Tests	6	3,978.90	<1	N.S.
Race × DI × Tests	3	1,287.61	<1	N.S.
SES × Race × DI × Tests	6	7,381.00	1.33	N.S.
Error (within)	369	5,536.64		

* Deprivation Index dichotomized.

Table 17–7

SES DIFFERENCES IN OVERALL TEST SCORE BY DEPRIVATION LEVEL (FIFTH GRADE)

	MORE DEPRIVATION			LESS DEPRIVATION		
SES Levels	$\overline{X}$	SD	N	$\overline{X}$	SD	N
I. Lower	454.22	94.00	38	513.83	69.78	13
II. Medium	490.18	81.45	23	526.23	97.23	25
III. Higher	536.08	52.55	6	533.11	72.87	30

Table 17–8

SIGNIFICANCE TESTS OF SES DIFFERENCES WITHIN DEPRIVATION LEVELS (FIFTH GRADE)

Within	df	F	P
More Deprivation	2	9.00	<.01
Less Deprivation	2	<1	N.S.

Table 17–8 (continued)

NEWMAN-KEULS COMPARISONS AMONG SES LEVELS WITHIN GREATER DEPRIVATION LEVELS

SES Levels	P
III vs. I	<.01
III vs. II	<.05
I vs. II	N.S.

Table 17–9

DIFFERENCES BETWEEN MORE AND LESS DEPRIVED (AS ASSESSED BY DEPRIVATION INDEX) ON GATES READING SCORE AS RELATED TO IQ LEVELS (FIFTH GRADE)

	DEPRIVATION LEVEL					
	MORE			LESS		
	$\overline{X}$	SD	N	$\overline{X}$	SD	N
IQ						
Higher	5.23	.60	24	5.33	.59	55
Lower	3.84	.85	59	4.46	1.14	22

Note: Interaction between IQ and Deprivation Index significant at .05 level.

context of social advantage and exacerbated in the context of social disadvantage.

A third example of the interactive influence of deprivation is afforded by the study of the combined effects of differences in socioeconomic status, race, and deprivation upon the test scores of the first-grade children. The three test scores are the marker variables for three factors derived from an analysis of a battery of cognitive tests administered to the first-grade sample. The factors are labeled intelligence, concept formation, and verbal fluency.

There is a significant interaction among the three independent variables. One interpretation of this significant interaction is that race, SES, and deprivation level define a category which differs from the others in terms of test scores. The statistical tests reveal that the differing category is the one defining the most advantaged grouping among the Negro children, i.e., those Negro children who are least deprived and in the highest socioeconomic category.* In order to show this

* Within the less-deprived category (but not in the more deprived category) simple effects of SES $\times$ race are significant ($p < .05$). Within the less-deprived category, and within the Negro group (but not within the white group), SES differences are significant by "simple effects" tests ($p < .01$). Again

more clearly, the mean test scores of the Negro and white children for each deprivation and SES category are shown in Table 17–10. It can be seen that the Negro children of higher SES level and lesser deprivation show a relatively higher mean score. It does *not* mean that these Negro children score significantly higher than those white children comparable in SES and deprivation level. The statistical tests reveal rather that the combined effects of higher SES and lowered deprivation have a significantly ameliorative effect among the Negro children.

Table 17–10

SES Differences in Overall Test Scores as a Function of Race and Deprivation Index (First Grade)

	NEGRO			WHITE		
SES Level	$\overline{X}$	SD	N	$\overline{X}$	SD	N
Lower						
More deprived	475.96	86.23	18	483.00	92.28	20
Less deprived	464.47	84.20	5	533.83	78.51	2
Medium						
More deprived	485.42	94.75	16	503.36	83.85	13
Less deprived	504.97	116.09	10	535.67	92.91	3
Higher						
More deprived	493.36	115.30	11	530.07	113.24	9
Less deprived	580.11	122.31	6	523.80	86.48	10

Note: Interaction between race, Deprivation Index, and SES level significant at .05 level.

SOME IMPLICATIONS

This paper has been concerned with social disadvantage from three viewpoints: (a) with the delineation of specific environmental factors which help to explain the disadvantaging effects of such global background factors as lowered socioeconomic status or membership in an underprivileged racial group; (b) with the description of a causal sequence, a developmental process whereby early environmental factors

within the less-deprived Negro group, higher SES level is significantly different from medium and lower SES levels ($p < .01$) in both Newman-Keuls comparisons, but medium and lower SES groups are not significantly different from one another.

manifest their disadvantaging effects upon later scholastic achievement and sense of competence through their adverse effects on the abilities underlying such achievements; and (c) with detailing ways in which social advantage may ameliorate the negative effects attributable to a cognitive factor such as intelligence or to social background factors such as socioeconomic status and race. Each of these concerns will be discussed in order.

  a. In the delineation of specific environmental conditions we have pointed out the importance of the child's interactions with adults in cognitively and motivationally stimulating settings. This emphasis is supported by the recent work carried out at the University of Chicago and reported by Bloom in his book, *Stability and Change in Human Characteristics*.[1] Thus, as reported by Bloom, Wolf has secured ratings of thirteen process variables descriptive of the interactions between parents and child and hypothetically related to intellectual growth. These items fall under the headings of parental press for academic achievement and for language development as well as provision for general learning. Wolf found a multiple correlation of .76 between ratings of the above factors and the IQ measures of 60 fifth-grade students. A similar study by Dave, also reported by Bloom, found a correlation of .80 between familial measures of the above type and achievement test performance of fourth-graders. In our study, the multiple *r* relating the six deprivational variables to reading is .49. The differences may be attributable to differences in instruments assessing social disadvantage, to the tests measuring achievement, and most of all to the attenuated number of predictor variables used in this as compared to the Dave study (six as compared to thirteen). Besides their emphasis on interaction with adults, the deprivational variables reveal another attribute—their specificity, i.e., their relatively slight degree of interrelation. This would suggest that remedial effects may best be attained by programs that direct attention to a number of specific areas and competencies rather than concentrate effort upon one. As suggested by the deprivational variables, such areas and competencies may be of a motivational, linguistic, and informational nature. The importance of parental motivation, it should be noted, emerges in our data at the first-grade level. Unfortunately, we did not measure reading readiness at the first-grade level, so that comparisons between first- and fifth-grade correlations between parental scholastic aspiration and achievement in school could not be made.

  b. Our results are consistent with a developmental sequence relating environmental conditions to the formation of certain abilities which in turn affect achievement and sense of competence. However, the results, in supplying empirical correlations between (1) Deprivation Index, (2) the self-concept measure, (3) test scores reflecting abilities, and (4) reading score reflecting achievement, are also consistent with a more complicated interactive model as well as one stressing a simple one-way progression of influence. Cultural deprivation, occasioned by the conditions associated with poverty, may result in some cognitive and learning deficits relative to the demands of the early grades. With early failure or difficulty in academic tasks, the child's self-confidence may be impaired so that learning becomes more difficult and unrewarding. The lowered achievement level may even feed back on the slower development of the original abilities. In any case, lowered abilities may produce lower achievements, and lowered achievements may induce diminished self-confidence which in turn feeds back upon the achievements and so on. If one adds the devaluations brought about by race prejudice superimposed on poverty prejudice, these processes may be accelerated.

At a more abstract level, the above process is reminiscent of Piaget's accommodation and assimilation paradigm[3, 5] and of Hunt's conceptions of intrinsic motivation.[4] Piaget's fundamental notion is that intelligence comprises a series of hierarchically arranged cognitive structures. The sensorimotor schemata of the early years are structures derived from the actual physical intractions with environmental objects. With continued interaction and with the development of linguistic and symbolic functions, the essentially motoric schemata become internalized as concrete operations. With these concrete operations, the child from about seven to eleven years can mentally organize, integrate, and differentiate the concrete world about him. With further development, the concrete operations themselves become organized into systems of formal operations. The latter represent mental processes which allow the individual to explore possibilities, pursue hypotheses, and make systematic connections within imagined realities. Within each of these levels there is a process of accommodation and assimilation. The mental structure accommodates to the variety of stimulation and problems presented to it. But it can accommodate only when there is a "match," in Hunt's terms, between the internal schema or operation and the external task or requirement. Only then will the internal structure assimilate the environment. If the environment poses problems that are too difficult, the structure will not be able to assimilate it and accommodation or mental growth will not take place. Frustration and withdrawal will. If the problems are too easy, boredom and disinterest will prevail. From this purview, the period from six to ten is one where important schemata are being strengthened and integrated. If there is a continually poor match between the child's schemata and the subject matter which these schemata are supposed to assimilate, there will be little constructive accommodation, and little growth of those underlying thought forms. The cumulative deficit in our study of the first- and fifth-graders may be the results of such a process.

c. Our final set of findings, dealing with ameliorative effects of the more advantageous circumstances implicit in the items making up the Deprivation Index, lends support to enrichment attempts. For these enrichment programs attempt to induce, by controlled intervention, some of the advantage accruing to certain groups "naturally." These findings specify the particular conditions under which socioeconomic, race, and intellective differences are more pronounced and when they are attenuated. One interpretation of these findings is that a background of greater advantage (low scores on the Deprivation Index) has a compensatory effect. Thus if race is associated with lowered-ability test scores, such decrements are minimized or vanish under conditions of stronger social advantage; or by extension, under conditions where learning environments have been substantially improved. Similarly, if lowered intelligence scores are associated with lowered reading scores, this decrement is also ameliorated under conditions of stronger social advantage. Increased educational opportunities may produce the same ameliorating effect, as suggested in a recent publication of the Office of Education.[2]

Though lowered socioeconomic status is associated with lowered test scores on intellective and language functions, interactional opportunities, as assessed by the Deprivation Index, provide for a counter-effect. In sum, to the degree that intervention attempts are capable of supplying the compensatory experiences implicit in the Deprivation Index, such attempts may be successful in reversing or ameliorating the cumulative deficit discussed above.

Pertinent to this point is the distinction between the effects of race and SES. Thus these two background factors show different relationships to the Lorge-Thorndike. The SES deficit begins earlier and is as pronounced among the younger first-graders as among the older fifth-graders. The decrement associated with race, however, begins later, is more cumulative and more pronounced among the older Negro children. Our sample selection as well as our mode of statistical analysis has aimed at separating these two factors—race and SES. But in society, they are confounded. Negroes tend to be poorer than whites. The implication is that the Negro child may be sequentially disadvantaged. Factors associated with lower SES may produce early deficit. In addition, later deficit may be produced by environmental factors associated with Negro status. Some of these environmental factors which are independent of the SES measure seem to be tapped by the Deprivation Index. The lack of correlation in our sample between race and SES, the significant relation between race and Deprivation Index, the loss of the cumulative race deficit when the Deprivation Index is controlled—these afford evidence for this interpretation.

REFERENCES

1. Bloom, B. *Stability and change in human characteristics.* New York: Wiley, 1964.
2. Coleman, J., *et al. Equality of educational opportunity.* Washington: U. S. Government Printing Office, 1966.
3. Flavell, J. H. *The developmental world of Jean Piaget.* Princeton, N.J.: Van Nostrand, 1963.
4. Hunt, J. McV. *Intelligence and experience.* New York: Ronald, 1961.
5. Piaget, J. *The psychology of intelligence.* Transl. from the French by M. Percy and D. E. Berlyne. London: Routledge & Paul, 1950.

18 /

The Role of Social Class in Language Development and Cognition

MARTIN DEUTSCH

The particular area of research on which we have been focusing at the Institute for Developmental Studies has as one of its objectives the delineation of the major dimensions through which environment is likely to operate in a manner inhibiting development. Another objective is to attempt to specify the cognitive and language areas that have been most influenced by unfavorable environmental circumstances. As we learn about the typology of cognitive and language deficiencies, we also learn something more about human learning and evolve methods that might be effective in facilitating development.

The delineation of the area of concern in this way reflects a basic thesis that human potential is not even close to full exploitation by the available educational structures and that the possibilities for development are most especially being neglected with regard to what Harrington has termed "The Other America." [2]

Simply obtaining relationships between social-class or ethnic attributes and intelligence or other singular factors has been historically useful, but inadequate in telling us how the structure of experience as mediated through particular environments influences the patterning of cognitive processes. Therefore, our attack on this problem has included an initial attempt to make a microanalysis of the environment, encompassing such molar data as the traditional information on the social structure of the family, communication, economic circumstances, the educational histories of the family members, their child-rearing practices, dominance-passivity patterns, sex role determinations, and the like. The attempt also has been made to analyze the activity structure of the home, the quality of interaction between adults and children, and the whole matrix of behavioral expectations, in terms of both immediate behavior and long-range educational and general goal aspirations. What we are attempting to do in this series of studies is to identify patterns in the context of background variables at two developmental stages, and to relate these background patterns to specific cognitive and linguistic patterns. The purpose, thus, is not simply to demonstrate the existence of cognitive and learning disabilities in association with disadvantaged environments, but to define both anomalies and orderliness in perceptual, linguistic, and conceptual processes, so that eventual compensatory action on the areas of disability can be based on empirical evidence.

In the study to be discussed here, emphasis was placed on the evaluation of linguistic variables, not only because language is the primary avenue for communication, absorption, and interpretation of the environment, but because it also reflects highly acculturated styles of thought and ideational modes for solving and not solving problems. It seems reasonable to conclude that as we study the background influences on qualitative variables in language and language development, we also are studying the effects of the same influences on cognitive development and problem-solving styles and abilities. As Bruner puts it in his introduction to Vygotsky's book *Thought and Language:*[7] "For it is the internalization of overt action that makes thought, and particularly the internalization of external dialogue that brings the powerful tool of language to bear on the stream of thought. Man, if you will, is shaped by the tools and instruments he comes to use, and neither the mind nor the hand alone can amount to much . . ."

Strong evidence can be adduced to support the assumption that it is the active verbal engagement of people who surround him which is the operative influence in the child's language development. The structuring of these verbal engagements in terms of the family's conditions and style of life, and the further relationship between the style of life and social-class membership leads to the analysis of children's language skills and verbal behavior in terms of their families' socioeconomic status. In the cognitive style of the lower-class family, Bernstein[1] points out, language is used in a convergent or restrictive fashion rather than a divergent, elaborative fashion. An exclamation or an imperative or a partial sentence frequently replaces a complete sentence or an explanation: if a child asks for something, the response is too frequently "yes," "no," "go away," "later," or simply a nod. The feedback is not such that it gives the child the articulated verbal parameters that allow him to start and fully develop normative labeling and identification of the environment. Family interaction data which we have gathered in both lower-class socially deprived and middle-class groups indicate that, as compared with the middle-class homes, there is a paucity of organized family activities in a large number of lower-class homes. As a result, there is less conversation, for example, at meals, as meals are less likely to be regularly scheduled family affairs. In Chapter 14 we reported that children from fatherless homes have significantly lower IQ scores by the time they get to the fifth grade than do children who come from intact homes, and we hypothesized that this finding was a consequence not so much of the absence of the father, as it was of the diminution of organized family activity.

The data to be discussed in this paper come from the "Verbal Survey." The population studied included a core sample of 292 children and an extended population of about 2,500 children of various racial and social-class groupings. Negro and white, lower- and middle-class children were included in a relatively well-balanced sample.

In general, we have found that lower-class children, Negro and white, compared with middle-class children, are subject to what we've labeled a "cumulative deficit phenomenon," which takes place between the first- and fifth-grade years. Though there are significant socioeconomic and race differences seen in measured variables at the first-grade level, it is important to note that they become more marked as the child progresses through school. While we can accept the notion that some of this cumulative deficiency is associated with inadequate early preparation because of corresponding environmental deficiencies, the adequacy of the school environment also must be questioned: in a model system, one should expect linearity in cognitive growth.

In a caste society it is very difficult to control for socioeconomic status, and it is possible that some of the Negro child's measured increasing deficit stems artificially from this incomplete control. At the same time, inferior caste must imprint itself on the child at an early age and is a constant presence in the environment.

As indicated above, the data to be reported here were collected on a balanced sample of children at two age levels, and it is some of the analysis and interpretation of a portion of these data which will now be discussed. In the "Verbal Survey" we assessed over 100 identifiable variables concerned with home background, language functioning, conceptual behavior, intelligence test performance, reading, general orientation, self-systems, various subcomponents of language, and assorted related factors. This paper will make reference (by no means exhaustively) to only 52 of these variables concerned with a range of cognitive functions and a few demographic measures, but with language variables at the core.

The entire correlational matrices will not be reproduced here. Rather, the overall patterning of results will be examined in terms of social-class, race, and developmental levels as more-or-less independent variables. Only those correlations which are significant at the .01 level or better will be considered as significant. For the size of the current samples, this means including correlations of .21 or higher (Table 18–1). A definition of each of the variables is listed in Table 18–2.

Table 18–1

COMPARISONS BETWEEN FIRST- AND FIFTH-GRADE "VERBAL SURVEY" SAMPLES: SIGNIFICANT CORRELATIONS WITH RACE AND SES [a]

	CORRELATIONS WITH RACE [b]		CORRELATIONS WITH SES [c]	
Variables	*First Grade* (N=127)	*Fifth Grade* (N=165)	*First Grade* (N=127)	*Fifth Grade* (N=165)
7—Age in months				—.21
8—L-T IQ Score		—.36	.42	.38
9—L-T subtest #1		—.34	.35	.25
10—L-T subtest #2		—.30	.26	.32
11—L-T subtest #3		—.30	.26	.38
12—L-T raw score		—.35	.34	.37
13—WISC Vocab. score		—.31	.22	.49
14—Gates score			(test not given)	.44
15—Verbal Ident., noun enumer. score	—.25	—.28		
16—Verbal Ident., action enumer. score	—.28	—.20		
17—Verbal Ident., combined enumer. score	—.27	—.27		
18—Verbal Ident., noun gestalt score			.33	.24
19—Verbal Ident., action gestalt score			.24	
20—Verbal Ident., combined gestalt score			.32	.27
21—PPVT raw score			.32	(test not given)
22—PPVT IQ			.33	(test not given)

Table 18–1 (continued)

COMPARISONS BETWEEN FIRST- AND FIFTH-GRADE VERBAL SURVEY SAMPLES: SIGNIFICANT CORRELATIONS WITH RACE AND SES [a]

Variables	CORRELATIONS WITH RACE [b]		CORRELATIONS WITH SES [c]	
	First Grade (N=127)	Fifth Grade (N=165)	First Grade (N=127)	Fifth Grade (N=165)
23—Concept Sort., # piles score	.21			
25—Concept Sort., verbal score			.23	
26—Concept Sort., verbal score/ # piles (ratio)	−.21			.23
29—Concept Form, percept. similarities scores				.22
35—Concept Form., verbaliz. score, class specificity	−.25	−.36	.26	.20
36—Concept Form., verbaliz. score, class generaliz.		−.24		.21
37—Concept Form., total verbaliz. score	−.24	−.32		.21
38—Word Knowledge score (Verbal Fluency)		−.24 −.24		
39—Verbal Fluency, all rhymes score		−.20	.24	.28
40—Verbal Fluency, meaningful rhymes		−.24	.28	.33
41—Verbal Fluency, sentence fluency		−.20	.25	
43—Orientation Scale		−.30	.36	.51
47—Wepman test of auditory discrimination [d]	.24		−.24	
48—Word Assoc., form class score				.27
49—Word Assoc., latency score		.35		
50—Cloze test, grammatical score			.26	.33
51—Cloze test, correct score			.25	.33
52—Cloze test, popular score			.30	.37

[a] Only correlations significant at $p < .01$ are shown.
[b] For purposes of coding, white was coded as 1 and Negro as 2.
[c] Higher index numbers denote higher SES.
[d] Error score.

On the first-grade level, lower social-class status is associated with poorer performance on all the IQ scores: the Lorge-Thorndike (L-T), the WISC vocabulary test, and the Peabody Picture Vocabulary Test (PPVT); the three scores on a Verbal Identification Test which have to do with a more abstract conceptualization of a visual stimulus; several rhyming, fluency, and verbal-explanation scores on a Verbal Fluency and a Concept Sorting Test; scores on a Cloze Test; and a score reflecting general environmental orientation (variables 8, 9, 10, 11, 12, 13, 18, 19, 20, 21, 22, 25, 35, 39, 40, 41, 43, 47, 50, 51, 52).

If for the first-grade subjects we examine the variables which correlate significantly with both SES and race, there are only two in addition to those which correlated only with SES. These are one verbalization score on the Concept Formation Test and scores on the Wepman test of auditory discrimination (variables 35, 47).

There are only six variables which relate to race but not SES. These variables are three enumeration scores on the Verbal Identification Test, two scores relating to the inclusiveness of grouping on the Concept Sorting Test, and a verbalization score on the Concept Formation Test (variables, 15, 16, 17, 23, 26, 27). The tasks on the Verbal Identification Test involved labeling and are measures highly reflective of experience and the specific availability of labels, whereas the Concept Sorting Test required a knowledge of categories including occupations, transportation, housing, and animals.

Table 18–2

BRIEF DESCRIPTION OF "VERBAL SURVEY" TEST MEASURES

Variable Number	Identification	Variable Number	Identification
7.	S's age in months at time of Lorge-Thorndike testing	17.	*Combined Enumeration Score* (15 + 16)—All the items identified correctly on the stimulus cards of the Verbal Identification test.
8–12.	Lorge-Thorndike IQ Score (Subjects 1, 2, 3, and Raw Score)		
13.	WISC Vocabulary Score	18.	*Noun Gestalt Score*—The measure of the child's ability to describe a scene with a single word when the scene is best described by a noun.
14.	Gates Reading Score		
		19.	*Action Gestalt Score*—The measure of the child's ability to describe a scene with a single word when the scene is best described by a verb.
	Verbal Identification Test— The child is shown 20 simple drawings one at a time and given a set to enumerate the objects in the pictures. The child is then shown the 20 pictures a second time and asked to give the one word that best describes each picture.		
		20.	*Combined Gestalt Score* (18 + 19)—The measure of the child's ability to describe the scenes of the Verbal Identification test with a single word.
15.	*Noun Enumeration Score*— The number of items identified correctly on those stimulus cards best described by a noun, e.g., kitchen.		
		21.	*PPVT Raw Score*—Peabody Picture Vocabulary Test. The number of words tried minus the number incorrect.
16.	*Action Enumeration Score*— The number of items identified correctly on those stimulus cards best described by a verb, e.g., saluting.	22.	*PPVT IQ Score*—Obtained from the appropriate tables in the PPVT manual.

Table 18–2 (continued)

BRIEF DESCRIPTION OF "VERBAL SURVEY" TEST MEASURES

Variable Number	Identification	Variable Number	Identification

Concept Sorting Test—
The child is presented 16 cards in random order (four each representing: modes of transportation, housing, occupations, and animals) and asked to sort the cards into piles. He also is asked to explain his grouping.

23. *Number of Piles Score*—The exact number of piles sorted. Four would be best. Usually anything above four indicates inadequacy at the task. This number has been primarily intended as a denominator for the other scores.

24. *Sort Score*—This score reflects the implicit quality of the child's sorting, e.g., sorting by class generalization receives more credit than functional pairings. Generally, the higher the score the better the quality.

25. *Verbalization Score*—For this score the child is asked to explain the basis of his sorting procedure. The basis of his sorting is evaluated and scored. Higher forms of classification, e.g., generalization vs. functional pairing, get higher scores.

26. 25/23 = Verbal Score Ratio
27. 24/23 = Sort Score Ratio

Concept Formation Test—
The child is presented with a booklet consisting of pictures representing concepts of identity, similarity, class specificity (persons or animals), and class generalization (living things). He is instructed to choose stimuli which belong together and to give a verbal explanation for the grouping.

28. *Perceptual Identification Score*—The number of correctly matched items when the intended basis for matching is perceptual identity, e.g., the same dog.

29. *Perceptual Similarity Score*—

The number of correctly matched items when the intended basis for matching is perceptual similarity, e.g., a collie with terriers.

30. *Class Specificity Score*—The number of items correctly matched when the intended basis for matching is that the items belong to the same class, e.g., a dog and a horse are both animals.

31. *Class Generality Score*—The number of items correctly matched when the items to be matched belong to different classes which are subclasses of a more general category, e.g., a dog and a rose are both living things.

32. *Total Choice Score*—The total number of items matched correctly (28 + 29 + 30 + 31).

33. *Verbalization Score, Perceptual-Identification Items*—The Verbalization Score is the evaluation of the child's expressed reason for putting two items together, with higher levels of generalization getting higher scores. This is the verbalization score for those items where the basis for matching is perceptual identity.

34. *Verbalization Score, Perceptual Similarity Items*—The evaluation of the child's expressed reason for putting together items when the basis of matching is perceptual similarity.

35. *Verbalization Score, Class Specificity Items*—The evaluation of the child's expressed reason for matching items when the intended basis for matching is class specificity.

36. *Verbalization Score, Class Generality Items*—The evaluation of the child's expressed reason for matching items when the

Table 18-2 (continued)

BRIEF DESCRIPTION OF "VERBAL SURVEY" TEST MEASURES

Variable Number	Identification	Variable Number	Identification
	intended basis for matching is class generality.		(1–10) of the most distant association accepted as going with the stimulus word.
37.	*Total Verbalization Score* (33 + 34 + 35 + 36.)	45.	*Association Score*—The number of associations accepted as going with the stimulus word.
	Verbal Fluency Test	46.	*Discrepancy Score* (44–45)—The most distant association minus the number of associations made.
38.	*Word Knowledge Score*—The number of words the child can give in 45 seconds.		
39.	*All Rhymes Score*—Total number of rhymes given (whether or not a response is a meaningful word) in response to specific stimuli.	47.	*Wepman Auditory Discrimination Test—Different Score*—This is an error score, and refers to errors made in identifying as different, pairs of words which have very similar sounds.
40.	*Meaningful Rhymes Score*—Total number of *meaningful rhymes* given by child in response to specific stimuli.		
41.	*Sentence Fluency Score*—The child is requested to make sentences using first one word, then the original word plus a second stimulus, and finally a sentence containing the first two stimuli plus a third. The sentences are evaluated for quality and organization.		*Word Association Test*
		48.	*Form Class Score*—The number of first-word responses which are of the same form class as the stimulus word.
		49.	*Latency Score*—The time in seconds before first association to each stimulus is given.
42.	*Difference Score*—All rhymes minus meaningful rhymes (39–40).		*Cloze Test*
43.	*Orientation Scale Test*—A measure of the child's general knowledge, e.g., what state does he live in?	50.	*Grammatical Score*—The number of fill-ins which are grammatically correct. These responses do not have to be contextually correct as well.
	Word Distance Test— To the same stimuli presented in the Word Association Test, the child is requested to state whether or not ten specific words go with each stimulus. The specific words were previously ranked for distance from stimulus.	51.	*Correct Score*—The number of contextually correct fill-ins including popular responses.
44.	*Distance Score*—The number	52.	*Popular Score*—The number of responses which correspond to the responses given most frequently by schoolteachers and medical students.

It might be noted that all the significant relationships were between poorer performance and lower-class status. The race differences are present and are in the direction of poorer performance by Negro children, but they are reflected in *only* eight of the possible 43 comparisons for the first-grade group.

It is important to note that the correlation with the Wepman auditory-discrimination test is associated with both SES and race. What might be operative here is the presence of dialect variations in the Negro group, influencing and limiting the communication possibilities in school, and possibly having direct relevance to the three enumeration scores that are associated only with race, as there may be a general contamination here of comprehension.

On examining similar relationships for the fifth-grade group, we find that all the IQ measures now no longer relate just to SES but also to race. Still relating only to SES are two gestalt scores involving abstract categorization of visual stimuli, and the scores on the Cloze Test, which are associated with the manipulation and syntactical control of language. Additional variables associated with SES for the fifth-grade sample are a Form-Class score on the Word Association Test, also probably associated with syntax and logical sequence; a perceptual similarities score on a Concept Formulation Test; and a score on a Concept Sorting Test which reflects the adequacy of categorizing visual stimuli (variables 48, 29, 26). The final variable which relates to SES is the reading score (variable 14)—a score which at the time of the "Verbal Survey" could not be obtained for the first-grade group. We now are completing the standardization of a Reading Prognosis Test for kindergarten and first-grade children, and are collecting data which will be parallel to those reported here for fifth-grade children.

For the fifth-grade sample, there are 12 variables which are related to both SES and race, as opposed to 3 variables for first-graders. What happens in terms of specific measures is that the Wepman correlation drops, no doubt for developmental reasons; the other 2 measures—both verbalization scores—remain and are joined by 10 additional variables, none of which was associated with race for the first-grade sample, but all of which were associated with SES. These 10 measures include all the IQ scores, 2 verbal fluency measures, and the general orientation score (variables 8, 9, 10, 11, 12, 13, 39, 40, 43). What this seems to indicate is that the deficit associated with lower SES status on these measures is joined by a deficit associated with race. A more exact breakdown of these shifts is currently underway by means of partial correlations and analyses of variance.

The variables for the fifth-grade sample associated with race but not SES include the same 3 enumeration scores as were found for the first-graders, but do not include the 2 categorization scores found at the first-grade level. However, a word knowledge and a sentence-fluency score have been added to this category, and, very interestingly, a latency score has also been added (variables 38, 41, 49). This last finding is consistent with some other data on expressive language behavior (see Chapter 10) and might indicate a hesitation phenomenon among Negro children when handling language material. This finding also could reflect a different temporal expectation in verbal interchange, and this might be a fruitful hypothesis to investigate.

Over all, of 42 measures for the first-grade sample, 6 correlated significantly with race alone, 19 with SES alone, and 2 with both. Of 43 scores for the fifth-grade sample, 6 correlated with race alone, 10 with SES alone, and 12 with both. This result means that significant correlations with race were found in 8 comparisons for the first-graders, and in 18 for the fifth-grade sample. The number of significant comparisons on SES for each group was 22. Also, for each group 15 measures were related to neither race nor SES. There was great overlap between the groups on these non-discriminating measures, and they tended to be the more concrete ones (first grade—variables 7, 24, 27, 28, 29, 30, 31, 32, 33, 34, 36, 38, 42, 48, 49; fifth grade—variables 19, 23, 24, 25, 27, 28, 30, 31, 32, 33, 34, 42, 44, 45, 46, 47).

If we now look for the functions underlying measures for which race is associated with poor performance, they are found in areas of abstraction, verbalization, and experientially dependent enumeration. It should be emphasized, however, that not all measures reflecting these functions related to race.[1]

In a paper by John[4] reporting on work done at the Institute, she suggests that the middle-class child has an advantage over the lower-class child in the amount of tutoring and help available to him in his home. She emphasizes that without such help it is very difficult for a child to acquire the more abstract and precise use of language. Indeed, in the data just discussed, what is found is a deficiency based on class and race in the measures which reflect abstract and categorical use of language, as opposed to denotative and labeling usage.

If the tripartite language ordering that we have used in formulating measures for our research is applied, it is found that as the complexity of the levels increases, from labeling, through relating, to categorizing, the negative effects of social disadvantage are enhanced. It is also true, in looking at the enumeration scores, that as labeling requirements become more complex and related to more diverse and variegated experience, lower-class people with more restricted experience are going to have more difficulty in supplying the correct labels. In Hunt's terms,[3] there is an inappropriate "match" between the child's intrinsic development and the external requirements.

In the formulation of Bernstein,[1] the cumulative deficiency in language functioning is the failure in development of an elaborated language system that has accurate grammatical order and logical modifiers, and is mediated through a grammatically complex sentence structure, which has frequent use of prepositions and impersonal pronouns, as well as a discriminative selection of adjectives and adverbs. These and other characteristics described by Bernstein are those which he feels give direction to the organization of thinking. The elaborated language code is differentiated from what he defines as the restricted language code, which is systematically used largely as the major speech form of the lower class. It is characterized by grammatically simple and often unfinished sentences, poor syntactical form, simple and repetitive use of conjunctions, the inability to hold a formal topic through speech sequences, a rigid and limited use of adjectives and adverbs, etc. In essence, he is describing a class-based language system that effectively denies the lower-class person the necessary verbal strategies to obtain vertical social mobility. This is probably more true in England, where Bernstein works, with its rigid class-oriented school system, than it is here. But in our society it might be particularly cogent for rural-to-urban migrants marked by caste factors or by the highly delineated social-class factors possessed, for example, by the Appalachian whites. In our society, if school is to be effective and these youngsters are not to be discharged into that very large group of unskilled unemployables, then mediating, expressive, and receptive language training should be a conscious part of curriculum organization. You just cannot become a computer technologist unless you can read the instructions and utilize the necessary mechanisms for symbolization and concept attainment. And for this you must have available an elaborated language system with appropriate mediators.

What makes the implications of the findings reported so significant is their apparent contribution to the cumulative deficit hypothesis. Also, the findings provide insight into the nature of the cumulative deficit. Essentially, it would appear that when one adds four years of a school experience to a poor environment, plus minority-group status, what emerge are children who are apparently less capable of handling standard intellectual and linguistic tasks. One also might postulate that when the Negro child broadens his environmental contacts by going to school (and to and from school) he is made more aware of his inferior caste status, and this awareness has the same depressing effect on his performance that his inferior class status had all along. The data indicate that being lower class, Negro or white, makes for lower language scores. Being Negro makes for lower scores. But being both lower class and Negro does not disproportionately make for lower language scores.

As indicated, these children have poorer capabilities in handling syntax. I would suggest that they are aware of their grammatical ineptness, and this awareness leads to a reticence and a hesitancy to communicate across social-class lines. This would mean that speech as Luria[5,6] conceives of it (as a single complex leading to changes in the stimulus field) is not operative for these children in the school situation. If language cannot be used as an elaborating form of communication, school loses much of its socializing and teaching capabilities, regardless of the curriculum content. As a consequence, for a significant proportion of these children, functional motivation may not exist in terms of the learning strategies demanded by the school situation. As a result, the negative properties associated with lower-class and minority-group status tend to become reinforced, and for these children, language becomes an effective tool only when it has adequate feedback properties in communicating with peers or others who share the particular subculture. In other words, language becomes intra-class contained. The breakdown in communication here is probably a major operative variable which leads for example to the high dropout rate; the student is no longer in communication with anything that is meaningful to him in the school. When teachers report they are frustrated with the learning attitudes and potentials of many of the disadvantaged children, they are responding objectively to a reality condition that, through their expectations, they have helped to produce.

It would seem that in the long run the most effective remedial and enrichment programming would have to follow developmental stages, and curriculum change should be introduced at the earliest possible time in the school experience in order to arrest the cumulative deficit, for as development goes on in the individual child, it probably is progressively more difficult to reverse the deficit, as there is more of it.

In a sense, we still know a minimum of what the school does and does not do to the child. The exciting aspect is that with more specific knowledge of developmental processes and of the influences of environmental factors and of special stimulating conditions on them, it should be possible to program stimulation in increasingly less amorphous ways and with methods that are appropriate to basic learning capabilities, so as to vitiate the effects of unfavorable environments.

REFERENCES

1. Bernstein, B. Language and social class. *Brit. J. Sociol.*, 1960, 11, 271–276.
2. Harrington, M. *The other America.* New York: Macmillan, 1962.
3. Hunt, J. McV. *Intelligence and experience.* New York: Ronald, 1961.
4. John, Vera P. The intellectual development of slum children: some preliminary findings. *Amer. J. Orthopsychiat.*, 1963, 33 (5), 813–822.
5. Luria, A. R. *The role of speech in regulation of normal and abnormal behavior.* New York: Liveright, 1961.
6. Luria, A. R., & Yudovich, F. Y. *Speech and development of mental processes in children.* London: Staples Press, 1959.
7. Vygotsky, L. S. *Thought and language.* Cambridge: MIT Press, 1962.

19 /

The Principal Issue

MARTIN DEUTSCH

In a sense there has been a shotgun wedding between education and social science, but it is still questionable whether the bride and groom will be able to establish the kind of relationship that will permit effective collaboration in the development of new knowledge and its application both to the school as a social system and to the learning process in the classroom.

It has been quite fashionable for intellectuals mechanically to characterize education as the apex of mediocrity, and work in the behavioral and social sciences typically has lost status if it has application to education. There can be little question that education has at least in part earned its image; but at the same time sneering scholasticism has helped create an automatic defensive posture in education. Both attitudes have impaired and minimized the interchange of experience and evolving knowledge.

In the last decade, a greatly intensified interchange has taken place, largely because of the series of social revolutions which have invaded the classroom. For the first time many social and behavioral scientists are finding themselves active participants in the educational system, though often with undefined status and role relationships, particularly with respect to decision-making processes. As a result of this lack of definition, there is a constant danger that the individual social scientist will become either entirely alienated or totally absorbed into the system.

Our nation has become more conscious of the pivotal role of education in "solving" major social problems. As education has become identified as a major avenue through which particular social goals may be attained, it has become the victim of a kind of magical orientation to which our culture is prone: identifying the problem is considered just a short step from solving it. Once education is seen as the key to alleviation of external pressures and internal social inequities, then, magically, the cure need only be applied.

The new explicit and distinct role assigned to education has created enormous pressures on a system which has had no built-in mechanisms to absorb, modify, codify, and accommodate to social change. Education is in many respects in an unenviable position, and one that necessitates the active engagement of the intellectual community with the full gamut of education's social responsibilities.

The changes taking place which create a whole new social context for educational innovation include accelerated communication of ideas and knowledge, international competition that places greater priority on accomplishment in some fields than in others, and, probably most important, the increasing demands of people in all industrializing nations for a greater participation in the rewards of a growing national productive capacity. These changes are occurring, further, in a context of massive urbanization, the civil rights struggle, a shifting in the ratio of demand for highly skilled workers to that for semi- and unskilled ones, and all the other by-products of an automating, technologically advancing society that is at the same time being forced to face its moral and social delinquencies.

Education is being asked to compensate not only for its own failures but for society's failures as well. Education's fault has been its inability to identify its own problems and its moral callousness in allowing massive failure and miserable educational conditions for a substantial segment of the school population. For example, segregated schools carry with them poor education, partly because there traditionally has been in them no middle-class group demanding quality. Generally speaking, education has been satisfied to offer an inferior intellectual diet in the urban ghetto, and the demand for change has come not from educators, but from external social forces demanding equality of opportunity. Much of the most recent dissonance between the intellectual community and the educational establishment (whatever either of those is) has arisen from intellectuals' consistent identification of the civil rights struggle as one of the most significant social events, together with the general apathy and passivity of educators in responding to it.

The changes that are taking place in education—whether in curriculum reform, early childhood programs, programmed instruction, and game techniques or in redistricting, educational parks, and meaningful social integration in the classroom—are for the most part being imposed or stimulated from the outside. It is too much to expect that a bureaucratic Neanderthal like the educational establishment could have devised and instituted its own program of reform and creative innovation. But now that we are approximately a decade away from the Supreme Court's decision in the *Brown* case and from Sputnik, it may be expected that education will develop its own inner velocity to meet social demands. If it is to have the respect it so often claims to deserve, certainly a good proportion of the next decade's innovations and the development of recent ones should come from the formal educational establishment. Also, having absorbed a decade of severe criticism and having almost achieved a new social status, the automatic defensive posture to external suggestion should be assumed less frequently and should be replaced by the development of techniques of analysis and incorporation of new strategies.

To place the responsibility for innovation on the schools is not to ignore or deny the ongoing participation of social scientists in education. On the contrary, the role for them can be an extremely important one, and one which the changes in education should make possible. The fact that the schools have been subjected to so much external pressure has done much to make them a more open system and one which can be more receptive (or less hostile) to potential contributions from the social and behavioral sciences.

One major area for this contribution has come to eclipse others. Currently it has been estimated that over 60 per cent of Negro and 20 per cent of white youth do not pass the armed forces general education test. Failure rates are related to the quality of education available to the young men taking the test. Such rates therefore represent serious failure on the part of education. Regular social science participation in the system offers the possibility of continual feedback about the effectiveness of educational programs. The classical correlation of per pupil expenditure with effectiveness of educational program can be spurious and therefore should not be relied on exclusively by either critics or defenders of the educational status quo. Low level of expenditure is most likely to be associated with poor educational products, though even here there are infrequent exceptional circumstances and teachers for whom other motivation replaces the desire for money. But high educational expenditure does not automatically re-

374 / The Principal Issue

sult in an above-the-mean product. Money may be a necessary ingredient, but quality education must be accomplished through the meshing of other elements. The fiction that money alone can change the products of education omits the essential human elements of involvement, high motivation, favorable expectations and attitudes, and the assumption by education of a professional responsibility for the results of its efforts.

The social scientist now on the scene can at least, if there is sufficient fidelity to the scientific perspective, supply the information by means of which educators can become aware of the social ramifications of their activities. Assuming that the social scientist does not become wholly part of the educational system, he can become the examiner of realities rather than fantasies and can join in a partnership that may substantially change both the educator and the social scientist.

So perhaps one of the most effective roles for the social scientist in the schools is the evaluation of the operation and consequences of educational planning and programming, with special reference to the concrete assumption of responsibility for meaningfully incorporating the needs of different racial and ethnic groups. This carries with it the responsibility for seeing the educational system both as part of the social system and as part of a historical process. And possibly most important is the social scientist's part in identifying middle-class ambivalence toward making the educational establishment as responsive to Harlem as it is to Westchester.

When all is said and done, education represents society's gift-horse for the aspirations of 60 to 70 per cent of the public school children in the next few decades. It may very well be the social scientist's role to assist the educator in making certain that it is not a Trojan horse.

In essence, this brief discussion has been saying that the most important considerations in education relate to establishing equality of opportunity for all, at least in the school system. Race and social class are essential factors in this process, and both education and the social sciences are fortunate that they have the opportunity to influence one another to make the social accommodations that are so patently necessary.

If the current evidence that integrated schools are of great importance to the Negro child and of only slightly less importance to the white child is borne out, the joint forces of the social sciences and education will be necessary. Social scientists and educators will need all their courage to criticize the old order and make radical renovations for the new.

In the light of the overriding importance of this issue, the other obvious areas in which social scientists can and do productively participate in education—curriculum reform, applications of learning theory, research into basic learning processes, etc.—seem to assume lesser urgency, though without the implication that work in these areas should be decreased. Our social problems are so enormous that failure to face up to them will keep education in the last century and make the social scientist an erstwhile consultant.

Conclusion

20 /

Brief Reflections on the Theory of Early Childhood Enrichment Programs

CYNTHIA P. DEUTSCH
AND MARTIN DEUTSCH

Enrichment programs need to be evolved as we obtain more knowledge about the patterning of intellectual capabilities at different developmental stages. With such knowledge we can devise appropriate methods, using the modern technologies, for the stimulation of maximum cognitive growth. It is obvious that satisfactory enrichment programs cannot be developed on an "instant" basis, though the social need is immediate. However, much can be done today, based on available techniques and the willingness of the educational apparatus to commit itself to taking the responsibility for the training of the child at an earlier age. With the application of new techniques, programs should become increasingly relevant to the needs of the child, and effective in securing change.

The emphasis on so-called disadvantaged children is dictated by the enormous problem of social inequality with its sequelae of interference with developmental potential. The educational apparatus has thus far been unable to provide these children with the necessary compensations that would lead to school performance consistent with their intrinsic capabilities. However, the emphasis placed on the particular problems of children from disadvantaged circumstances is accompanied by the recognition that the formulations about cognitive processes and educational procedures have application to children from all backgrounds.

There are several basic theoretical assumptions which are at the foundation of our thinking and our programming at the Institute for Developmental Studies.

The first of these is that environment plays a major role in the

development of cognitive skills and of the functional use of intellectual capabilities, such as learning how to learn. The probability is that
the environmental role is greatest in the large central area of the continuum of intellectual skill, with biological factors making their greatest contribution at the lowest and at the highest ends. Environment influences the development of cognitive processes as well as the content
of thought and ideas. The assumption is that processes develop as a
result of either the *interaction* between the neural substrate and the
environmental stimuli, or as a result of the *impact* of the external stimuli on the neural substrate.

The second assumption is that the impact of different aspects of
the environment is different for different functions at different times.
A corollary is that environmental influences on development of particular functions are greatest at particular times. One hypothesis is that
the times when the influence is greatest are those when the functions
being influenced are having their period of most rapid growth; presumably this functional growth is correlated with the period of most
rapid growth and consolidation of the neural substrate which sub-
sumes the particular function. Since the neural substrate remains
functional even in a more consolidated form, after its period of most
rapid development, this amounts to an optimal-time, rather than a
critical-time, hypothesis: a much more optimistic position with respect to influencing functional growth.

A second corollary to this assumption is that the various psychological functions have different "adequate stimuli," so that not only are
certain functions more open to influence at certain times, but also the
kinds of stimuli which influence development in one area may not do
so—or may do so to a lesser degree—in another area.

A third assumption is that some types of environments are consistently more stimulating to cognitive development than are others.
In general, the social-class rubric yields consistent categories in this
respect, with the lower-class and slum environments contributing
fewer, less well timed, or less adequate stimuli to cognitive development than do the middle- and upper-class environments.

A fourth assumption is that cognitive development proceeds by
stages, and it is probable that these stages follow a consistent order.
This assumption would be especially true within particular areas; it
would be, perhaps, less true for the timing or progression of different,
relatively independent abilities. There is a variety of somewhat conflicting views of stages in cognitive development. While Piaget's seems

to offer the most logical basis for formulating enrichment programs, we do not espouse or follow one to the exclusion of others from consideration. This assumption relates only to the *existence* of stages, not to their specific definition. The correct identification of the stages will still involve a massive empirical effort.

A fifth assumption, related to the fourth, is that some kinds of skills or abilities are basic to others, and that, in general, there are fewer basic skills than there are more specific ones. This relationship would be diagrammed as an inverted pyramid, with each basic skill contributing to a number of adjacent specific ones, and those specific ones, in turn, being basic to some which are narrower and more specific. This basic-specific progression pertains both to temporal relationships and to generality of functions. For example, visual discrimination must develop before reading can be acquired, but visual-discrimination ability underlies artistic skill, driving ability, and various other functions as well as reading.

These theoretical assumptions about environment and development underlie our programmatic formulations and provide the source of many of the hypotheses investigated in our basic research projects.

There are also some assumptions, or hypotheses, which rest on those stated above and directly underlie the action research and demonstration programs which we conduct.

One such major assumption is that the proper task for early childhood education of disadvantaged children is the identification of the stimulation lacks in the environment; the diagnosis of the areas of retardation in cognitive development of the children; the prescription of particular stimuli, strategies, and techniques for their presentation in order to accelerate the development of the retarded functions; and the evaluation of the efficiency of the techniques used. We will discuss each of these activities in turn, recognizing that this procedure creates the impression of a rather artificial separation of each from the others. This separation is being allowed in the interest of clarity of exposition; in practice, most of the activities should be strongly interrelated, and a recycling and feedback process is constantly in operation.

First, let us consider the identification of the stimulation lacks in the environment: This identification involves some knowledge about slum environments, family structure in various disadvantaged groups, child-rearing practices, and the atmosphere in different homes. Also, since stimulation lacks are in part inferred from functional retardations and poor performance in various skills, some of this diagnosis must go on concurrently. A relevant element in the analysis of the environment is the fact that social-class groups are far from homogeneous on most parameters, and they are undoubtedly heterogeneous in the provision of cognitive stimuli for their children. This heterogeneity can be put to good use in the process of determining stimulus-behavior relationships. An instrument currently being developed and analyzed at the Institute is the "Deprivation Index." Its purpose is to subdivide larger social-class groupings into smaller deprivation levels in a way which will be meaningful for predicting children's performance on verbal and intellective measures. (The most complete description of this Index is to be found in Chapter 16.) The goal is the development of instruments which will subdivide groups into smaller and smaller units in order to define specific background stimulation and behavioral development relationships.

Let us proceed to the diagnosis of the areas of retardation in particular children and in groups of children. This diagnosis involves application of a number of techniques, more or less well suited to the purpose, and broad-scale normative studies of cognitive abilities of children at various ages. Standarized tests have been used largely for holistic measures such as IQ, though use has also been made of subtest patterning on such tests as the Illinois Test of Psycholinguistic Abilities. Specific measures of particular functions have also been employed, many of them while still in experimental stages. Especially with these measures, however, large groups of children from different background categories must be tested in order to obtain some picture of the relative strengths and weaknesses to be found in different populations. Among the measures in this category are modifications of some of Piaget's techniques, the Kendler and Osler concept-formation paradigms, the Continuous Performance Test (to measure vigilance or attention), the Wepman Test of Auditory Discrimination and some specially constructed auditory discrimination measures, and the like. (An Institute for Developmental Studies Index of Tests gives pertinent data about each one used, including a description of the samples to which it was administered.)

An important question raised by the decision to seek out the areas of retardation in development is: On what level does one seek deficits? If only the most complex areas, such as reading, are analyzed, then the factors which may contribute to deficits might be missed. On the other hand, if only the smallest definable components, such as visual perception of the diagonal, are measured, then a great deal of time might be spent in seeking procedures to train a skill that may not be too important to overall functioning and that, perhaps, would develop as a by-product of some other training procedure anyway. This is one situation in which the middle ground truly seems the best answer—at least initially until it can be tested. The middle ground between perception of the diagonal and reading, for example, might be visual discrimination.

With the necessity to prescribe particular techniques for the stimulation of the functions found to be retarded we arrive at one of the most difficult points of procedure, and the one about which probably the least is known. Essentially, the problem is one of curriculum formulation, and a certain amount of trial and error is inevitable. However, certain further assumptions, prescriptions, caveats, and requirements underlie our development of training techniques.

It is easy to assume that the kinds of experiences which should be provided are those which the child has lacked; it is this assumption which lies behind taking children on various trips—to the zoo, to museums, and the like—and expecting that development will be stimulated in response to the trips (more about this latter expectation later). The assumption is not a true one, however: Experiences missed at one age or developmental level cannot be retrieved at another. In order to conduct a special enrichment program, one must assume that functions which would have developed, or developed more fully, in response to the missed stimulation can later be retrieved. But development at a later time must be stimulated by experiences which are consistent with the child's level of development, cognitive organization, and knowledge at the later, rather than at the earlier, time. Here, the theoretical assumption, stated earlier, that cognitive development proceeds in stages, is relevant. The formulation of curriculum procedures would be consistent with the cognitive level, or stage, achieved by the child at that time. This will be recognized as a variant of Hunt's concept of the "match."

The concept is also a clinical truism: If an adult is suffering poor interpersonal relationships because his childhood deprivation of parental love and attention prevented his working out initial identifications and relationships with his parents, it would not be therapeutic, even if it were possible, to treat the adult as a child and re-create the primary family—i.e., to supply at twenty-five the exact experiences which he lacked at five or ten. Instead, the aim must be to help him develop, by a method appropriate to his adult level, the same skills he would have learned years before by a method appropriate to the childhood years. The same principle holds true for the formulation of compensatory educational procedures. There is no logic in assuming that a simple supplying *now* of what was missing *then* will have a beneficial effect on the current deficit areas. The experiences and stimuli to be presented in order to ameliorate retardation in function must be appropriate both to the child's developmental level and to his background of experience and knowledge. These experiences and stimuli must also be appropriate to the level of generality of the skill to be stimulated and developed. Here the whole body of theory and evidence on generalization of response and transfer of training is relevant, though some caution must be exercised in translating procedures into those appropriate for disadvantaged children. Often tasks which are apparently simple ones, composed of single units, are in reality much more complex and must be carefully analyzed and adapted before they can be applied.

Another principle of curriculum development is that the simple provision of a particular experience is typically not sufficient: it must be structured and labeled, and the aspects relevant for the knowledge it is to convey or the function it is to stimulate must be pointed up. And this structure and emphasis must be meaningful for the child, in terms of his previous experience and understanding. This point was illustrated particularly strongly for us when we had the opportunity to speak to a number of children of migrant families. These children had traveled thousands of miles in cars and trucks, and at age ten or twelve had made several round trips between Oregon and Texas. Yet they were not able to answer simple geographical questions, such as on mileage or travel time between particular points. Their vast travel experience was cognitively meaningless in these terms because it had never been made meaningful to them: simply experiencing it was not enough. Some of our major reservations about the efficacy of brief and redundant programs stem from this point.

At this point it seems appropriate to review briefly what we consider essential for the intervention environment and curriculum. The environment would demand development and stimulate it along certain parameters. The environment would include sensorimotor stimulation, opportunities for making perceptual discriminations, interacting with a verbally adequate adult, receiving some individual attention, linking words and objects and meaningfully relating them in stories or to varying experiential contexts, being assisted in experiencing positive self-identifications, being encouraged toward task perseverance, and being helped to receive both tangible and verbal rewards for relatively competent performance. Such an environment includes stimulation which would be demanding of responses consistent with achieved developmental capabilities, and which would have sufficient and continual feedback from adults.

As for the evaluation of the effects of curriculum techniques, the testing problems are similar to those discussed under diagnosis, except that the measures used also have to be capable of registering the particular changes which are sought. What can be used here, of course, are achievement measures as well as retesting on particular experimental procedures. Perhaps the most important point about evaluation is the necessity for analyzing performance in both as small units as possible and in their interactions. Often a particular component skill can be the only apparent one to be affected by a particular training procedure, and yet analysis of skill interaction patterns will reveal changes in various of the more complex ones as well. This information could be invaluable, not only for its feedback into curriculum planning, but also for the insight it yields into the relationships among particular functions and skills.

Another element to be considered in evaluating the effects of special programs is time. There is no reason to suppose, ipso facto, that all effects will be immediately visible, nor that immediate gains will be maintained. It is possible that continuing enrichment programs in the elementary years will be necessary if these gains are not to be lost. It is highly likely that certain functions need a long time to mature once they are stimulated, while others develop at a fairly rapid rate. It is also likely that some curricula will stimulate development in areas which seem far removed from the content. Further, it is eminently plausible to assume that stimulation of a basic function at a time later than that at which it would ordinarily develop might not automatically yield the consequent development of the more specific skills which it underlies. Many similar questions can be formulated, all pointing to the necessity of an evaluation over time in order to ascertain the effects of an intervention program: to yield the information of which it is capable, evaluation must go on over a period of years.

The use of evaluation techniques constructed for particular populations and now used for disadvantaged children in and outside of enrichment programs raises the further question of whether artificial ceilings are not being imposed on the children's measurement. More experimentation needs to be done with restandardizing old tests on this population.

Following from these statements and assumptions (and a number of others which have not been discussed), our enrichment program is under constant evaluation and is constantly in evolution. In the 1965–66 school year, there were special classes for nursery-age children, for kindergarteners, and to a limited extent for first- and second-graders. The plan is to carry special enrichment through the third grade for as many children as possible in several successive groups of children, and then to continue follow-up evaluations through the sixth grade. When we began the program, we believed that such a time trajectory was necessary; now we know that it is essential.

Our initial results indicate that IQ as well as achievement levels and various verbal functions can be significantly increased as a result of special enrichment programs. But, so far, these findings also indicate that simple increases in content, such as vocabulary, do not necessarily imply or beget improvement in the more abstract and conceptual functions.

We are now preparing for what we call the "second generation" of research on early childhood education. We believe that the first level of research and demonstration has shown the possibility of arresting or retarding the accumulation of deficit (in Chapter 14, Deutsch and Brown have characterized it as a "cumulative deficit") to which these children are almost certainly subject in the absence of special programs. The task now is to refine both the diagnostic instruments and the curriculum techniques so that the disadvantaged children can produce performances which substantially overlap with the middle-class norms.

The final goal would demand a further, or "third generation" of research; that is, to develop methods and curricula to enhance the cognitive functioning of all children, and to come closer to insuring that each individual's intellectual potential will have opportunity to reach its maximum growth and usefulness.

These defined goals are consistent with a step-like approach to enrichment programming, which is, in turn, related to the definition of stages in cognitive development. Through the formulation of stages in enrichment, and then their evaluation, application of programs to children can contribute to theoretical understanding of cognitive stages. It is this kind of process that provides the feedback which enables the continuing evolution of both practice and research.

Contrary to some statements appearing from time to time in the popular press—and to views held on occasion by some government agencies—work in early childhood stimulation is far from done: it is in fact just beginning to develop the necessary prototypical models.

Acknowledgments

Chapter 1, "Social Intervention and the Malleability of the Child," was first presented as the fourth annual School of Education Lecture at Cornell University, Ithaca, New York, May 6, 1965.

Chapter 2, "Some Psychosocial Aspects of Learning in the Disadvantaged," is reprinted from *Teachers College Record*, **67** (4), (January, 1966), 260–265. It is based on a paper presented at the Boston University Developmental Conference on the Teaching of the Disadvantaged, June, 1964.

Chapter 3, "The Disadvantaged Child and the Learning Process," is reprinted from A. Harry Passow (Ed.), *Education in Depressed Areas* (New York: Teachers College Press, 1963), pp. 163–179. Copyright 1963 by Teachers College, Columbia University.

Chapter 4, "Facilitating Development in the Preschool Child: Social and Psychological Perspectives," is reprinted from the *Merrill-Palmer Quarterly of Behavior and Development*, **10** (3), (July, 1964), 249–263. It is based on a paper presented at the Arden House Conference on Pre-School Enrichment of Socially Disadvantaged Children, December, 1962, Arden House, Harriman, New York.

Chapter 5, "Nursery Education: The Influence of Social Programming on Early Development," is reprinted from *The Journal of Nursery Education* (published by the National Association for the Education of Young Children), **18** (3), (April, 1963). It is based on a talk presented at the Conference of the National Association for Nursery Education, Philadelphia, October 27, 1962.

Chapter 6, "Minority Groups and Class Status as Related to Social and Personality Factors in Scholastic Achievements," is reprinted from *Monographs of the Society for Applied Anthropology* (1960), No. 2, Chs. 1, 4, 5, 7, 8.

Chapter 7, "Early Social Environment and School Adaptation," is reprinted from *Teachers College Record*, **66** (8), (May, 1965), 699–706.

Chapter 8, "Learning in the Disadvantaged," is reprinted from Herbert J. Klausmeier and Chester W. Harris (Eds.), *Analyses of Concept Learning* (New York: Academic Press, 1966), pp. 189–204. It was first presented as a talk at the Conference on Analyses of Conceptual Learning at the Research and Development Center for Learning and Re-education, The University of Wisconsin, Madison, Wisconsin, October, 1965.

Chapter 9, "The Social Context of Language Acquisition," is reprinted from the *Merrill-Palmer Quarterly of Behavior and Development*, **10** (3), (July, 1964), 265–275. It is based on a paper presented at the Arden House Conference on Pre-School Enrichment of Socially Disadvantaged Children, December, 1962, Arden House, Harriman, New York.

Chapter 10, "Communication of Information in the Elementary School Classroom," is an abridged version of Cooperative Research Project No. 908 as compiled for the Office of Education, U.S. Department of Health, Education and Welfare, by the Institute for Developmental Studies, 1964.

Chapter 11, "The Relationship of Auditory and Visual Functioning to Reading Achievement in Disadvantaged Children," is an abridged and adapted version of Cooperative Research Project No. 1099 as compiled for the Office of Education, U.S. Department of Health, Education and Welfare, by the Institute for Developmental Studies, 1963.

Chapter 12, "Auditory Discrimination and Learning: Social Factors," is reprinted from the *Merrill-Palmer Quarterly of Behavior and Development,* **10** (3), (July, 1964), 277–296. It is based on a paper presented at the Arden House Conference on Pre-School Enrichment of Socially Disadvantaged Children, December, 1962, Arden House, Harriman, New York.

Chapter 13, "Dimensions of the School's Role in the Problems of Integration," is reprinted from Gordon J. Klopf and Israel A. Laster (Eds.), *Integrating the Urban School* (New York: Teachers College Press, 1963), pp. 29–44. Copyright 1963 by Teachers College, Columbia University.

Chapter 14, "Social Influences in Negro-White Intelligence Differences," is reprinted from the *Journal of Social Issues,* **20** (2), (April, 1964), 24–95. An earlier version of this paper was read at the biennial meeting of the Society for Research in Child Development, Berkeley, California, April, 1963.

Chapter 15, "Race and Social Class as Separate Factors Related to Social Environment," is reprinted from the *American Journal of Sociology,* **70** (4), (January, 1965), 471–476. Copyright 1965 by the University of Chicago. This is a slightly expanded version of a paper read at the annual meeting of the American Psychological Association, 1963.

Chapter 16, "Some Effects of Social Class and Race on Children's Language and Intellectual Abilities," is a revised version of a paper read at the biennial meeting of the Society for Research in Child Development, Minneapolis, Minnesota, March, 1965.

Chapter 17, "Social Disadvantage as Related to Intellective and Language Development." A preliminary report of the data in this paper was presented at the Conference on Cultural Deprivation and Enrichment Programs, Yeshiva University, New York, April, 1965. The research was sponsored by grants from the Taconic Foundation and the National Institute of Mental Health, and was supported by the United States Office of Education and the Office of Economic Opportunity. An expanded version of this paper can be found in Martin Deutsch, Arthur Jensen, and Irwin Katz (Eds.), *Social-Class, Race, and Psychological Development* (New York: Holt, Rinehart, and Winston, in press).

Chapter 18, "The Role of Social Class in Language Development and Cognition," is reprinted from the *American Journal of Orthopsychiatry,* **35** (1), (January, 1965), 78–87. First presented as a talk at the annual meeting of the American Orthopsychiatric Association, Chicago, 1964.

Chapter 19, "The Principal Issue," is reprinted from the *Harvard Educational Review,* **36** (4), (Fall, 1966), 492–495.

Chapter 20, "Brief Reflections on the Theory of Early Childhood Enrichment Programs," was first presented as a talk at the Pre-School Education Conference sponsored by the Committee on Learning and the Educational Process of the Social Science Research Council, Chicago, February, 1966.

Index

abstract concepts, 16, 23
abstract verbal symbols, 26–27
abstraction, 22, 25, 26; race and, 366
academic performance, *see* scholastic achievement
accommodation and assimilation paradigm, 354–355
achievement motivation, 5, 6, 287; *see also* motivation
achievement orientation, 10, 43
active-constructive behavior, 114, 119
active-destructive behavior, 114
acuity, auditory and visual, 234
adaptation, school, early social environment and, 133–134
adult-child interaction, 7, 48, 49, 83–84, 95, 165, 167–168, 339, 353, 357, 359
alienation, school-child, 5, 36, 41–42, 65, 77, 135–137, 337–338
American Psychological Association, 291
Anastasi, Anne, 177
animal experiments, 31, 261–262, 264
A/R ratio, 99–100, 108
armed forces general education test, failures in, 373
Ashton-Warner, Sylvia, 174
attentional processes, 8, 15, 27, 45, 48, 50, 51, 56, 155–158
attentional shifting, 237; teacher's interpretation of, 287
auditory acuity, 234
auditory decoding, 151
auditory discrimination, advanced processes of, 274; critical times for learning of, 265; environment and, 48, 262–263, 265, 275; and hearing, 259–261; and learning process, 259–276; optimal time for development of, 264–266; preschool training programs for, 22, 69, 71–72, 85, 139, 154–155, 266; and reading, 233–256, 267–276; signal-to-noise ratio and, 153–154, 261–263, 265, 275; tests for, 14–15, 154–155, 181, 238–241, 243–246, 266–274, 382; and verbal abilities, 269–270, 273–274, 276
auditory mechanisms, three-function analysis of, 274
auditory memory span, testing of, 240–241
auditory recognition, 233, 260–262, 274
auditory sensory apparatus, 260
auditory stimuli, 235–239; *see also* auditory discrimination
auditory-visual stimulation, 235, 238
autoinstructional devices, need for, 35–37
automatic promotion policy, 93*n*.
automation, effects of, 59, 62, 141, 372

background variables, *see* environment
Baltimore language study, 152
behavioral sciences, cognitive development and, 60–61, 81, 124, 292; and education, 37, 56–57, 60–61, 77, 292–293, 371, 373; and sociopsychological processes, 89

Bereiter, Carl, 152

Bernstein, B., 24, 37, 52, 70, 149, 152, 164, 167, 177–178, 217, 223, 228, 358, 367

bimodal reaction-time apparatus, 237–238, 241–243, 251, 271

Binet IQ, 13, 14

Bloom, B., 9, 10, 353

Bloom, Richard D., 309

broken homes, 14; and cumulative deficit, 221; and dropouts, 62; IQ and, 295–306, 359; in Negro community, 43, 63, 90, 102, 105–106, 108, 110, 311; and scholastic achievement, 103–108, 127, 130

Brown, Bert R., 177, 221, 295, 319

Brown, R., 170

Brown case, 373

Bruner, J. S., 31, 32, 67–68, 152, 358

bussing, 293–294

canal-boat children, study of, 126–127

Carol, Bernard, 210*n.*

caste status, 17, 18, 284, 359, 367, 368

categorizing, of concepts, 83, 84; of visual stimuli, 365

channeling, attentional, 156

Cherry, C., 265

Cherry-Peisach, Estelle, 177, 210*n.*

chi-square analyses, 100, 201–203, 310, 311*n.*

child-rearing practices, 72, 357, 381

civil rights movement, 4, 372

Clarke, A. D. B., 31, 32

Clarke, A. M., 31, 32

class status, *see* socioeconomic status

classifications of perceptions, 25

closed-end status orientation, 24

Clown technique, 181–189, 200–202, 221–223, 226–228

Cloze procedure, 204–215, 224–227

Cloze tests, 342, 347, 362, 364, 365

cluttering, 270

cognitive development, attitudinal system in, 47; behavioral sciences and, 60–61, 81, 124, 292; contentual aspects of, 45–48, 50, 52; critical-time period, 9, 67, 265, 275, 380; discrimination and, 81; enrichment programs for, *see* enrichment pro-

grams; environment and, 9–14, 18, 31–34, 39–55, 62–74, 163, 281–282, 291–292, 319–322, 337–356, 379–387; formal aspects of, 45–47, 52; optimal-time period, 9, 67, 265–266, 275, 380; preoperational stage, 9, 22, 25, 67; race and, 42–44, 46–47, 319–335; self-concept and, 35, 54–55, 81, 106, 123; socioeconomic status and, 18, 39–44, 46–55, 63–69, 77–86, 158–161, 319–335, 357–369; stages in, 9–10, 53, 67, 380–381, 383; *see also* learning process

cognitive orientation, 20–21, 102

cognitive stimulation, 66–68, 73, 81–83

Columbia Mental Maturity Scale (CMMS), 16

communication gap, family-child, 83–84, 149–150; teacher-child, 52, 368

community sociology, teacher training in, 141

compensatory programs, *see* enrichment programs

competence motivation, 35, 66, 290; *see also* motivation

concept(s), abstract, 16, 23; categorizing of, 83, 84; mediational, 23; symbolic, 23; temporal, 24; time, 48–49

concept formation, 69; Deprivation Index and, 351–352; language development and, 53, 70, 83, 84

Concept Formation Test, 362, 363, 365

Concept Sorting Test, 170–171, 361–363, 365

Continuous Performance Test (CPT), 157–158, 238–239, 243–245, 272–274, 382

coping, 24, 26, 45, 66, 68, 106, 134, 140

covert language, 164, 172

critical-time hypothesis, 9, 263–265, 275, 380

cross-modal reaction time, 241, 271–272

crowding ratio, 94, 100, 128

cultural deprivation, 31, 102, 354; *see also* environment

cultural-relativism hypothesis, 159, 160

cultural variables, 91
culture-free tests, 46–47
cumulative deficit, alienation and,
  337–338; broken homes and, 221;
  Deprivation Index and, 344–345;
  deprivational factors in, 304–305,
  324, 331, 345; enrichment programs
  and, 14, 17–19, 27, 338, 368, 386;
  and race, 345, 359; socioeconomic
  status and, 345, 359, 367–368

Dave, R. H., 353
Dawe, Helen C., 221
deficit-evaluation approach, 11–12
DeHirsch, Katrina, 274–275
delinquency, 3; school conditions and,
  55; human sciences and, 60; scholastic retardation and, 92
denigration, 63
denotative usage, 366
deprivation, cultural, 31, 102, 354;
  economic, 31, 32, 43–44, 46, 59–60,
  68–69, 77; of parental love, 31, 383;
  sensory, 67–68; social, 5, 10, 14, 41,
  40–44, 59, 77, 90, 127, 298, 320–
  324; sociocultural, 42–43, 324;
  stimulus, 10–12, 44–50, 64, 67, 72,
  80, 85, 102, 153, 381–387; visual,
  153; see also environment; socioeconomic status
Deprivation Index, 149, 296, 321–
  335, 382; and concept formation,
  351–352; and cumulative deficit,
  344–345; enrichment programs and,
  13–14, 16–19, 355; and IQ, 349,
  351; and race, 19–20, 348–352,
  355–356; and self-concept, 346–
  358; and socioeconomic status, 18–
  19, 348–352, 355–356; and verbal
  fluency, 351–352
Deutsch, Cynthia P., 147, 259, 379
Deutsch, Martin, 3, 31, 39, 59, 77, 89,
  133, 177, 221, 233, 237, 250, 281,
  295, 309, 319, 327, 357, 371, 379
dialects, 37, 78, 178, 225, 261, 365
Digit Span test, 96, 101–102, 109,
  241, 247–248, 267, 273, 274
discrimination, and cognitive development, 81; job, 3; see also integration
dominance-passivity patterns, 357
Dreger, R. M., 306
dropouts, 5, 31, 39; broken homes

and, 62; communication breakdown
  and, 368; early school experiences
  and, 102, 135, 138; female, 141–
  142; school conditions and, 55–56;
  socioeconomic status and, 39

early childhood programs, see enrichment programs
economic deprivation, 31, 32, 43–44,
  46, 59–60, 68–69, 77; see also environment
education, behavioral sciences and, 37,
  56–57, 60–61, 77, 292–293, 371,
  373; contemporary problems of, 60–
  61; expenditures for, 373–374; human sciences and, 60, 61, 285; politically oriented bureaucracies and,
  286, 294, 373; reforms in, 283, 372–
  373, 375; and social change, 4–7,
  59–62, 133, 281–294, 371–375; social sciences and, 56–57, 61, 89,
  130–131, 286–287, 371, 373–375
Eells, K., 167
effectance motivation, 66
elaborated language, 177–178, 223,
  358, 367
elementary classroom language studies, see language studies
enrichment programs, behavioral sciences and, 292–293; and cumulative deficit, 14, 17–19, 27, 338, 368,
  386; Deprivation Index and, 13–14,
  16–19, 355; evaluation techniques,
  385–386; first-goal, 20–23, 26; goals
  of, 19–21, 386; and IQ, 386; preschool, see preschool enrichment
  programs; "second generation" curriculum, 12–19, 23, 386; second-
  goal, 23–27; storytelling, 25–26;
  theory of, 379–387; third-goal, 27–
  28
enumeration, race and, 366
environment, and auditory discrimination, 48, 262–263, 265, 275; and
  cognitive development, 9–14, 18,
  31–34, 39–55, 62–74, 163, 281–
  282, 291–292, 319–322, 337–356,
  379–387; coping with, 24, 26, 45,
  66, 68, 106, 134, 140; and language
  development, 163–174, 337–356;
  motivation and, 90; operant control
  over, 173; and reading achievement,

environment (*cont'd*)
338–344, 349, 351; and school adaptation, 133–143; and self-concept, 90; stimulation lacks in, 10–12, 44–50, 64, 67, 72, 80, 85, 102, 153, 381–387; and visual discrimination, 47–48, 152–153; *see also* socioeconomic status
environmental orientation, 24, 69–72
environmental parameters, 17, 21
environmental stimulation, 21
Ervin, Suzan, 225n.
expressive language study, 52, 178–203, 214–219, 221–223, 366; *see also* language studies
extraneous words, 220

failure(s), in armed forces general education test, 373; school, *see* school failure; social, 3–4
Family Atmosphere Index, 95, 100, 101n.
family-child interaction, 7, 48, 49, 83–84, 95, 165, 167–168, 339, 353, 357, 359
Fantz, R. L., 153
feedback, 4, 21, 24, 48, 51, 81, 168–170, 173, 358–359, 368, 381, 385, 386
female dropouts, 141–142
figure drawing, 95–96
figure-ground relationships, 47, 261
foreign languages, learning of, 263–265
form perception, 153
Fowler, W., 66–67, 73, 79, 81–82, 264, 303
Freedman, A., 237, 250
Friedman, R. M., 240
Fromm, Erich, 131
frustration, childhood, 47–48, 54–55, 84, 90, 355; economic, 135; job, 135; and motivation, 54–55
functional motivation, 368

Gates Reading tests, 181, 235, 236, 267, 268, 271, 340, 342, 347–349, 351
generalizations, 26, 170
generic transfer, 68
Gesell, Arnold, 164
Gestalt perceptual theory, 262

ghettos, urban, 372
Goldstein, Leo S., 163
Goodman, C. C., 152
Gordon, H., 126
Gray, Susan W., 152
Gresham's Law, 265
Gulliksen, H., 331n.
gypsy children, study of, 126–127

Hardy, W. G., 260, 274
Harrington, M., 357
Headstart, 4, 12–13
hearing, auditory discrimination and, 259–261
Hebb, Donald O., 164, 172
Hernández-Peón, R., 261
hesitation phenomena, 228, 366, 368
Hess, R. D., 24
Higher Horizons program, 4
home-family orientation, 65, 134
human sciences, 60, 61, 285
Hunt, J. McV., 10, 28, 45, 64, 72, 74, 149, 164, 354, 367, 383
hyperactivity, teacher's interpretation of, 287

Illinois Test of Psycholinguistic Abilities (ITPA), 14–16, 151, 152, 154, 382
inadequate development, Wepman's category of, 269
in-service teacher training, 284, 287–288
Institute for Developmental Studies, 13, 23, 42, 48–51, 53, 79, 149, 154, 157, 159, 180n., 235, 291, 338 357, 367, 379, 382
integration, 89; aim of, 294; bussing and, 293–294; caste barriers to, 281; community ambivalence toward, 283–284; heterogeneous grouping and, 288–289; homogeneous grouping and, 288–289; and IQ, 291–292; and motivation, 290–291; power prerogatives and, 287; role of school in, 281–294; and self-concept, 287, 289–291; social-class barriers to, 281, 287; social sciences and, 287; and track system, 289; value system and, 284, 285
intellectual development, *see* cognitive development

intelligence, *see* IQ
Intelligence and Experience, 149
interactive variable, 322
intervention programs, *see* enrichment programs
intrinsic motivation, 354
ipsi-modal reaction time, 241-271
IQ, and bimodal reaction time, 242–243; broken homes and, 295–306, 359; of canal-boat children, 126–127; Deprivation Index and, 349, 351; and discrimination skills, 246; enrichment programs and, 386; of gypsy children, 126–127; integration and, 291–292; and memory span, 247–248; race and, 295–306, 325–328, 355–356, 365; and reading achievement, 253–254; and serial learning, 250; socioeconomic status and, 295–306, 325–328, 344–345, 355, 361, 365
Irwin, O. C., 177

Jensen A. R., 10, 149, 150, 171
job discrimination, 3
job frustration, 135
job insecurity, 107, 141
job-opportunity structure, shifting of, 5, 59, 62, 77, 142, 284, 372
John, Vera P., 163, 367

Katz, Phyllis A., 233, 272–273
Kendler, H., 171
Kendler, Tracy S., 171
Kendler concept-formation paradigm, 151, 382
kindergarten, *see* preschool enrichment programs
Klineberg, O., 221, 291, 319
Kluckhohn, Florence, 102
Kornetsky, C., 157–158

label acquisition, 165–166
labeling, and language development, 50, 51, 84, 150, 163; receptive, 166–169; socioeconomic status and, 358–359, 362, 366–367; training in, 22, 71, 85
labor demand, changes in, 5, 59, 62, 77, 142, 284, 372
Landreth, Catherine, 223
language(s), covert, 164, 172; elab-orated, 177–178, 223, 358, 367; foreign, learning of, 263–265; formal, 52, 70; informal, 52, 70; and learning, 37; Osgood's model of, 164; overt, 164, 172; receptive, 37; restricted, 178, 223, 358, 367
language acquisition, social context of, 163–174
language development, and concept formation, 53, 70, 83, 84; dialects and, 37, 78, 178, 225, 261, 365; environment and, 163–174, 337–356; and labeling, 50, 51, 84, 150, 163; maturational approach to, 164; modern psychological theories of, 164, 172; phoneme comparison, 14–15, 154; preschool training programs for, 70–72, 84, 139, 151–152, 167–171, 173–174; and problem solving, 53, 70, 150, 177; race and, 19, 179–230, 319–335, 365, 368; sex differences and, 179–230; socioeconomic status and, 18, 48, 50–53, 63, 70–71, 149–152, 166–173, 177–230, 319–335, 357–369; syntax, 15, 24, 37, 51, 52, 71, 150, 365, 368; *see also* verbal abilities
language facility and fluency, acquisition of, 51, 177
language stimulation, 71, 82–84
language studies, Baltimore, 152; Clown technique, 181–189, 200–202, 221–223, 226–228; Cloze procedure, 204–215, 224–227; educational implications, 227–228; expressive, 52, 178–203, 214–219, 221–223, 366; factor-analysis approach, 192–200, 219; IDS, 149–152; receptive, 52, 203–214, 224–230; research implications 228; Rocket technique, 181–189, 200–202, 221–223, 226–227; sentence length factor, 200, 220; type-token ratio, 198–199, 270; verbal output, 192, 195–198, 219–220
language symbolization, 45, 50, 72–73
language variables, 358–360
learning process, auditory discrimination and, 259–276; disadvantaged child and, 147–161; environmental factors in, 40–44; language and, 37;

learning process (*cont'd*)
  psychological aspects of, 31–37, 44–55; school conditions and, 55–57, 128–131; self-concept and, 35, 54–55, 81, 106, 123; *see also* cognitive development
Lee, E. S., 303
Levinson, Alma, 177
linguistic variables, 358–360
Loban, W., 187
logical abilities, 53
Lorge-Thorndike tests, 181–184, 189–191, 204–206, 210–212, 229–230, 236, 242–244, 246–248, 268, 296–297, 300–306, 324–328, 331, 333, 334, 340, 342, 344–347, 349, 355, 361
Lorge-Thorndike Word Book, 266
Luria, A. R., 172, 368

McCarthy, Dorothea A., 165n.
Martin, W., 86
mazes, 187
mediational concepts, 23
memory, 48–49; training of, 71, 84
memory drum, 157
memory span, testing of, 240–241, 247–248
mental health, 3; human sciences and, 60; teacher training in, 141
mental health centers, 4–5
Menyuk, Paula, 218
Merton, Robert, 107
Miller, K. S., 306
Milner, Brenda, 273
Milner, Esther, 83, 167
minority groups, *see* race; socioeconomic status
Mirsky, A. F., 157–158
"mom-ism," 74, 142
monitoring, 238
Montessori, Maria, 69–70
motivation, achievement, 5, 6, 287; competence, 35, 66, 290; effectance, 66; environment and, 90; frustration and, 54–55; functional, 368; integration and, 290–291; intrinsic, 354; negative, 123, 127, 155; parental, 17, 33, 55, 140, 332, 339, 342, 344, 353; positive, 55; rewards and, 21, 33, 45, 49, 80–81, 102, 107–108, 134, 384–385

motor coordination, 264
motor learning, 164
Myklebust, H. R., 262
Myrdal, G., 309

nativism-empiricism controversy, 153
Negative Family Atmosphere, Index of, 95, 100, 103, 105
negative motivation, 123, 127, 155
negative self-concept, 35, 101, 105–106, 123, 126, 127, 346–348
Negative Self-Image, Index of, 95, 100, 101, 105
Negro children, self-concept and, 43, 54–55, 81, 101, 106; *see also* race
Negro community, broken homes in, 43, 63, 90, 102, 105–106, 108, 110, 311; *see also* broken homes
neurophysiological immaturity, 274–275
Newman-Keuls comparisons among means, 347–349, 351
nonsense syllables, 148
North-Hatt study, 310, 312, 313
nursery schools, 7, 13, 20, 21, 77–86, 266; *see also* preschool enrichment programs

Object Assembly subtest, 150
occupational aspiration, 62, 95; race and, 108, 111–113, 314–316; socioeconomic status and, 137
optimal-time hypothesis, 9, 67, 263–266, 275, 380
orientation, achievement, 10, 43; closed-end status, 24; cognitive, 20–21, 102; environmental, 24, 69–72; home-family, 65, 134; preschool enrichment programs and, 8; school-faculty, 65; spatial, 139; temporal, 139; time, 36, 49
Orientation Scale, 49, 267, 268, 340–342
Osgood, Charles E., 15–16, 164
Osler concept-formation paradigm, 382
Other America, The, 357
overindulgence, parental, 128
overt language, 164, 172
overt verbalization, 24

parent-child interaction, 7, 48, 49, 83–

84, 95, 165, 167–168, 339, 353, 357, 359

parental love, deprivation of, 31, 383

parental motivation, 17, 33, 55, 140, 332, 339, 342, 344, 353

parental overindulgence, 128

Pasamanick, B., 276

passive-constructive behavior, 114

passive-destructive behavior, 114

pattern-making, 274

Peabody Picture Vocabulary Test (PPVT), 13, 152, 166–167, 170, 268, 361

Pearson product-moment correlations, 246

perceptions, classifications of, 25

perceptual discrimination, see visual discrimination

personality variables, 91, 92

phonemes, 14–15, 154

Piaget, J., 9, 22, 45, 53, 64, 67, 68, 73, 354, 380–382

Picture Completion subtest, 150

positive motivation, 55; see also motivation

positive self-attitudes, 123

positive self-concept, 106, 140

preschool enrichment programs, 6–12, 20–23, 26, 62–74; auditory discrimination training, 22, 69, 71–72, 85, 139, 154–155, 266; Headstart, 4, 12–13; importance of, 79, 137–139; language training, 70–72, 84, 139, 151–152, 167–171, 173–174; memory training, 71, 84; nursery, 7, 13, 20, 21, 77–86, 266; and orientation, 8; prospects for, 142–143; psychological and social perspectives, 62–74; semantic discrimination training, 85; visual discrimination training, 12, 22, 69, 85, 139; see also enrichment programs

problem-solving abilities, 8, 16, 27, 50, 53, 70, 150, 177, 358

processing, 274

Project Headstart, 4, 12–13

Psychological Bulletin, 81–82

Raab, Shirley, 237, 250

race, and abstraction, 366; and cognitive development, 42–44, 46–47, 319–335; cumulative deficit and, 345, 359; dependent variables associated with, 311–317; Deprivation Index and, 19–20, 348–352, 355–356; and enumeration, 366; IQ and, 295–306, 325–328, 355–356, 365; and language development, 19, 179–230, 319–335, 365, 368; and occupational aspirations, 108, 111–113, 314–316; reading achievement and, 267–272; and scholastic achievement, 89–131, 140; and self-concept, 43, 54–55, 81, 101, 106; self-identification and, 106–108, 110–111; sex-role delineations and, 107–108; and verbal abilities, 319–335; Verbal Survey and, 18, 359–369; and verbalization, 18, 19, 366

Rand report, 10

rapport, increasing of, 135–137

Raven Progressive Matrices, 150

reaction time, bimodal, 237–238, 241–243, 251, 271; cross-modal, 241, 271–272; ipsi-modal, 241, 271

readiness, 135–136, 139, 264

reading, auditory discrimination and, 233–256, 267–276; environment and, 338–344, 349, 351; Deprivation Index and, 349, 351; early analysis of deficits in, 11; and IQ, 253–254; parent-child conversation and, 339; race and, 267–272; remedial, 130, 154–155, 233; skills involved in, 233, 254, 341; socioeconomic status and, 48, 158–159, 236, 254–255, 267–272, 324, 339–342; teaching of, 233–234; visual discrimination and, 233–256, 381

Reading Prognosis Test (RPT), 235–236, 365

reading-readiness tests, 275

reality testing, 50

receptive labeling, 166–169

receptive language, 37

receptive language study, 52, 203–214, 224–230; see also language studies

recognition, auditory, 233, 260–262, 274

redundancies, 179, 218, 270

reforms, educational, 283, 372–373, 375

reinforcement, 24, 26, 45, 48, 85, 288;
absence of, 80–81; positive, 70;
self-, 49, 52

remedial programs, 51–52, 69, 368;
reading, 130, 154–155, 233

restricted language, 178, 223, 358,
367

retention, 274

reticular system, 261–262

reward system, 21, 33, 45, 49, 80–81,
102, 107–108, 134, 384–385

Rocket technique, 181–189, 200–202,
221–223, 226–227

Rosvold, H. E., 157–158, 238

Roswell-Chall word-parts test, 267

Salzinger, Kurt, 181n.

Schneiderman, Norma, 215

scholastic achievement, broken homes
and, 103–108, 127, 130; and self-
attitudes, 105–106; and self-concept, 105–106; sex differences and,
108–110; socioeconomic status and,
89–131, 339

school adaptation, early social environment and, 133–143

school conditions, dropouts and, 55–
56; and learning process, 55–57,
128–131

school dropouts, *see* dropouts

school-faculty orientation, 65

school failure, 3, 31; effects of on child,
134–135; socioeconomic status and,
39, 66, 68–69, 133–135

school integration, *see* integration

Scott, J. P., 67, 79, 264, 265

self-attitudes, 90, 92, 95; internalized,
90; positive, 123; scholastic achievement and, 105–106

self-concept, and cognitive development, 35, 54–55, 81, 106, 123; Deprivation Index and, 346–348; differentiated, 63–64; environment
and, 90; and integration, 287, 289–
291; learning process and, 35, 54–
55, 106, 123; negative, 35, 101,
105–106, 123, 126, 127, 346–348;
Negro child and, 43, 54–55, 81, 101,
106; positive, 106, 140; and scholastic achievement, 105–106

self-fulfilling prophecy, 8, 33, 107

self-identification, positive, 21; race
and, 106–108, 110–111

self-identity, destruction of, 5–6;
knowledge of, 54

self-image, *see* self-concept

self-reinforcement, 49, 52

semantic discrimination training, 85

seminars, 92–93, 96–97, 115, 121–122

Senden, M. von, 153

sensorimotor stimulation, 21

sensory deprivation, 67–68

sensory modalities, 26, 156

sensory transmission, 261

Sentence Completion Test, 95, 100–
101, 106–107

serial learning, 241, 248–250, 252–
254, 270

SES, *see* socioeconomic status

sex differences, language development
and, 179–230; and receptive language, 226; and scholastic achievement, 108–110

sex-role delineations, race and, 107–
108

Shipman, Virginia C., 24

Siegel, Jay, 210n.

signal-to-noise ratio, 153–154, 261–
263, 265, 275

single-channel vigilance tasks, 244–
245, 253

size discrimination, 69–70

skilled labor, demand for, 5, 59, 62,
77, 284, 372

social change, education and, 4–7, 59–
62, 133, 281–294, 371–375; *see
also* integration

social class designations, 16–17; *see
also* socioeconomic status

social environment, *see* environment

social failure, 3–4

social intervention, *see* enrichment programs

social psychology, 56, 89

social sciences, education and, 56–57,
61, 89, 130–131, 286–287, 371,
373–375; and integration, 287; and
sociopsychological processes, 89

sociocultural deprivation, 42–43, 324

socioeconomic status, cognitive development and, 18, 39–44, 46–55, 63–
69, 77–86, 158–161, 319–335, 357–
369; and cumulative deficit, 345,

359, 367–368; dependent variables associated with, 311–317; Deprivation Index and, 18–19, 348–352, 355–356; and dropouts, 39; and IQ, 295–306, 325–328, 344–345, 355, 361, 365; labeling and, 358–359, 362, 366–367; and language development, 18, 48, 50–53, 63, 70–71, 149–152, 166–173, 177–230, 319–335, 357–369; occupational aspirations and, 137; and reading achievement, 48, 158–159, 236, 254–255, 267–272, 324, 339–342; and scholastic achievement, 89–131, 339; school adaptation and, 133–143; and school failure, 39, 66, 68–69, 133–135; and verbal abilities, 319–335; Verbal Survey and, 18, 359–369; *see also* environment

Socioeconomic Status, Index of, 180

sociometric index, 94, 110

sociology, 61; community, teacher training in, 141

sociopsychological processes, 89

S–O–R paradigm, 147

spatial organization, 47

spatial orientation, 139

speech, *see* language; language development

speech tests, 261

Stability and Change in Human Characteristics, 9, 353

Stanford Achievement Test, 94, 98–100, 103, 108, 116

status, need for, 6

status mobility, 107

stimulus deprivation, 10–12, 44–50, 64, 67, 72, 80, 85, 102, 153, 381–387

stimulus-field manipulation, 157–158, 368

stimulus-field organization, 152, 156

stimulus modalities, 235, 237–239, 241–243, 250–251, 271

storytelling, 25–26

Supreme Court decisions, 89, 281, 373

Suttcliffe, J. P., 311*n*.

Sutton, S., 237

symbolic concepts, 23

symbolization, language, 45, 50, 72–73

syntactical deficiency, 15, 24, 37, 51, 150; race and, 365, 368; socioeconomic status and, 52, 71, 365, 368

task completion, 21, 45, 49, 63–64

Taylor, W. L., 206

teacher-child communication gap, 52, 368

teacher shortage, 89

teacher training, 56, 136; in community sociology, 141; in mental health, 141; in-service, 284, 287–288; seminars, 92–93, 96–97, 115, 121–122

teaching machines, 62

Templin, Mildred C., 164, 177, 214–216, 219–220

temporal concept, 24

temporal orientation, 139

Thought and Language, 358

time concept, 48–49

time orientation, 36, 49

track system, 289

tutoring, 366

type-token ratio, 198–199, 270

United States Census of Housing, 296, 323

urban ghettos, 372

urbanization, 77, 372

value system(s), 102, 107, 111; and integration, 284, 285

verbal abilities, 51; auditory discrimination and, 269–270, 273–274, 276; race and, 319–335; socioeconomic status and, 319–335; *see also* language development

verbal fluency, 51, 342; Deprivation Index and, 351–352

Verbal Fluency Test, 362, 364

Verbal Identification Test, 361, 362

verbal mediation, 24–25, 27, 150, 163, 164, 171–173

verbal parameters, 358–359

Verbal Survey, 16–18, 295, 338; and race, 18, 359–369; and socioeconomic status, 18, 359–369

verbal symbols, abstract, 26–27

verbalization, overt, 24; race and, 18, 19, 366

vigilance tasks, 157, 238, 250, 252–254; single-channel, 244–245, 253
visual acuity, 234
visual-deprivation experiments, 153
visual discrimination, environment and 47–48, 152–153; figure-ground relationships, 47, 261; form perception, 153; Gestalt perceptual theory, 262; preschool training programs for, 12, 22, 69, 85, 139; and reading, 233–256, 381; size, 69–70; spatial organization, 47; tests for, 157–158, 238–241, 243–246, 272–274
visual memory span, testing of, 241
visual-motor association, 151
visual stimuli, 150, 235–240; categorizing of, 365
vocabulary development, 24, 27, 71, 164, 165
vocal encoding, 151
Vygotsky, L., 53, 164–165, 358

Washington, Booker T., 111
watch-keeping, 238
Wattenberg, W., 122

Wechsler-Bellevue Vocabulary Scale, 341
Wechsler Intelligence Scale for Children, 150, 247–248, 267; Comprehension subtest, 268; Information subtest, 268; Vocabulary subtest, 267–268, 324, 328–332, 340, 342, 344–345, 361
welfare cases, 14, 32, 62, 141
Wepman Auditory Discrimination Test, 14–15, 154, 181, 214, 266–271, 273, 362, 365, 382
White, R. W., 35, 66, 290
white children, *see* race
Whiteman, Martin, 309, 319, 327
Whorf, Benjamin, 53
Williams, H. M., 214, 215
Winer, B. J., 201n., 325
withdrawal, 42, 287–288, 355
Wolf, R. M., 353
word association tests, 346–347, 364, 365
Word Distance Test, 346–347, 364

Young, F. M., 177